Angel Sanctuary™

story and art by Kaori Yuki
vol.3

Angel Sanctuary

Vol. 3
Shôjo Edition

STORY AND ART BY KAORI YUKI

Translation/JN Productions
English Adaptation/Marv Wolfman
Touch-up & Lettering/James Hudnall
Cover, Graphics & Design/Izumi Evers
Editor/William Flanagan
Supervising Editor/Frances E. Wall

Editor in Chief, Books/Alvin Lu
Editor in Chief, Magazines/Marc Weidenbaum
VP of Publishing Licensing/Rika Inouye
VP of Sales/Gonzalo Ferreyra
Sr. VP of Marketing/Liza Coppola
Publisher/Hyoe Narita

Tenshi Kinryou Ku by Kaori Yuki

Printed in Canada

Published by VIZ Media, LLC
P.O. Box 77010
San Francisco, CA 94107

Shôjo Edition
10 9 8 7 6 5 4
First printing, July 2004
Fourth printing, August 2007

www.viz.com
store.viz.com

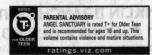

Angel Sanctuary ™

story and art by Kaori Yuki   vol.3

The Story Thus Far

High-school student Setsuna Mudo is always in trouble. When
he isn't getting into fights with local punks, he's talking back
to teachers or hanging around his juvenile delinquent friend
Sakuya Kira. Setsuna always considered his problems, including a romantic love for his younger sister, Sara, to be just his
bad luck, but it turns out there's more to it than that...

Setsuna is the reincarnation of a female angel, Alexiel, who
rebelled against God. Two demons from Hell, the quick-tem-
pered but noble female demon Kurai and the vampy male
demon Arachne, have come to Earth to find Alexiel's soul and
recruit their former leader back into the cause. But Setsuna
will have none of it. He just wants to be left alone so he can
brood over his sister.

The high-level angel Rosiel, twin brother of Alexiel, would also
like to free Alexiel's soul from Setsuna's human body, but his
inducements are twisted and evil. He initiates several schemes
including kidnapping Sara to force Setsuna to use his Angelic
powers in order to save her, and hanging up pictures that
exposes Setsuna's incestuous love for all the world to see.
This move forces Sara's and Setsuna's mother to go to
extreme lengths to separate the couple—she arranges to move
to England and bring Sara with her.

Meanwhile, one of Rosiel's schemes has forced Setsuna, tem-
porarily overtaken by the power of Alexiel, to kill a human,
and as the police get involved in the matter, Setsuna becomes
their prime suspect!

Contents

Characters

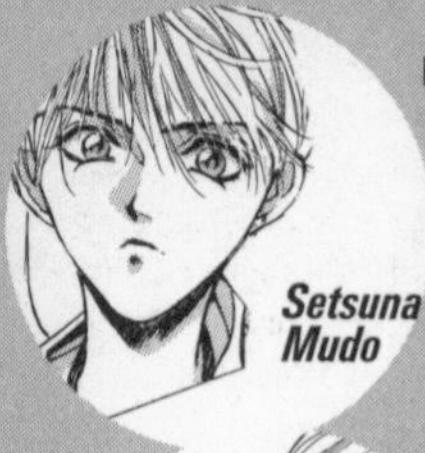
Setsuna Mudo

Main character. A high school student who is the reincarnation of the female angel Alexiel. He is in love with his sister, Sara.

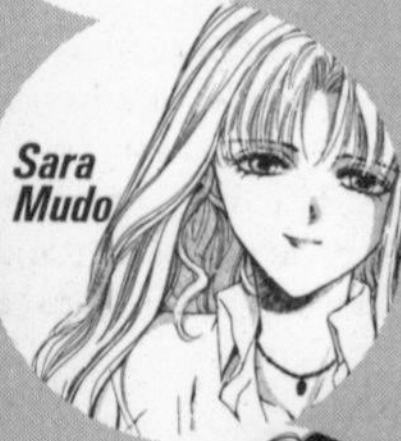
Sara Mudo

Setsuna's younger sister, troubled because she is in love with her older brother.

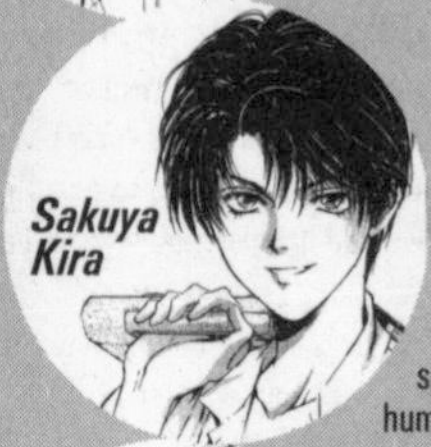
Sakuya Kira

A "big brother" figure to Setsuna; a combination of an immortal spirit and a human.

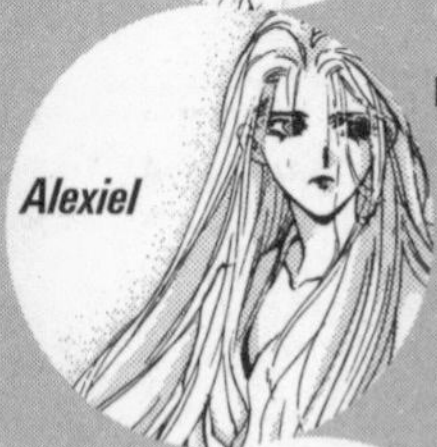
Alexiel

Legendary organic angel, second only to God in Heaven.

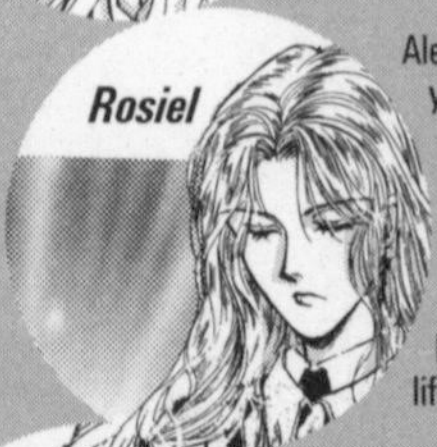
Rosiel

Alexiel's younger twin brother. Rosiel is after Setsuna Mudo's life.

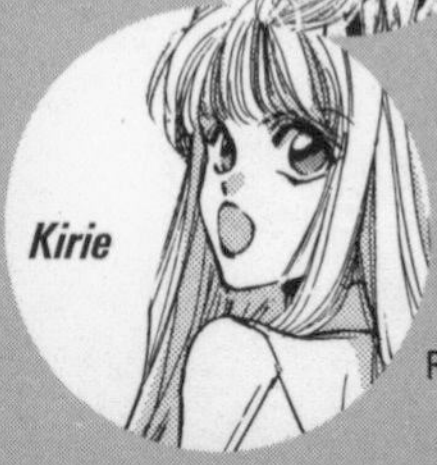
Kirie

Archangel candidate in Heaven who faithfully serves Rosiel.

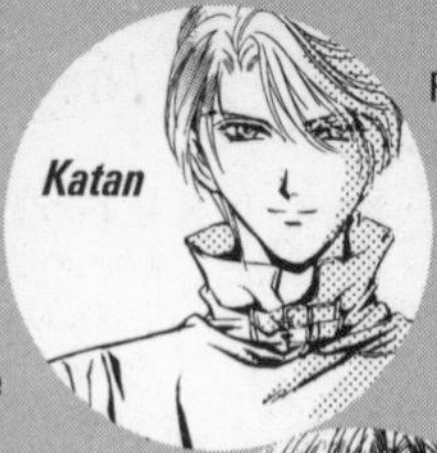
Katan

Rosiel's subordinate who carried out the Angel Sanctuary Plan.

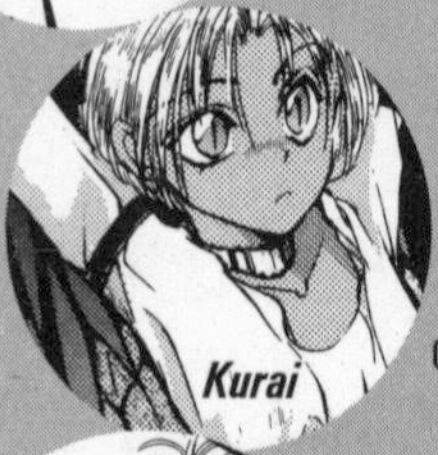
Kurai

Demon battling Heaven; 14th Princess of Gehenna.

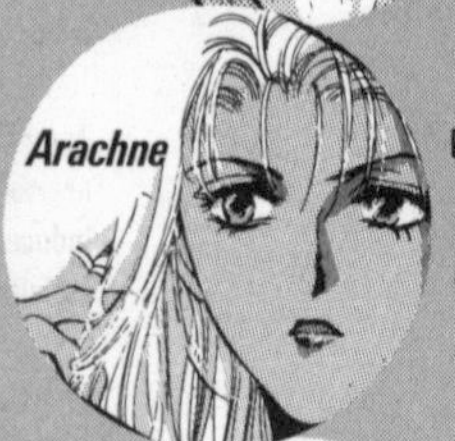
Arachne

Demon cousin of Kurai; beautiful, but male.

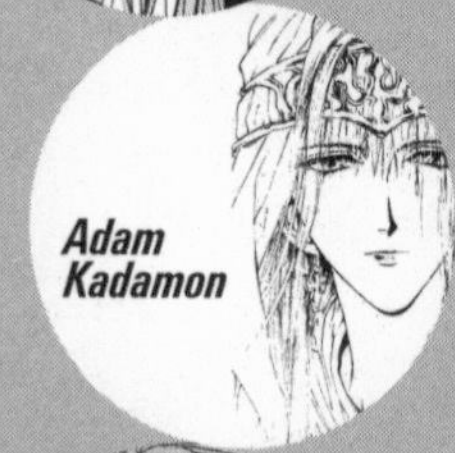
Adam Kadamon

God's ultimate creation and legendary holy hermit.

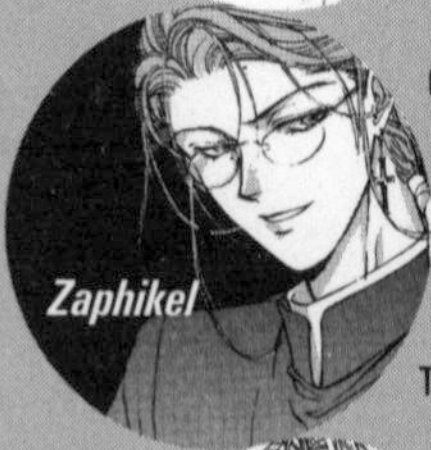
Zaphikel

One of the Seven Great Angels of Heaven; holds the position of Great Thrones.

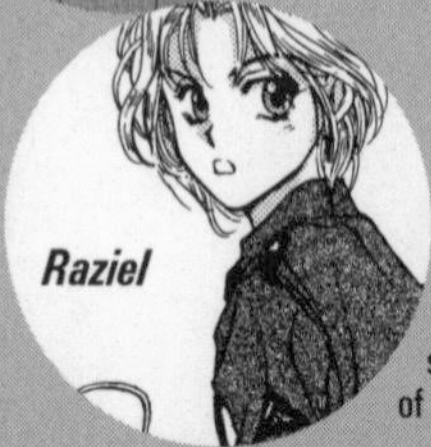
Raziel

Archangel candidate in Heaven; subordinate of Zaphikel.

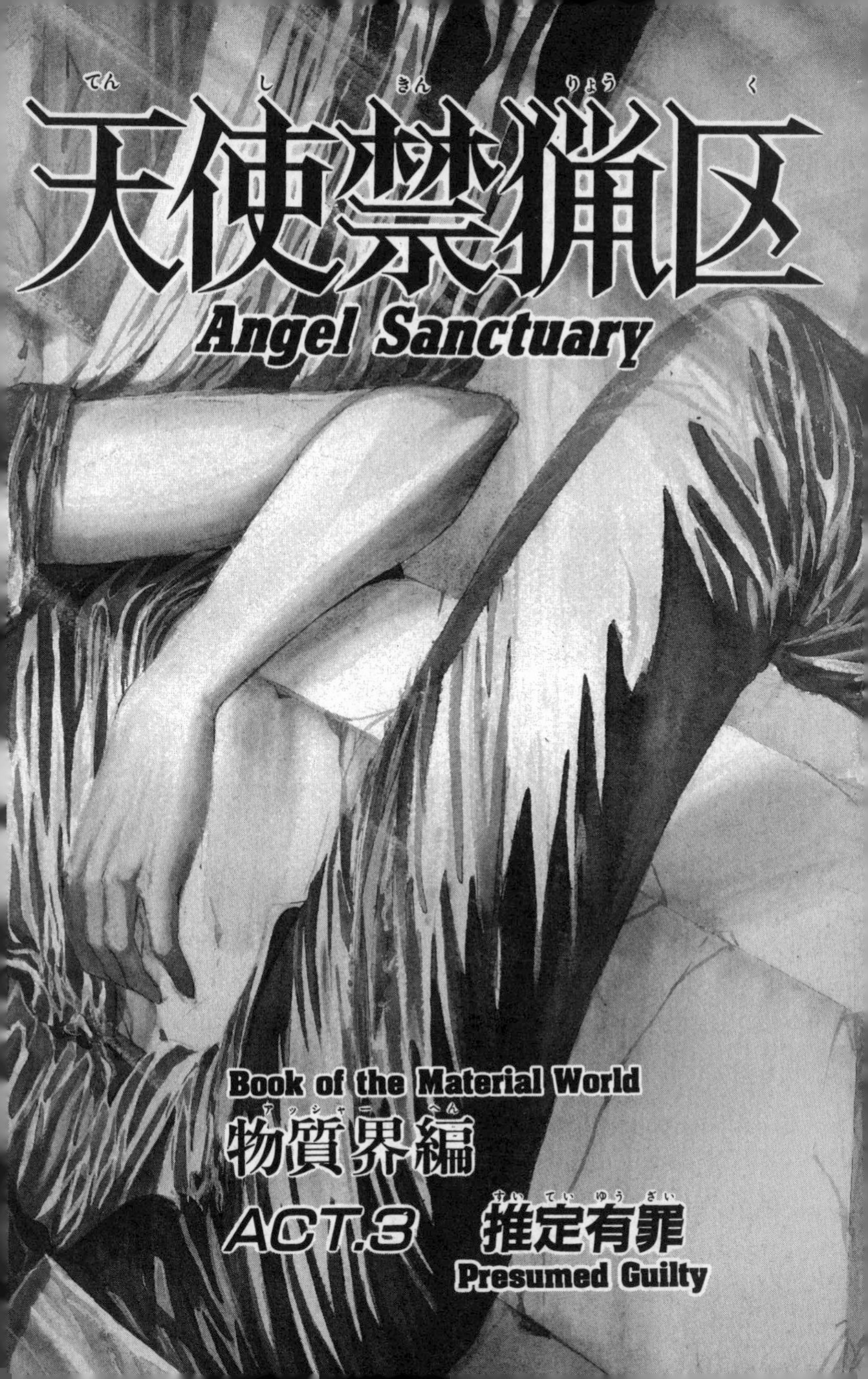
天使禁猟区
Angel Sanctuary
Book of the Material World
物質界編
ACT.3 推定有罪
Presumed Guilty

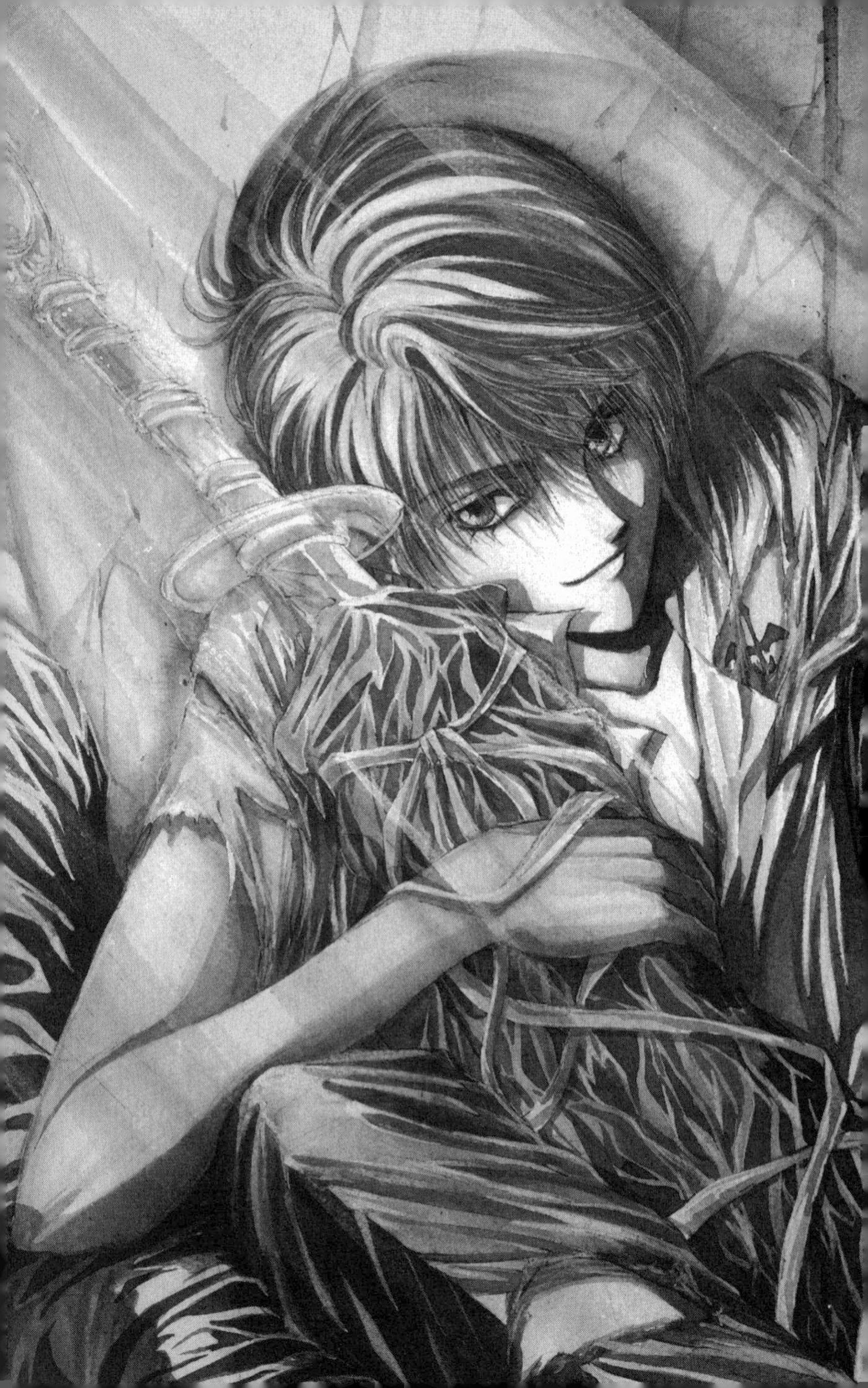

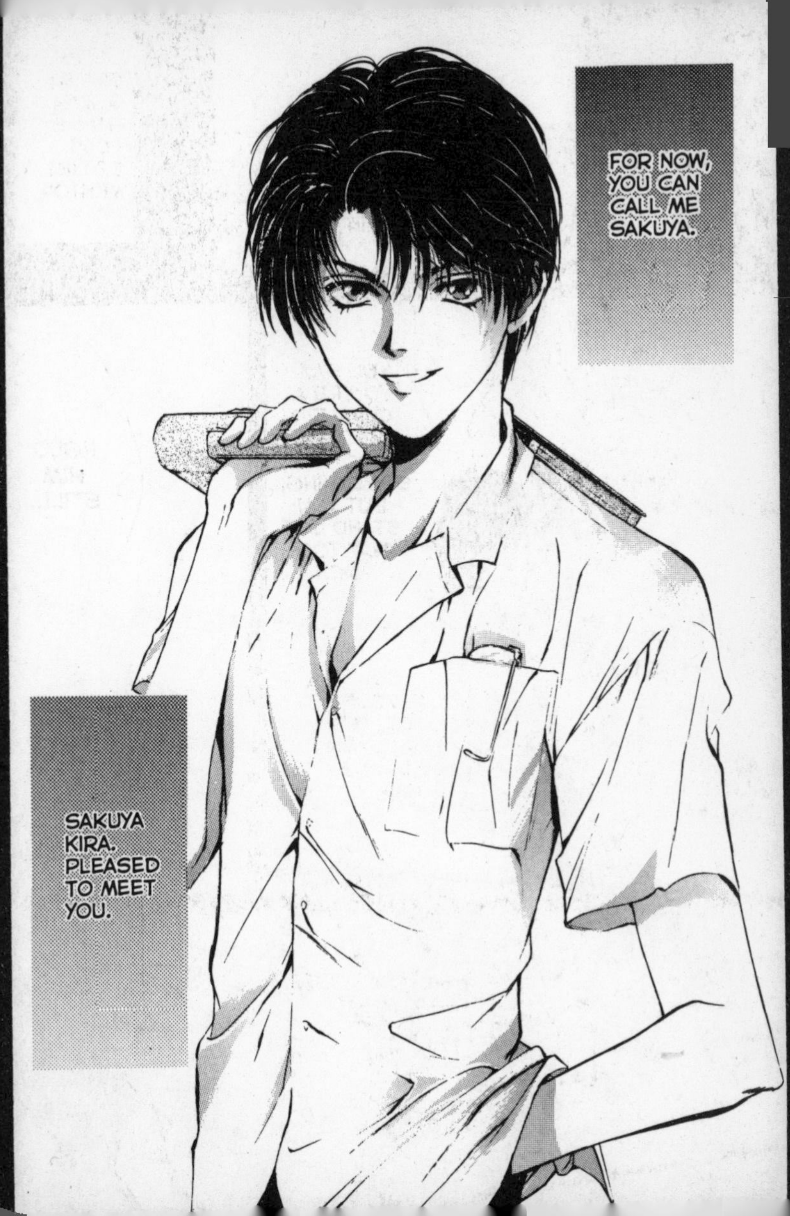
FOR NOW, YOU CAN CALL ME SAKUYA.
SAKUYA KIRA. PLEASED TO MEET YOU.

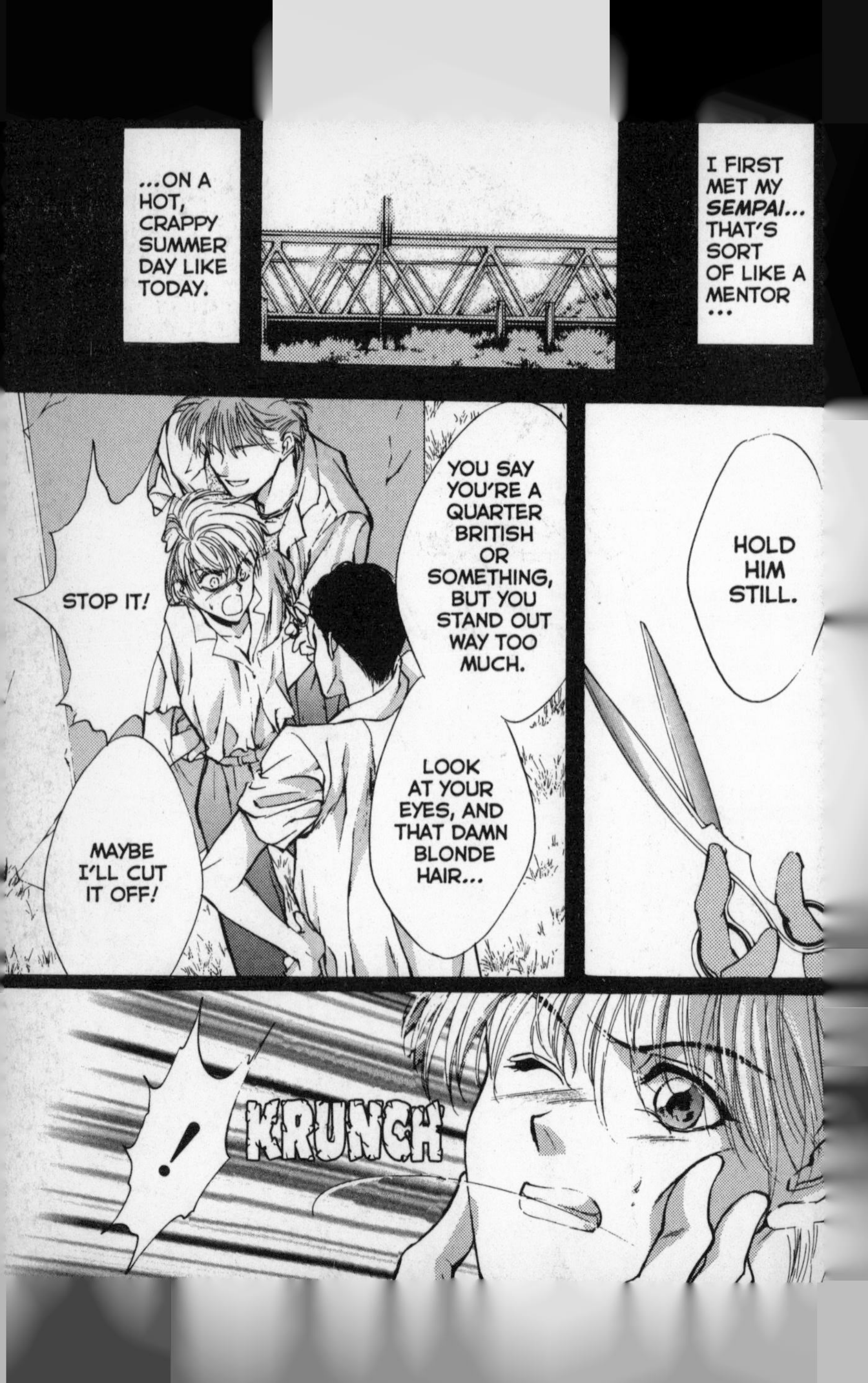
I FIRST MET MY *SEMPAI*... THAT'S SORT OF LIKE A MENTOR ...
...ON A HOT, CRAPPY SUMMER DAY LIKE TODAY.
HOLD HIM STILL.
YOU SAY YOU'RE A QUARTER BRITISH OR SOMETHING, BUT YOU STAND OUT WAY TOO MUCH.
LOOK AT YOUR EYES, AND THAT DAMN BLONDE HAIR...
STOP IT!
MAYBE I'LL CUT IT OFF!
KRUNCH
!

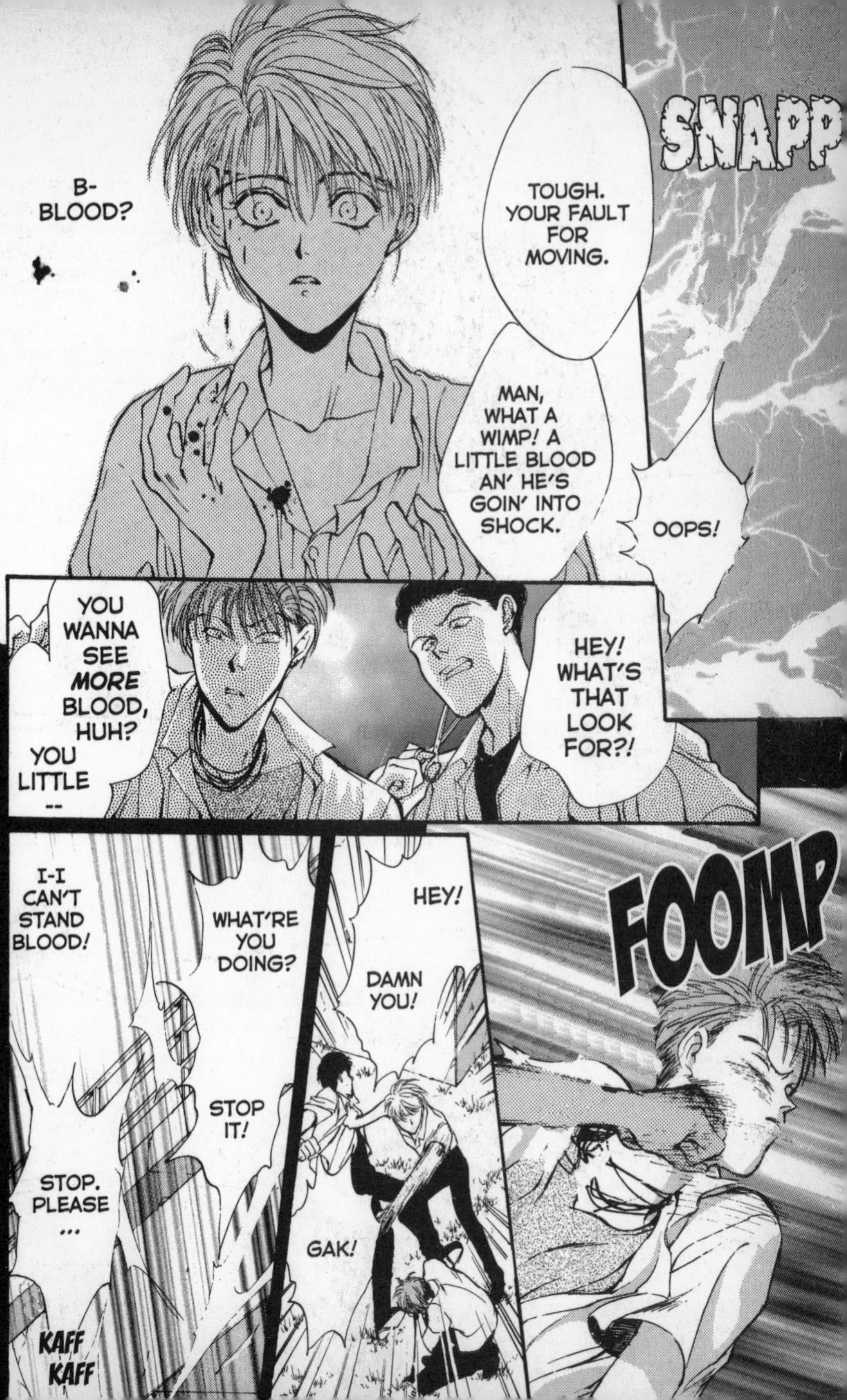
SNAPP
OOPS!
TOUGH. YOUR FAULT FOR MOVING.
MAN, WHAT A WIMP! A LITTLE BLOOD AN' HE'S GOIN' INTO SHOCK.
B- BLOOD?
HEY! WHAT'S THAT LOOK FOR?!
YOU WANNA SEE *MORE* BLOOD, HUH? YOU LITTLE --
FOOMP
HEY!
WHAT'RE YOU DOING?
DAMN YOU!
STOP IT!
GAK!
I-I CAN'T STAND BLOOD!
STOP. PLEASE ...
KAFF KAFF

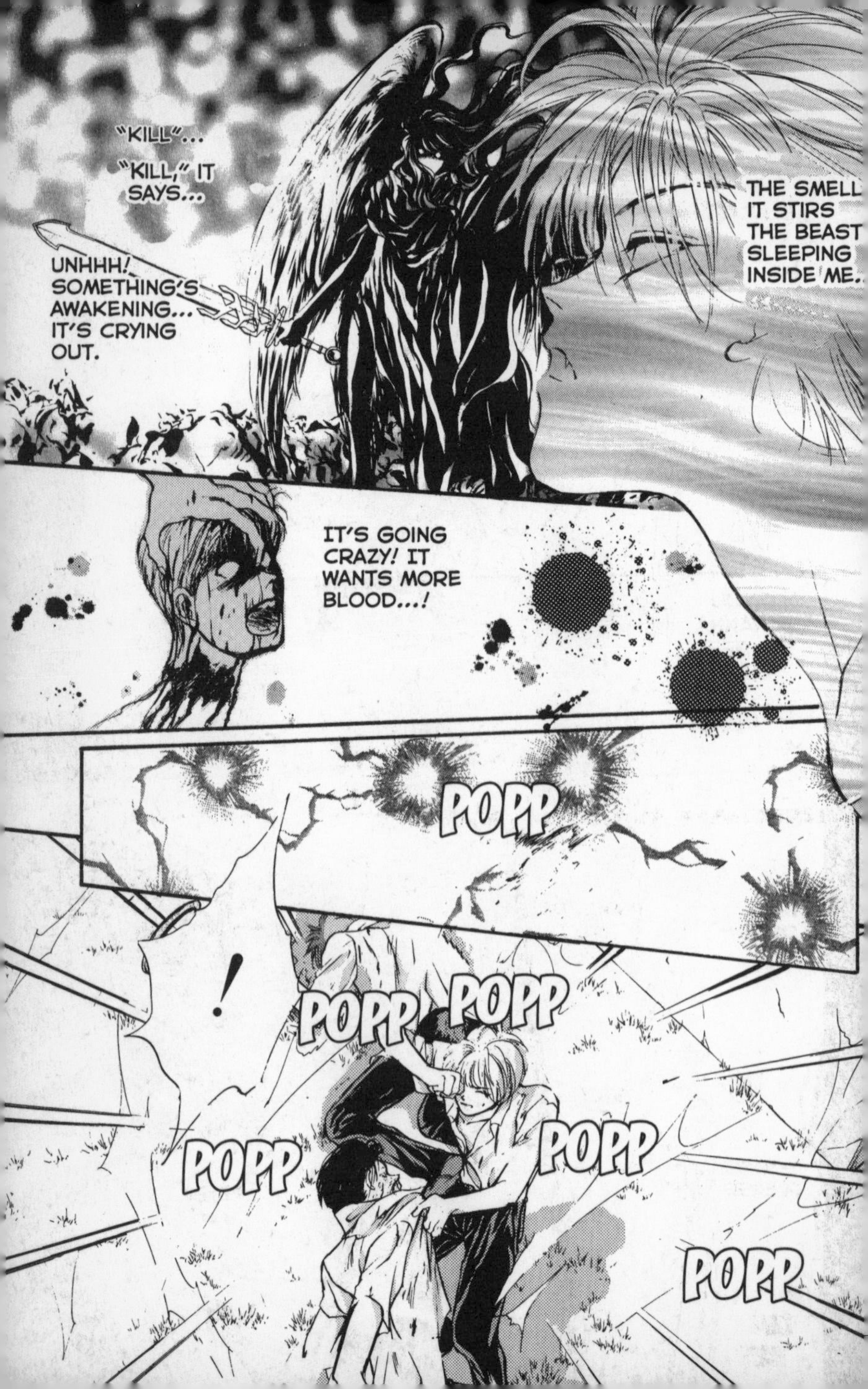
THE SMELL IT STIRS THE BEAST SLEEPING INSIDE ME...
"KILL"...
"KILL," IT SAYS...
UNHHH! SOMETHING'S AWAKENING... IT'S CRYING OUT.
IT'S GOING CRAZY! IT WANTS MORE BLOOD...!
POPP
!
POPP
POPP
POPP
POPP
POPP

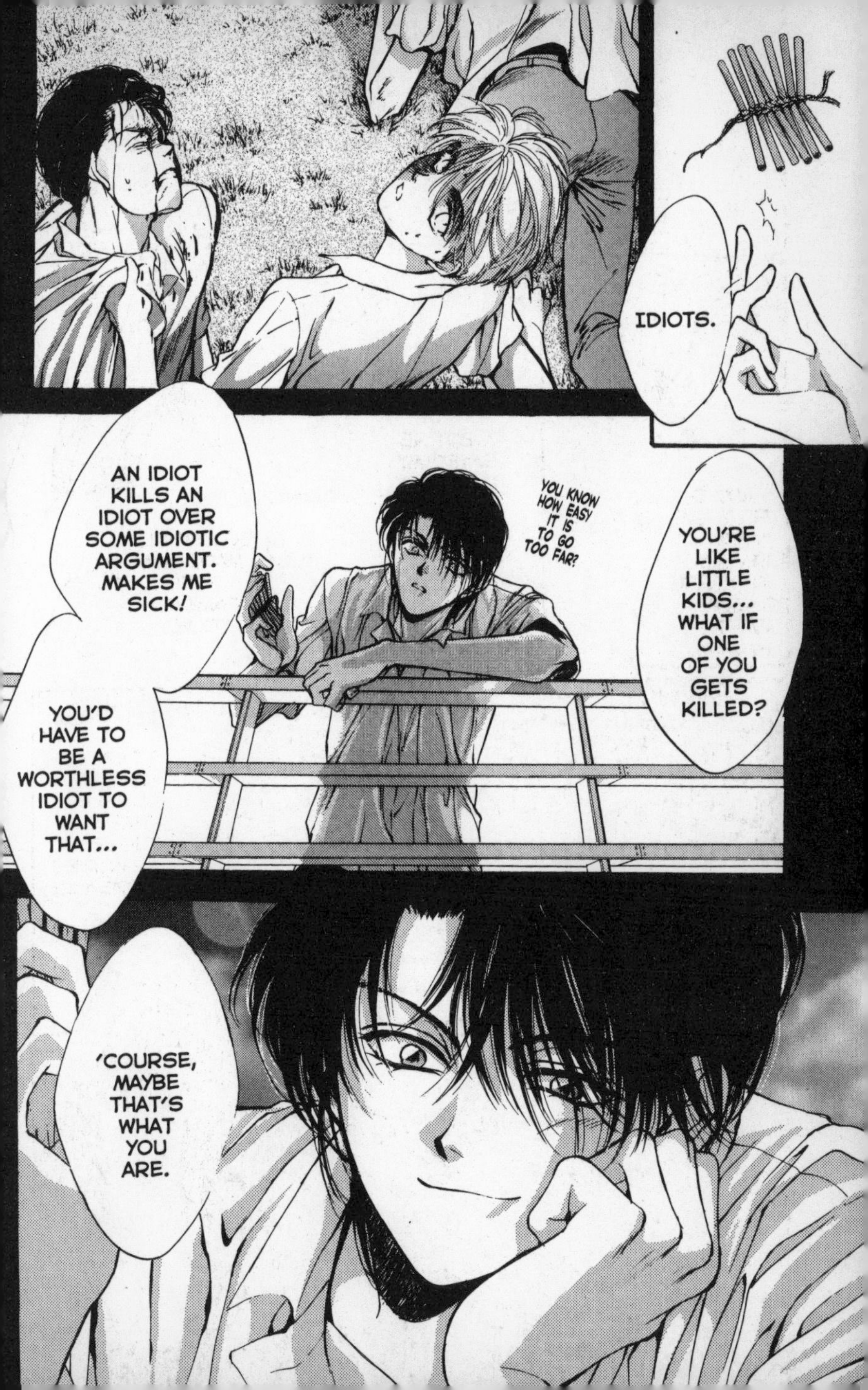
IDIOTS.
YOU'RE LIKE LITTLE KIDS... WHAT IF ONE OF YOU GETS KILLED?
YOU KNOW HOW EASY IT IS TO GO TOO FAR?
AN IDIOT KILLS AN IDIOT OVER SOME IDIOTIC ARGUMENT. MAKES ME SICK!
YOU'D HAVE TO BE A WORTHLESS IDIOT TO WANT THAT...
'COURSE, MAYBE THAT'S WHAT YOU ARE.

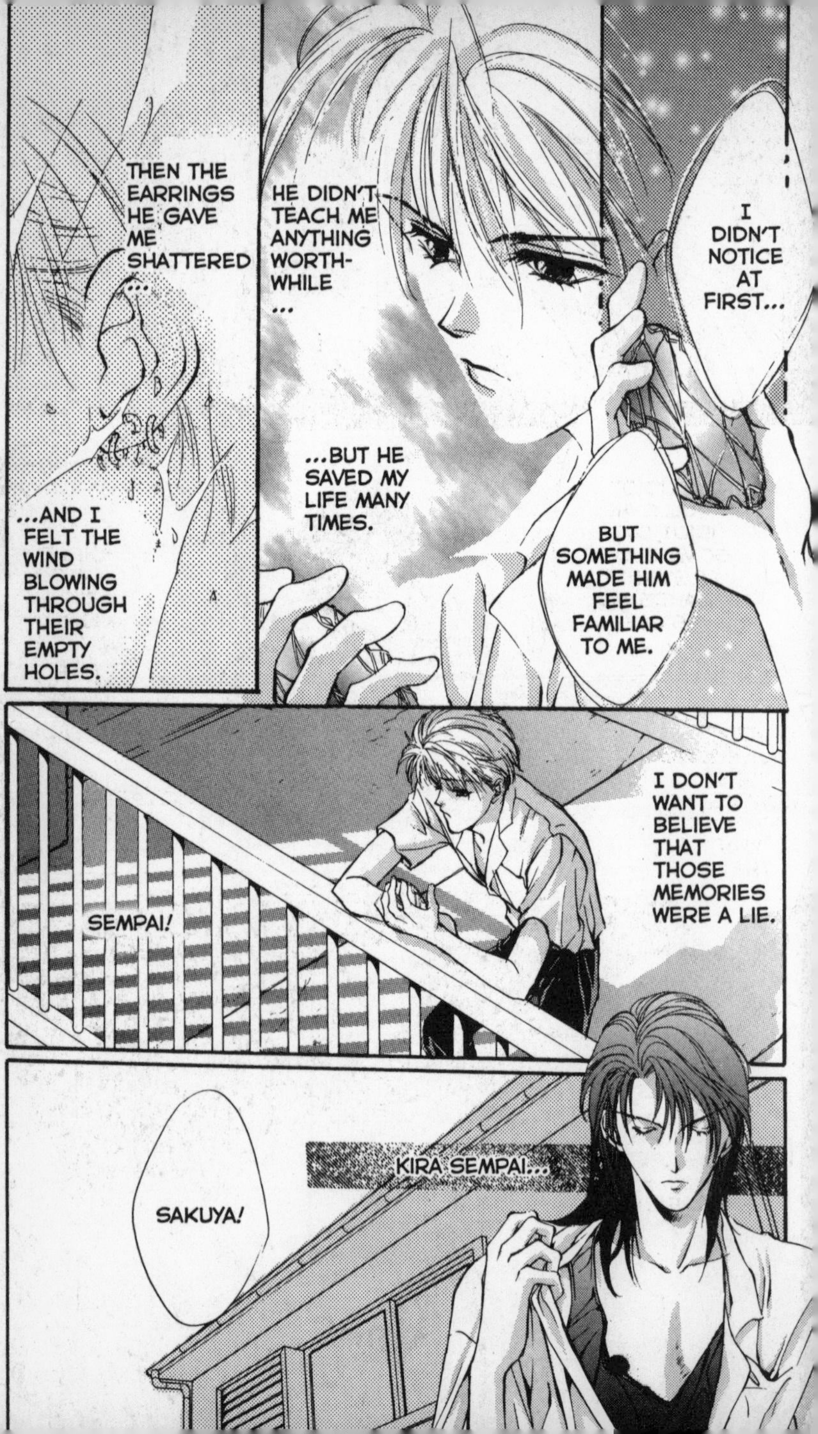
I DIDN'T NOTICE AT FIRST...
BUT SOMETHING MADE HIM FEEL FAMILIAR TO ME.
HE DIDN'T TEACH ME ANYTHING WORTHWHILE...
...BUT HE SAVED MY LIFE MANY TIMES.
THEN THE EARRINGS HE GAVE ME SHATTERED...
...AND I FELT THE WIND BLOWING THROUGH THEIR EMPTY HOLES.
I DON'T WANT TO BELIEVE THAT THOSE MEMORIES WERE A LIE.
SEMPAI!
KIRA SEMPAI...
SAKUYA!

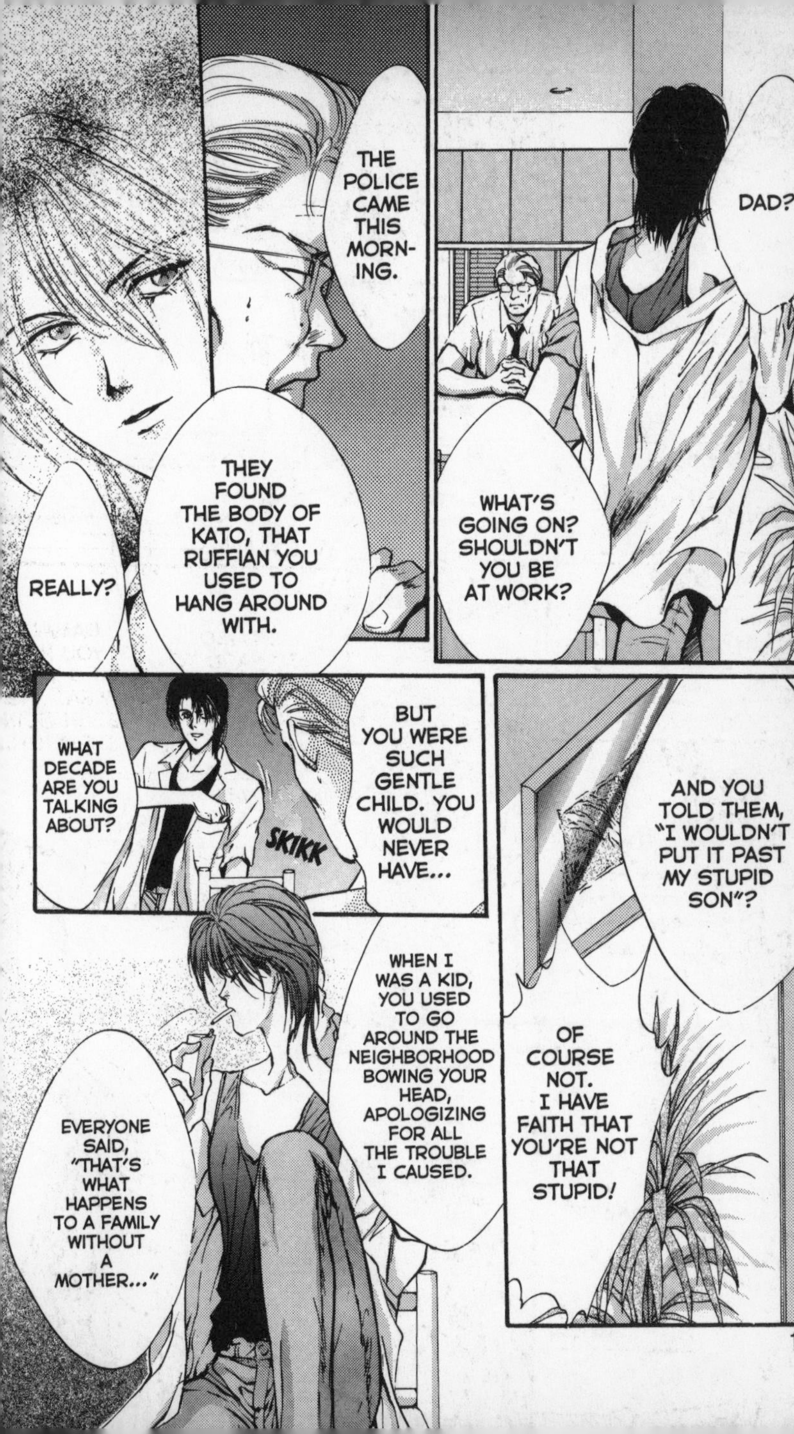
DAD?
WHAT'S GOING ON? SHOULDN'T YOU BE AT WORK?
THE POLICE CAME THIS MORN-ING.
THEY FOUND THE BODY OF KATO, THAT RUFFIAN YOU USED TO HANG AROUND WITH.
REALLY?
AND YOU TOLD THEM, "I WOULDN'T PUT IT PAST MY STUPID SON"?
OF COURSE NOT. I HAVE FAITH THAT YOU'RE NOT THAT STUPID!
BUT YOU WERE SUCH GENTLE CHILD. YOU WOULD NEVER HAVE...
SKIKK
WHAT DECADE ARE YOU TALKING ABOUT?
WHEN I WAS A KID, YOU USED TO GO AROUND THE NEIGHBORHOOD BOWING YOUR HEAD, APOLOGIZING FOR ALL THE TROUBLE I CAUSED.
EVERYONE SAID, "THAT'S WHAT HAPPENS TO A FAMILY WITHOUT A MOTHER..."

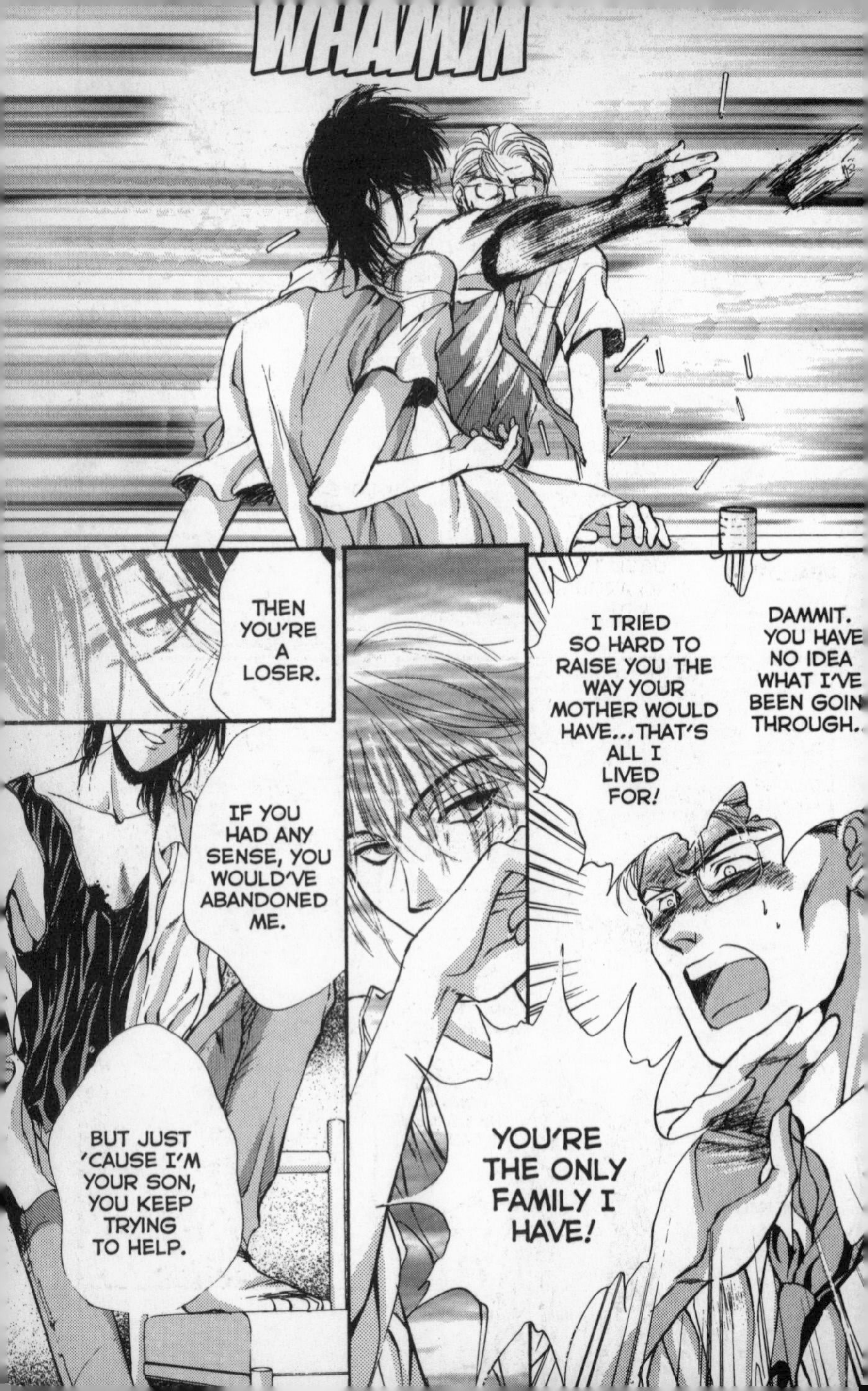
WHAMM
DAMMIT. YOU HAVE NO IDEA WHAT I'VE BEEN GOIN THROUGH.
I TRIED SO HARD TO RAISE YOU THE WAY YOUR MOTHER WOULD HAVE...THAT'S ALL I LIVED FOR!
YOU'RE THE ONLY FAMILY I HAVE!
THEN YOU'RE A LOSER.
IF YOU HAD ANY SENSE, YOU WOULD'VE ABANDONED ME.
BUT JUST 'CAUSE I'M YOUR SON, YOU KEEP TRYING TO HELP.

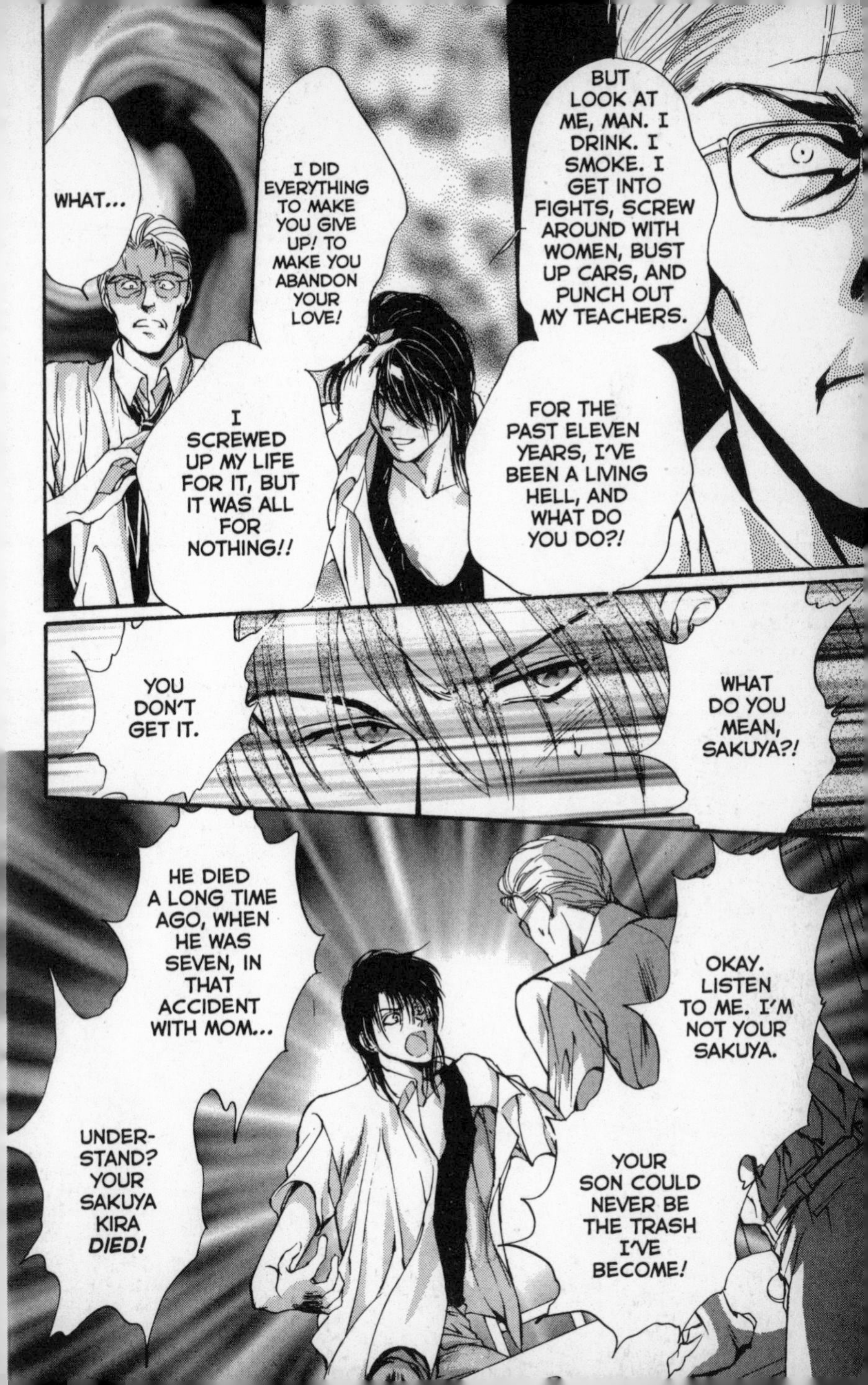
BUT LOOK AT ME, MAN. I DRINK. I SMOKE. I GET INTO FIGHTS, SCREW AROUND WITH WOMEN, BUST UP CARS, AND PUNCH OUT MY TEACHERS.
FOR THE PAST ELEVEN YEARS, I'VE BEEN A LIVING HELL, AND WHAT DO YOU DO?!
I DID EVERYTHING TO MAKE YOU GIVE UP! TO MAKE YOU ABANDON YOUR LOVE!
I SCREWED UP MY LIFE FOR IT, BUT IT WAS ALL FOR NOTHING!!
WHAT...
WHAT DO YOU MEAN, SAKUYA?!
YOU DON'T GET IT.
OKAY. LISTEN TO ME. I'M NOT YOUR SAKUYA.
YOUR SON COULD NEVER BE THE TRASH I'VE BECOME!
HE DIED A LONG TIME AGO, WHEN HE WAS SEVEN, IN THAT ACCIDENT WITH MOM...
UNDER-STAND? YOUR SAKUYA KIRA *DIED*!

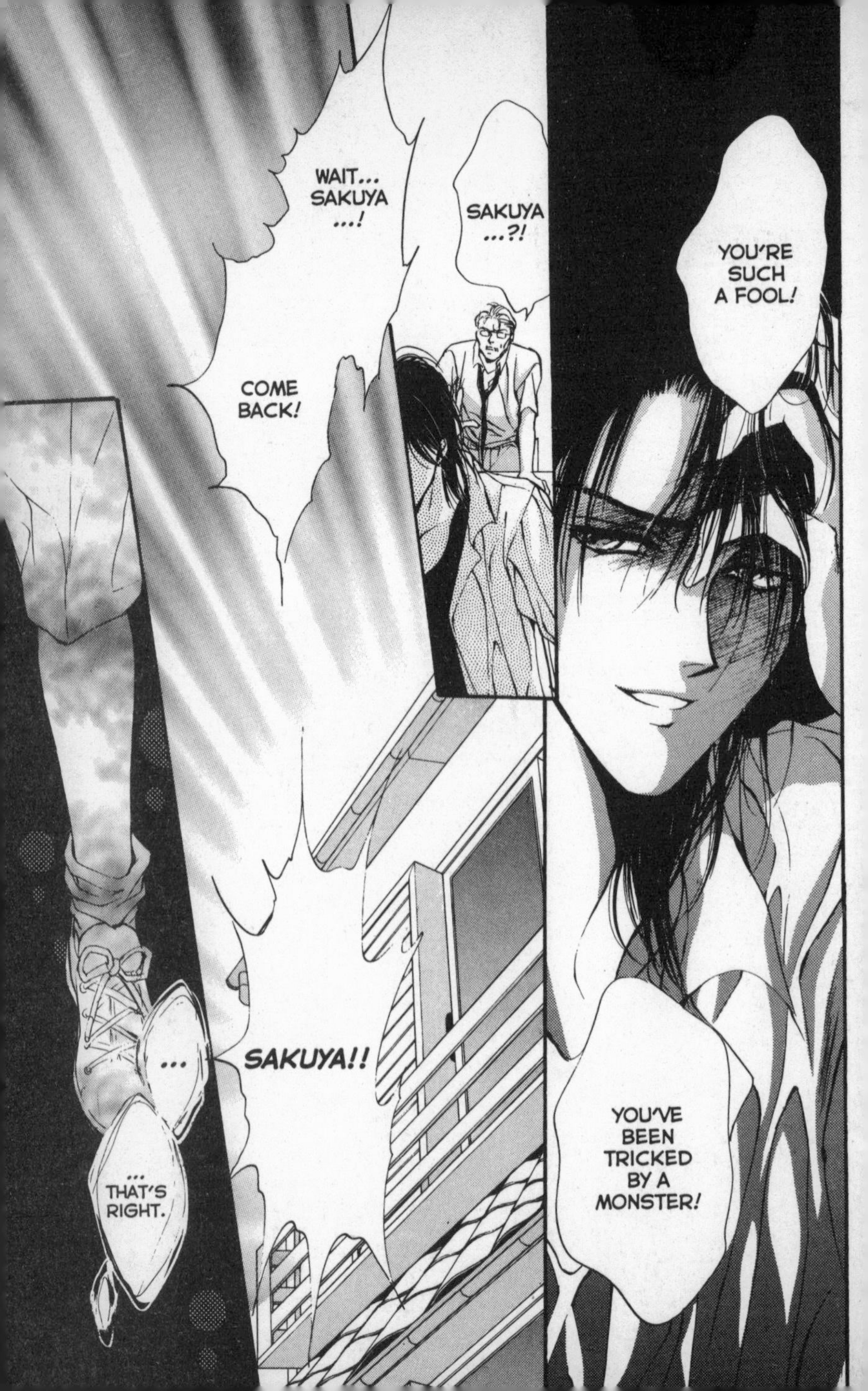
YOU'RE SUCH A FOOL!
YOU'VE BEEN TRICKED BY A MONSTER!
SAKUYA ...?!
WAIT... SAKUYA ...!
COME BACK!
SAKUYA!!
...
... THAT'S RIGHT.

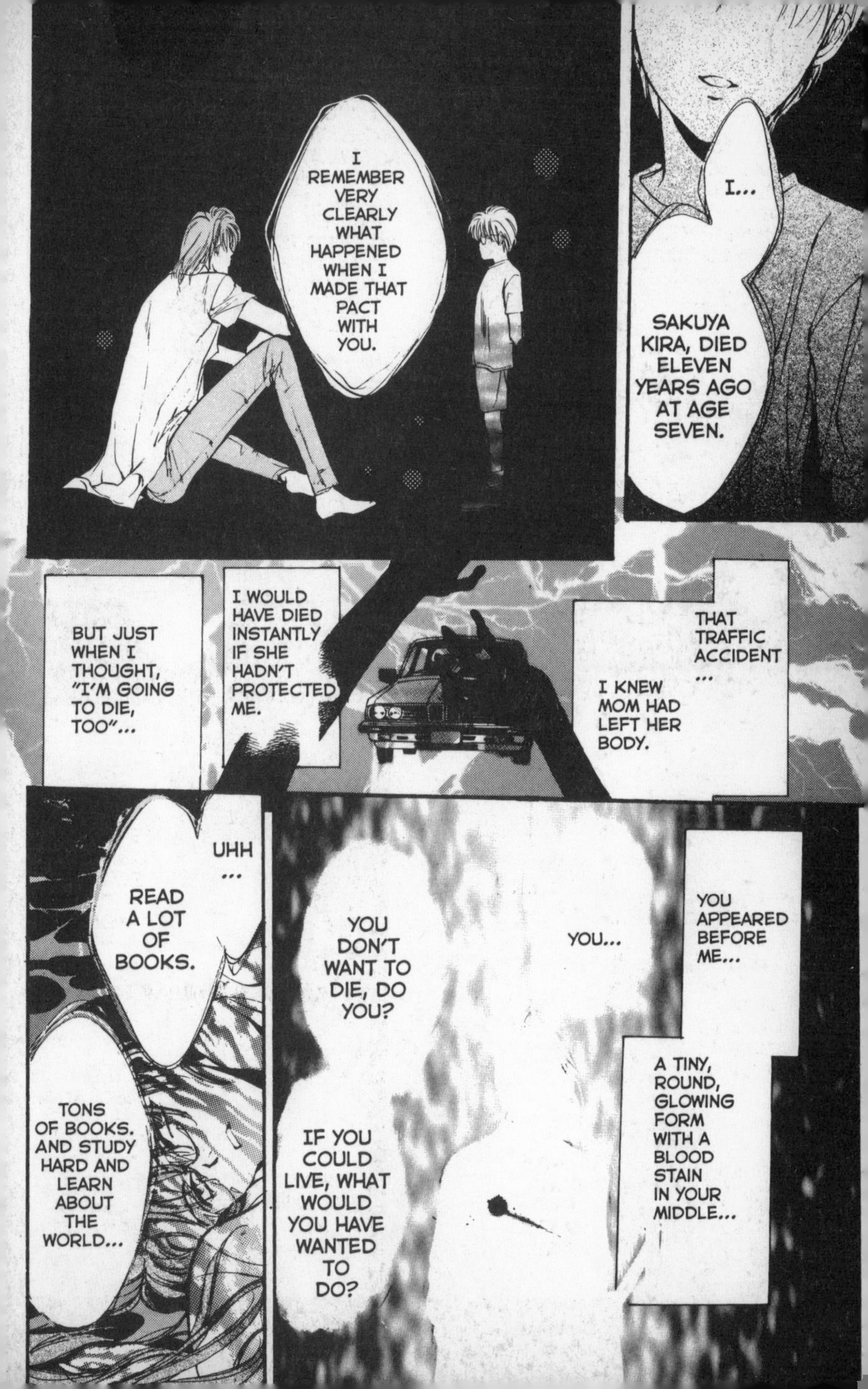
I...
SAKUYA KIRA, DIED ELEVEN YEARS AGO AT AGE SEVEN.
I REMEMBER VERY CLEARLY WHAT HAPPENED WHEN I MADE THAT PACT WITH YOU.
THAT TRAFFIC ACCIDENT...
I KNEW MOM HAD LEFT HER BODY.
I WOULD HAVE DIED INSTANTLY IF SHE HADN'T PROTECTED ME.
BUT JUST WHEN I THOUGHT, "I'M GOING TO DIE, TOO"...
YOU APPEARED BEFORE ME...
A TINY, ROUND, GLOWING FORM WITH A BLOOD STAIN IN YOUR MIDDLE...
YOU...
YOU DON'T WANT TO DIE, DO YOU?
IF YOU COULD LIVE, WHAT WOULD YOU HAVE WANTED TO DO?
UHH...
READ A LOT OF BOOKS.
TONS OF BOOKS. AND STUDY HARD AND LEARN ABOUT THE WORLD...

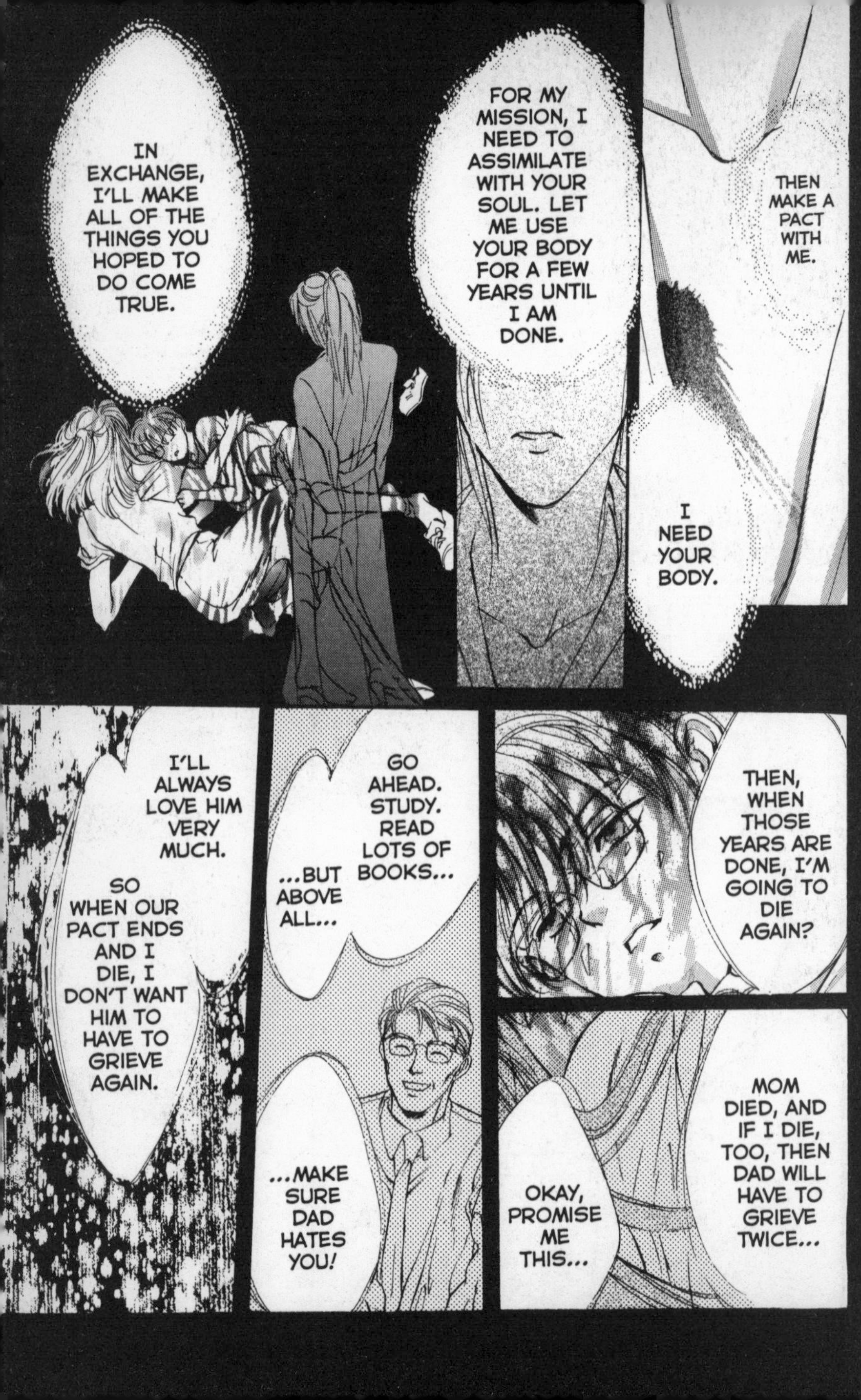
THEN MAKE A PACT WITH ME.
I NEED YOUR BODY.
FOR MY MISSION, I NEED TO ASSIMILATE WITH YOUR SOUL. LET ME USE YOUR BODY FOR A FEW YEARS UNTIL I AM DONE.
IN EXCHANGE, I'LL MAKE ALL OF THE THINGS YOU HOPED TO DO COME TRUE.
THEN, WHEN THOSE YEARS ARE DONE, I'M GOING TO DIE AGAIN?
MOM DIED, AND IF I DIE, TOO, THEN DAD WILL HAVE TO GRIEVE TWICE...
OKAY, PROMISE ME THIS...
GO AHEAD. STUDY. READ LOTS OF BOOKS...
...BUT ABOVE ALL...
...MAKE SURE DAD HATES YOU!
I'LL ALWAYS LOVE HIM VERY MUCH.
SO WHEN OUR PACT ENDS AND I DIE, I DON'T WANT HIM TO HAVE TO GRIEVE AGAIN.

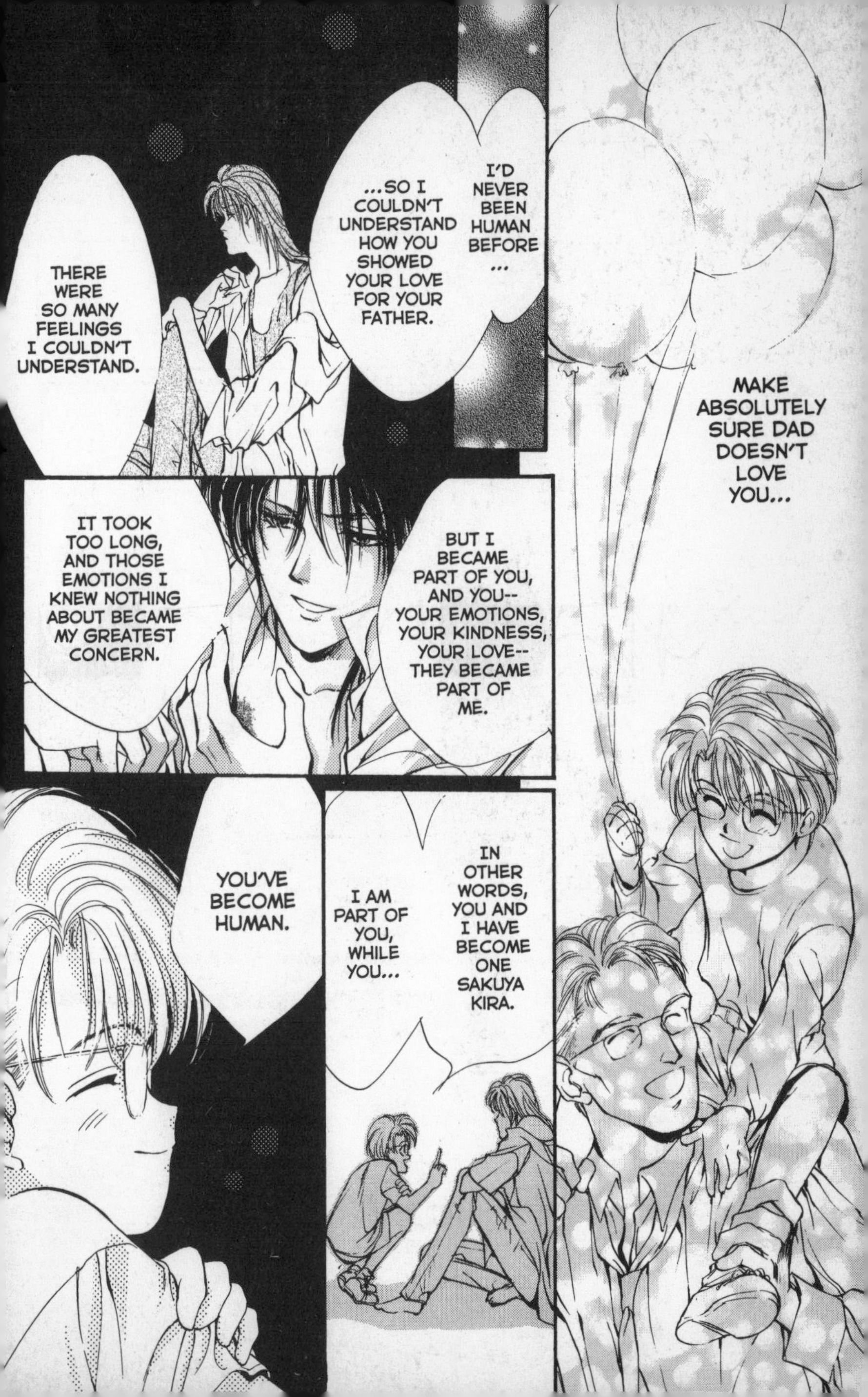
MAKE ABSOLUTELY SURE DAD DOESN'T LOVE YOU...
I'D NEVER BEEN HUMAN BEFORE ...
...SO I COULDN'T UNDERSTAND HOW YOU SHOWED YOUR LOVE FOR YOUR FATHER.
THERE WERE SO MANY FEELINGS I COULDN'T UNDERSTAND.
BUT I BECAME PART OF YOU, AND YOU-- YOUR EMOTIONS, YOUR KINDNESS, YOUR LOVE-- THEY BECAME PART OF ME.
IT TOOK TOO LONG, AND THOSE EMOTIONS I KNEW NOTHING ABOUT BECAME MY GREATEST CONCERN.
IN OTHER WORDS, YOU AND I HAVE BECOME ONE SAKUYA KIRA.
I AM PART OF YOU, WHILE YOU...
YOU'VE BECOME HUMAN.

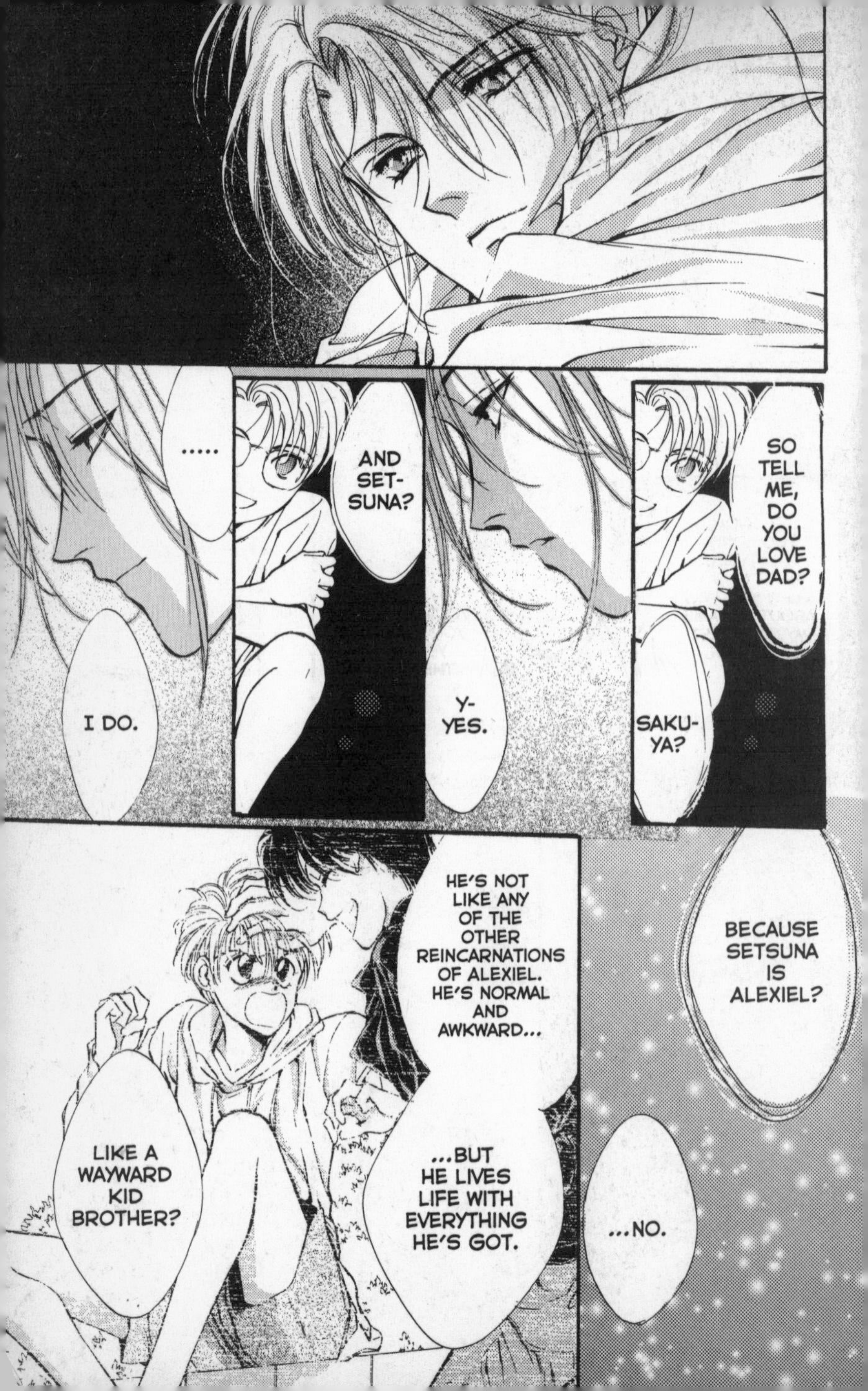
SO TELL ME, DO YOU LOVE DAD?
SAKU-YA?
Y-YES.
AND SET-SUNA?
.....
I DO.
BECAUSE SETSUNA IS ALEXIEL?
...NO.
HE'S NOT LIKE ANY OF THE OTHER REINCARNATIONS OF ALEXIEL. HE'S NORMAL AND AWKWARD...
...BUT HE LIVES LIFE WITH EVERYTHING HE'S GOT.
LIKE A WAYWARD KID BROTHER?

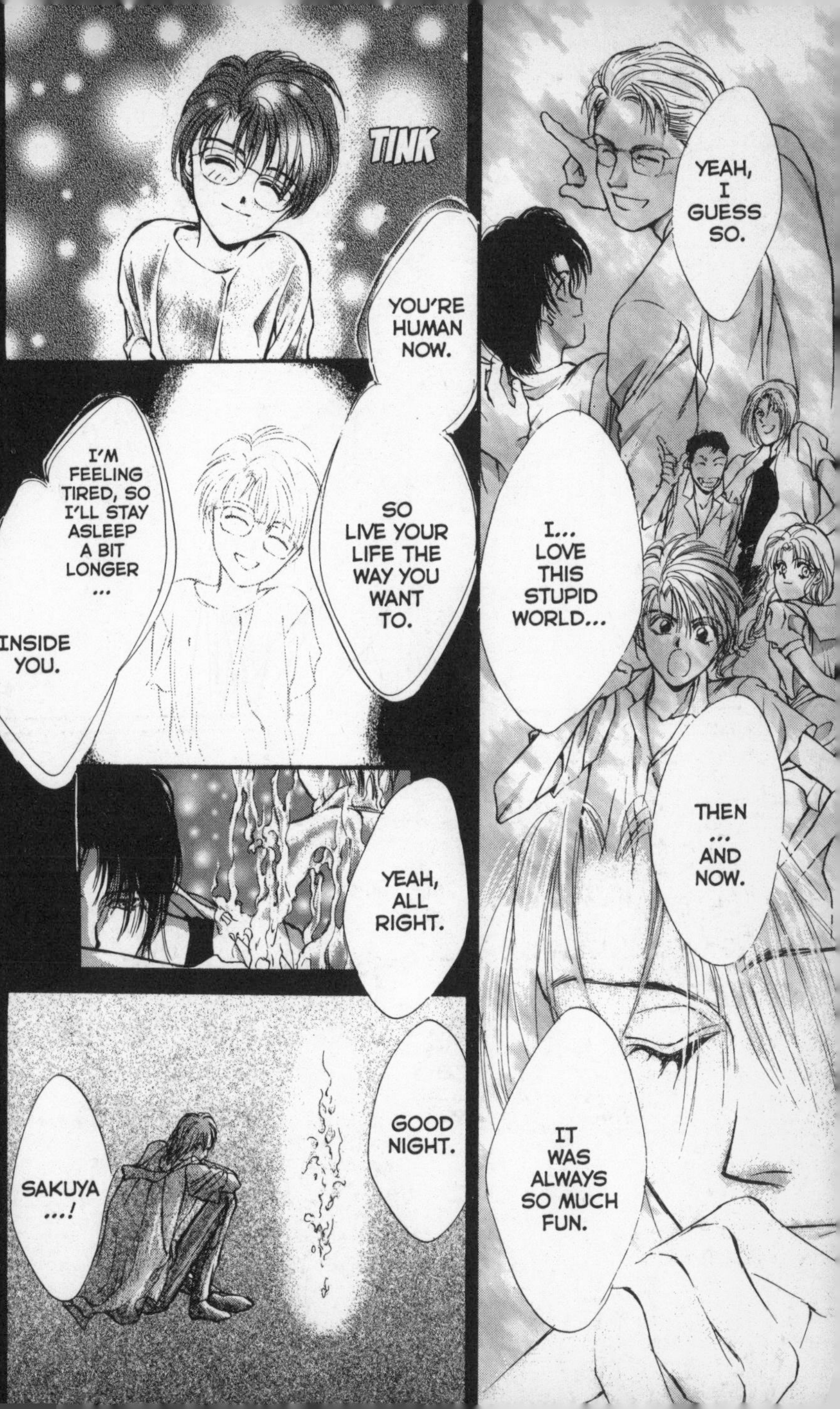
YEAH, I GUESS SO.
I... LOVE THIS STUPID WORLD...
THEN ... AND NOW.
IT WAS ALWAYS SO MUCH FUN.
TINK
YOU'RE HUMAN NOW.
SO LIVE YOUR LIFE THE WAY YOU WANT TO.
I'M FEELING TIRED, SO I'LL STAY ASLEEP A BIT LONGER ...
INSIDE YOU.
YEAH, ALL RIGHT.
GOOD NIGHT.
SAKUYA ...!

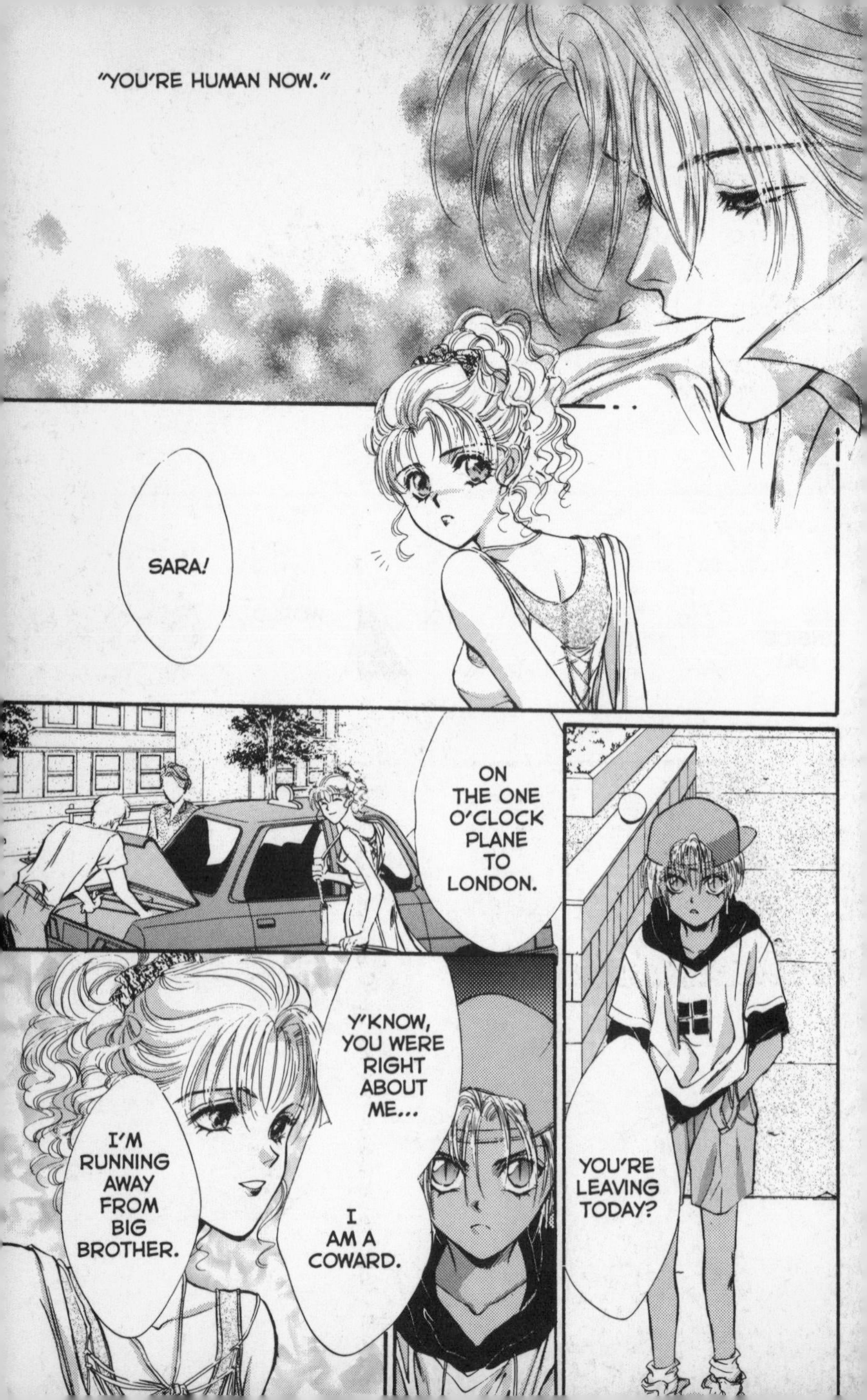
"YOU'RE HUMAN NOW."
SARA!
YOU'RE LEAVING TODAY?
ON THE ONE O'CLOCK PLANE TO LONDON.
Y'KNOW, YOU WERE RIGHT ABOUT ME...
I AM A COWARD.
I'M RUNNING AWAY FROM BIG BROTHER.

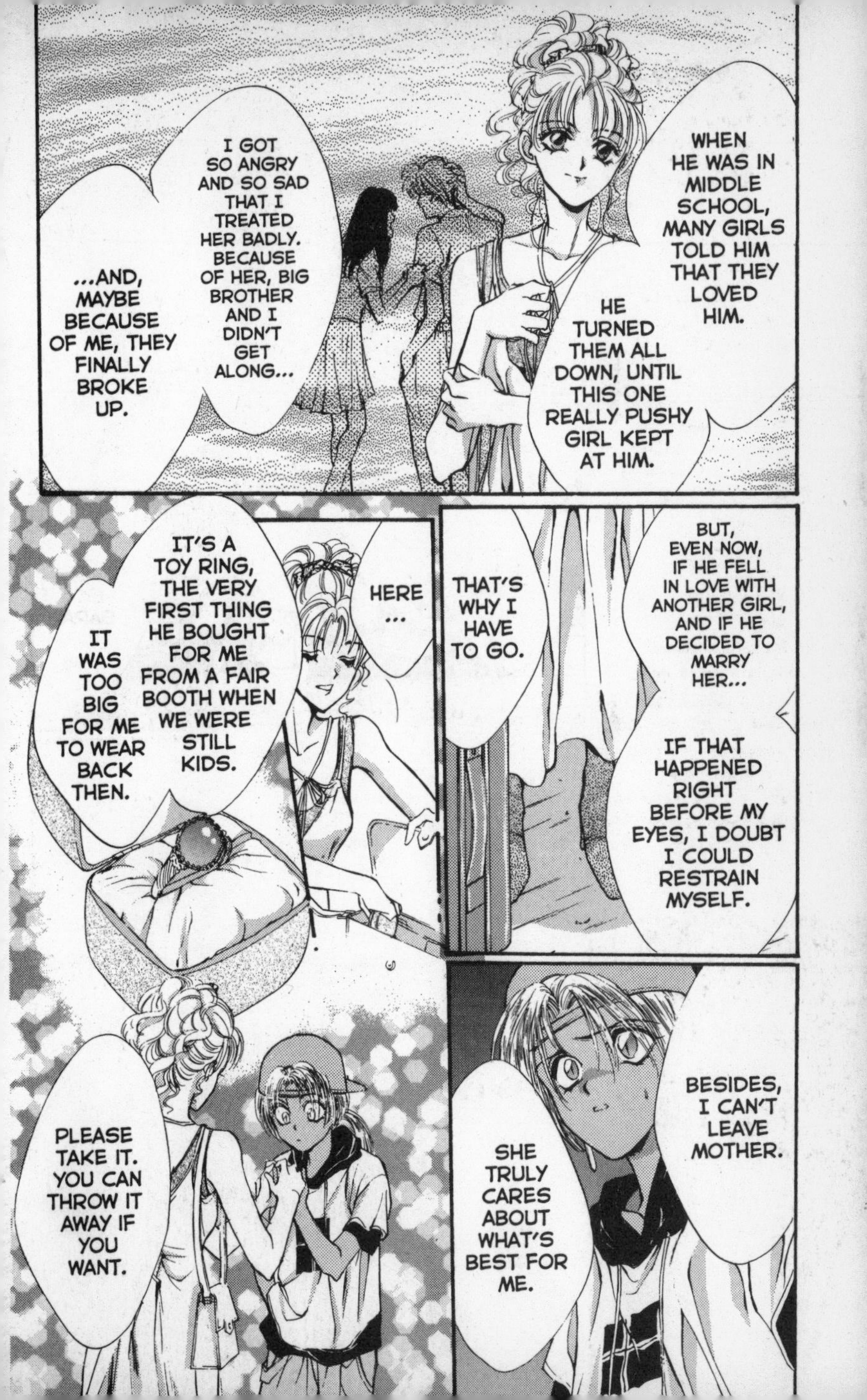
WHEN HE WAS IN MIDDLE SCHOOL, MANY GIRLS TOLD HIM THAT THEY LOVED HIM.
HE TURNED THEM ALL DOWN, UNTIL THIS ONE REALLY PUSHY GIRL KEPT AT HIM.
I GOT SO ANGRY AND SO SAD THAT I TREATED HER BADLY. BECAUSE OF HER, BIG BROTHER AND I DIDN'T GET ALONG...
...AND, MAYBE BECAUSE OF ME, THEY FINALLY BROKE UP.
BUT, EVEN NOW, IF HE FELL IN LOVE WITH ANOTHER GIRL, AND IF HE DECIDED TO MARRY HER...
IF THAT HAPPENED RIGHT BEFORE MY EYES, I DOUBT I COULD RESTRAIN MYSELF.
THAT'S WHY I HAVE TO GO.
HERE...
IT'S A TOY RING, THE VERY FIRST THING HE BOUGHT FOR ME FROM A FAIR BOOTH WHEN WE WERE STILL KIDS.
IT WAS TOO BIG FOR ME TO WEAR BACK THEN.
BESIDES, I CAN'T LEAVE MOTHER.
SHE TRULY CARES ABOUT WHAT'S BEST FOR ME.
PLEASE TAKE IT. YOU CAN THROW IT AWAY IF YOU WANT.

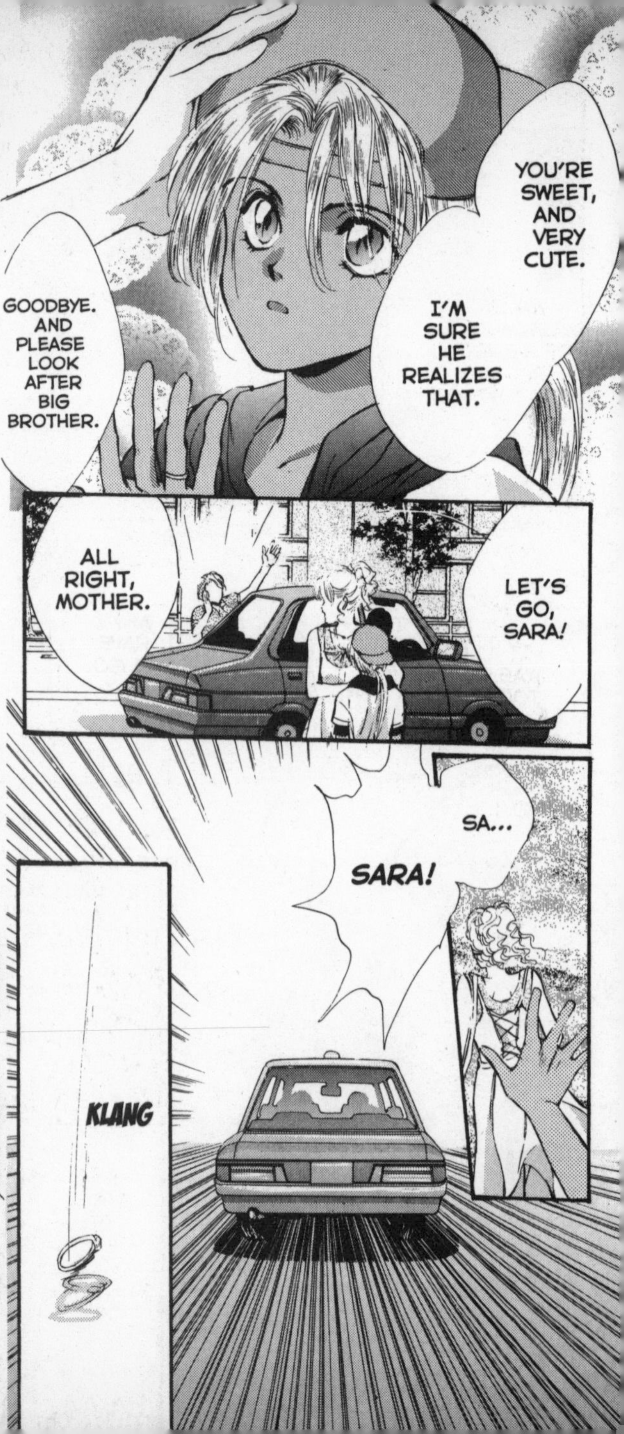
YOU'RE SWEET, AND VERY CUTE.
I'M SURE HE REALIZES THAT.
GOODBYE. AND PLEASE LOOK AFTER BIG BROTHER.
LET'S GO, SARA!
ALL RIGHT, MOTHER.
SA...
SARA!
KLANG

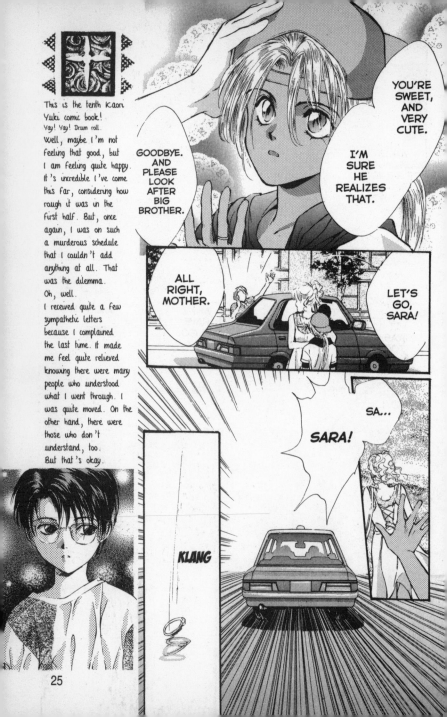

This is the tenth Kaori Yuki comic book!
Yay! Yay! Drum roll.
Well, maybe I'm not feeling that good, but I am feeling quite happy. It's incredible I've come this far, considering how rough it was in the first half. But, once again, I was on such a murderous schedule that I couldn't add anything at all. That was the dilemma.
Oh, well.
I received quite a few sympathetic letters because I complained the last time. It made me feel quite relieved knowing there were many people who understood what I went through. I was quite moved. On the other hand, there were those who don't understand, too.
But that's okay.

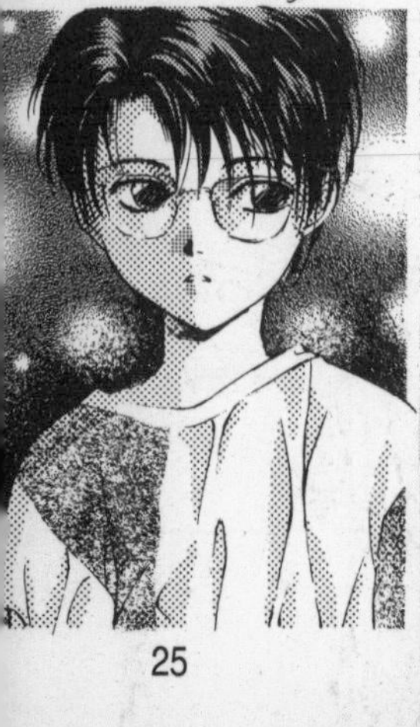

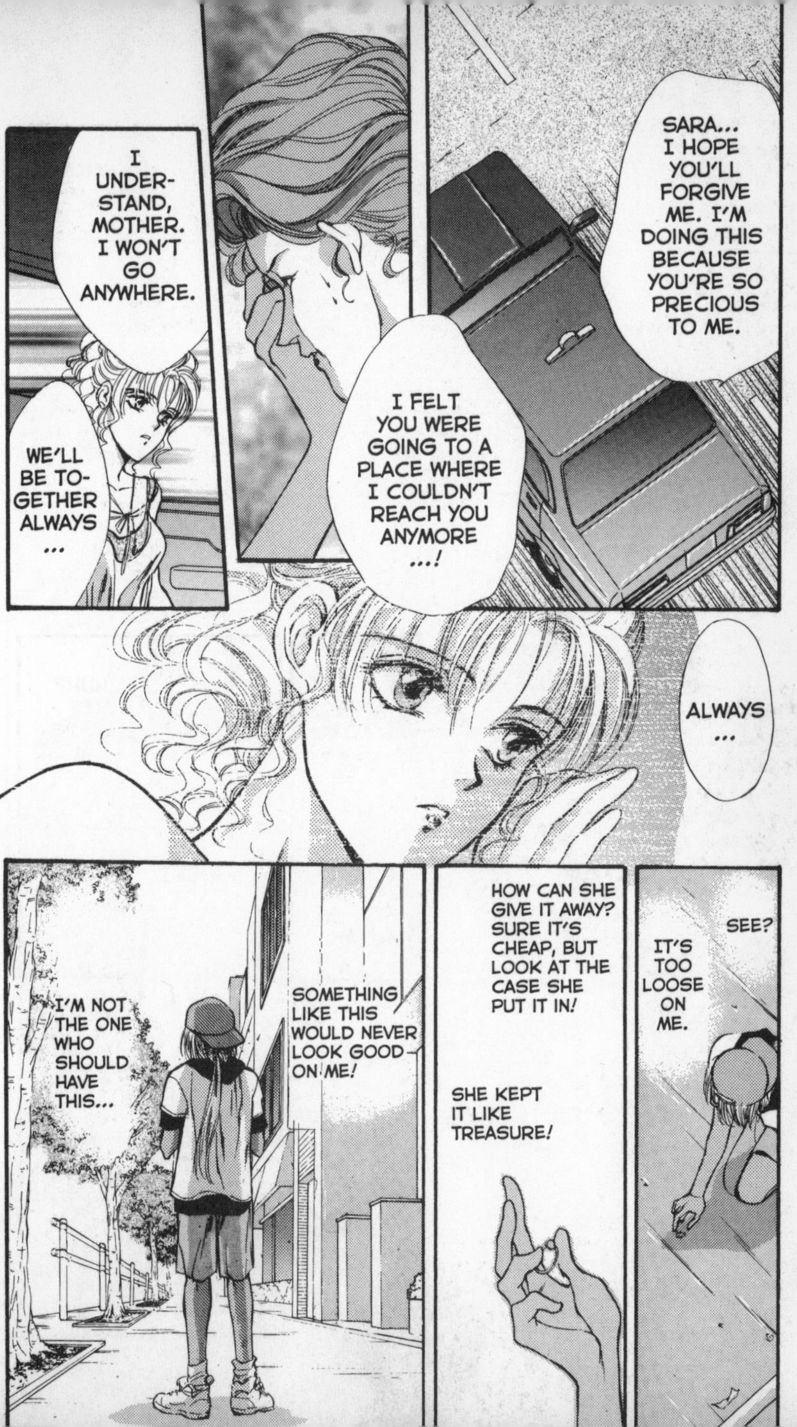
SARA... I HOPE YOU'LL FORGIVE ME. I'M DOING THIS BECAUSE YOU'RE SO PRECIOUS TO ME.
I FELT YOU WERE GOING TO A PLACE WHERE I COULDN'T REACH YOU ANYMORE ...!
I UNDER-STAND, MOTHER. I WON'T GO ANYWHERE.
WE'LL BE TO-GETHER ALWAYS ...
ALWAYS ...
SEE?
IT'S TOO LOOSE ON ME.
HOW CAN SHE GIVE IT AWAY? SURE IT'S CHEAP, BUT LOOK AT THE CASE SHE PUT IT IN!
SHE KEPT IT LIKE TREASURE!
SOMETHING LIKE THIS WOULD NEVER LOOK GOOD ON ME!
I'M NOT THE ONE WHO SHOULD HAVE THIS...

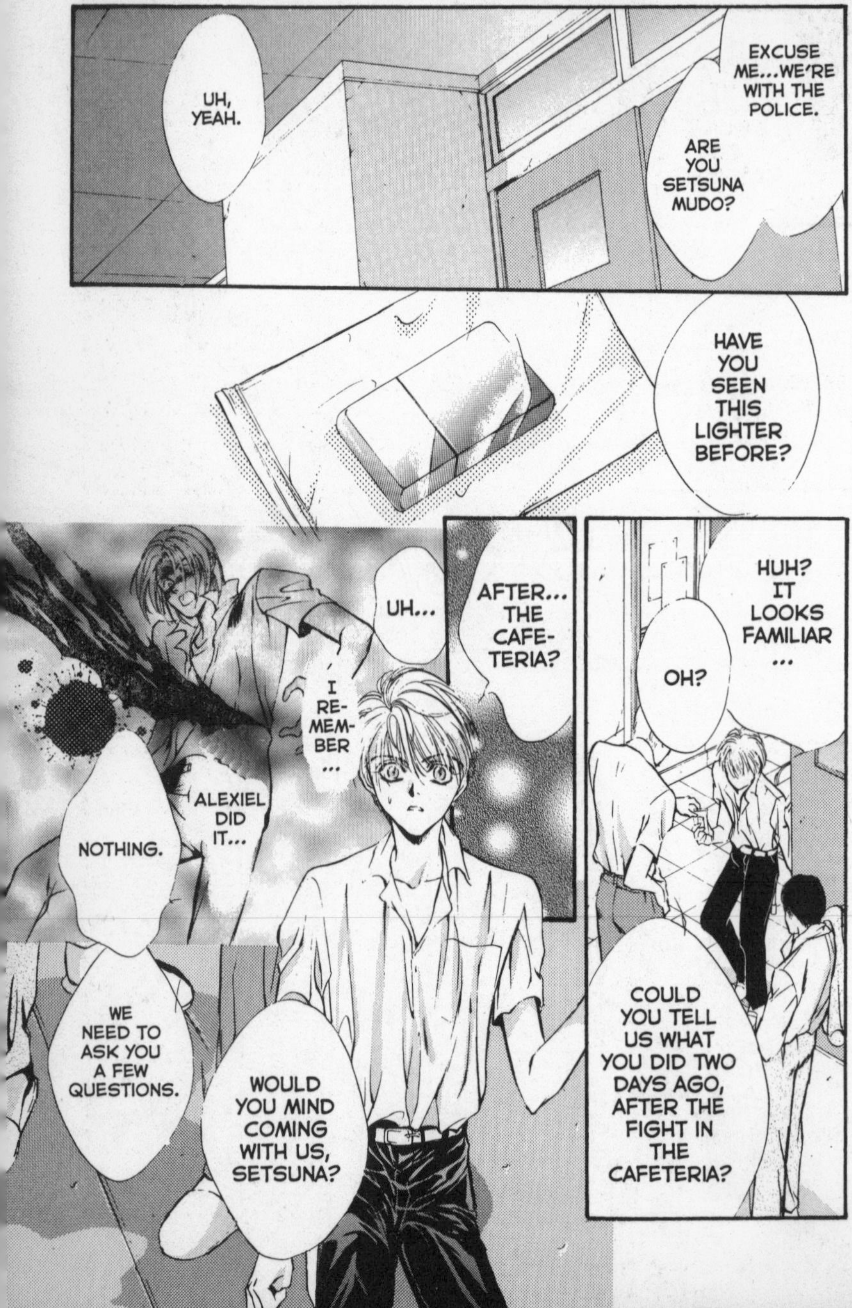
EXCUSE ME...WE'RE WITH THE POLICE.
ARE YOU SETSUNA MUDO?
UH, YEAH.
HAVE YOU SEEN THIS LIGHTER BEFORE?
HUH? IT LOOKS FAMILIAR...
OH?
COULD YOU TELL US WHAT YOU DID TWO DAYS AGO, AFTER THE FIGHT IN THE CAFETERIA?
AFTER... THE CAFETERIA?
UH...
I REMEMBER...
ALEXIEL DID IT...
NOTHING.
WOULD YOU MIND COMING WITH US, SETSUNA?
WE NEED TO ASK YOU A FEW QUESTIONS.

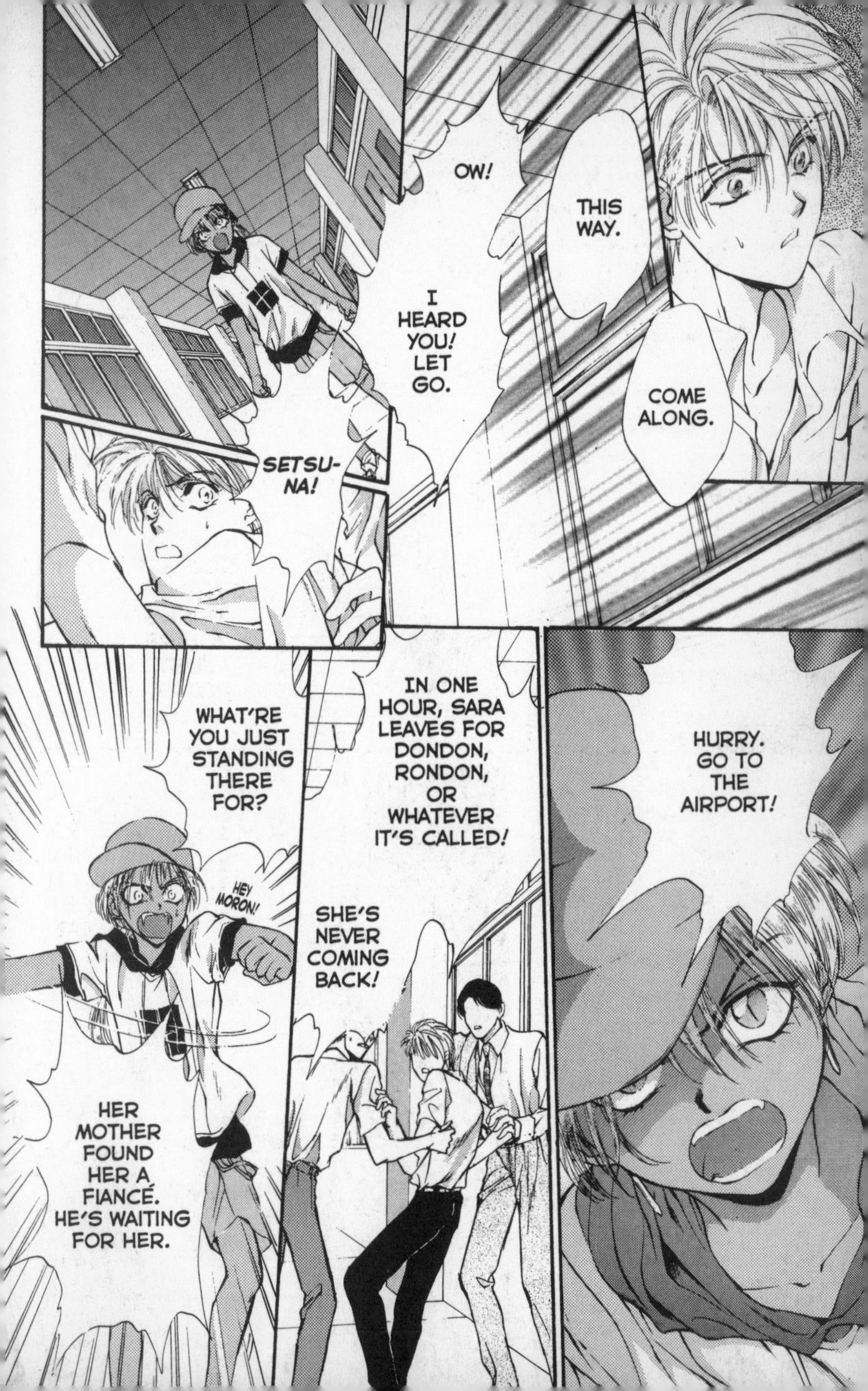
THIS WAY.
COME ALONG.
OW!
I HEARD YOU! LET GO.
SETSU-NA!
HURRY. GO TO THE AIRPORT!
IN ONE HOUR, SARA LEAVES FOR DONDON, RONDON, OR WHATEVER IT'S CALLED!
SHE'S NEVER COMING BACK!
WHAT'RE YOU JUST STANDING THERE FOR?
HEY MORON!
HER MOTHER FOUND HER A FIANCÉ. HE'S WAITING FOR HER.

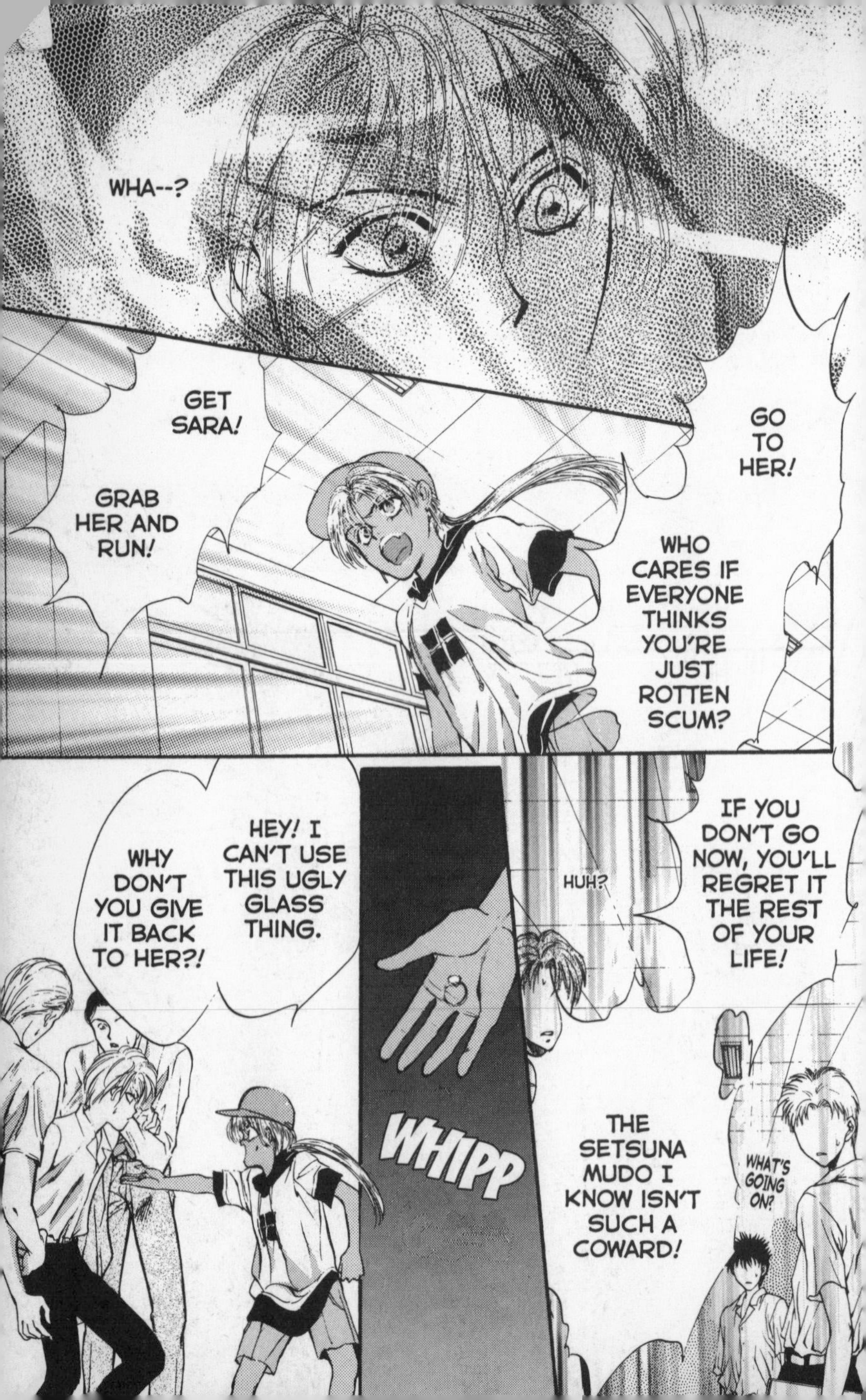
WHA--?
GO TO HER!
WHO CARES IF EVERYONE THINKS YOU'RE JUST ROTTEN SCUM?
GET SARA!
GRAB HER AND RUN!
IF YOU DON'T GO NOW, YOU'LL REGRET IT THE REST OF YOUR LIFE!
HUH?
THE SETSUNA MUDO I KNOW ISN'T SUCH A COWARD!
WHAT'S GOING ON?
WHIPP
HEY! I CAN'T USE THIS UGLY GLASS THING.
WHY DON'T YOU GIVE IT BACK TO HER?!

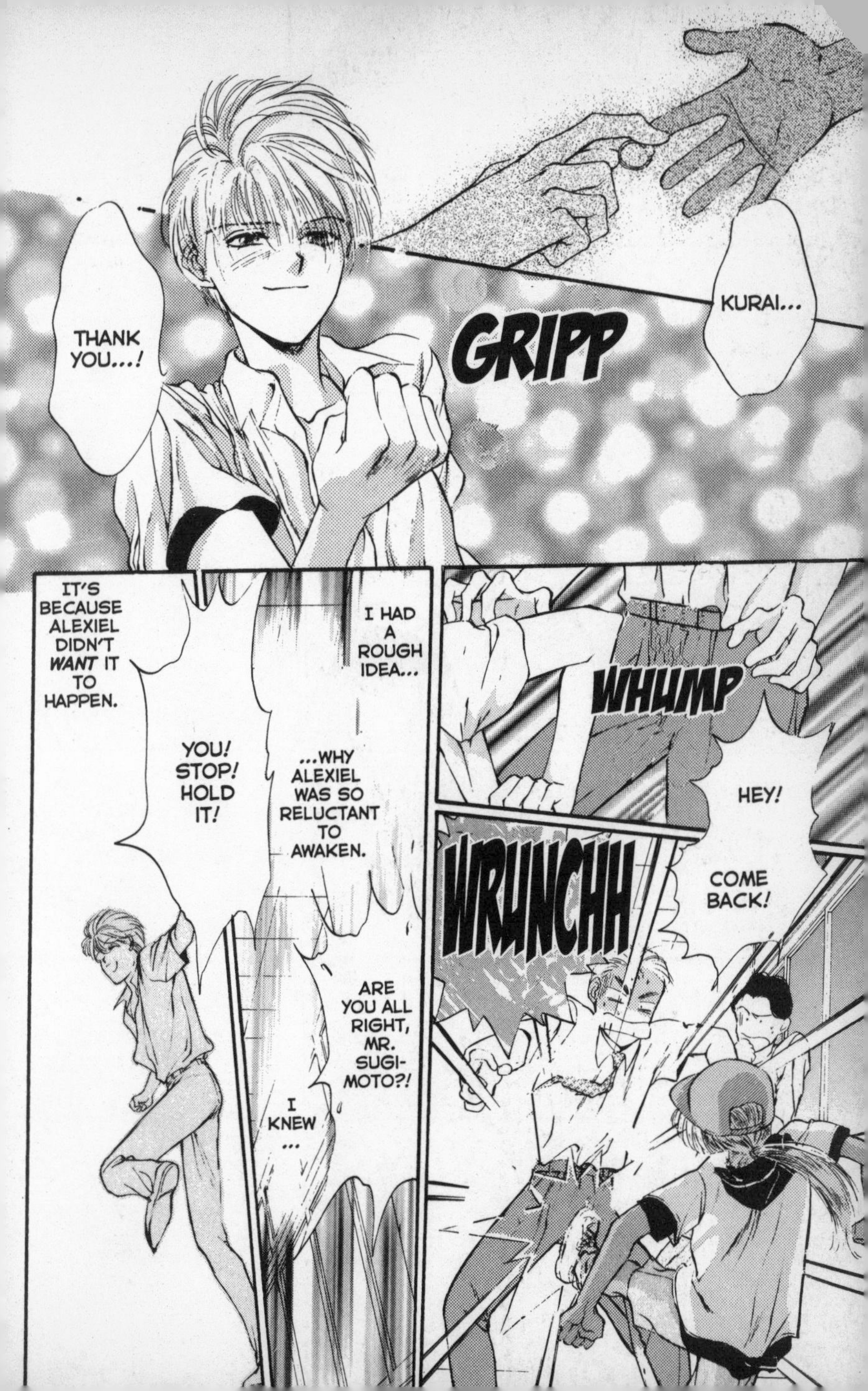
KURAI...
GRIPP
THANK YOU...!
WHUMP
HEY!
COME BACK!
WRUNCHH
ARE YOU ALL RIGHT, MR. SUGI-MOTO?!
I HAD A ROUGH IDEA...
...WHY ALEXIEL WAS SO RELUCTANT TO AWAKEN.
I KNEW...
IT'S BECAUSE ALEXIEL DIDN'T *WANT* IT TO HAPPEN.
YOU! STOP! HOLD IT!

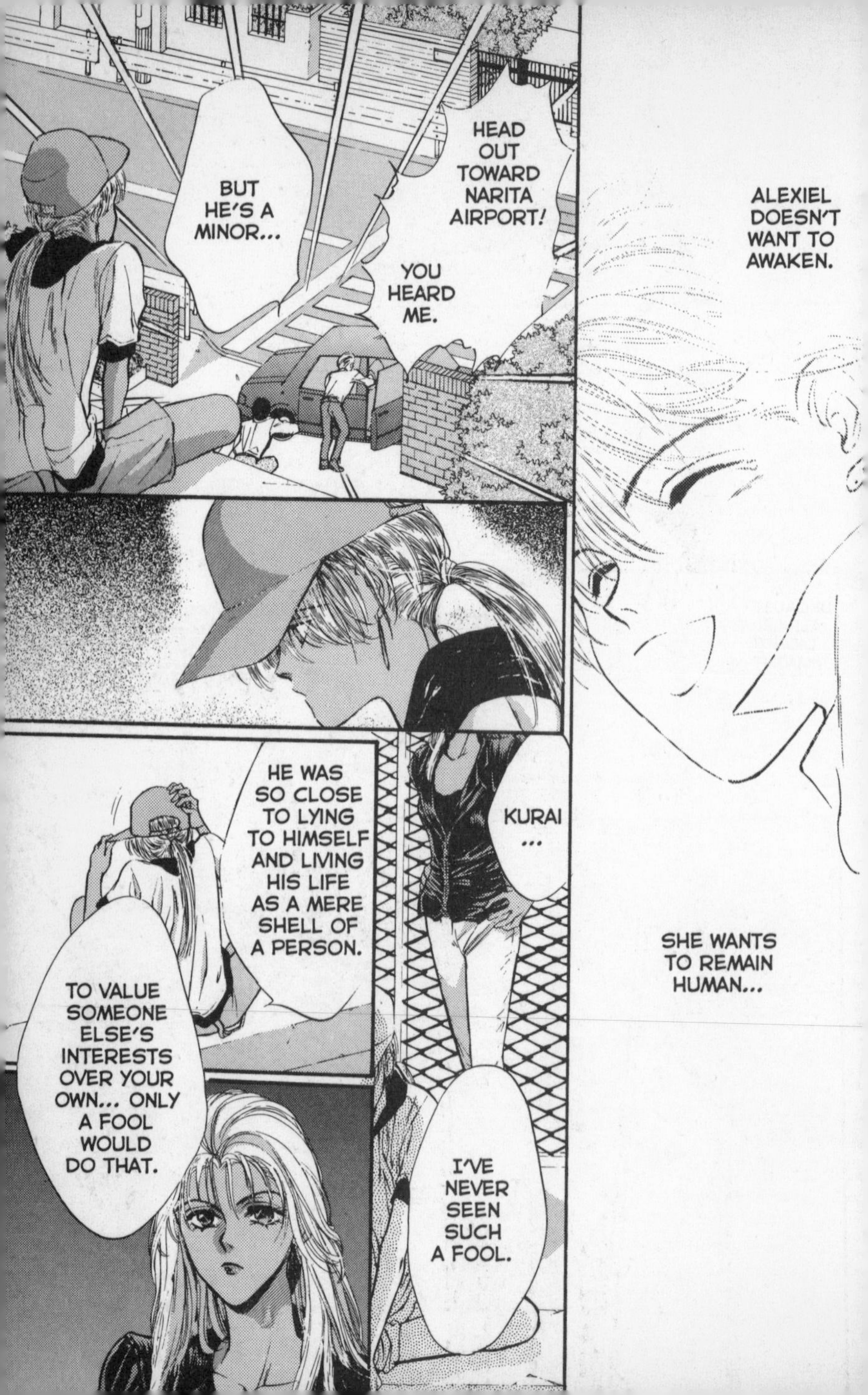
ALEXIEL DOESN'T WANT TO AWAKEN.
SHE WANTS TO REMAIN HUMAN...
HEAD OUT TOWARD NARITA AIRPORT!
BUT HE'S A MINOR...
YOU HEARD ME.
KURAI...
HE WAS SO CLOSE TO LYING TO HIMSELF AND LIVING HIS LIFE AS A MERE SHELL OF A PERSON.
TO VALUE SOMEONE ELSE'S INTERESTS OVER YOUR OWN... ONLY A FOOL WOULD DO THAT.
I'VE NEVER SEEN SUCH A FOOL.

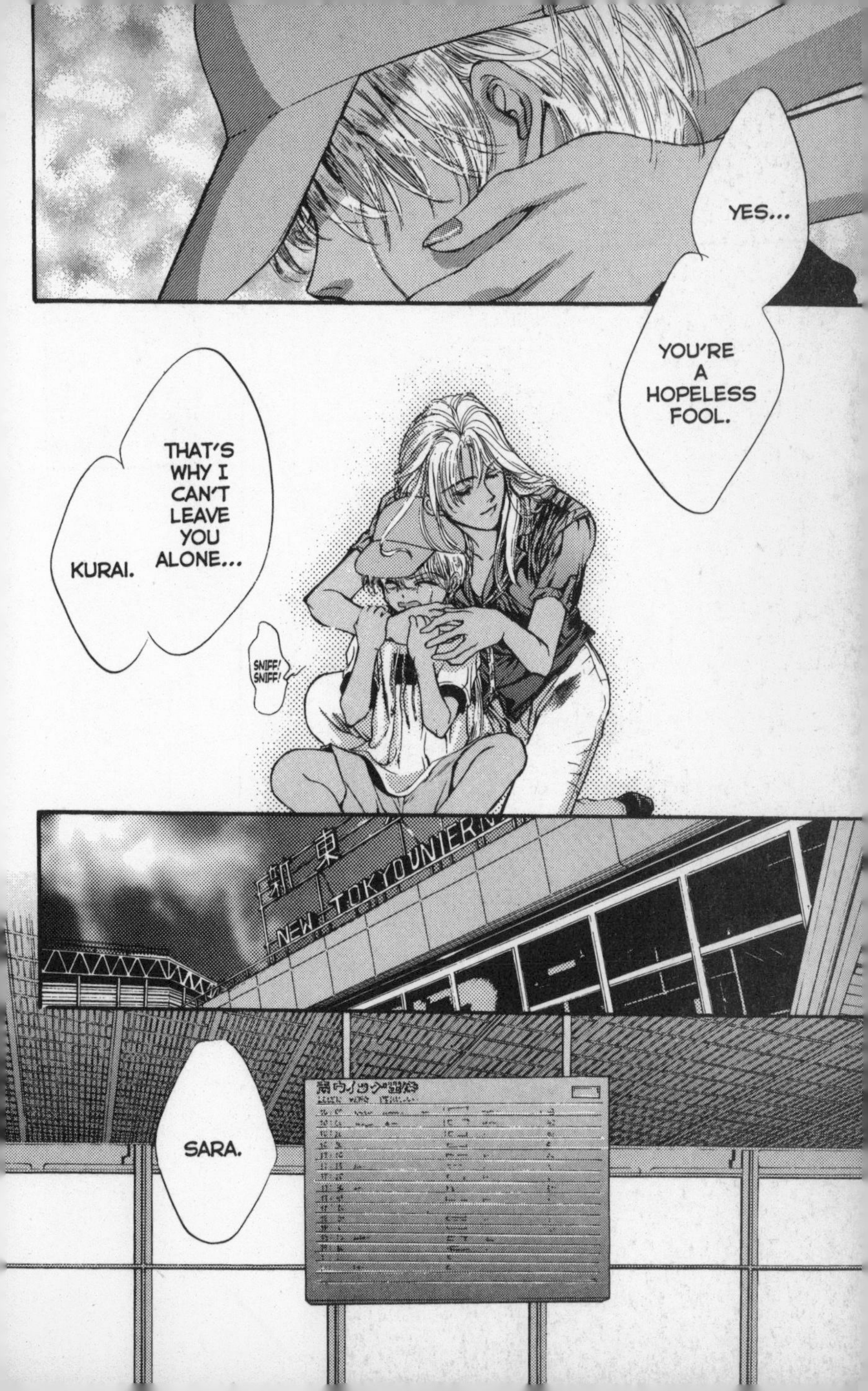

YES...
YOU'RE A HOPELESS FOOL.
THAT'S WHY I CAN'T LEAVE YOU ALONE...
KURAI.
SNIFF! SNIFF!
NEW TOKYO
SARA.

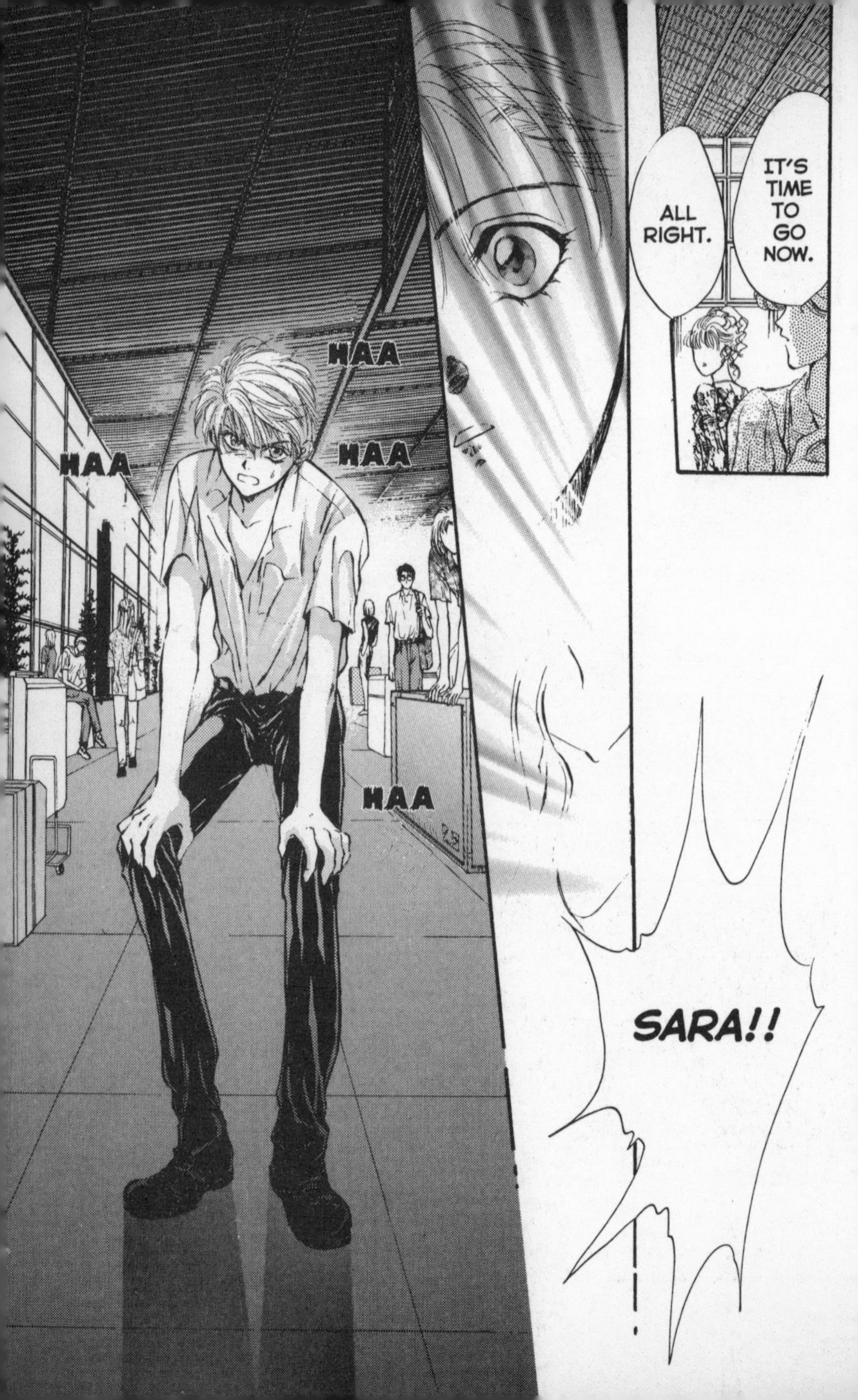
IT'S TIME TO GO NOW.
ALL RIGHT.
SARA!!
HAA
HAA
HAA
HAA

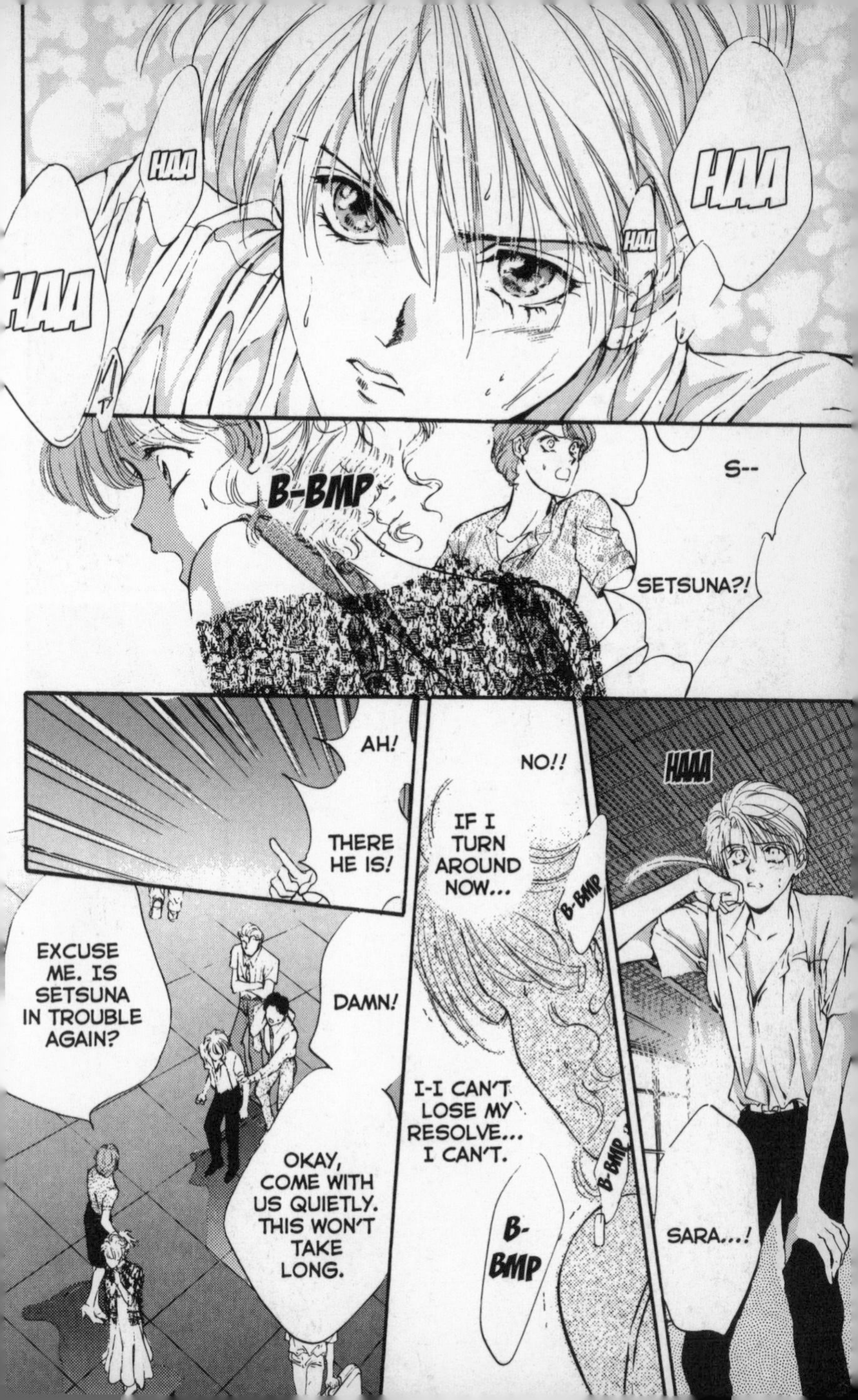
HAA
HAA
HAA
HAA
S--
SETSUNA?!
B-BMP
HAAA
SARA...!
NO!!
IF I TURN AROUND NOW...
B-BMP
I-I CAN'T LOSE MY RESOLVE... I CAN'T.
B-BMP
B-BMP
AH!
THERE HE IS!
DAMN!
EXCUSE ME. IS SETSUNA IN TROUBLE AGAIN?
OKAY, COME WITH US QUIETLY. THIS WON'T TAKE LONG.

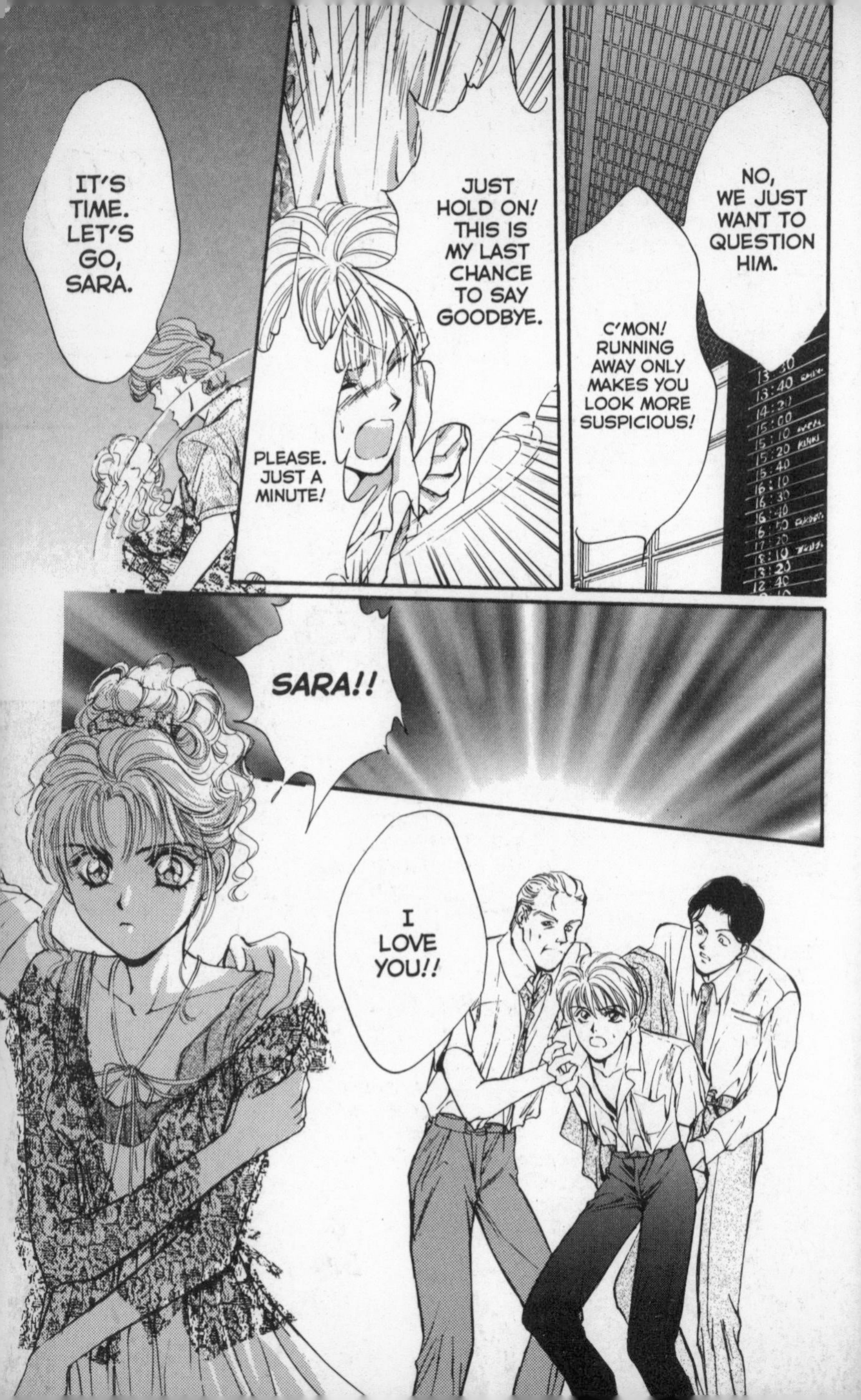
NO, WE JUST WANT TO QUESTION HIM.
C'MON! RUNNING AWAY ONLY MAKES YOU LOOK MORE SUSPICIOUS!
JUST HOLD ON! THIS IS MY LAST CHANCE TO SAY GOODBYE.
PLEASE. JUST A MINUTE!
IT'S TIME. LET'S GO, SARA.
SARA!!
I LOVE YOU!!

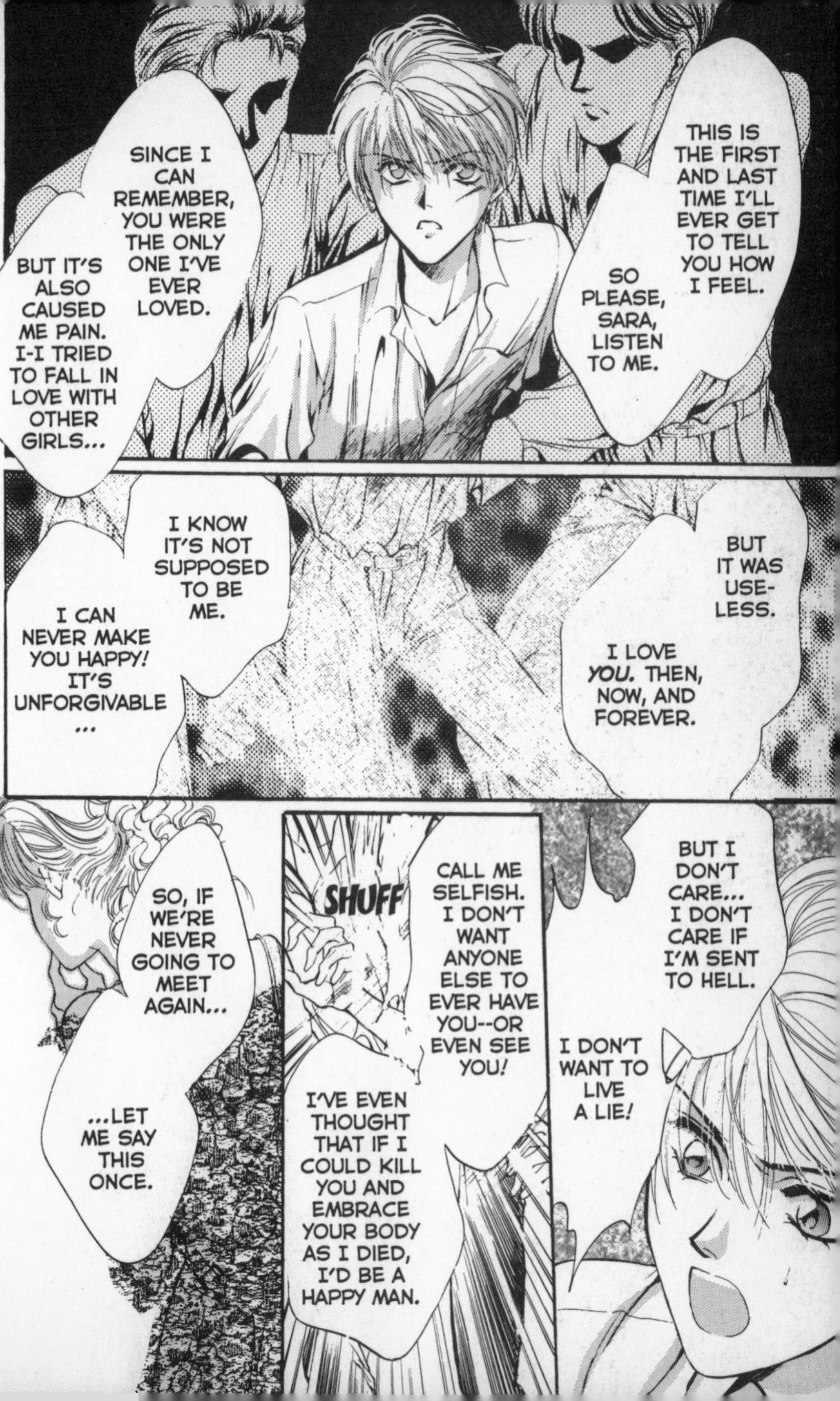
THIS IS THE FIRST AND LAST TIME I'LL EVER GET TO TELL YOU HOW I FEEL.
SO PLEASE, SARA, LISTEN TO ME.
SINCE I CAN REMEMBER, YOU WERE THE ONLY ONE I'VE EVER LOVED.
BUT IT'S ALSO CAUSED ME PAIN. I-I TRIED TO FALL IN LOVE WITH OTHER GIRLS...
BUT IT WAS USE-LESS.
I LOVE *YOU.* THEN, NOW, AND FOREVER.
I KNOW IT'S NOT SUPPOSED TO BE ME.
I CAN NEVER MAKE YOU HAPPY! IT'S UNFORGIVABLE...
BUT I DON'T CARE... I DON'T CARE IF I'M SENT TO HELL.
I DON'T WANT TO LIVE A LIE!
SHUFF
CALL ME SELFISH. I DON'T WANT ANYONE ELSE TO EVER HAVE YOU--OR EVEN SEE YOU!
I'VE EVEN THOUGHT THAT IF I COULD KILL YOU AND EMBRACE YOUR BODY AS I DIED, I'D BE A HAPPY MAN.
SO, IF WE'RE NEVER GOING TO MEET AGAIN...
...LET ME SAY THIS ONCE.

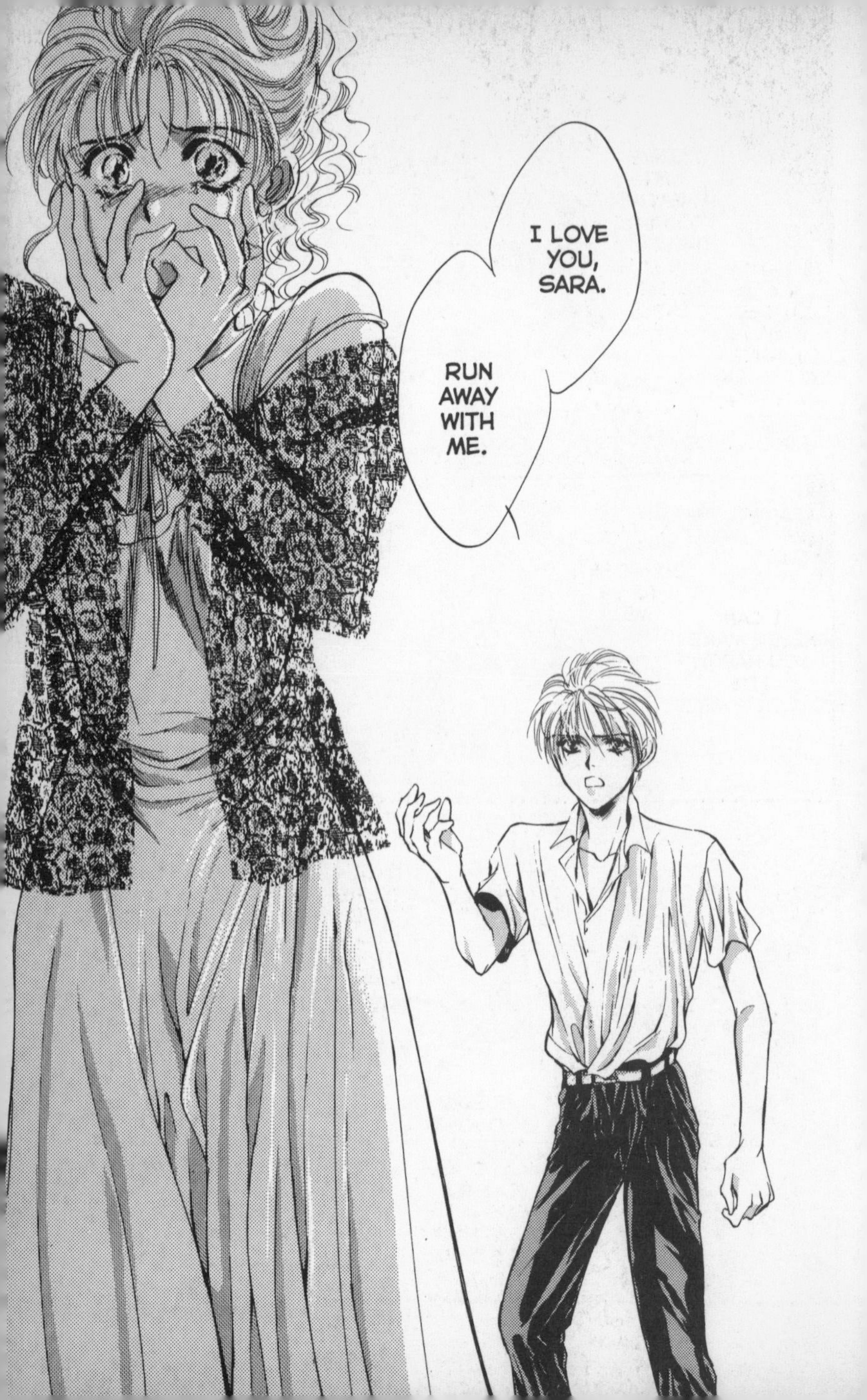
I LOVE YOU, SARA.
RUN AWAY WITH ME.

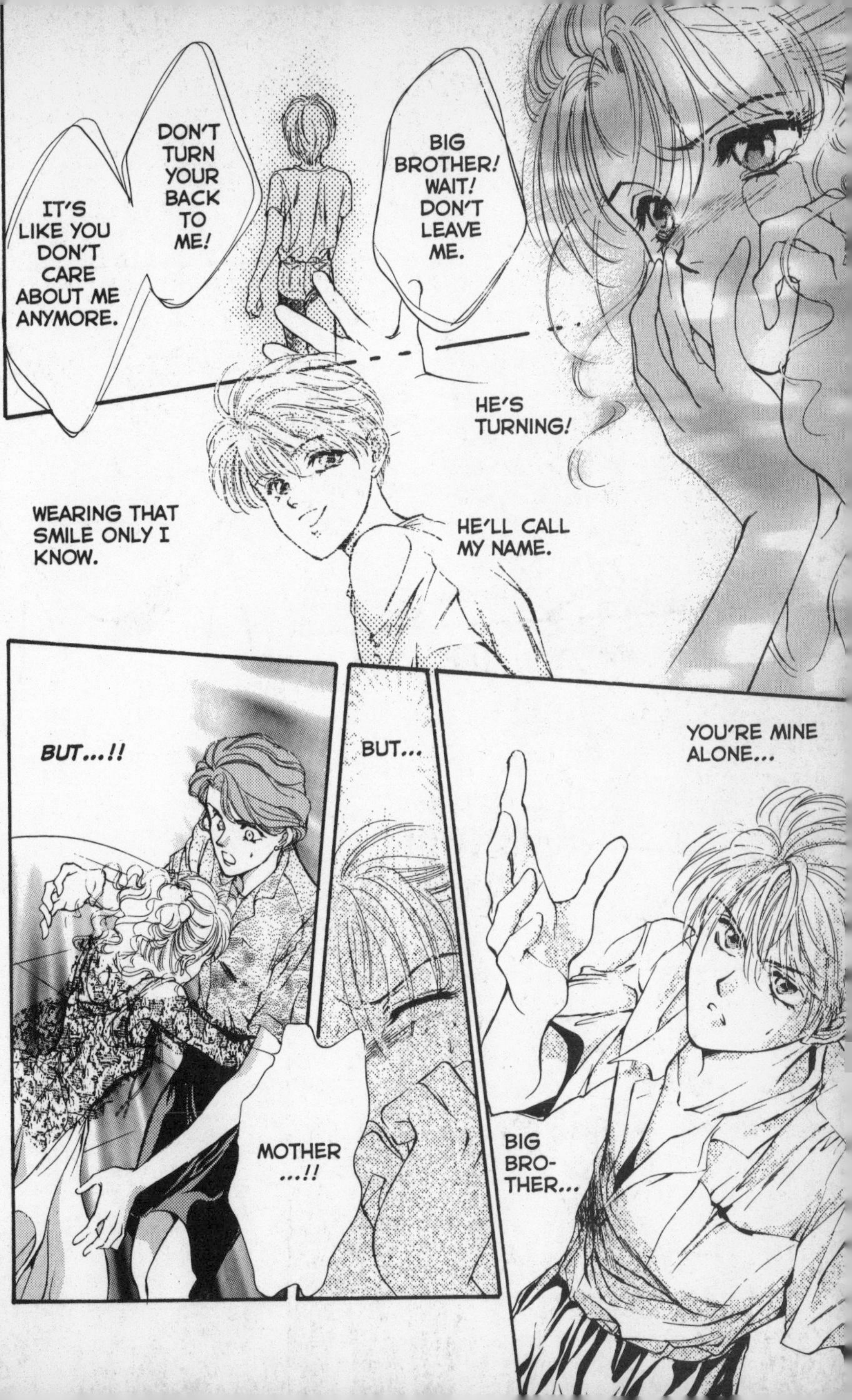
BIG BROTHER! WAIT! DON'T LEAVE ME.
DON'T TURN YOUR BACK TO ME!
IT'S LIKE YOU DON'T CARE ABOUT ME ANYMORE.
HE'S TURNING!
HE'LL CALL MY NAME.
WEARING THAT SMILE ONLY I KNOW.
YOU'RE MINE ALONE...
BIG BRO-THER...
BUT...
MOTHER...!!
BUT...!!

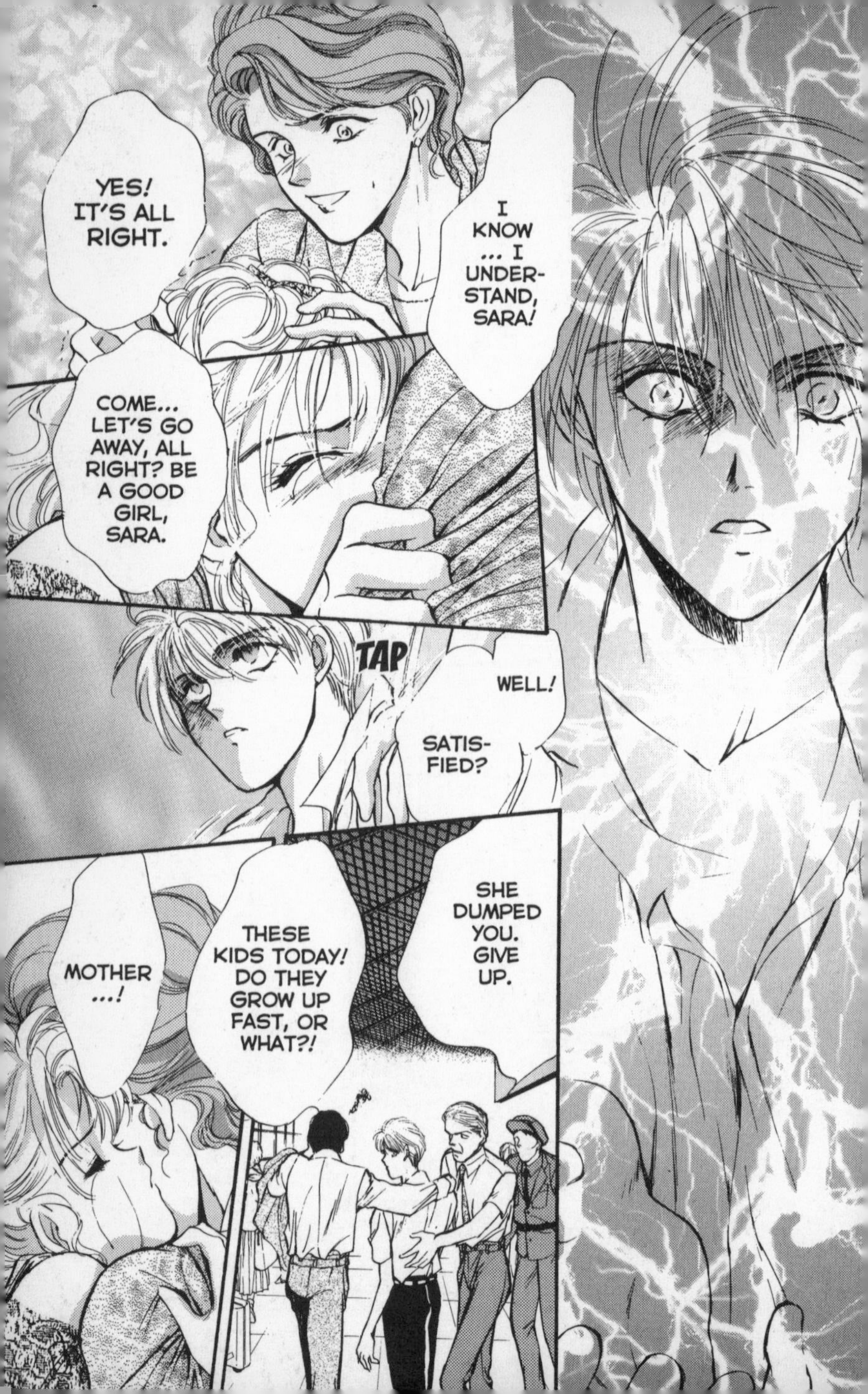
I KNOW ... I UNDERSTAND, SARA!
YES! IT'S ALL RIGHT.
COME... LET'S GO AWAY, ALL RIGHT? BE A GOOD GIRL, SARA.
TAP
WELL!
SATIS-FIED?
SHE DUMPED YOU. GIVE UP.
THESE KIDS TODAY! DO THEY GROW UP FAST, OR WHAT?!
MOTHER ...!

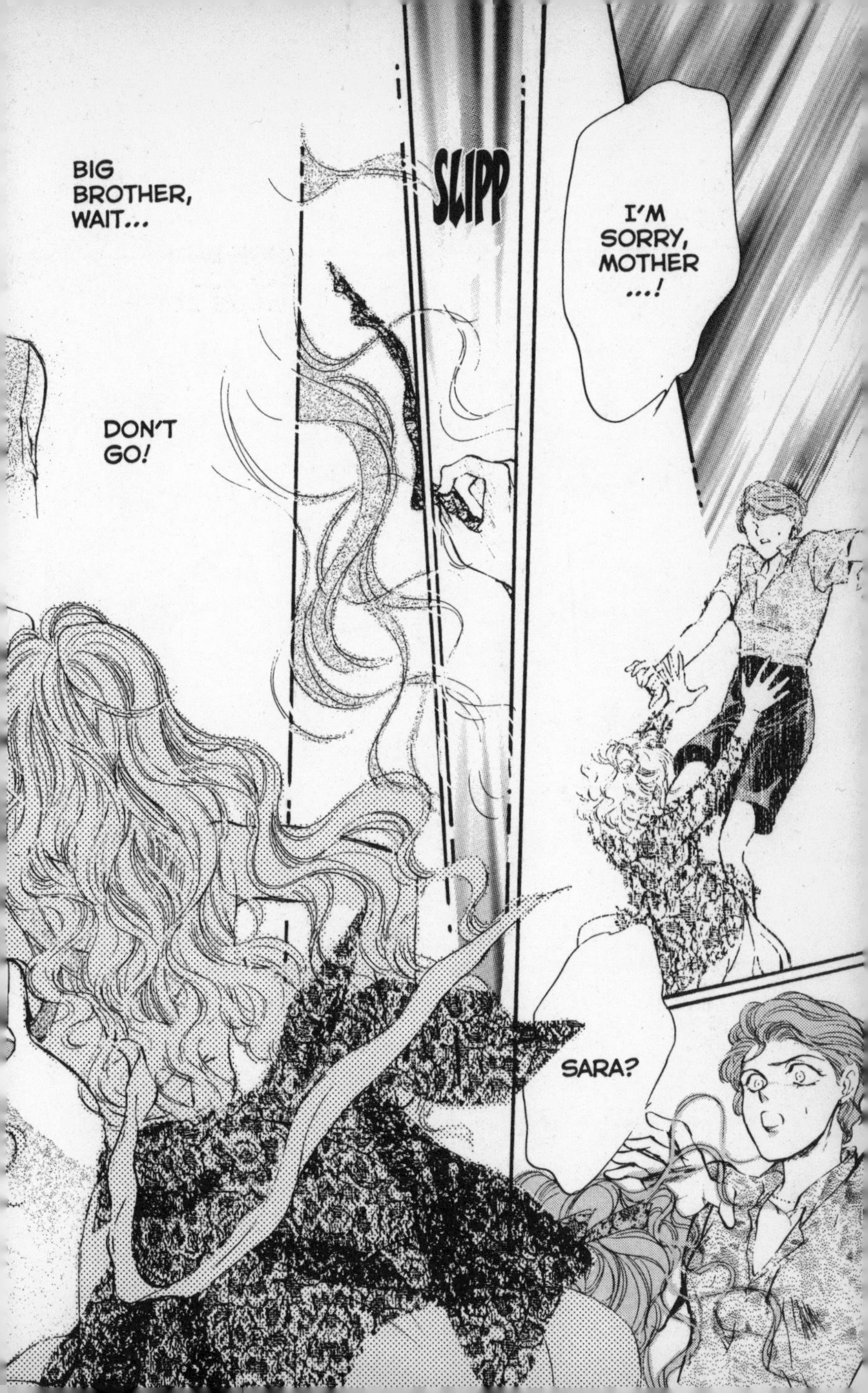
I'M SORRY, MOTHER...!
SARA?
SLIPP
BIG BROTHER, WAIT...
DON'T GO!

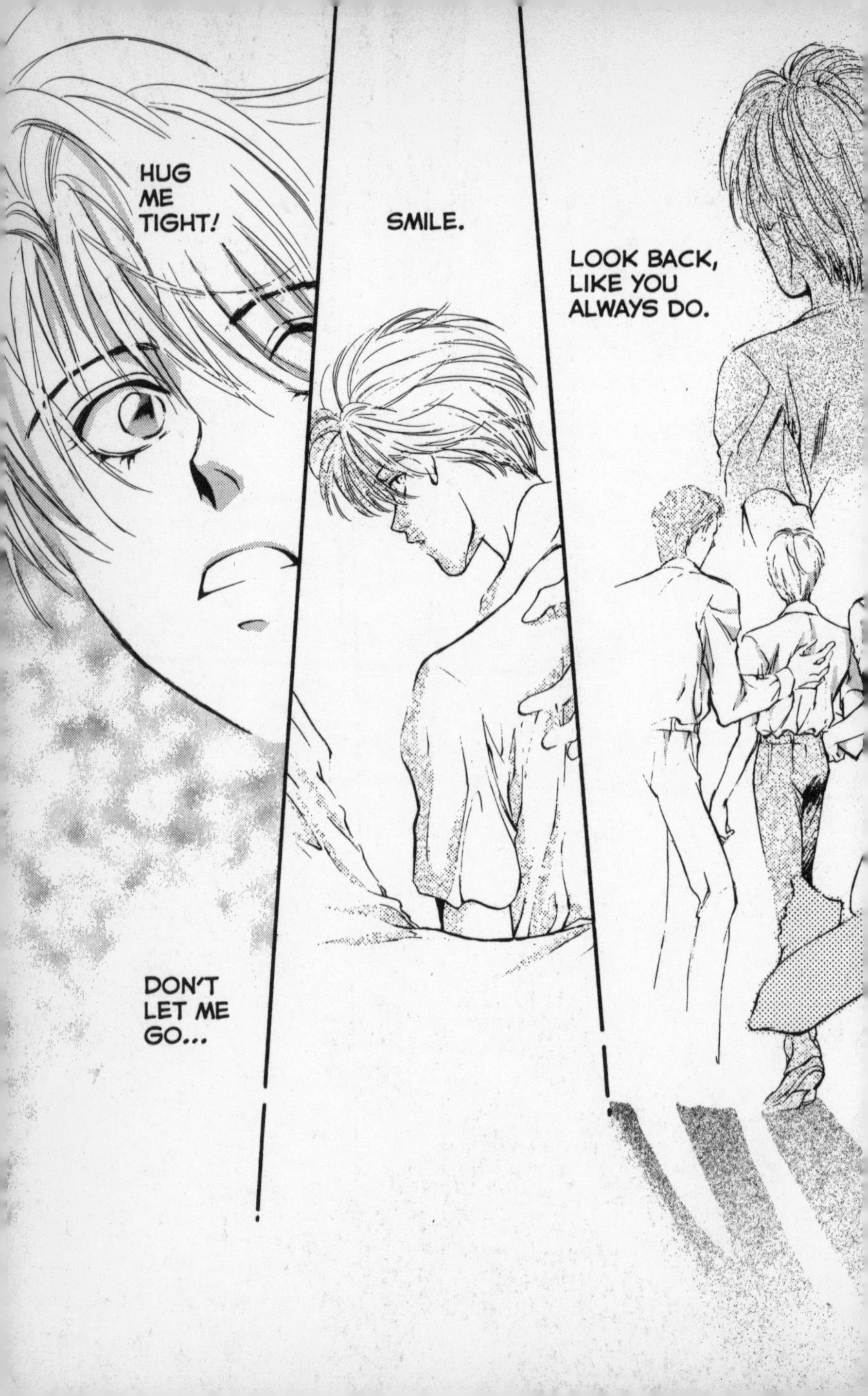
LOOK BACK, LIKE YOU ALWAYS DO.
SMILE.
HUG ME TIGHT!
DON'T LET ME GO...

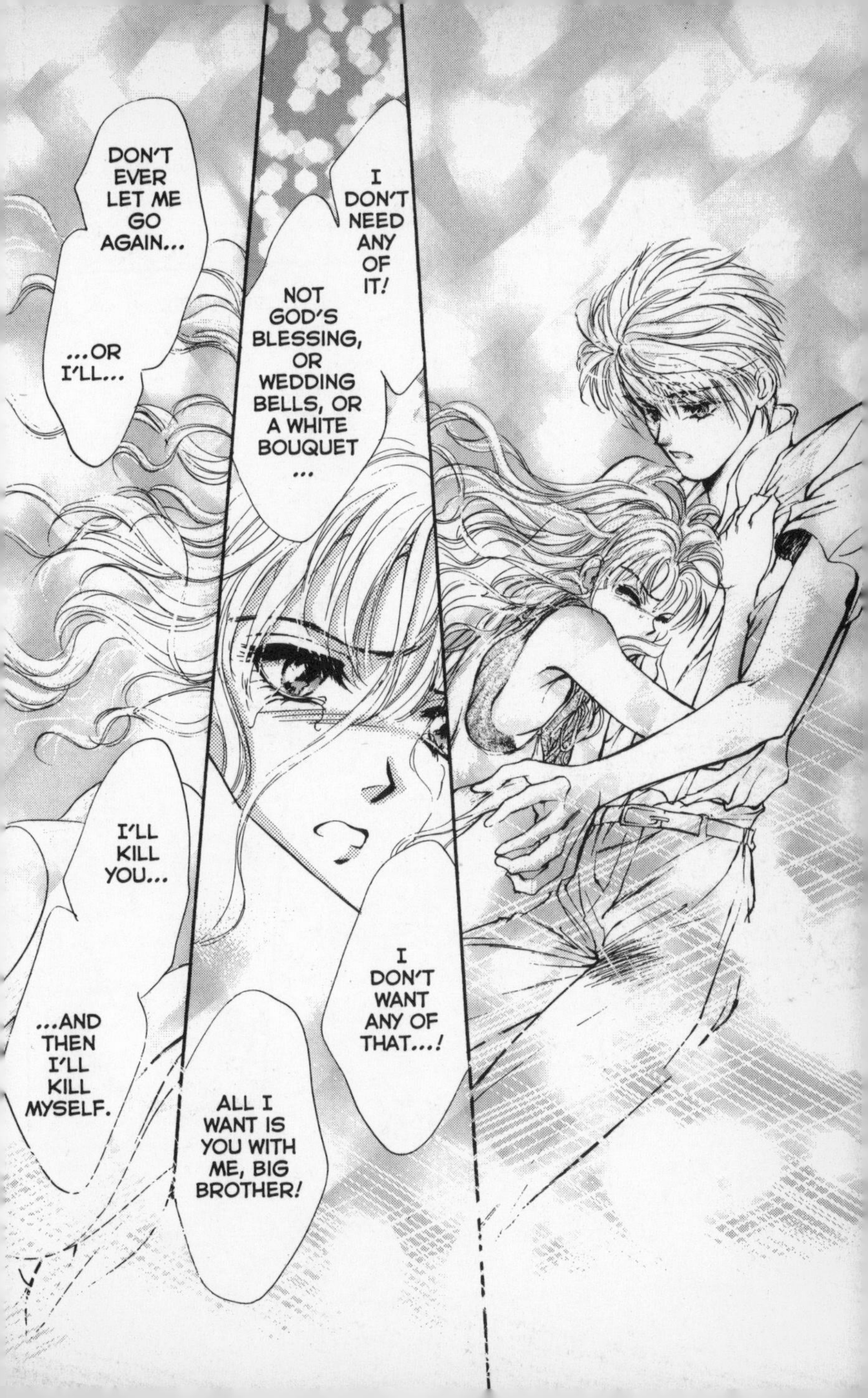
I DON'T NEED ANY OF IT!
NOT GOD'S BLESSING, OR WEDDING BELLS, OR A WHITE BOUQUET ...
I DON'T WANT ANY OF THAT...!
ALL I WANT IS YOU WITH ME, BIG BROTHER!
DON'T EVER LET ME GO AGAIN...
...OR I'LL...
I'LL KILL YOU...
...AND THEN I'LL KILL MYSELF.

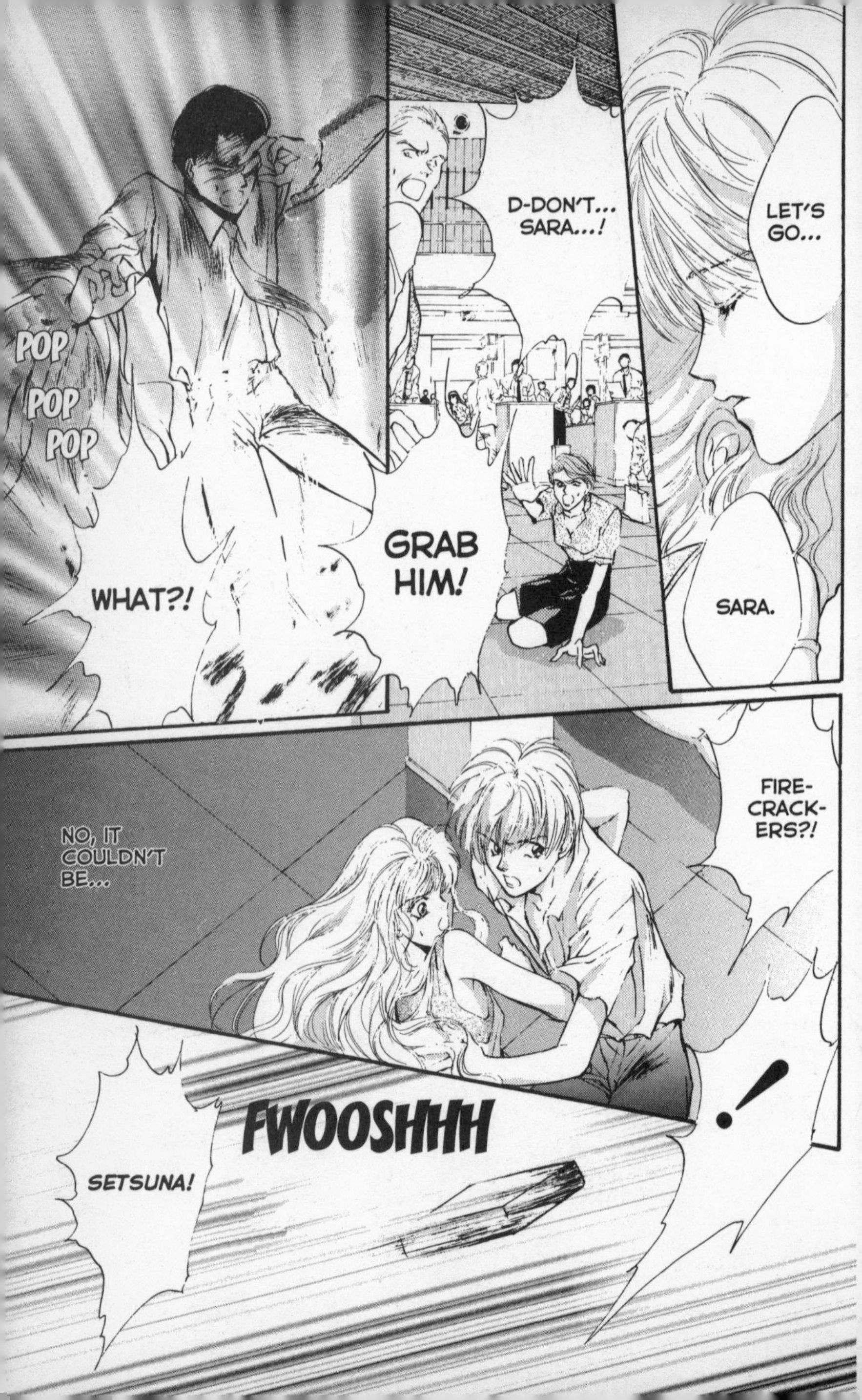
LET'S GO...
SARA.
D-DON'T... SARA...!
GRAB HIM!
POP
POP
POP
WHAT?!
FIRE-CRACK-ERS?!
NO, IT COULDN'T BE...
!
FWOOSHHH
SETSUNA!

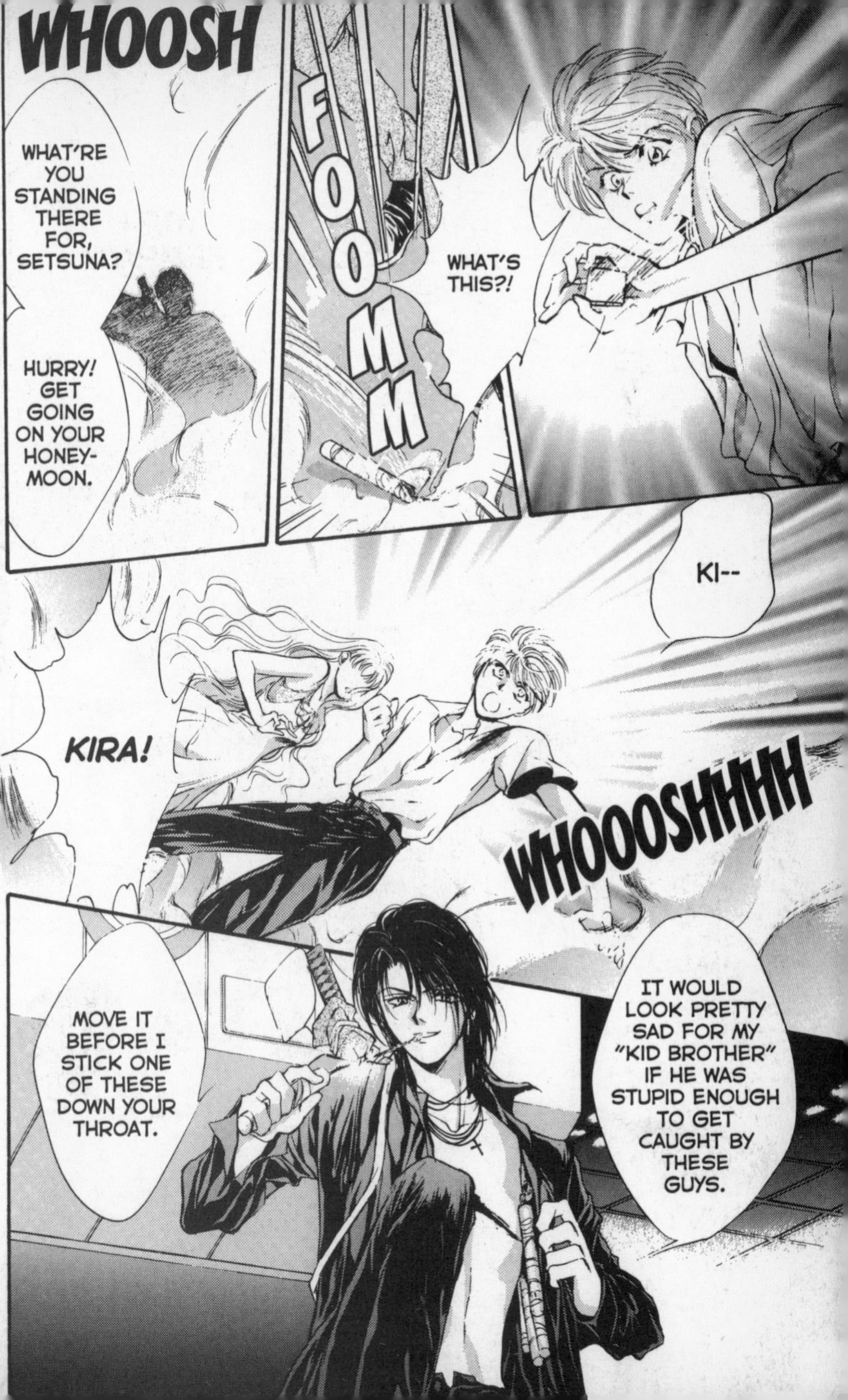
WHAT'S THIS?!
FOOOMM
WHOOSH
WHAT'RE YOU STANDING THERE FOR, SETSUNA?
HURRY! GET GOING ON YOUR HONEY-MOON.
KI--
WHOOOSHHHH
KIRA!
IT WOULD LOOK PRETTY SAD FOR MY "KID BROTHER" IF HE WAS STUPID ENOUGH TO GET CAUGHT BY THESE GUYS.
MOVE IT BEFORE I STICK ONE OF THESE DOWN YOUR THROAT.

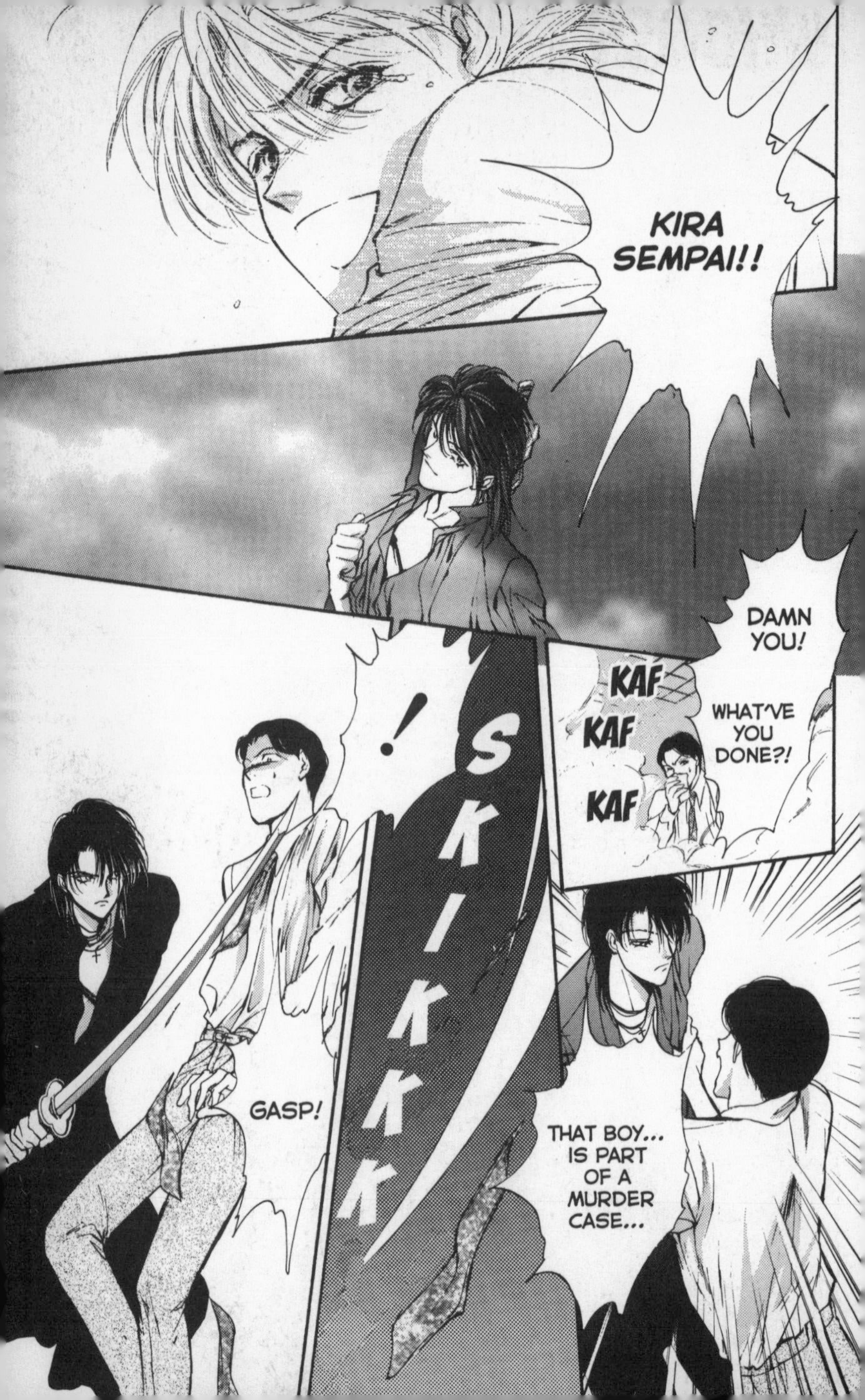
KIRA SEMPAI!!
DAMN YOU!
KAF
KAF
KAF
WHAT'VE YOU DONE?!
THAT BOY... IS PART OF A MURDER CASE...
!
SKIKKK
GASP!

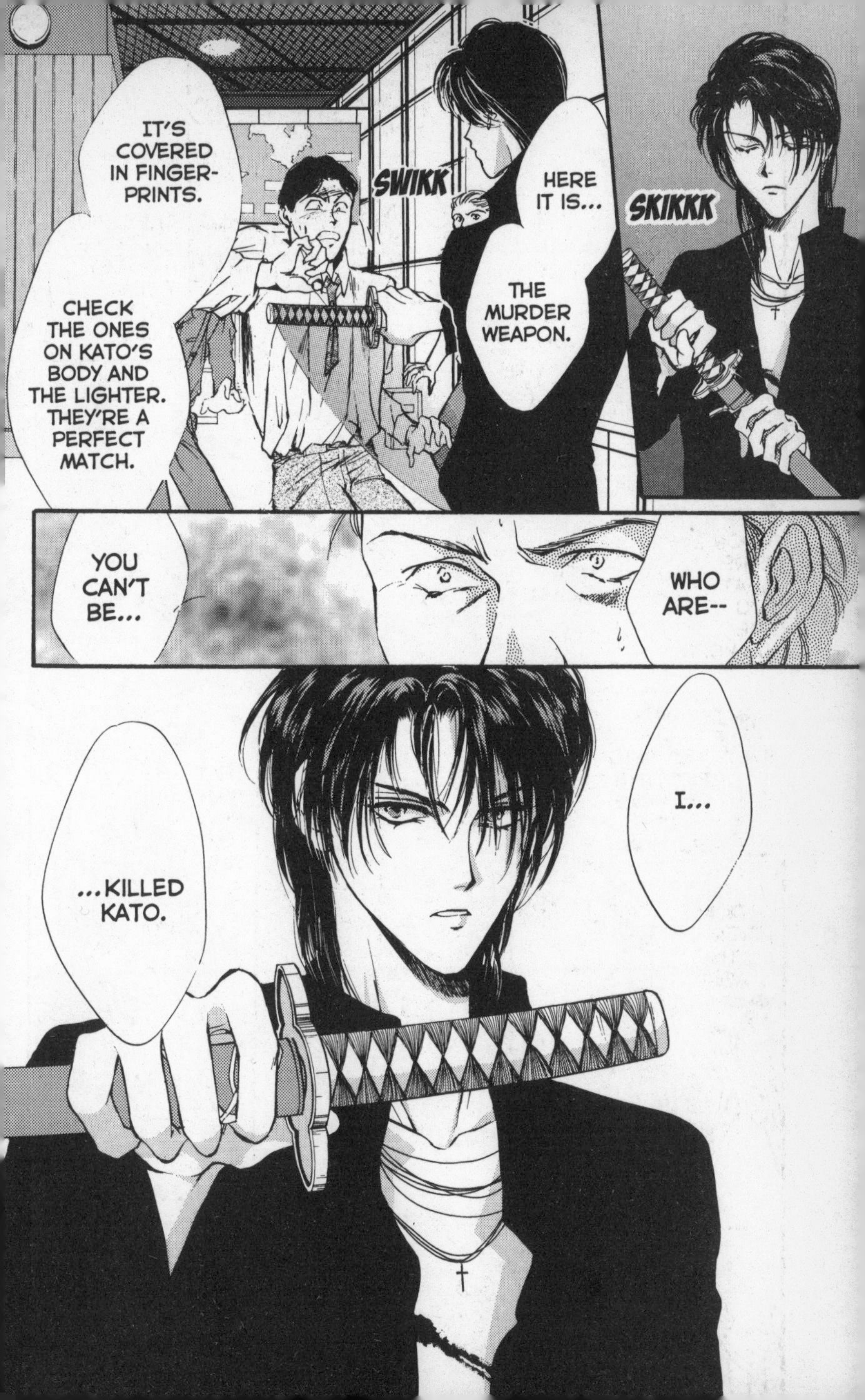
SKIKKK
HERE IT IS...
THE MURDER WEAPON.
SWIKK
IT'S COVERED IN FINGER-PRINTS.
CHECK THE ONES ON KATO'S BODY AND THE LIGHTER. THEY'RE A PERFECT MATCH.
WHO ARE--
YOU CAN'T BE...
I...
...KILLED KATO.

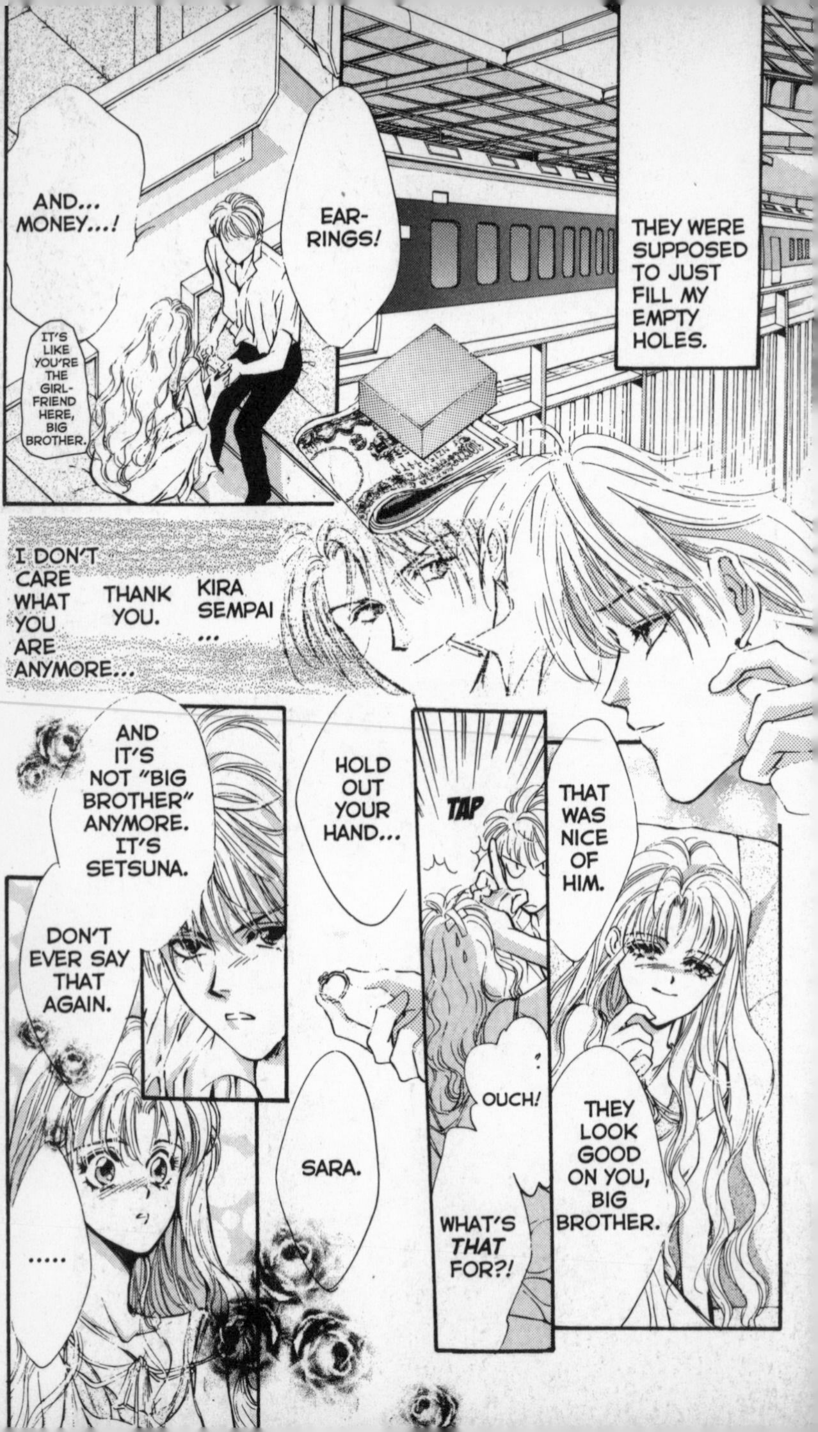
THEY WERE SUPPOSED TO JUST FILL MY EMPTY HOLES.
EAR-RINGS!
AND... MONEY...!
IT'S LIKE YOU'RE THE GIRL-FRIEND HERE, BIG BROTHER.
KIRA SEMPAI ...
THANK YOU.
I DON'T CARE WHAT YOU ARE ANYMORE...
THAT WAS NICE OF HIM.
THEY LOOK GOOD ON YOU, BIG BROTHER.
TAP
?
OUCH!
WHAT'S *THAT* FOR?!
HOLD OUT YOUR HAND...
SARA.
AND IT'S NOT "BIG BROTHER" ANYMORE. IT'S SETSUNA.
DON'T EVER SAY THAT AGAIN.
.....

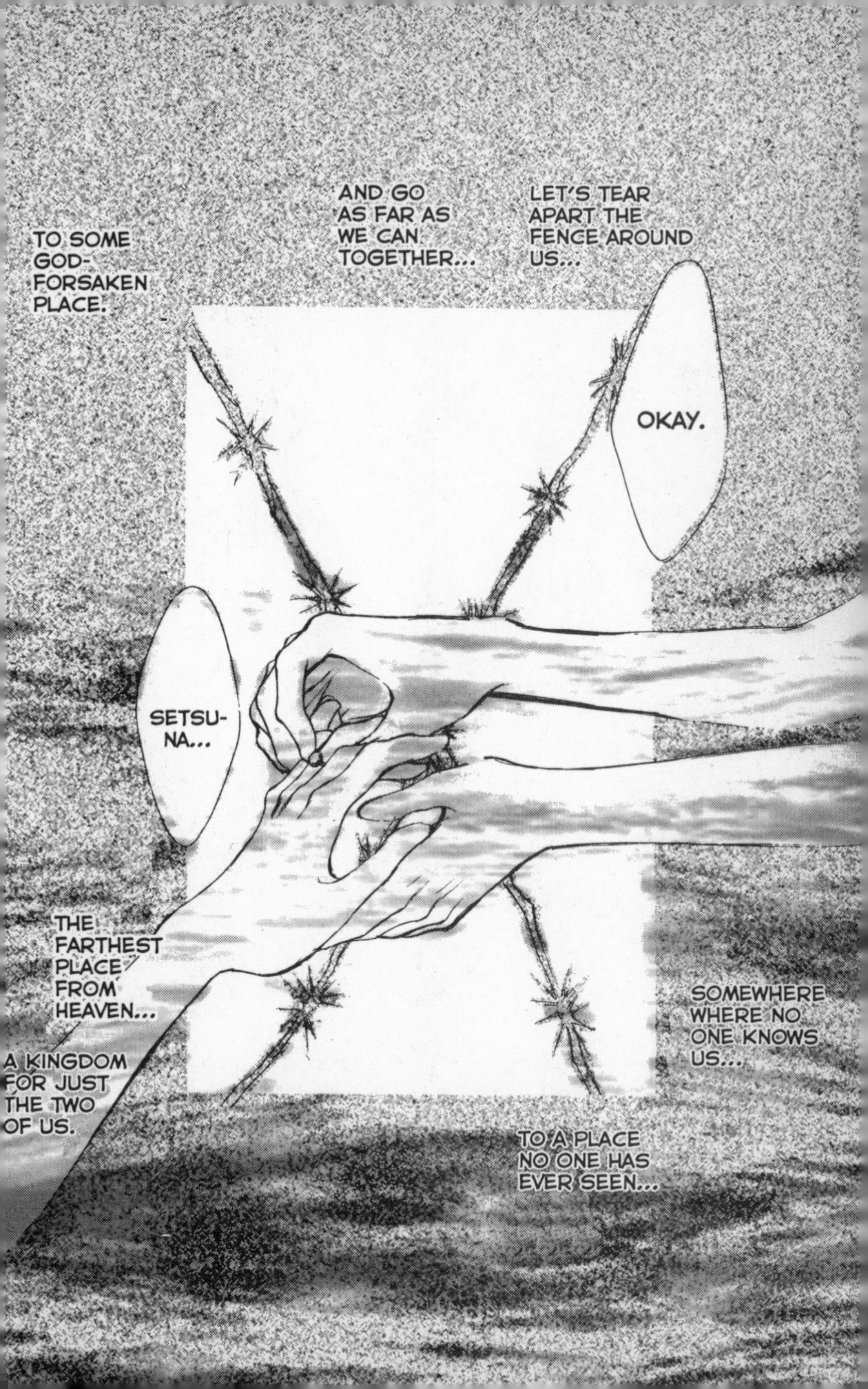
LET'S TEAR APART THE FENCE AROUND US...
AND GO AS FAR AS WE CAN TOGETHER...
TO SOME GOD-FORSAKEN PLACE.
OKAY.
SETSU-NA...
SOMEWHERE WHERE NO ONE KNOWS US...
THE FARTHEST PLACE FROM HEAVEN...
TO A PLACE NO ONE HAS EVER SEEN...
A KINGDOM FOR JUST THE TWO OF US.

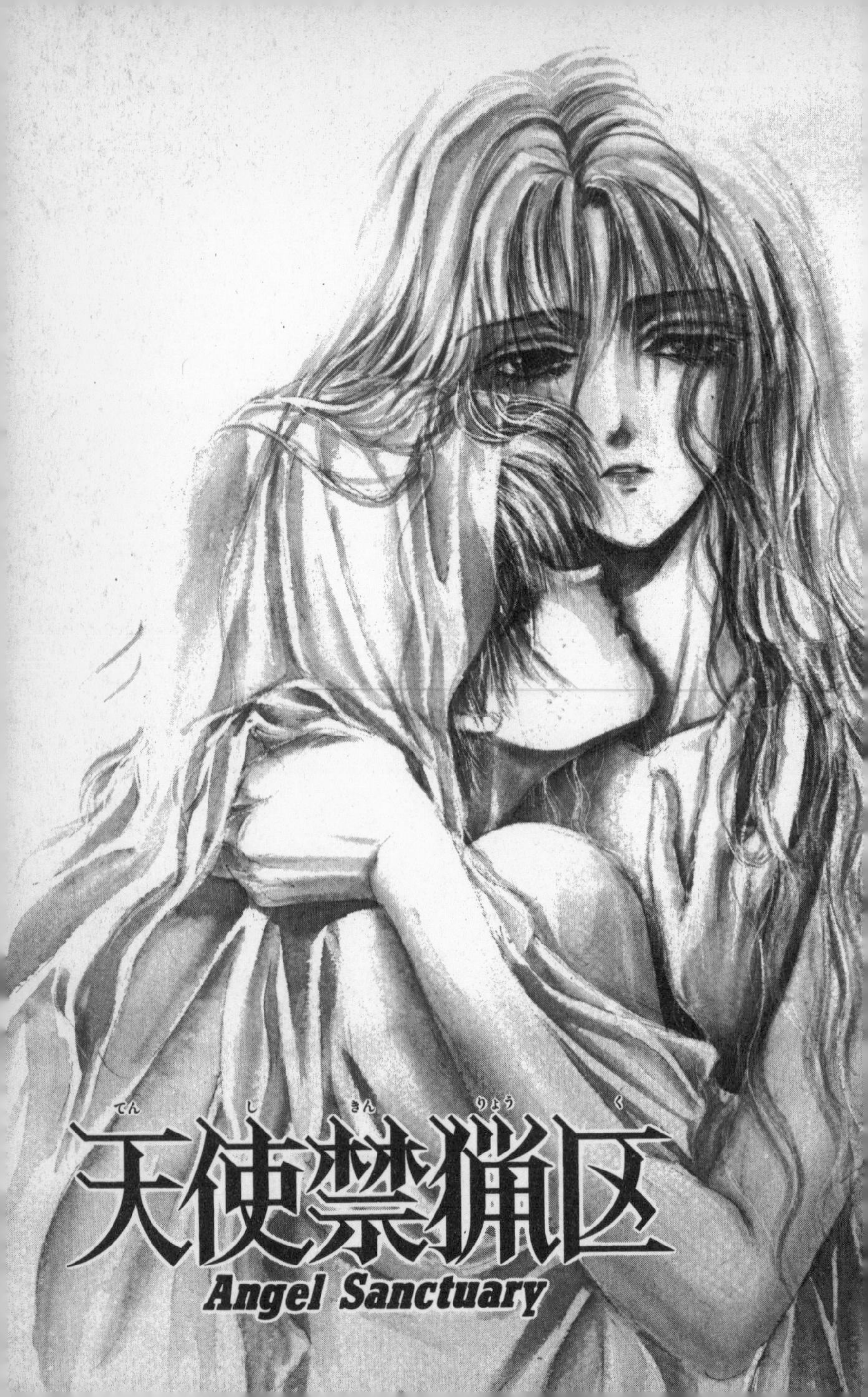
天使禁猟区（てんしきんりょうく）
Angel Sanctuary

NESTLED IN
THE WING,
WE SLOWLY
CLOSE OUR
EYES...

WHEN WE
AWAKE
FROM OUR
DROWSINESS,
WE REALIZE...

...THAT THIS
WAS ALL
A DREAM...

THE NIGHTMARE
IS OVER.

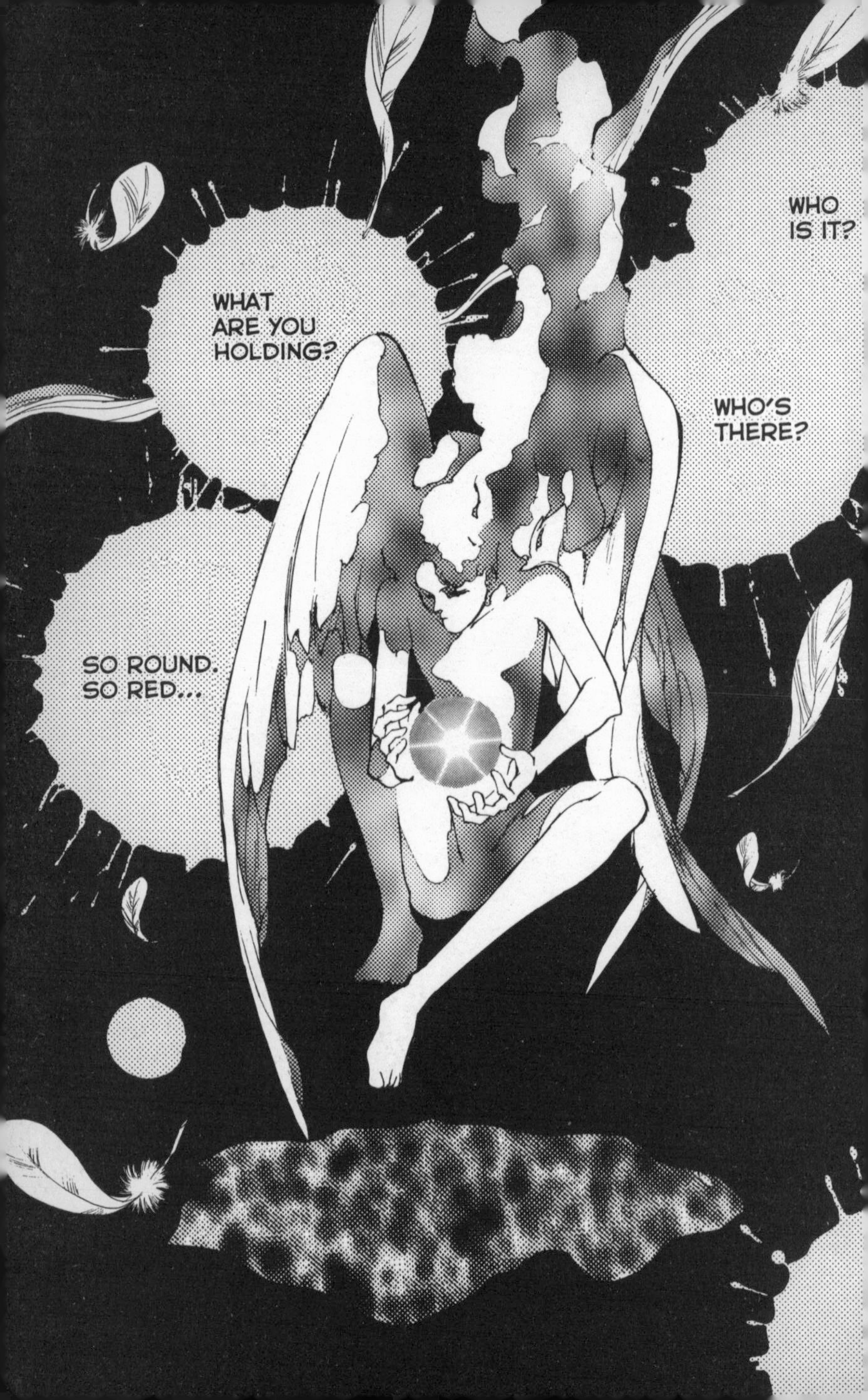
WHO IS IT?
WHO'S THERE?
WHAT ARE YOU HOLDING?
SO ROUND. SO RED...

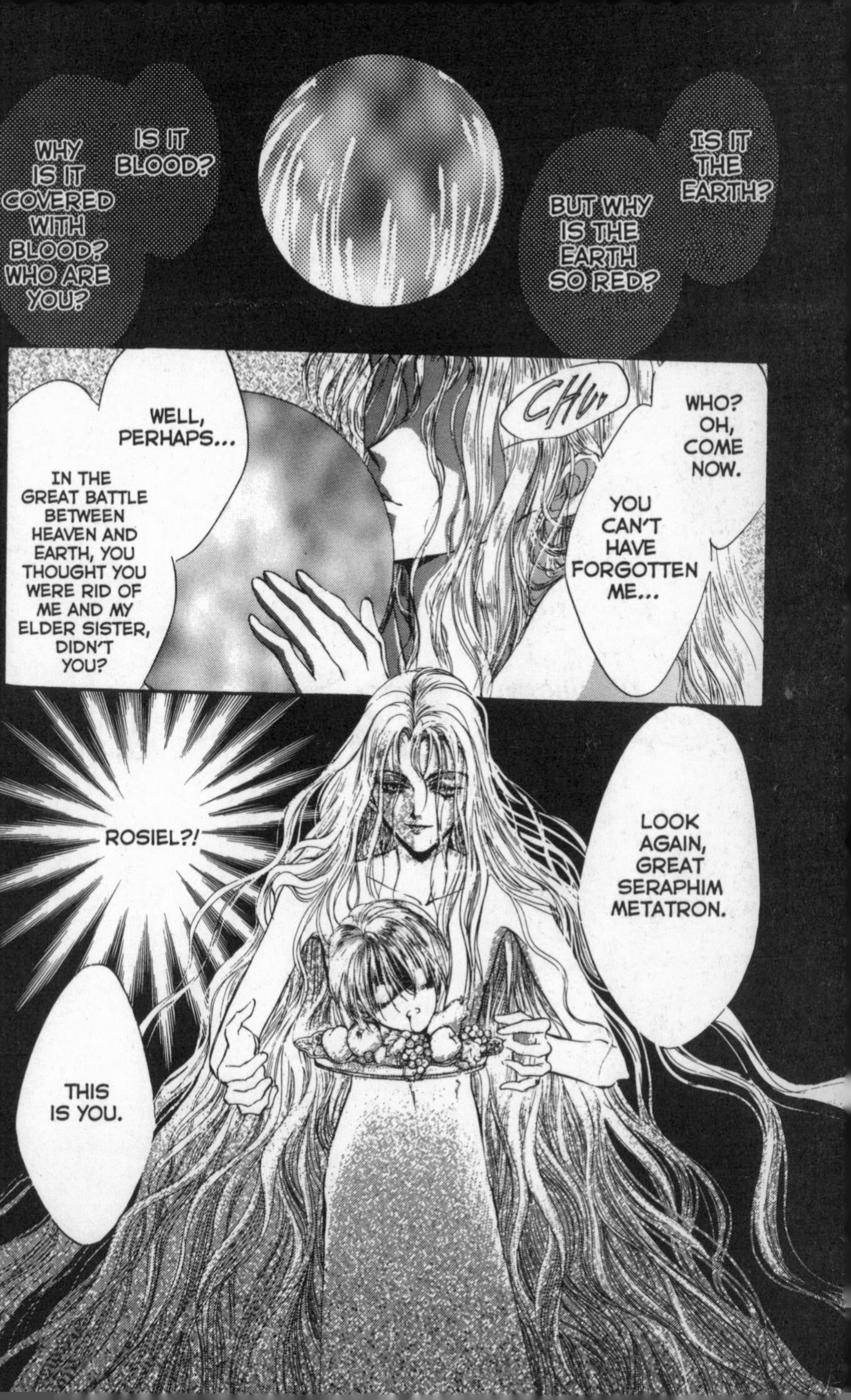
IS IT THE EARTH?
BUT WHY IS THE EARTH SO RED?
IS IT BLOOD?
WHY IS IT COVERED WITH BLOOD? WHO ARE YOU?
CHU
WHO? OH, COME NOW.
YOU CAN'T HAVE FORGOTTEN ME...
WELL, PERHAPS...
IN THE GREAT BATTLE BETWEEN HEAVEN AND EARTH, YOU THOUGHT YOU WERE RID OF ME AND MY ELDER SISTER, DIDN'T YOU?
LOOK AGAIN, GREAT SERAPHIM METATRON.
ROSIEL?!
THIS IS YOU.

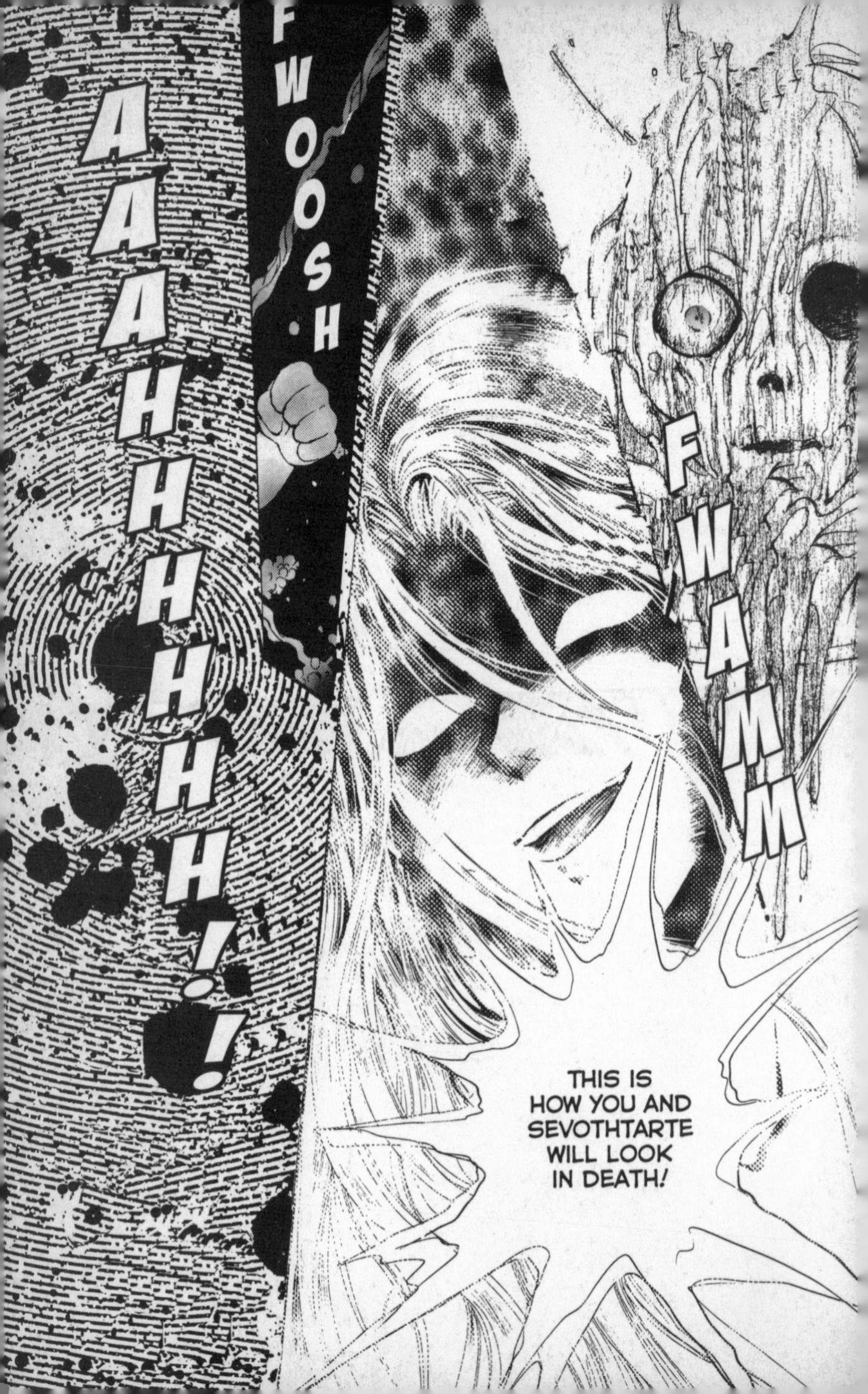
FWAMM
THIS IS HOW YOU AND SEVOTHTARTE WILL LOOK IN DEATH!
FWOOSH
AAAHHHHHH!!

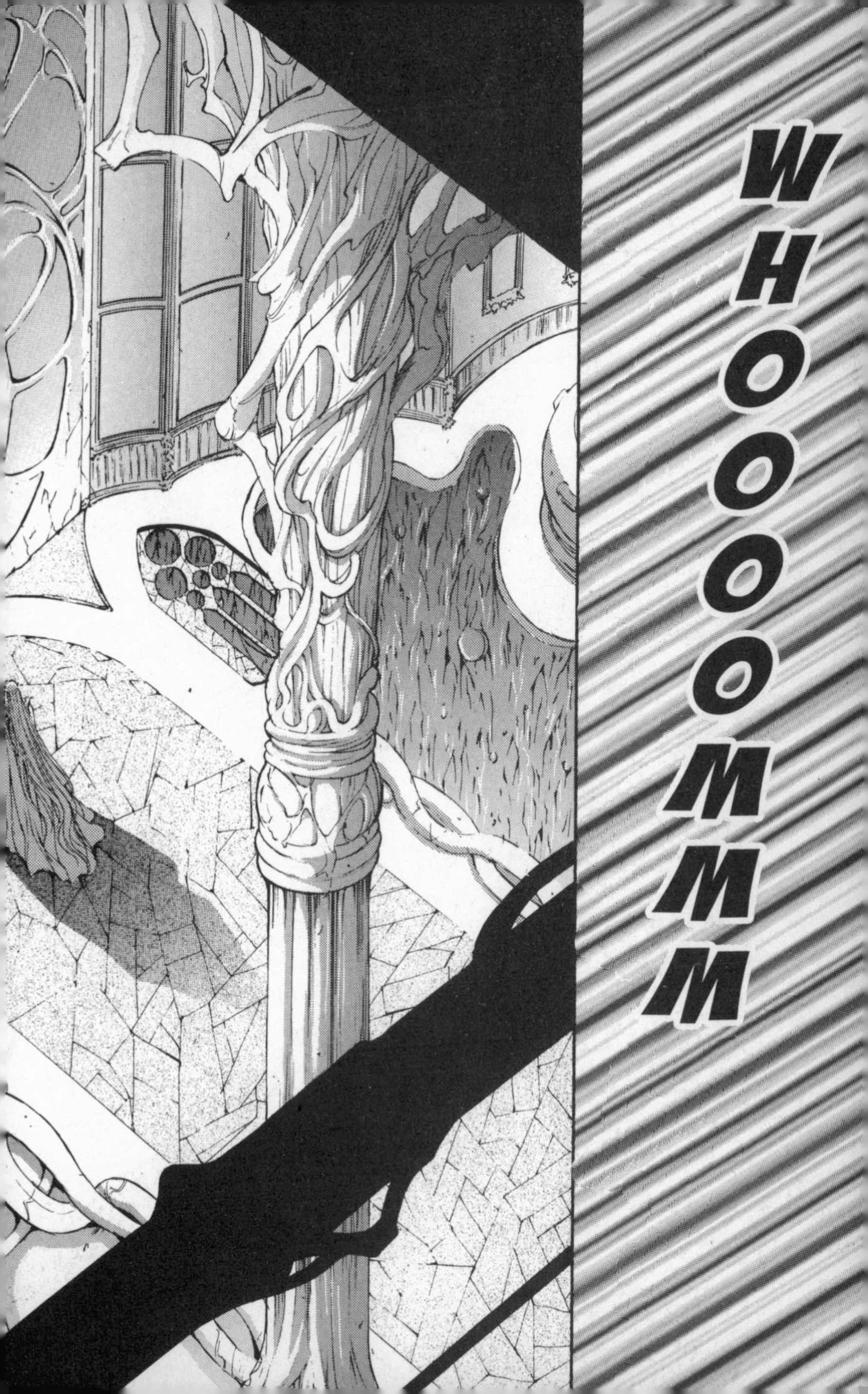
WHOOOOOMMM

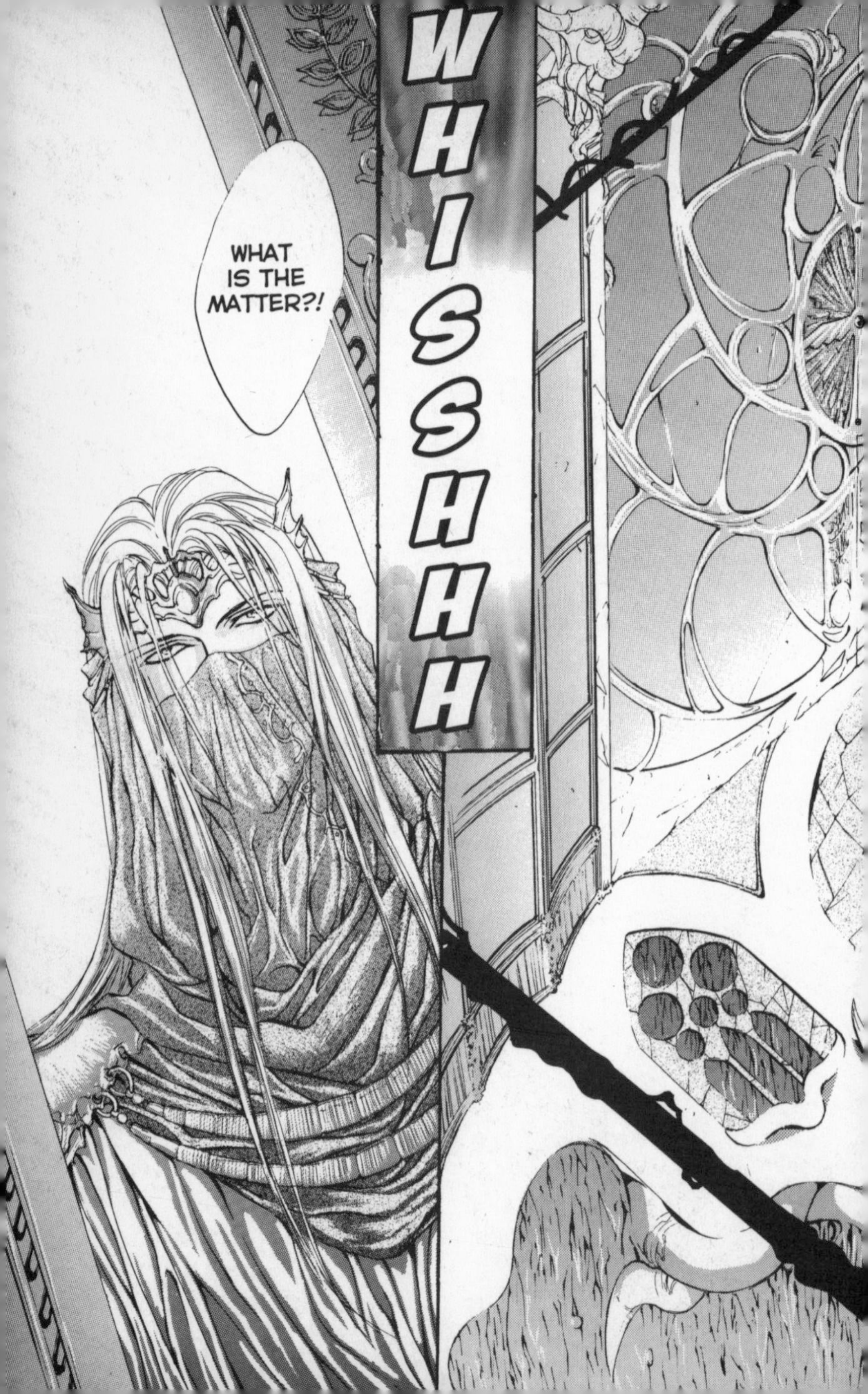
WHISHHH
WHAT IS THE MATTER?!

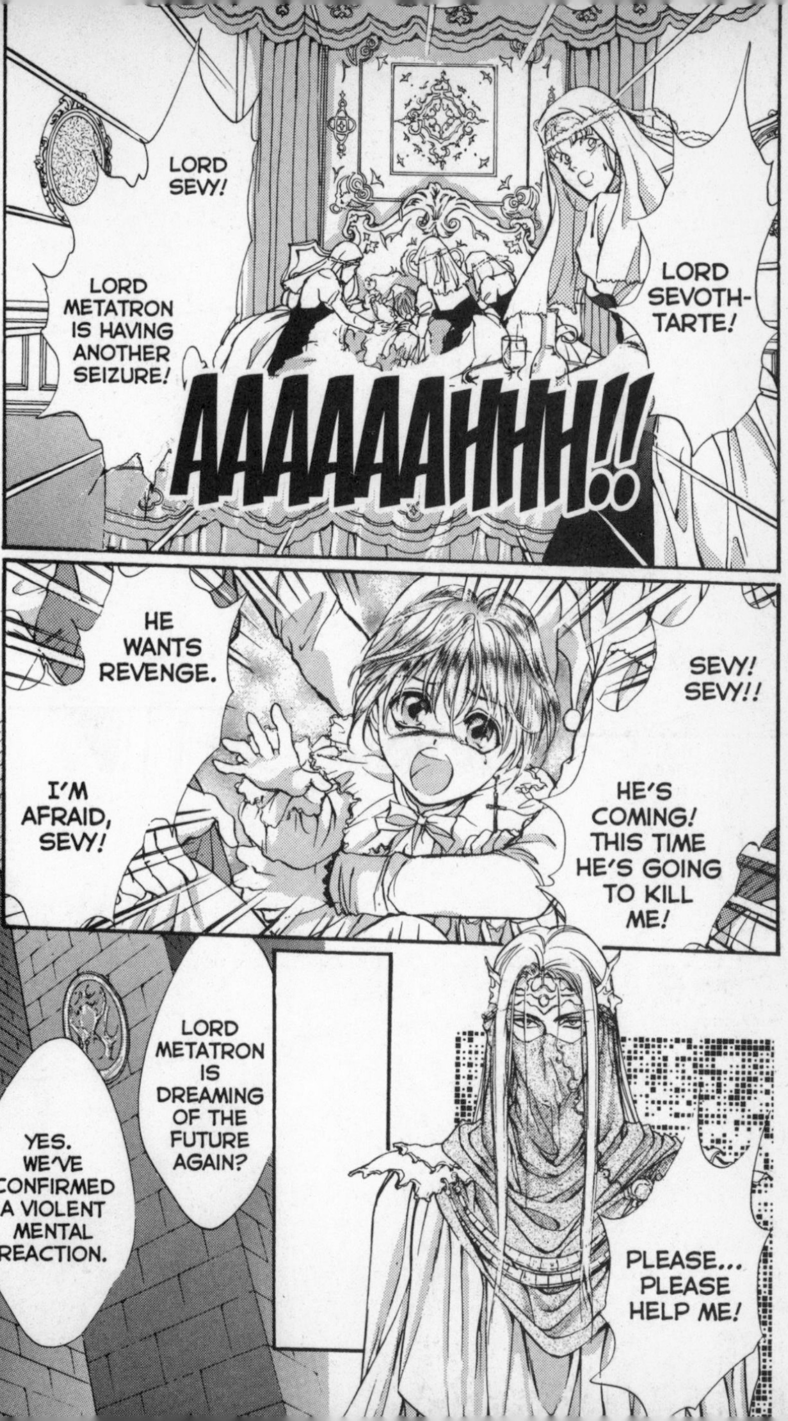
LORD SEVOTH-TARTE!
LORD SEVY!
LORD METATRON IS HAVING ANOTHER SEIZURE!
AAAAAAHHH!!
SEVY! SEVY!!
HE'S COMING! THIS TIME HE'S GOING TO KILL ME!
HE WANTS REVENGE.
I'M AFRAID, SEVY!
PLEASE... PLEASE HELP ME!
LORD METATRON IS DREAMING OF THE FUTURE AGAIN?
YES. WE'VE CONFIRMED A VIOLENT MENTAL REACTION.

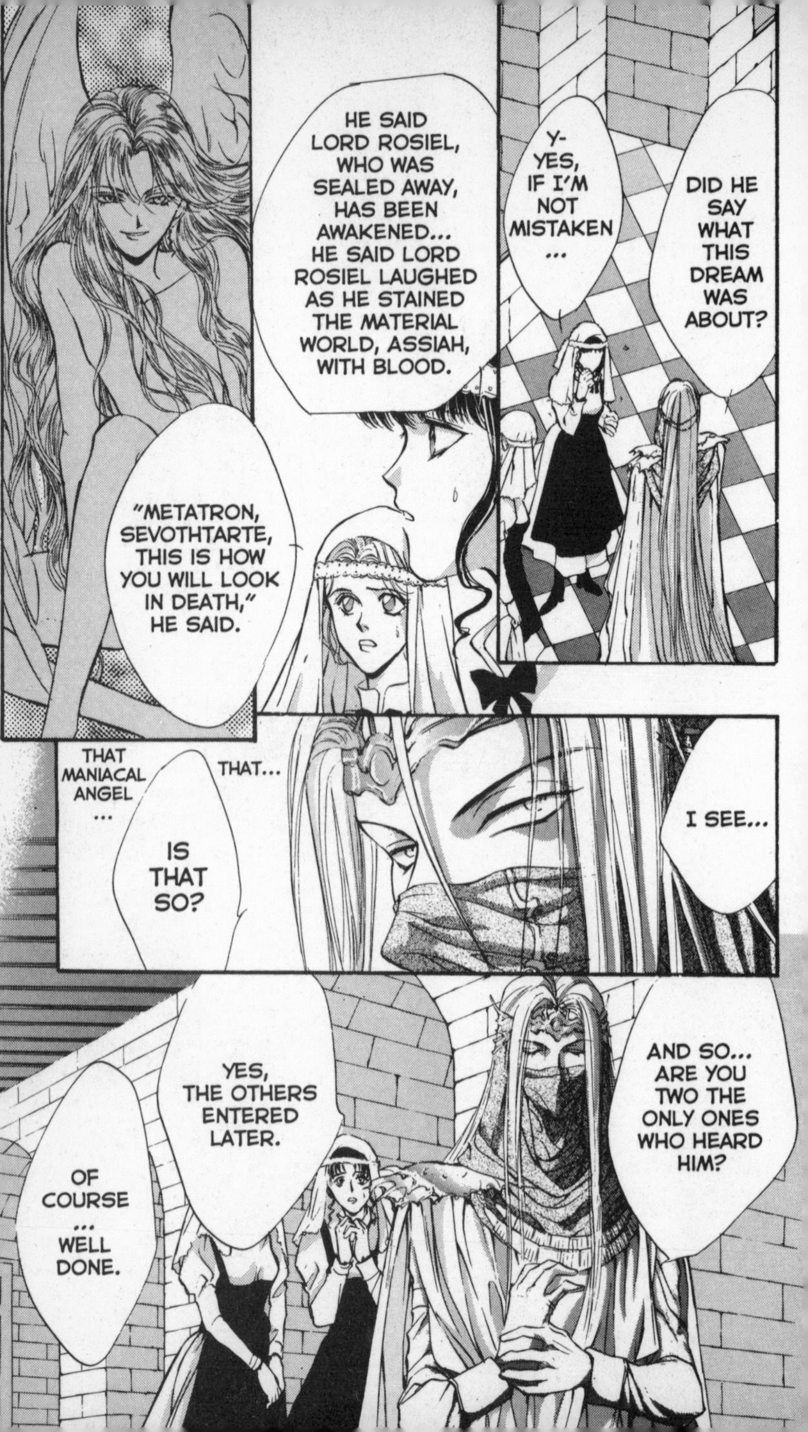
DID HE SAY WHAT THIS DREAM WAS ABOUT?
Y-YES, IF I'M NOT MISTAKEN...
HE SAID LORD ROSIEL, WHO WAS SEALED AWAY, HAS BEEN AWAKENED... HE SAID LORD ROSIEL LAUGHED AS HE STAINED THE MATERIAL WORLD, ASSIAH, WITH BLOOD.
"METATRON, SEVOTHTARTE, THIS IS HOW YOU WILL LOOK IN DEATH," HE SAID.
I SEE...
IS THAT SO?
THAT...
THAT MANIACAL ANGEL...
AND SO... ARE YOU TWO THE ONLY ONES WHO HEARD HIM?
YES, THE OTHERS ENTERED LATER.
OF COURSE... WELL DONE.

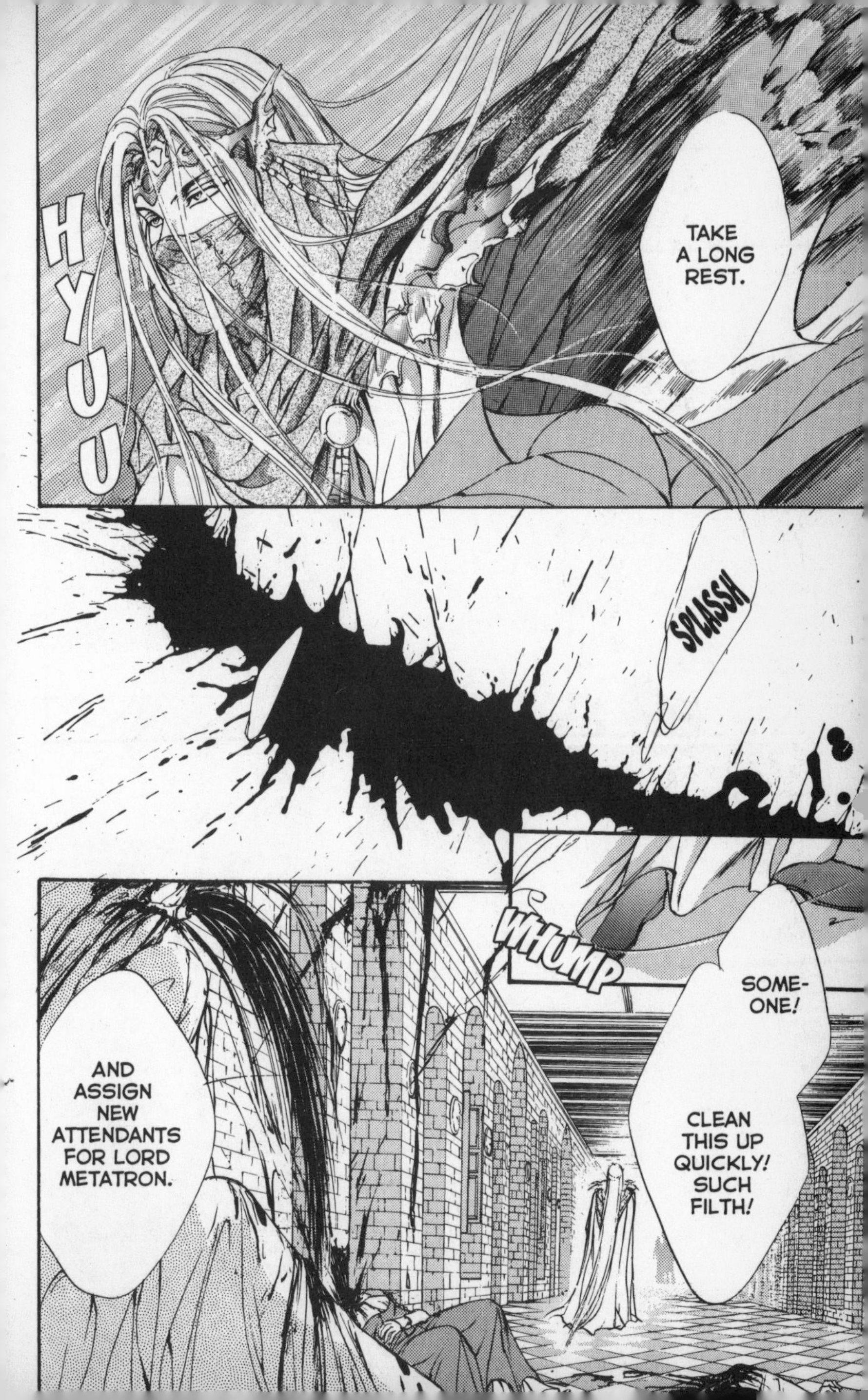
TAKE A LONG REST.
HYUU
SPLASSH
WHUMP
SOME-ONE!
CLEAN THIS UP QUICKLY! SUCH FILTH!
AND ASSIGN NEW ATTENDANTS FOR LORD METATRON.

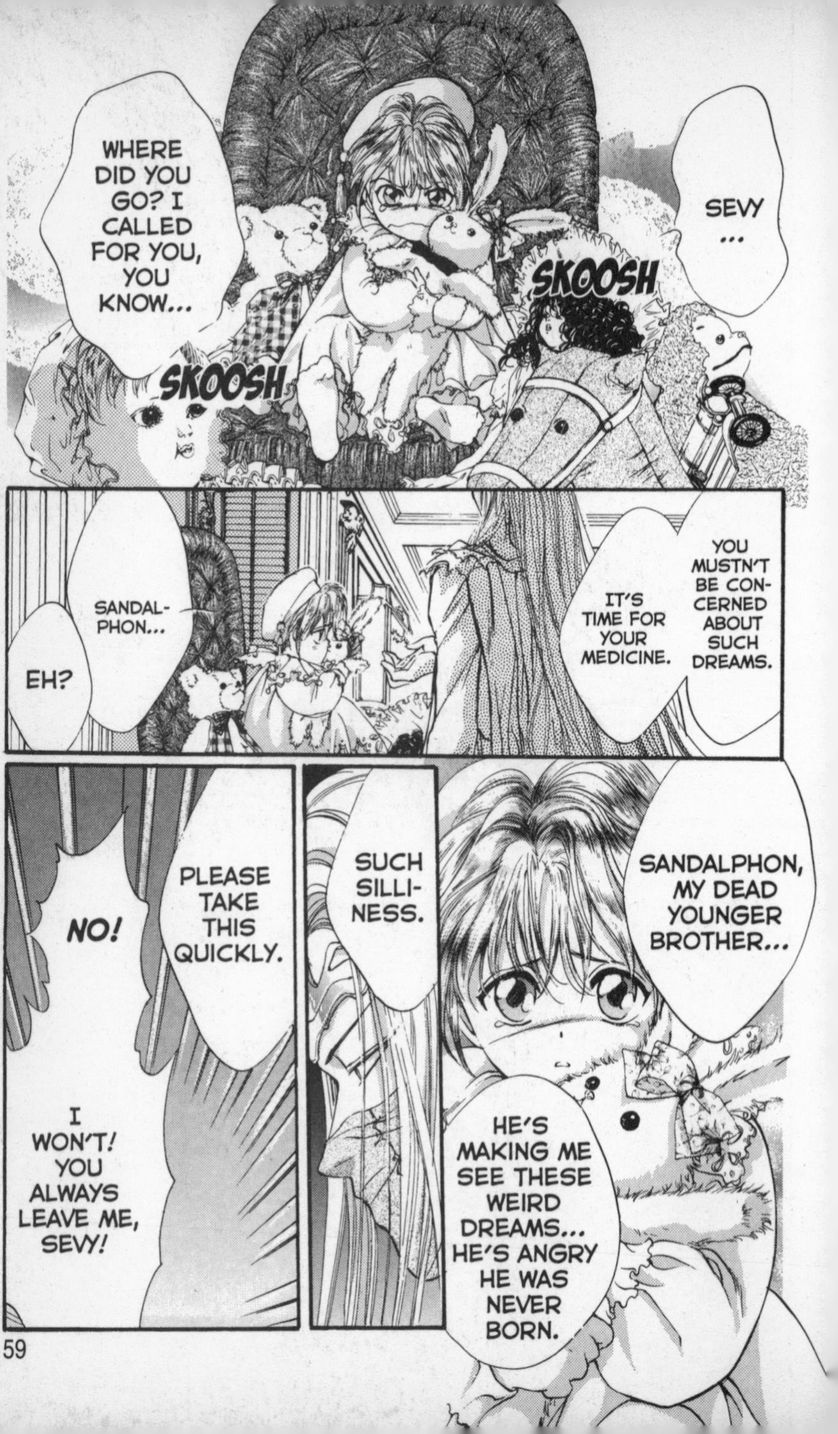
SEVY ...
SKOOSH
WHERE DID YOU GO? I CALLED FOR YOU, YOU KNOW...
SKOOSH
YOU MUSTN'T BE CONCERNED ABOUT SUCH DREAMS.
IT'S TIME FOR YOUR MEDICINE.
SANDALPHON...
EH?
SANDALPHON, MY DEAD YOUNGER BROTHER...
SUCH SILLINESS.
HE'S MAKING ME SEE THESE WEIRD DREAMS... HE'S ANGRY HE WAS NEVER BORN.
PLEASE TAKE THIS QUICKLY.
NO!
I WON'T! YOU ALWAYS LEAVE ME, SEVY!

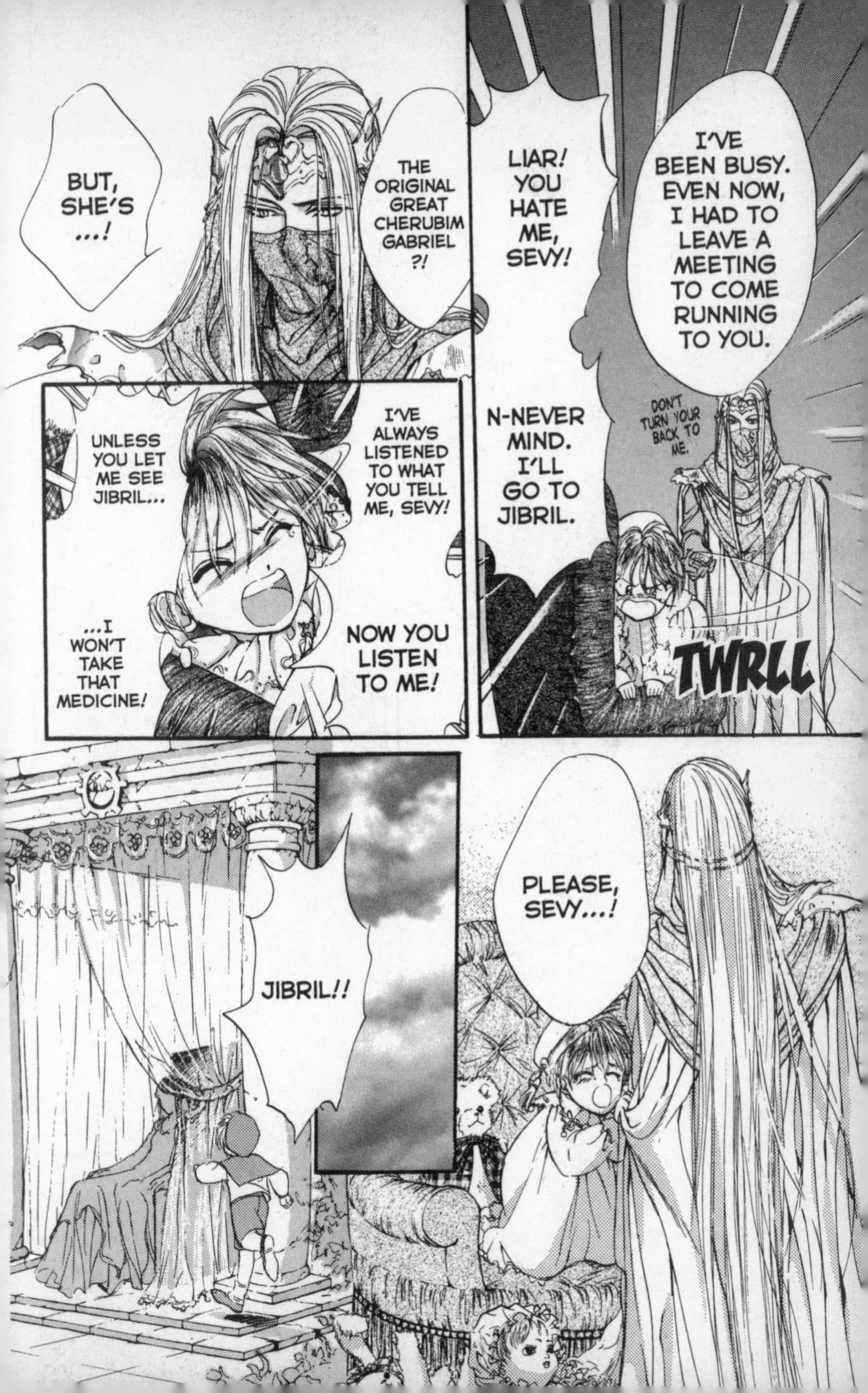
I'VE BEEN BUSY. EVEN NOW, I HAD TO LEAVE A MEETING TO COME RUNNING TO YOU.
LIAR! YOU HATE ME, SEVY!
DON'T TURN YOUR BACK TO ME.
N-NEVER MIND. I'LL GO TO JIBRIL.
TWRLL
THE ORIGINAL GREAT CHERUBIM GABRIEL ?!
BUT, SHE'S ...!
I'VE ALWAYS LISTENED TO WHAT YOU TELL ME, SEVY!
UNLESS YOU LET ME SEE JIBRIL...
NOW YOU LISTEN TO ME!
...I WON'T TAKE THAT MEDICINE!
PLEASE, SEVY...!
JIBRIL!!

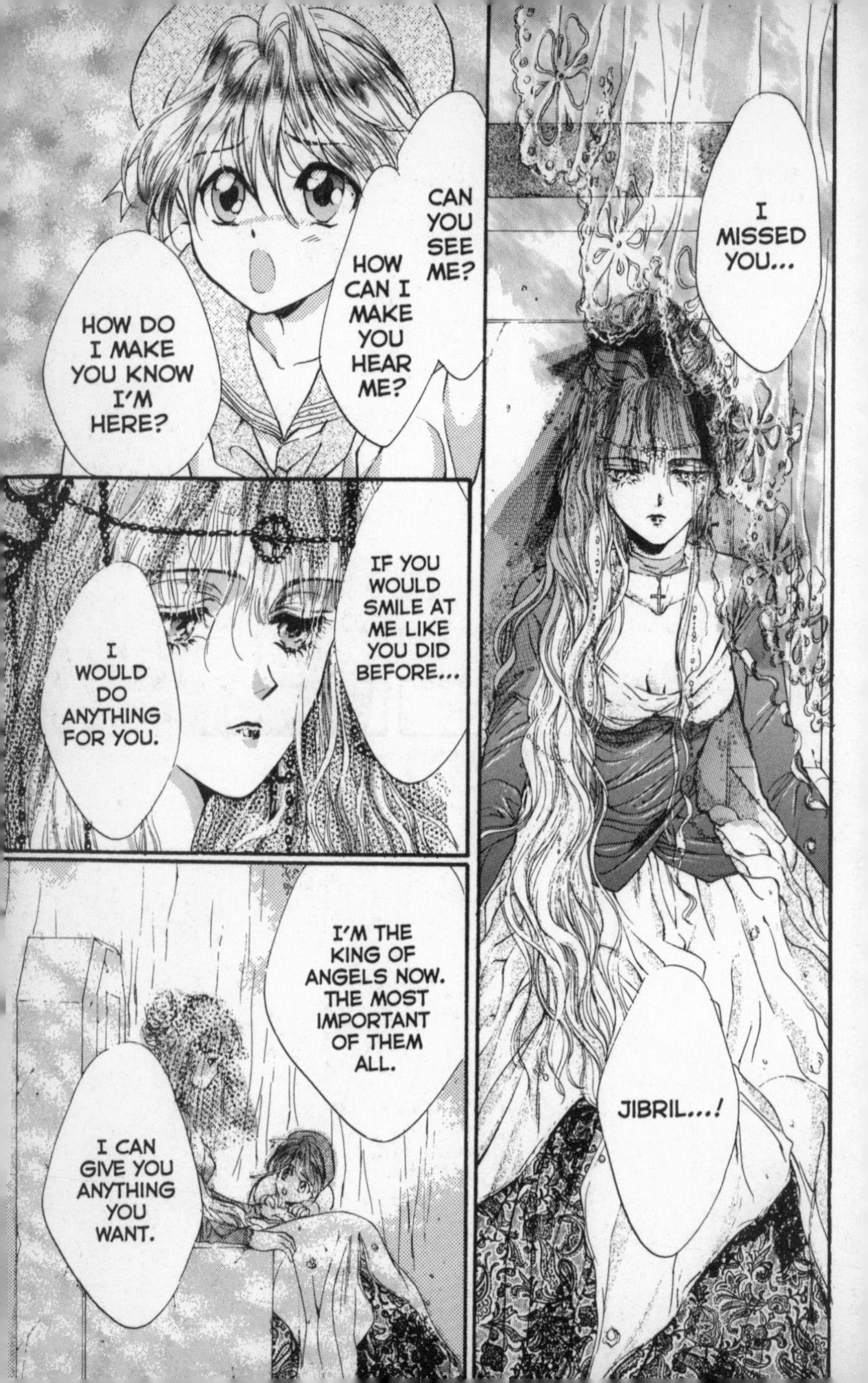
I MISSED YOU...
JIBRIL...!
CAN YOU SEE ME?
HOW CAN I MAKE YOU HEAR ME?
HOW DO I MAKE YOU KNOW I'M HERE?
IF YOU WOULD SMILE AT ME LIKE YOU DID BEFORE...
I WOULD DO ANYTHING FOR YOU.
I'M THE KING OF ANGELS NOW. THE MOST IMPORTANT OF THEM ALL.
I CAN GIVE YOU ANYTHING YOU WANT.

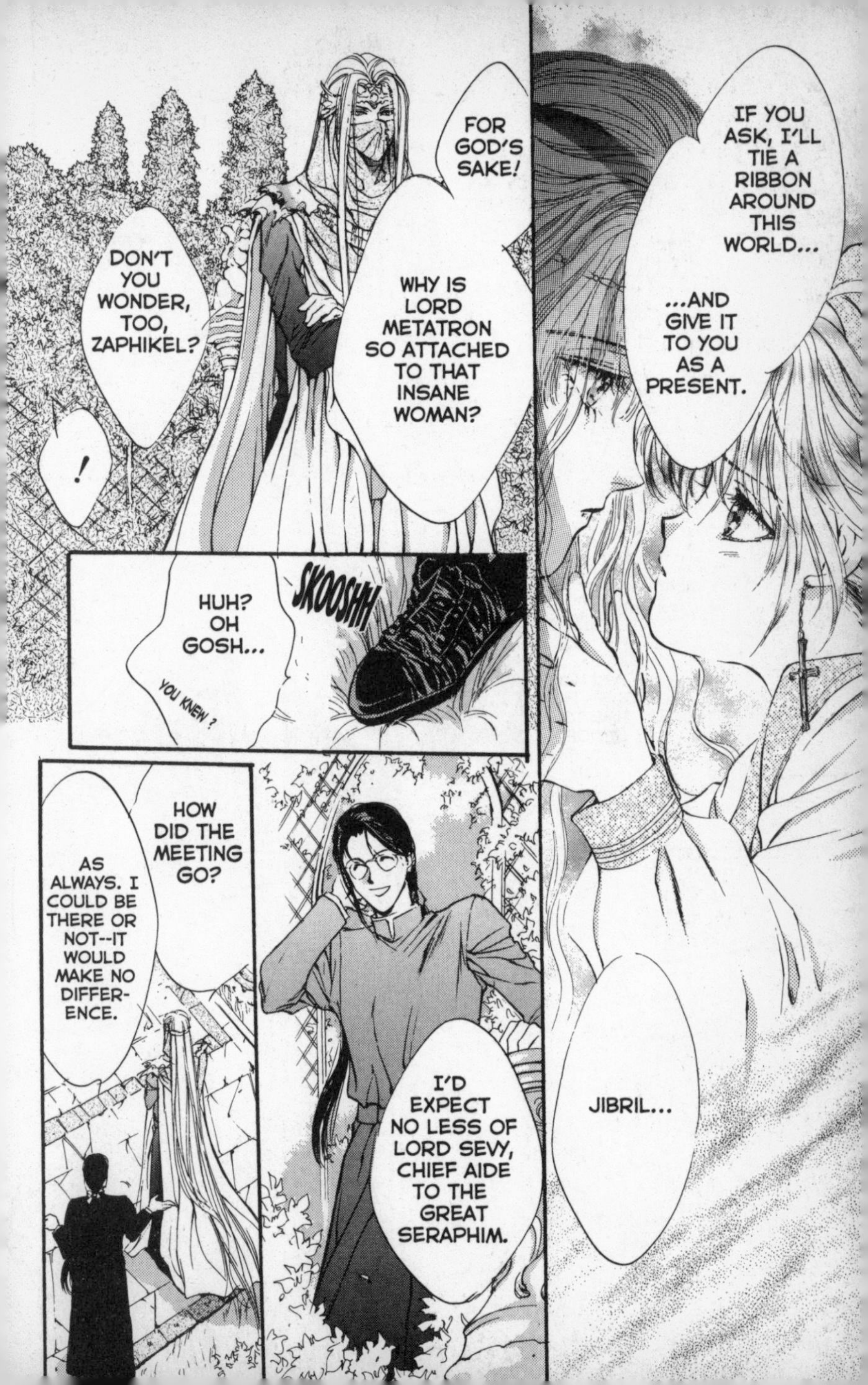
IF YOU ASK, I'LL TIE A RIBBON AROUND THIS WORLD...
...AND GIVE IT TO YOU AS A PRESENT.
JIBRIL...
FOR GOD'S SAKE!
WHY IS LORD METATRON SO ATTACHED TO THAT INSANE WOMAN?
DON'T YOU WONDER, TOO, ZAPHIKEL?
!
SKOOSHH
HUH? OH GOSH...
YOU KNEW ?
HOW DID THE MEETING GO?
AS ALWAYS. I COULD BE THERE OR NOT--IT WOULD MAKE NO DIFFERENCE.
I'D EXPECT NO LESS OF LORD SEVY, CHIEF AIDE TO THE GREAT SERAPHIM.

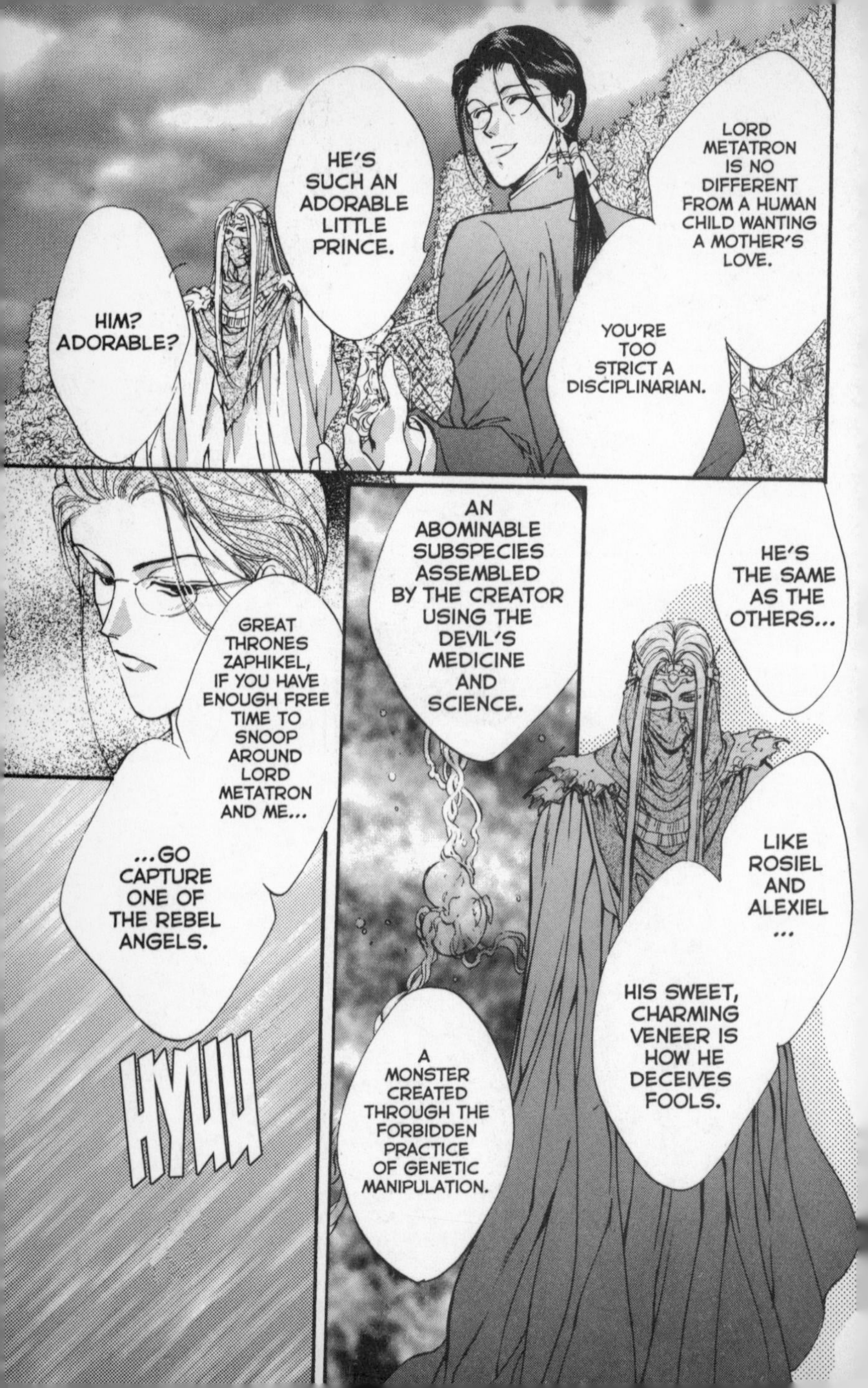
LORD METATRON IS NO DIFFERENT FROM A HUMAN CHILD WANTING A MOTHER'S LOVE.
YOU'RE TOO STRICT A DISCIPLINARIAN.
HE'S SUCH AN ADORABLE LITTLE PRINCE.
HIM? ADORABLE?
HE'S THE SAME AS THE OTHERS...
LIKE ROSIEL AND ALEXIEL ...
HIS SWEET, CHARMING VENEER IS HOW HE DECEIVES FOOLS.
AN ABOMINABLE SUBSPECIES ASSEMBLED BY THE CREATOR USING THE DEVIL'S MEDICINE AND SCIENCE.
A MONSTER CREATED THROUGH THE FORBIDDEN PRACTICE OF GENETIC MANIPULATION.
GREAT THRONES ZAPHIKEL, IF YOU HAVE ENOUGH FREE TIME TO SNOOP AROUND LORD METATRON AND ME...
...GO CAPTURE ONE OF THE REBEL ANGELS.
HYUU

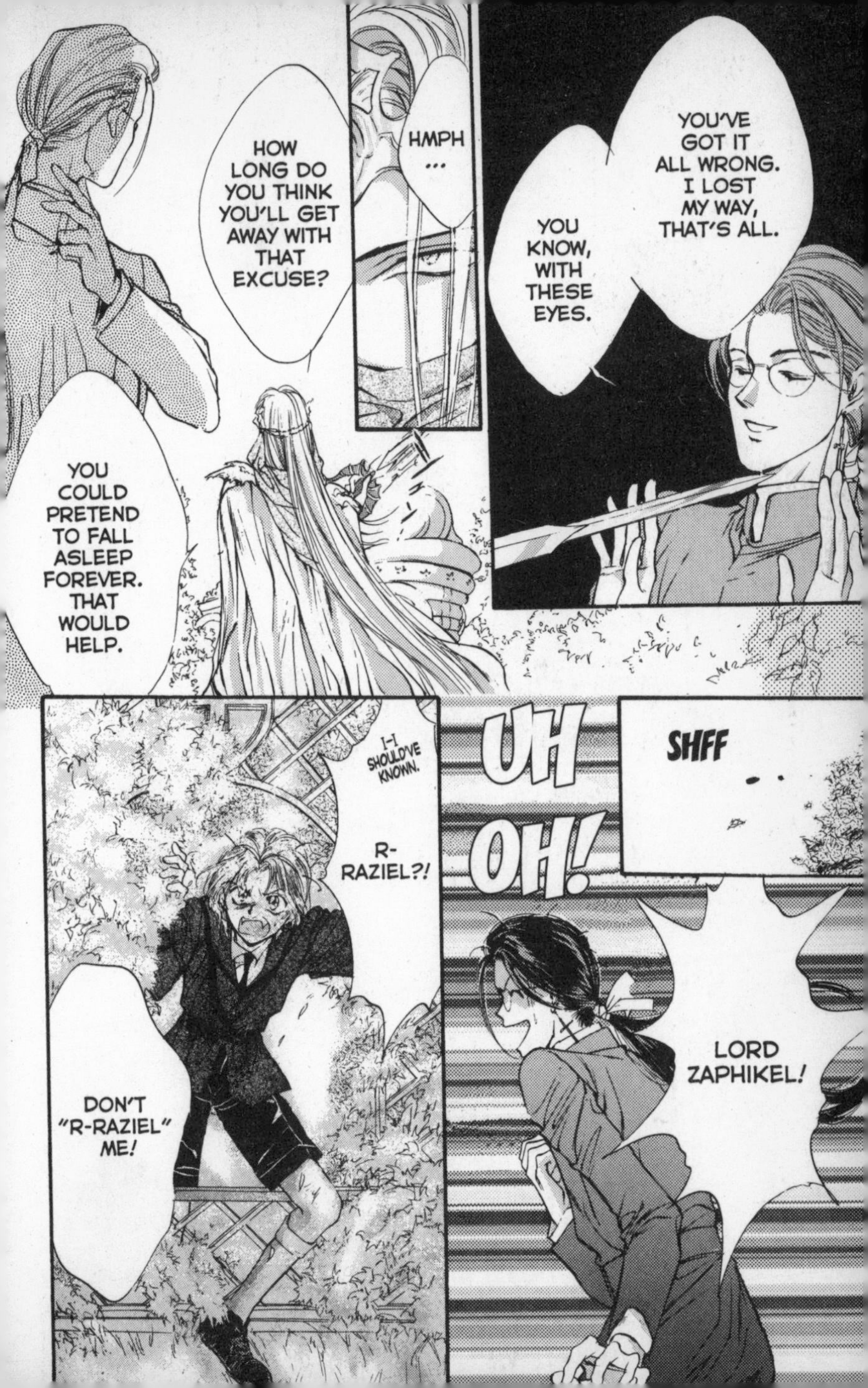
YOU'VE GOT IT ALL WRONG. I LOST MY WAY, THAT'S ALL.
YOU KNOW, WITH THESE EYES.
HMPH ...
HOW LONG DO YOU THINK YOU'LL GET AWAY WITH THAT EXCUSE?
YOU COULD PRETEND TO FALL ASLEEP FOREVER. THAT WOULD HELP.
SHFF
UH OH!
LORD ZAPHIKEL!
I-I SHOULD'VE KNOWN.
R-RAZIEL?!
DON'T "R-RAZIEL" ME!

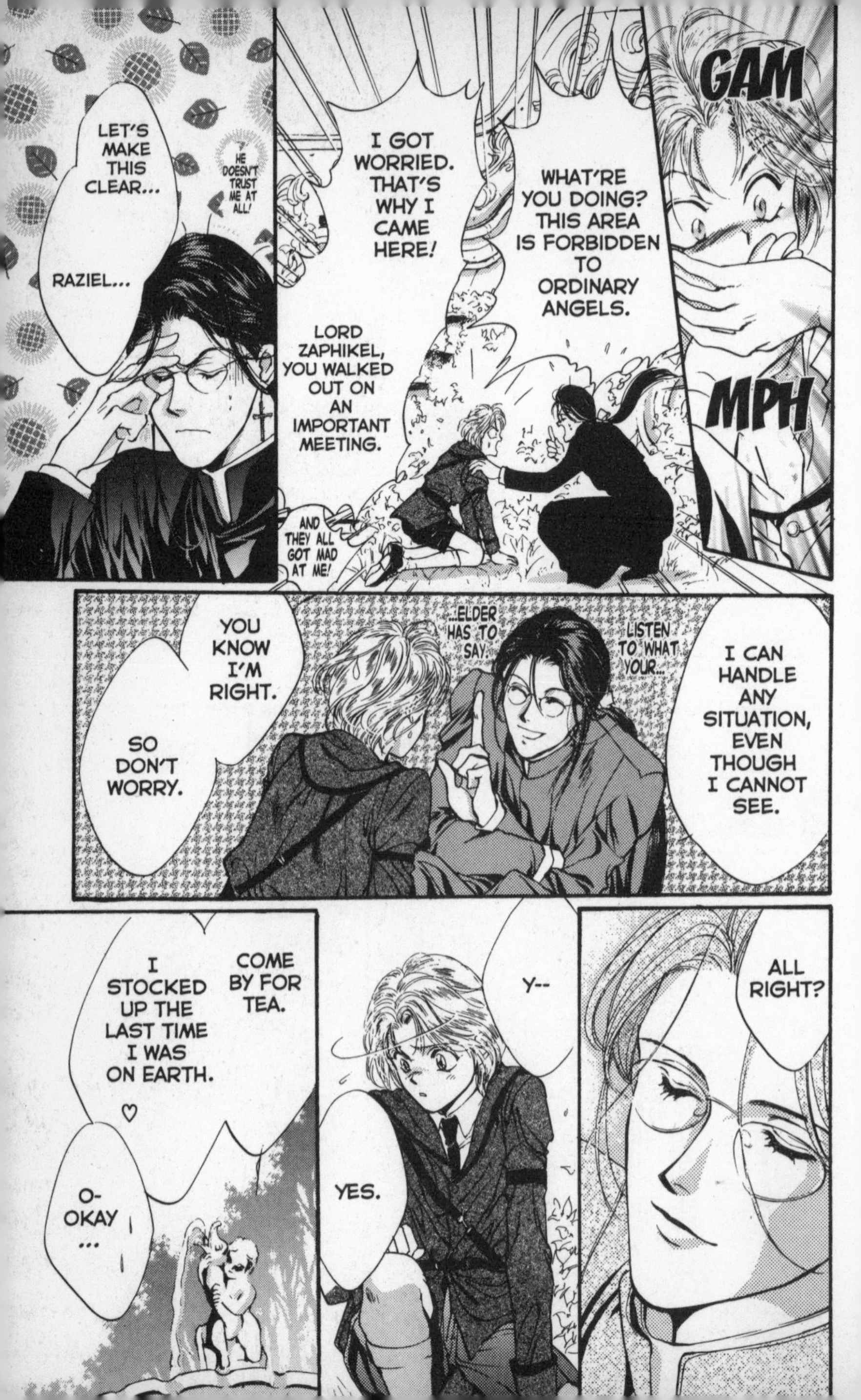
GAM
MPH
WHAT'RE YOU DOING? THIS AREA IS FORBIDDEN TO ORDINARY ANGELS.
I GOT WORRIED. THAT'S WHY I CAME HERE!
LORD ZAPHIKEL, YOU WALKED OUT ON AN IMPORTANT MEETING.
AND THEY ALL GOT MAD AT ME!
LET'S MAKE THIS CLEAR...
HE DOESN'T TRUST ME AT ALL!
RAZIEL...
I CAN HANDLE ANY SITUATION, EVEN THOUGH I CANNOT SEE.
LISTEN TO WHAT YOUR...
...ELDER HAS TO SAY.
YOU KNOW I'M RIGHT.
SO DON'T WORRY.
ALL RIGHT?
Y--
YES.
COME BY FOR TEA.
I STOCKED UP THE LAST TIME I WAS ON EARTH. ♡
O-OKAY...

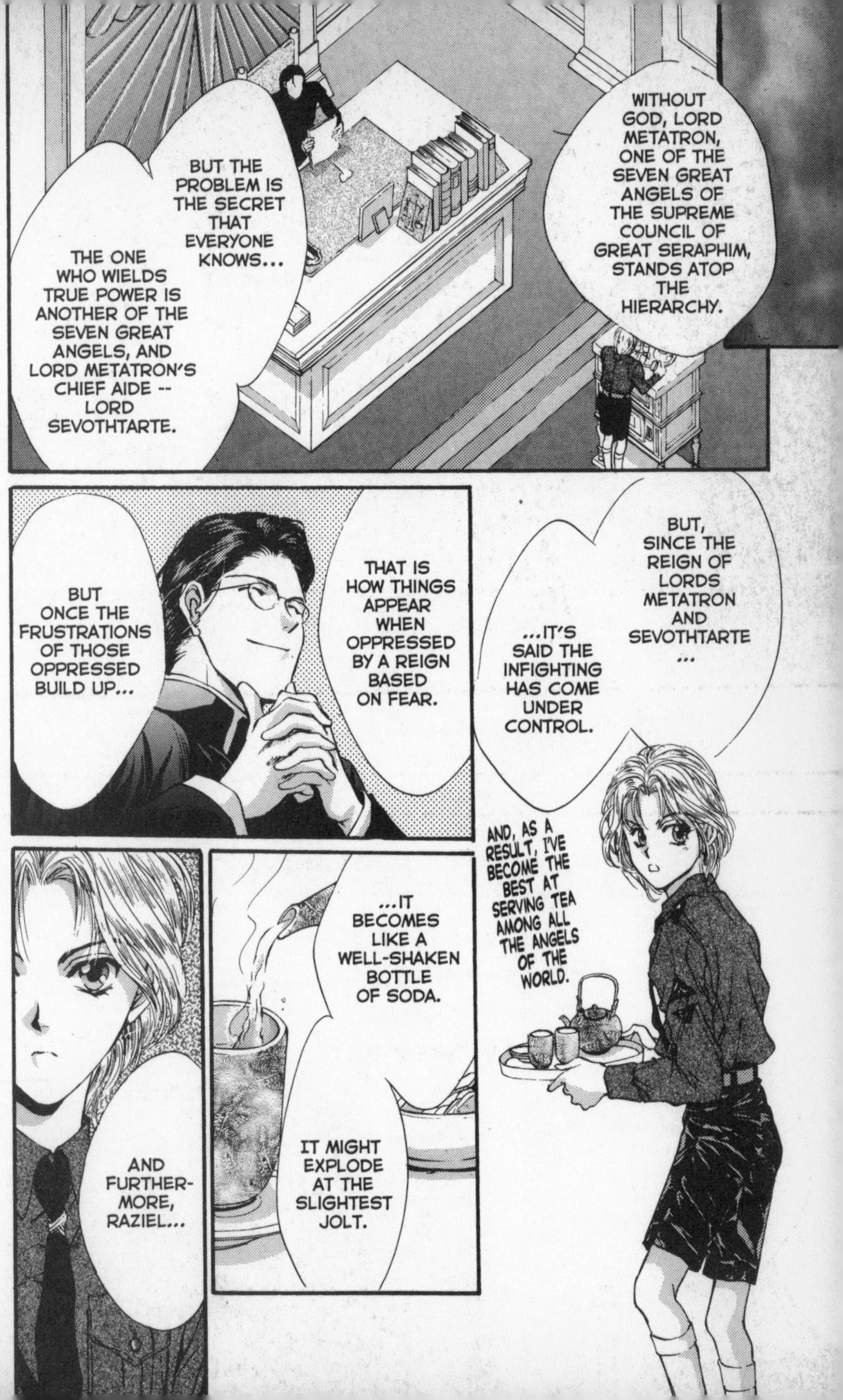
WITHOUT GOD, LORD METATRON, ONE OF THE SEVEN GREAT ANGELS OF THE SUPREME COUNCIL OF GREAT SERAPHIM, STANDS ATOP THE HIERARCHY.
BUT THE PROBLEM IS THE SECRET THAT EVERYONE KNOWS...
THE ONE WHO WIELDS TRUE POWER IS ANOTHER OF THE SEVEN GREAT ANGELS, AND LORD METATRON'S CHIEF AIDE -- LORD SEVOTHTARTE.
BUT, SINCE THE REIGN OF LORDS METATRON AND SEVOTHTARTE ...
...IT'S SAID THE INFIGHTING HAS COME UNDER CONTROL.
THAT IS HOW THINGS APPEAR WHEN OPPRESSED BY A REIGN BASED ON FEAR.
BUT ONCE THE FRUSTRATIONS OF THOSE OPPRESSED BUILD UP...
AND, AS A RESULT, I'VE BECOME THE BEST AT SERVING TEA AMONG ALL THE ANGELS OF THE WORLD.
...IT BECOMES LIKE A WELL-SHAKEN BOTTLE OF SODA.
IT MIGHT EXPLODE AT THE SLIGHTEST JOLT.
AND FURTHER-MORE, RAZIEL...

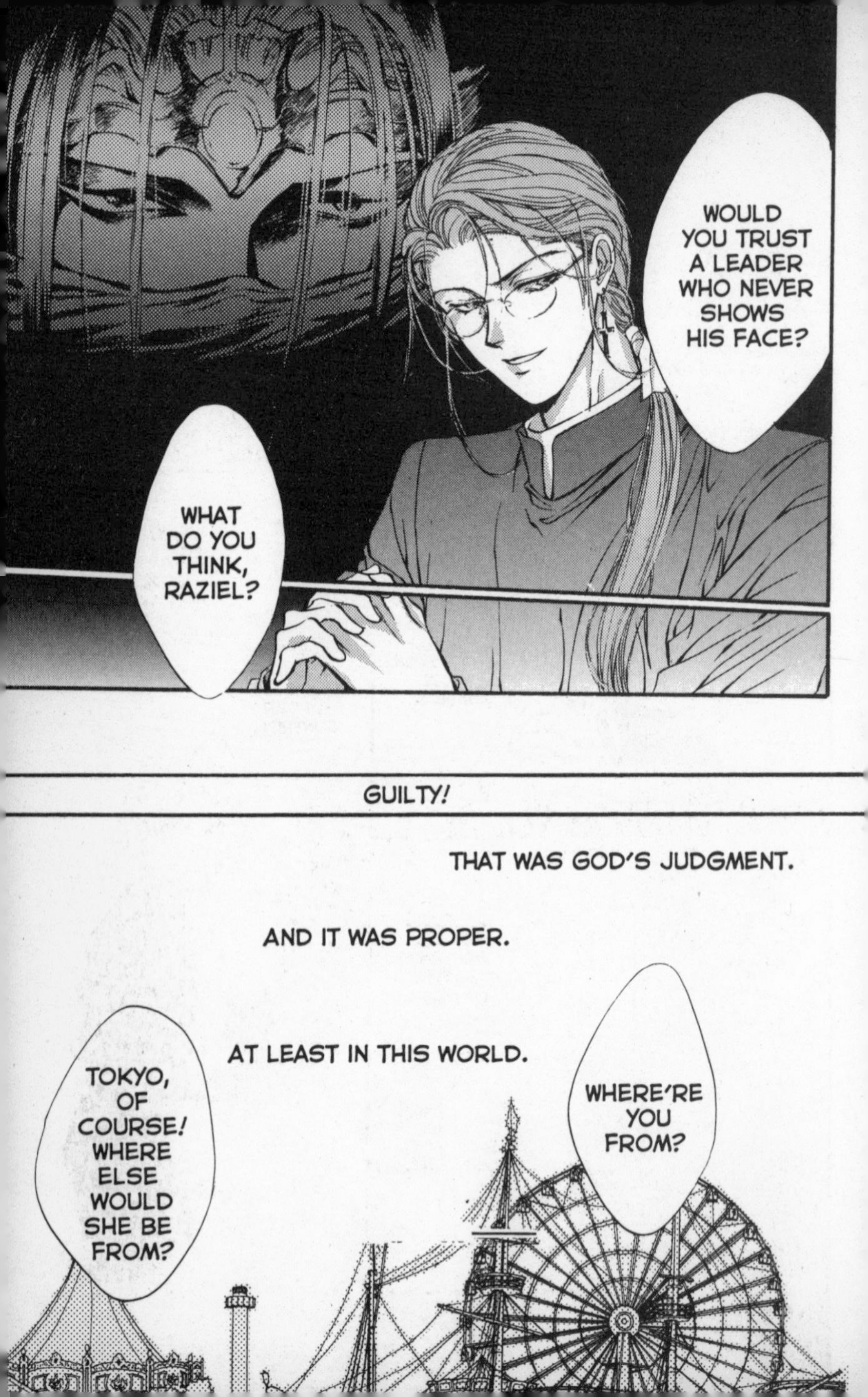
WOULD YOU TRUST A LEADER WHO NEVER SHOWS HIS FACE?
WHAT DO YOU THINK, RAZIEL?
GUILTY!
THAT WAS GOD'S JUDGMENT.
AND IT WAS PROPER.
AT LEAST IN THIS WORLD.
WHERE'RE YOU FROM?
TOKYO, OF COURSE! WHERE ELSE WOULD SHE BE FROM?

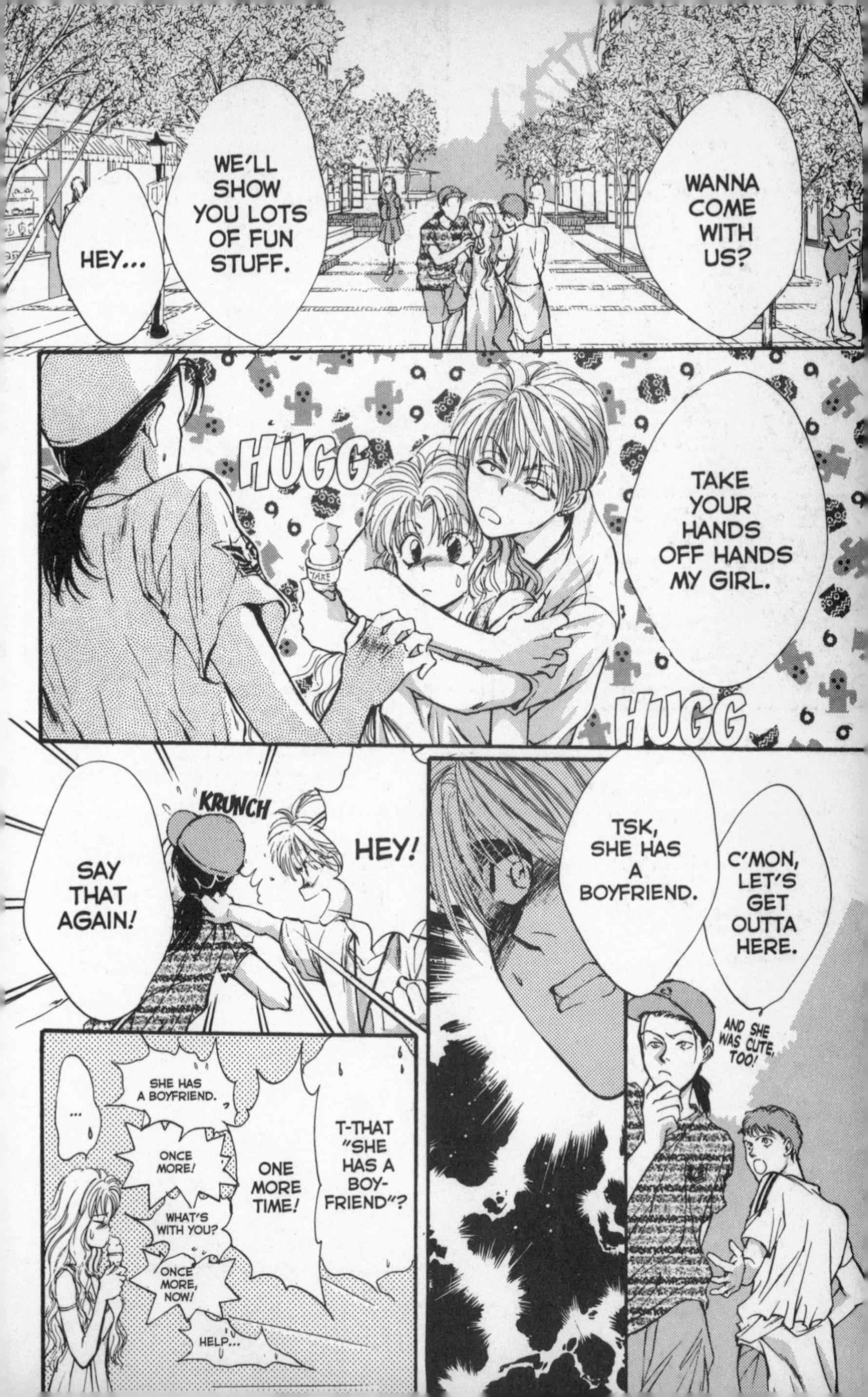
WANNA COME WITH US?
WE'LL SHOW YOU LOTS OF FUN STUFF.
HEY...
HUGG
TAKE YOUR HANDS OFF HANDS MY GIRL.
HUGG
TSK, SHE HAS A BOYFRIEND.
C'MON, LET'S GET OUTTA HERE.
AND SHE WAS CUTE, TOO!
HEY!
KRUNCH
SAY THAT AGAIN!
T-THAT "SHE HAS A BOY-FRIEND"?
ONE MORE TIME!
SHE HAS A BOYFRIEND.
...
ONCE MORE!
WHAT'S WITH YOU?
ONCE MORE, NOW!
HELP...

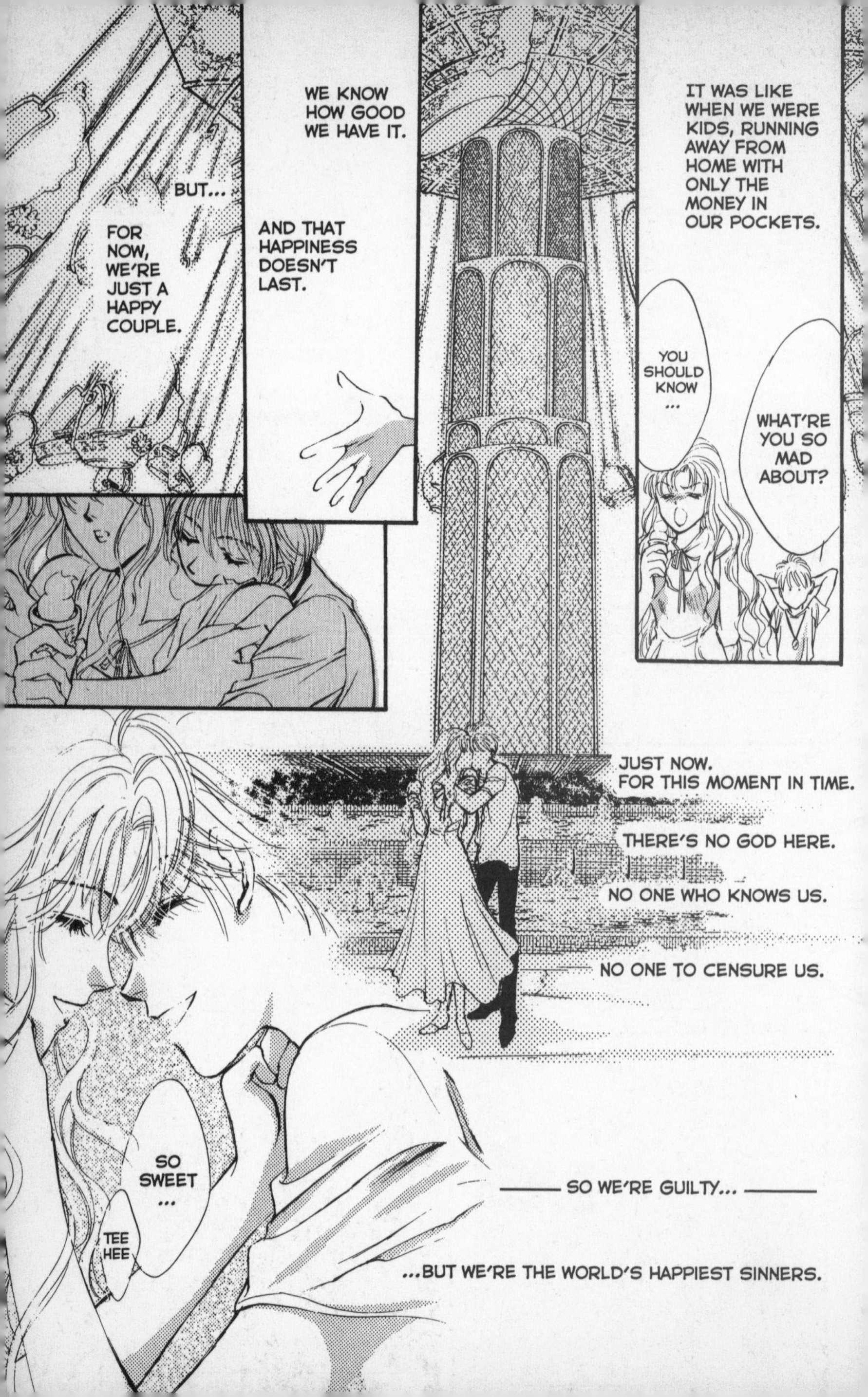
IT WAS LIKE WHEN WE WERE KIDS, RUNNING AWAY FROM HOME WITH ONLY THE MONEY IN OUR POCKETS.
WHAT'RE YOU SO MAD ABOUT?
YOU SHOULD KNOW ...
WE KNOW HOW GOOD WE HAVE IT.
AND THAT HAPPINESS DOESN'T LAST.
BUT...
FOR NOW, WE'RE JUST A HAPPY COUPLE.
JUST NOW.
FOR THIS MOMENT IN TIME.
THERE'S NO GOD HERE.
NO ONE WHO KNOWS US.
NO ONE TO CENSURE US.
—— SO WE'RE GUILTY... ——
...BUT WE'RE THE WORLD'S HAPPIEST SINNERS.
SO SWEET ...
TEE HEE

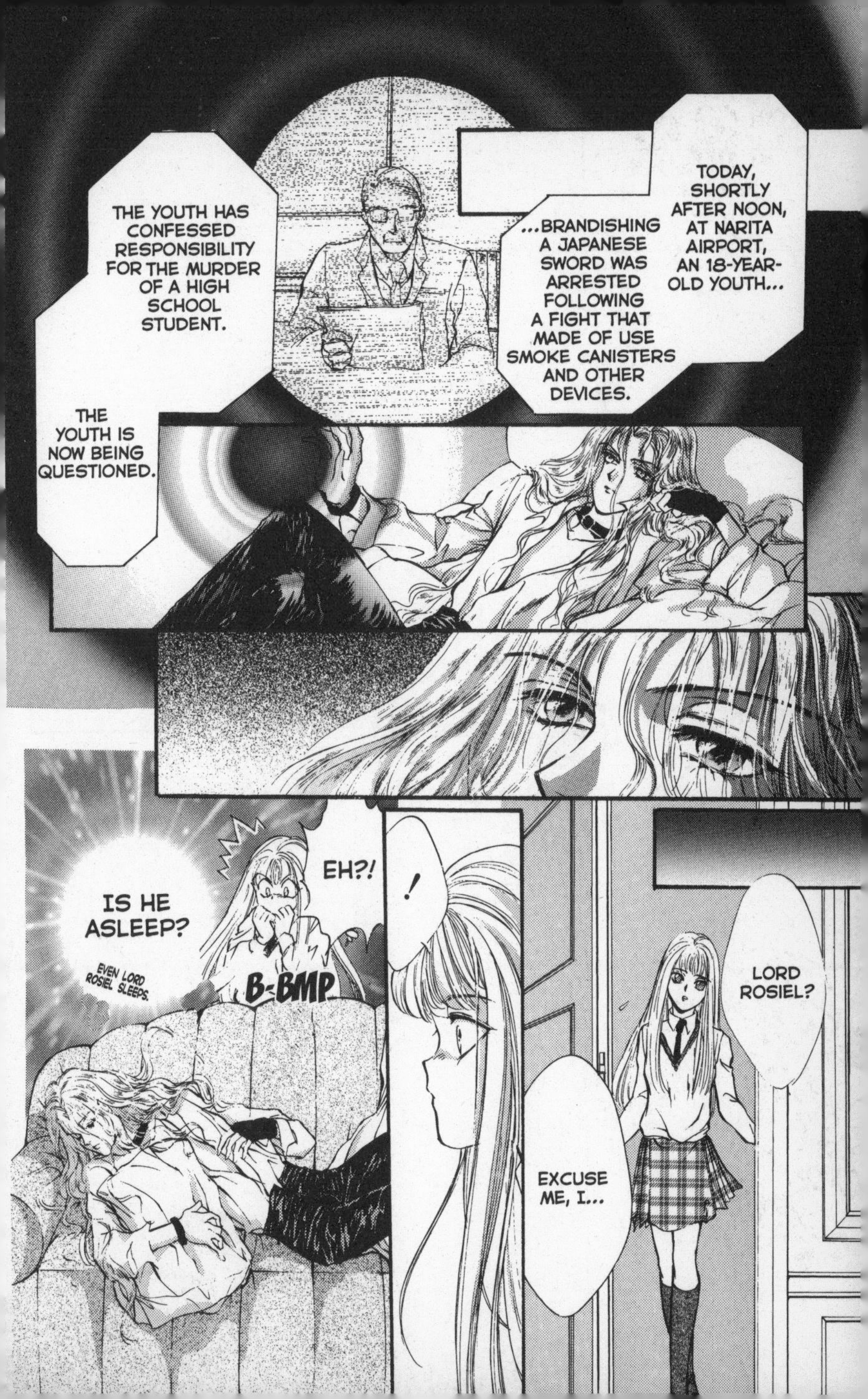
TODAY, SHORTLY AFTER NOON, AT NARITA AIRPORT, AN 18-YEAR-OLD YOUTH...
...BRANDISHING A JAPANESE SWORD WAS ARRESTED FOLLOWING A FIGHT THAT MADE OF USE SMOKE CANISTERS AND OTHER DEVICES.
THE YOUTH HAS CONFESSED RESPONSIBILITY FOR THE MURDER OF A HIGH SCHOOL STUDENT.
THE YOUTH IS NOW BEING QUESTIONED.
LORD ROSIEL?
EXCUSE ME, I...
!
EH?!
IS HE ASLEEP?
B-BMP
EVEN LORD ROSIEL SLEEPS.

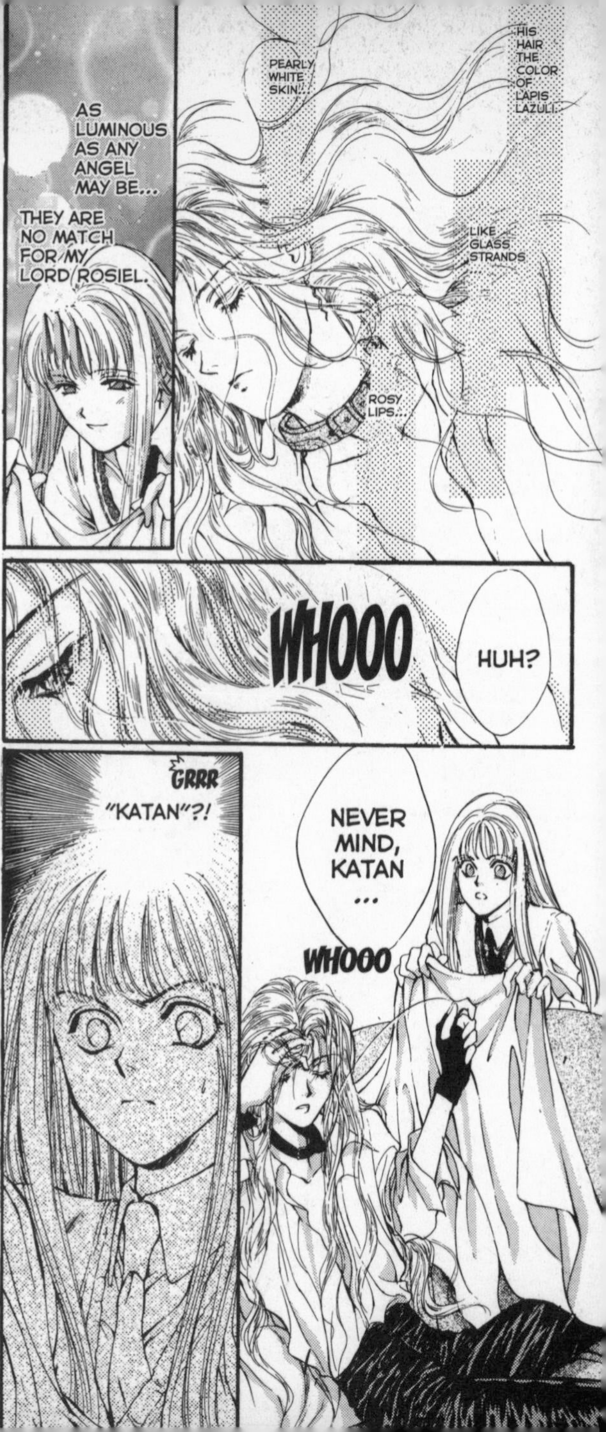
HIS HAIR THE COLOR OF LAPIS LAZULI...
PEARLY WHITE SKIN...
LIKE GLASS STRANDS
ROSY LIPS...
AS LUMINOUS AS ANY ANGEL MAY BE...
THEY ARE NO MATCH FOR MY LORD ROSIEL.
HUH?
WHOOO
NEVER MIND, KATAN...
WHOOO
GRRR
"KATAN"?!

I had decided long ago that Setsuna and Sara would elope, but I was concerned whether readers would say, "It's okay, since they love each other so much and have gone through so much pain." There is, after all, no doubt that it isn't right. Their parents would cry, too. I tend to think they jumped the gun, myself. But I think no one can say with absolute certainty that there aren't couples who awaken to the realization of their true love! I doubt that would convince everyone, though. I wish that as long as they don't trouble those around them, we could let it go. The price they pay is so much greater and so much more painful than other lovers that there is no comparison.

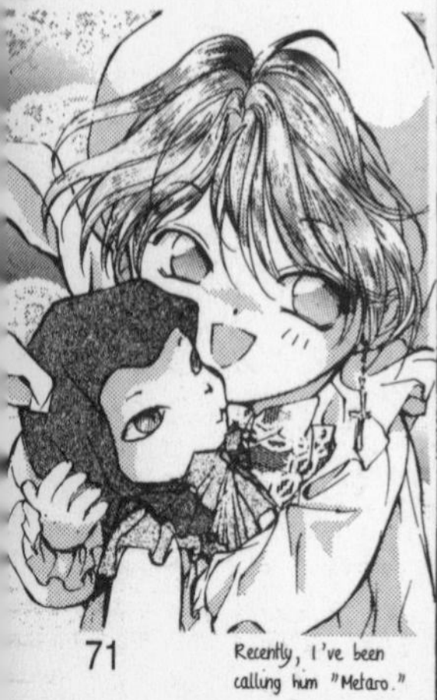

Recently, I've been calling him "Metaro."

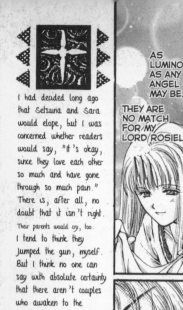

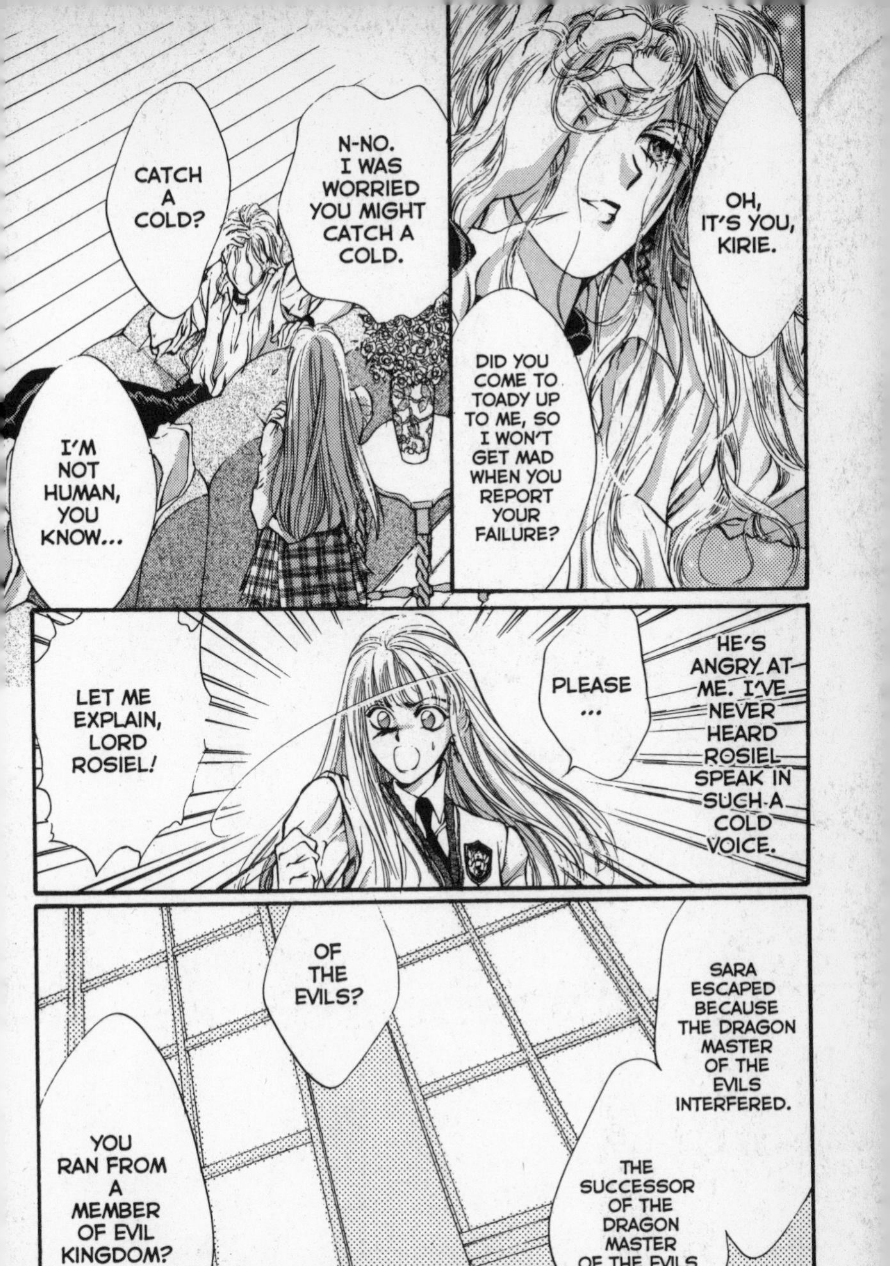
OH, IT'S YOU, KIRIE.
DID YOU COME TO TOADY UP TO ME, SO I WON'T GET MAD WHEN YOU REPORT YOUR FAILURE?
N-NO. I WAS WORRIED YOU MIGHT CATCH A COLD.
CATCH A COLD?
I'M NOT HUMAN, YOU KNOW...
HE'S ANGRY AT ME. I'VE NEVER HEARD ROSIEL SPEAK IN SUCH A COLD VOICE.
PLEASE ...
LET ME EXPLAIN, LORD ROSIEL!
SARA ESCAPED BECAUSE THE DRAGON MASTER OF THE EVILS INTERFERED.
THE SUCCESSOR OF THE DRAGON MASTER OF THE EVILS IS ALIVE!
OF THE EVILS?
YOU RAN FROM A MEMBER OF EVIL KINGDOM?

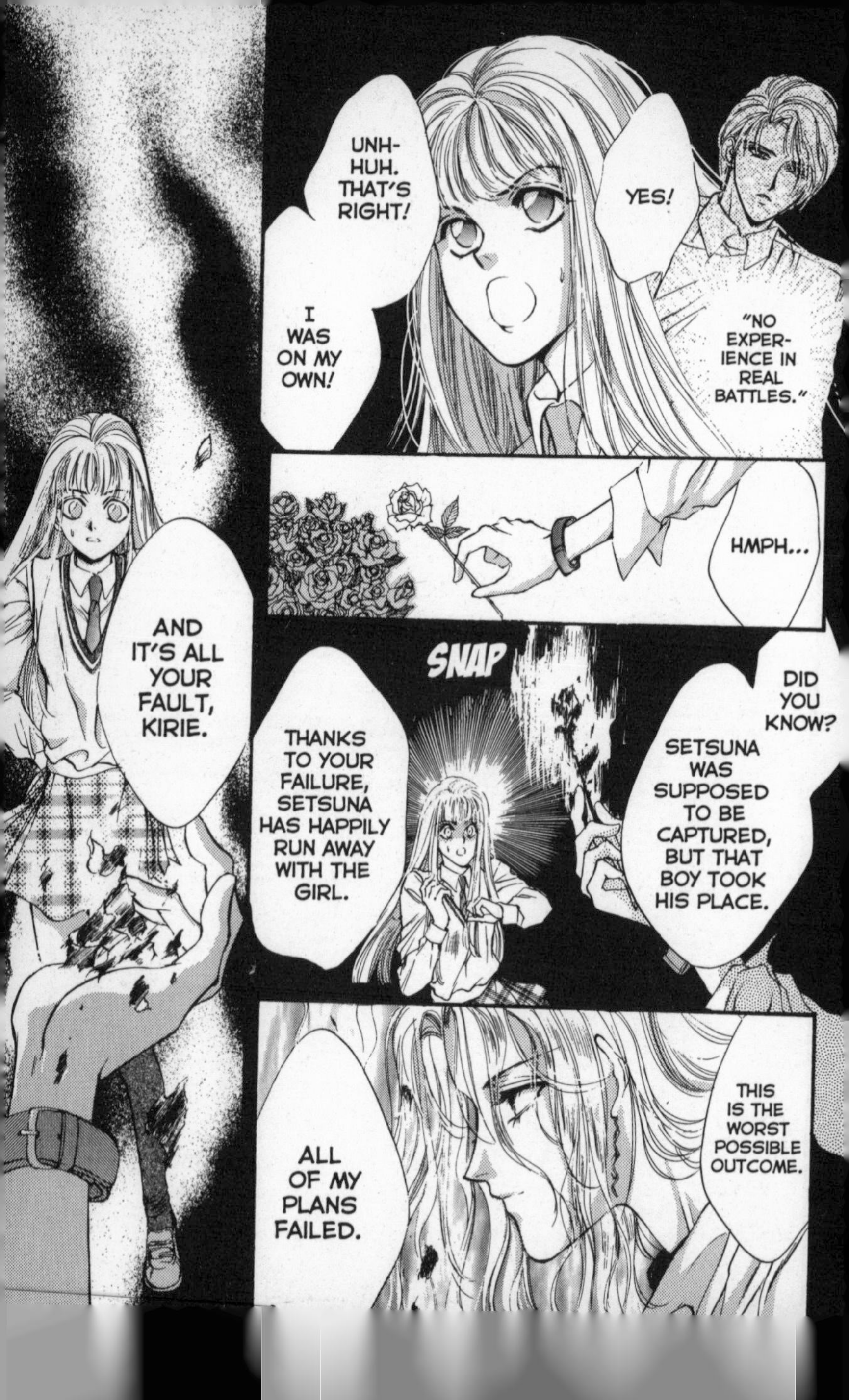
YES!
"NO EXPERIENCE IN REAL BATTLES."
UNH-HUH. THAT'S RIGHT!
I WAS ON MY OWN!
HMPH...
DID YOU KNOW?
SETSUNA WAS SUPPOSED TO BE CAPTURED, BUT THAT BOY TOOK HIS PLACE.
SNAP
THANKS TO YOUR FAILURE, SETSUNA HAS HAPPILY RUN AWAY WITH THE GIRL.
THIS IS THE WORST POSSIBLE OUTCOME.
ALL OF MY PLANS FAILED.
AND IT'S ALL YOUR FAULT, KIRIE.

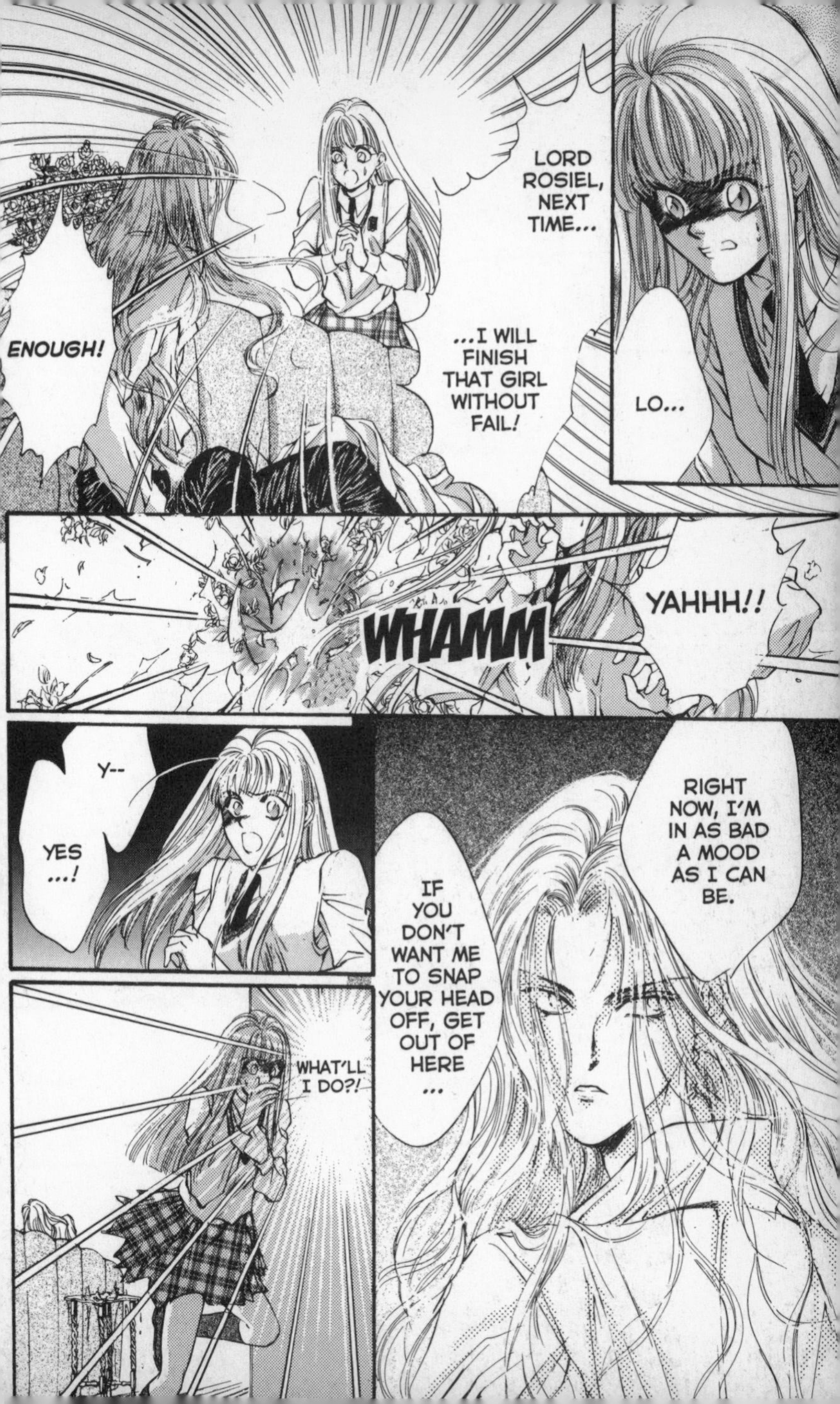
LO...
LORD ROSIEL, NEXT TIME...
...I WILL FINISH THAT GIRL WITHOUT FAIL!
ENOUGH!
YAHHH!!
WHAMM
RIGHT NOW, I'M IN AS BAD A MOOD AS I CAN BE.
IF YOU DON'T WANT ME TO SNAP YOUR HEAD OFF, GET OUT OF HERE ...
Y--
YES ...!
WHAT'LL I DO?!

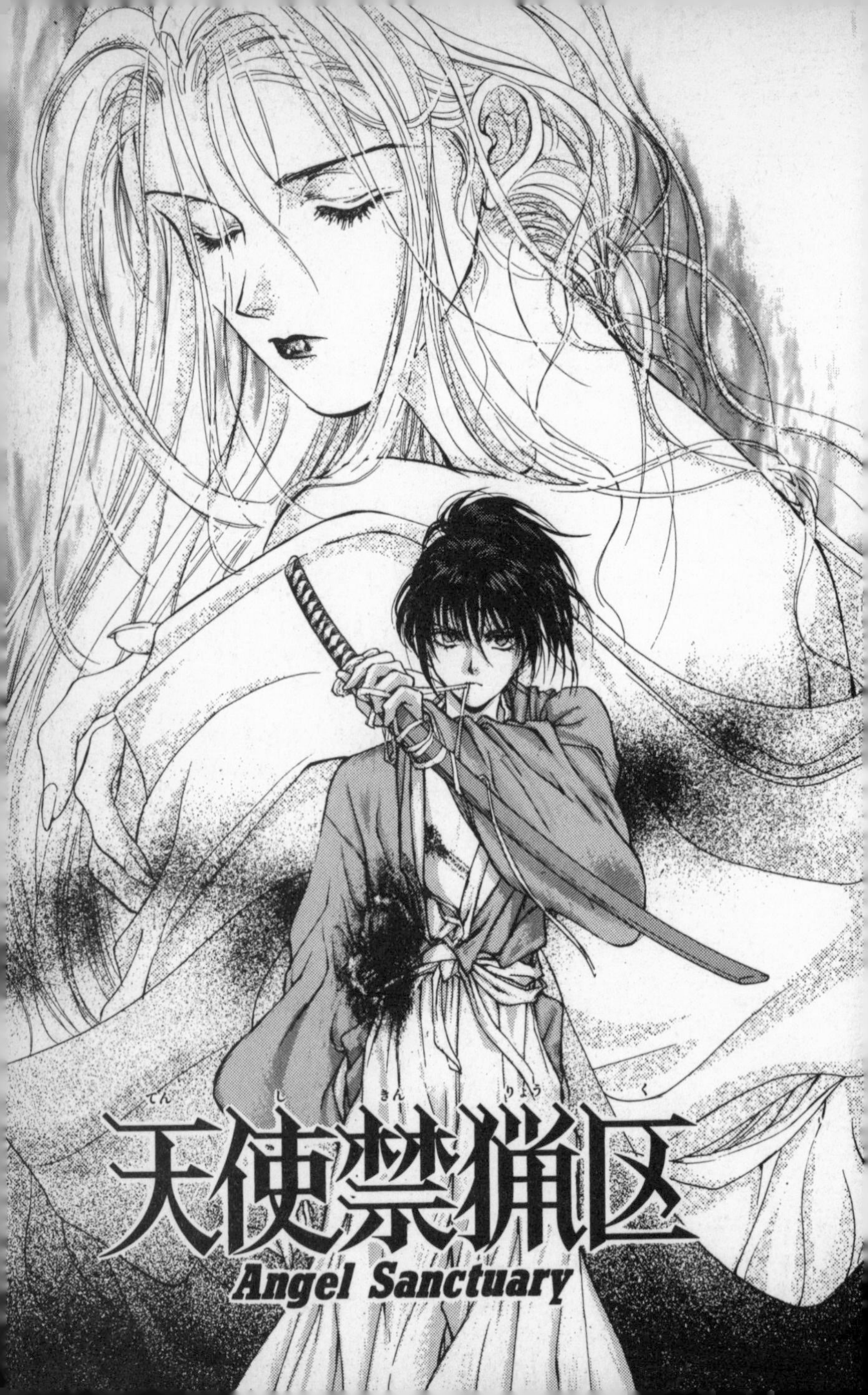
てん し きん りょう く
天使禁猟区
Angel Sanctuary

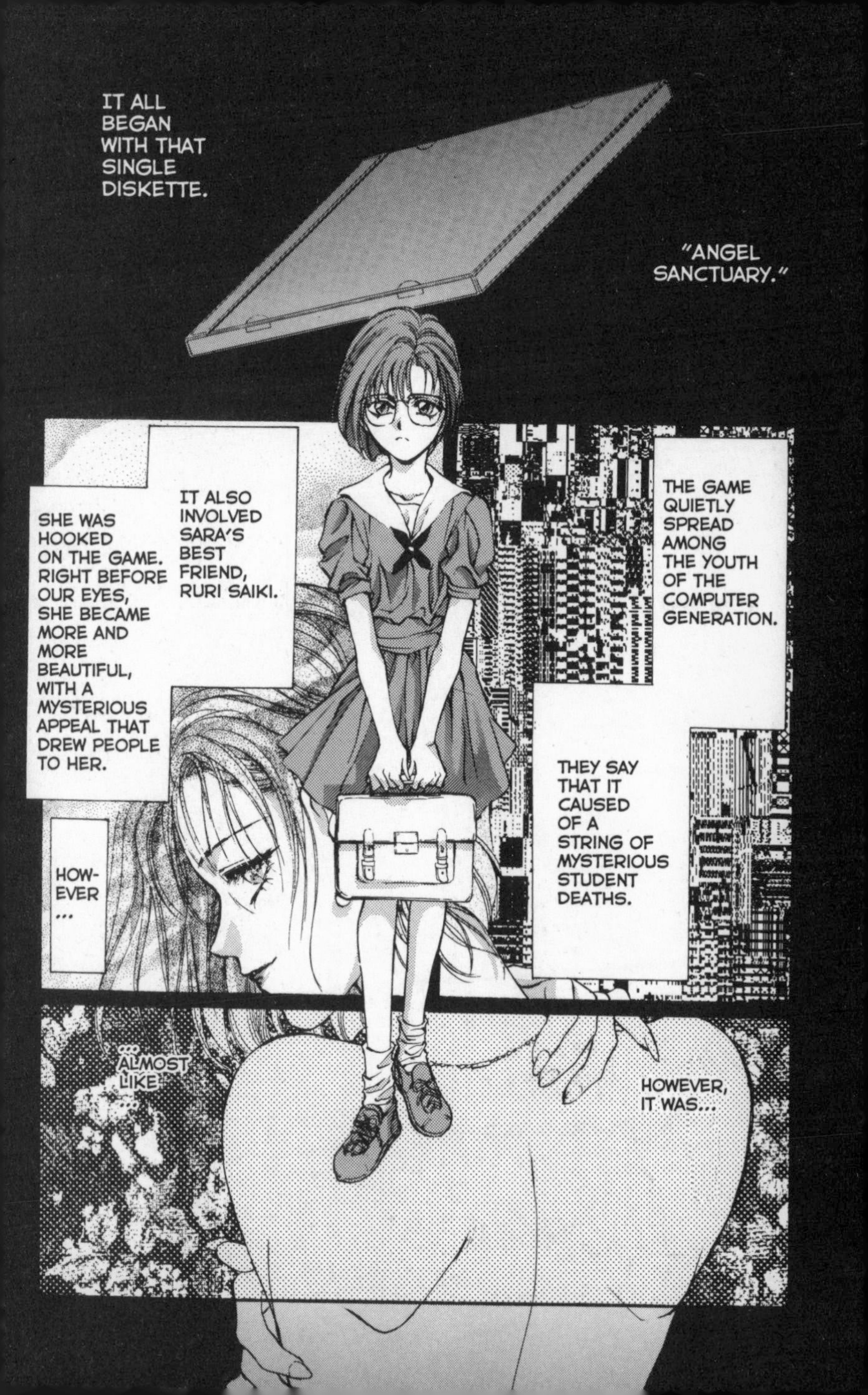
IT ALL BEGAN WITH THAT SINGLE DISKETTE.
"ANGEL SANCTUARY."
THE GAME QUIETLY SPREAD AMONG THE YOUTH OF THE COMPUTER GENERATION.
THEY SAY THAT IT CAUSED OF A STRING OF MYSTERIOUS STUDENT DEATHS.
IT ALSO INVOLVED SARA'S BEST FRIEND, RURI SAIKI.
SHE WAS HOOKED ON THE GAME. RIGHT BEFORE OUR EYES, SHE BECAME MORE AND MORE BEAUTIFUL, WITH A MYSTERIOUS APPEAL THAT DREW PEOPLE TO HER.
HOW-EVER ...
HOWEVER, IT WAS...
...ALMOST LIKE

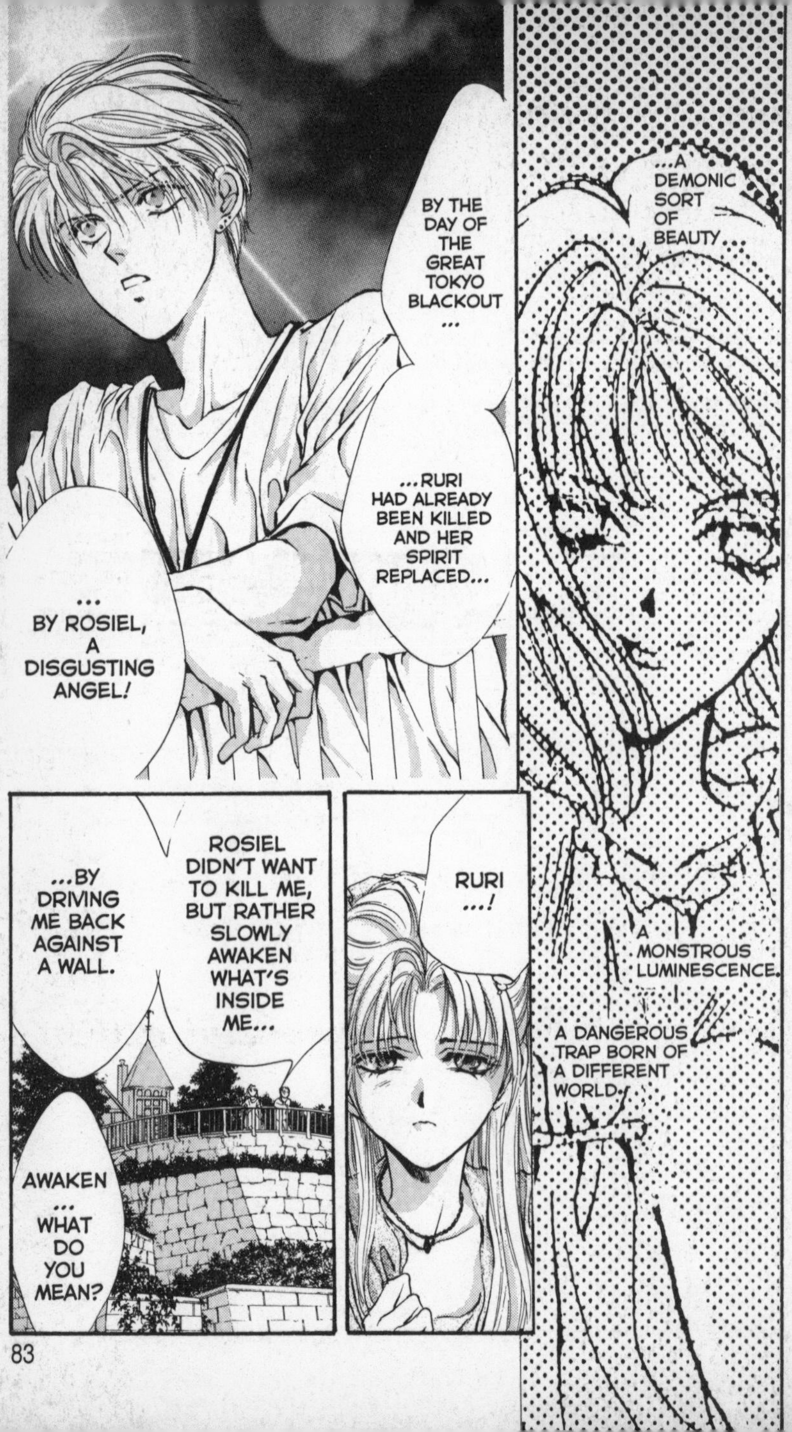
...A DEMONIC SORT OF BEAUTY...
A MONSTROUS LUMINESCENCE.
A DANGEROUS TRAP BORN OF A DIFFERENT WORLD.
BY THE DAY OF THE GREAT TOKYO BLACKOUT...
...RURI HAD ALREADY BEEN KILLED AND HER SPIRIT REPLACED...
...BY ROSIEL, A DISGUSTING ANGEL!
RURI...!
ROSIEL DIDN'T WANT TO KILL ME, BUT RATHER SLOWLY AWAKEN WHAT'S INSIDE ME...
...BY DRIVING ME BACK AGAINST A WALL.
AWAKEN... WHAT DO YOU MEAN?

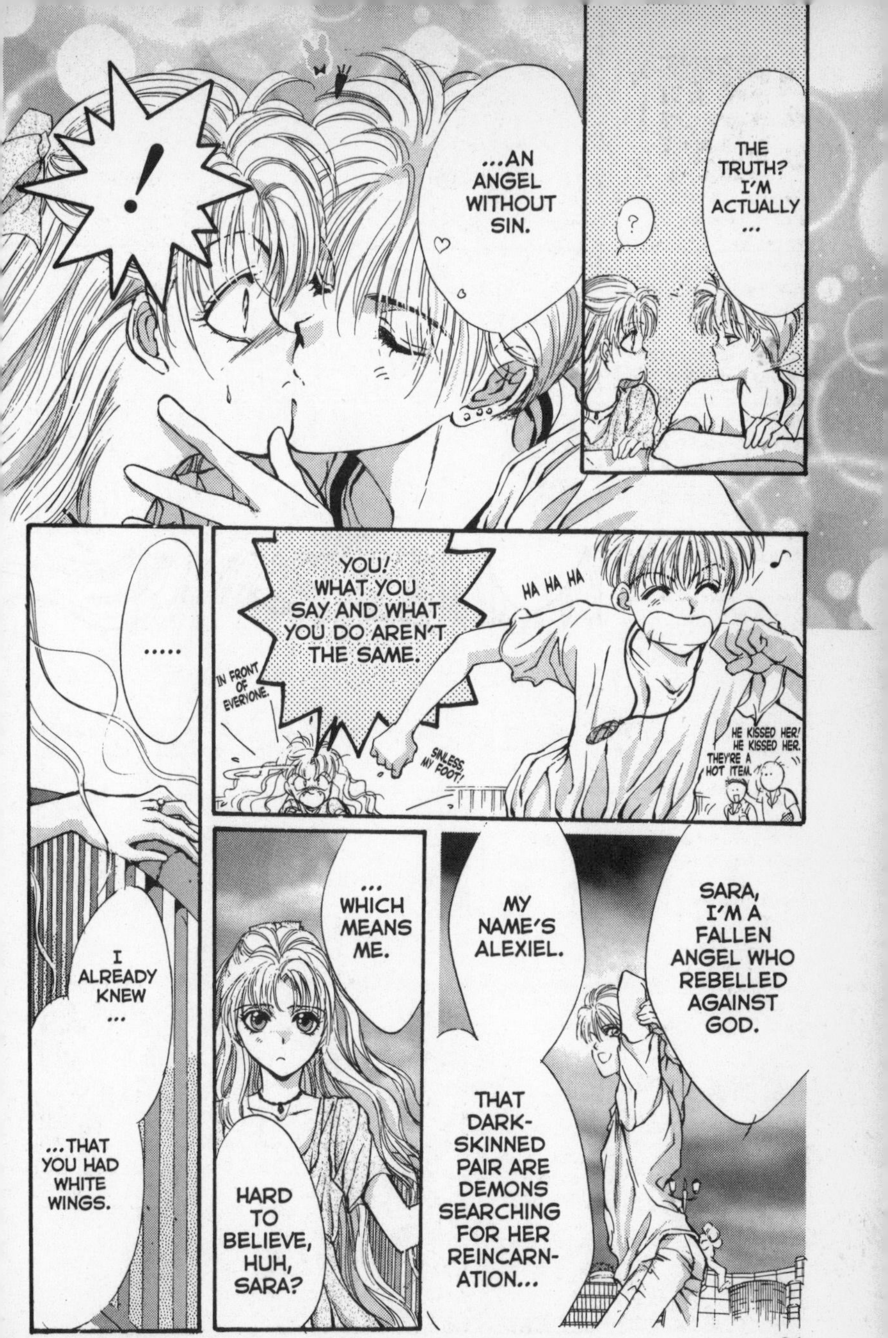
THE TRUTH? I'M ACTUALLY ...
?
...AN ANGEL WITHOUT SIN.
!
HE KISSED HER! HE KISSED HER.
THEY'RE A HOT ITEM.
HA HA HA
YOU! WHAT YOU SAY AND WHAT YOU DO AREN'T THE SAME.
IN FRONT OF EVERYONE.
SINLESS, MY FOOT!
SARA, I'M A FALLEN ANGEL WHO REBELLED AGAINST GOD.
MY NAME'S ALEXIEL.
THAT DARK-SKINNED PAIR ARE DEMONS SEARCHING FOR HER REINCARN-ATION...
... WHICH MEANS ME.
HARD TO BELIEVE, HUH, SARA?
.....
I ALREADY KNEW ...
...THAT YOU HAD WHITE WINGS.

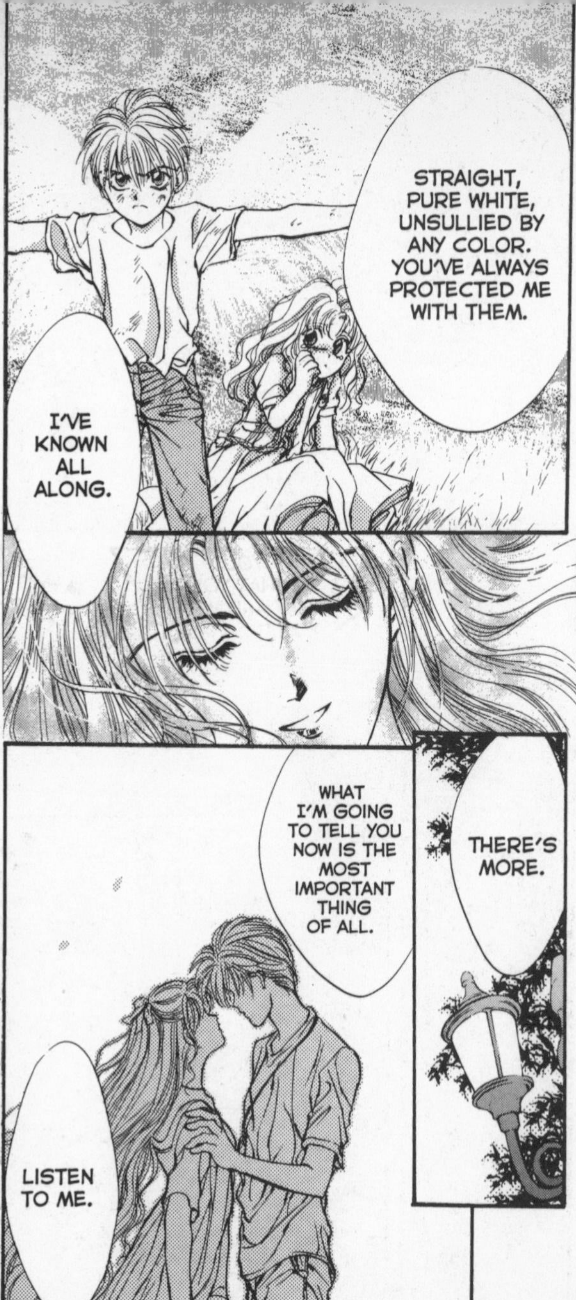
STRAIGHT, PURE WHITE, UNSULLIED BY ANY COLOR. YOU'VE ALWAYS PROTECTED ME WITH THEM.
I'VE KNOWN ALL ALONG.
THERE'S MORE.
WHAT I'M GOING TO TELL YOU NOW IS THE MOST IMPORTANT THING OF ALL.
LISTEN TO ME.

I remember being told by my assistant, my editor, and also my readers, that they liked the two students on the facing page who said, "He kissed her, he kissed her."

Not that it's all that important or anything.

The moral this time is "it's completely rational to do something I'm not familiar with." I suppose people who are familiar with the subject will have a lot to say about it, but it's none of their business! With regard to the question, "Is Arachne in love with Kira?" I'll leave it as "no comment."

I wouldn't say Arachne hates him, though.

I wanted to spend a lot of time describing Kira and Setsuna's previous lives, but as it was so unrelated to the main theme, that part of the story has become quite compact.

It's completely different from how I had intended it!

It was a lot of fun depicting such a flashy Arachne.

Do you think he actually went out in public looking like that?!

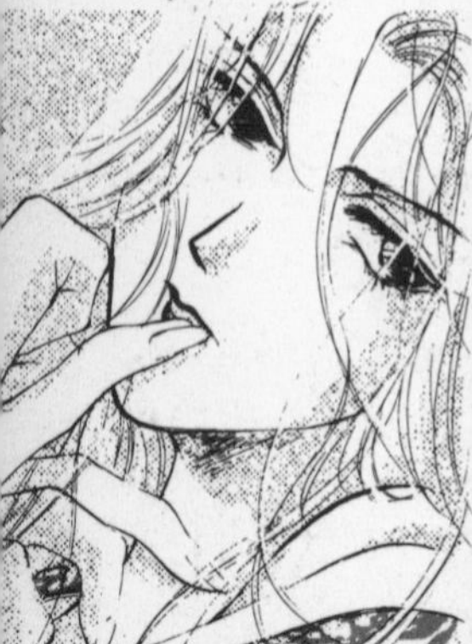

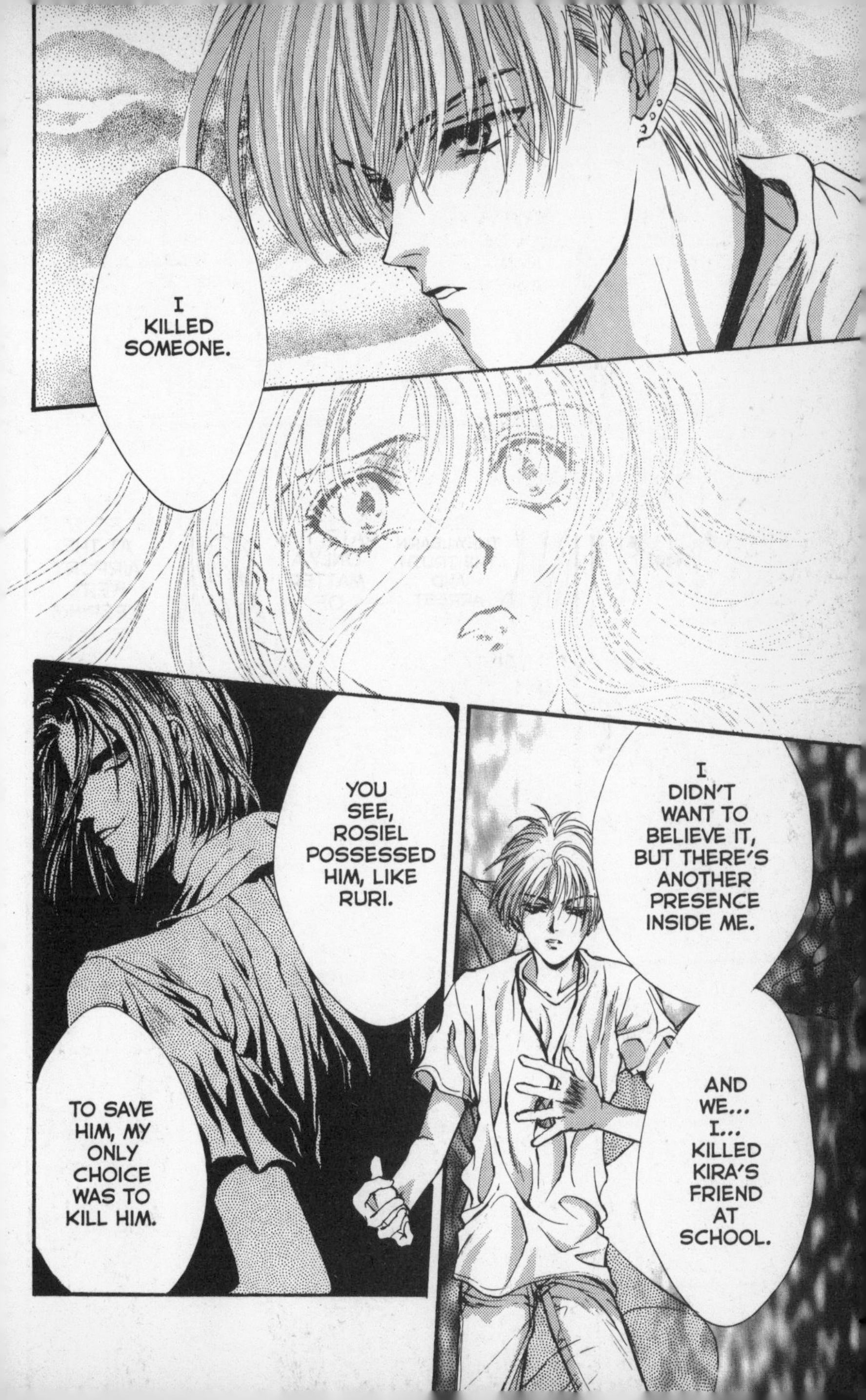
I KILLED SOMEONE.
I DIDN'T WANT TO BELIEVE IT, BUT THERE'S ANOTHER PRESENCE INSIDE ME.
AND WE... I... KILLED KIRA'S FRIEND AT SCHOOL.
YOU SEE, ROSIEL POSSESSED HIM, LIKE RURI.
TO SAVE HIM, MY ONLY CHOICE WAS TO KILL HIM.

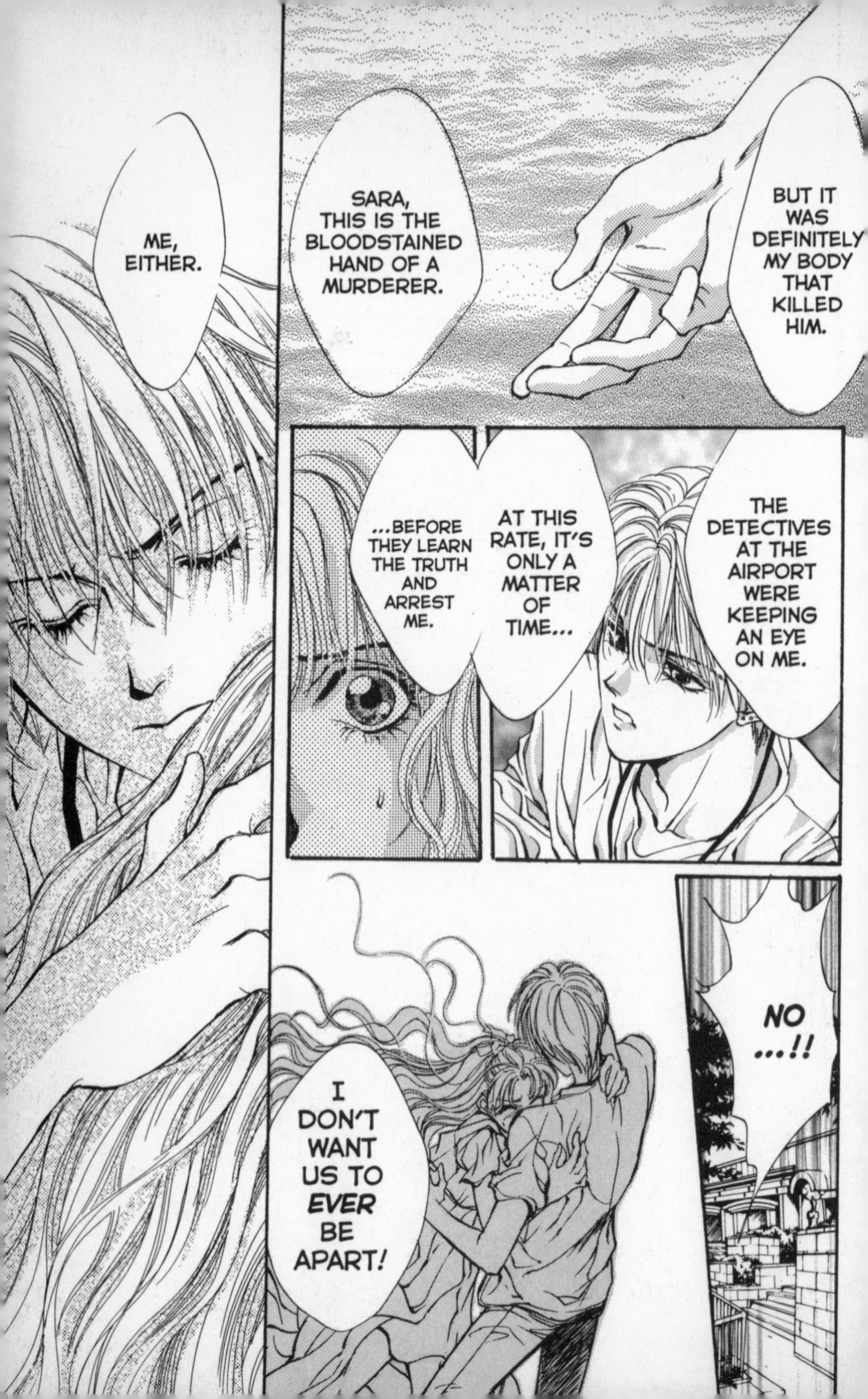
BUT IT WAS DEFINITELY MY BODY THAT KILLED HIM.
SARA, THIS IS THE BLOODSTAINED HAND OF A MURDERER.
THE DETECTIVES AT THE AIRPORT WERE KEEPING AN EYE ON ME.
AT THIS RATE, IT'S ONLY A MATTER OF TIME...
...BEFORE THEY LEARN THE TRUTH AND ARREST ME.
NO ...!!
I DON'T WANT US TO *EVER* BE APART!
ME, EITHER.

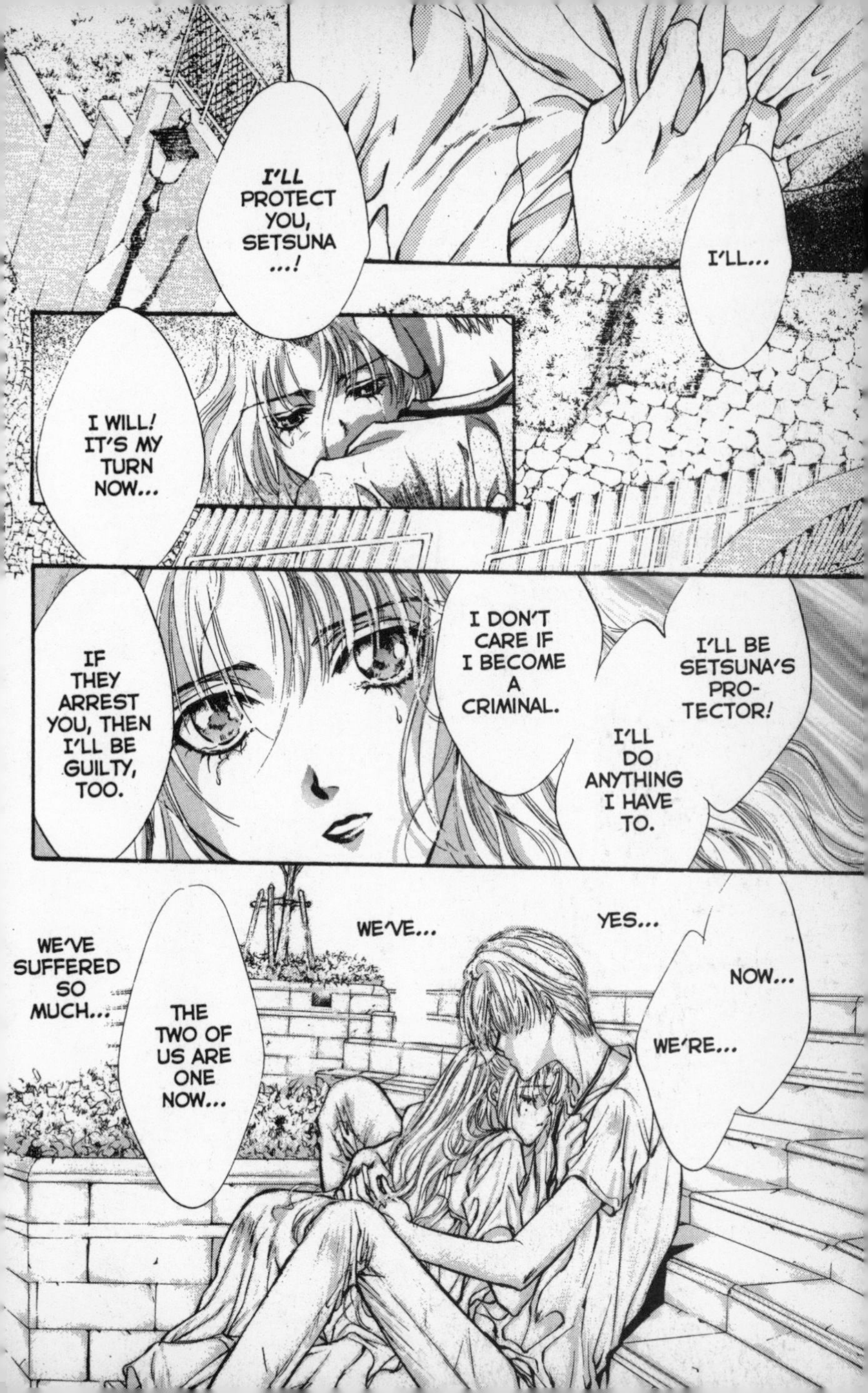
I'LL...
I'LL PROTECT YOU, SETSUNA ...!
I WILL! IT'S MY TURN NOW...
I'LL BE SETSUNA'S PRO-TECTOR!
I'LL DO ANYTHING I HAVE TO.
I DON'T CARE IF I BECOME A CRIMINAL.
IF THEY ARREST YOU, THEN I'LL BE GUILTY, TOO.
YES...
NOW...
WE'RE...
THE TWO OF US ARE ONE NOW...
WE'VE...
WE'VE SUFFERED SO MUCH...

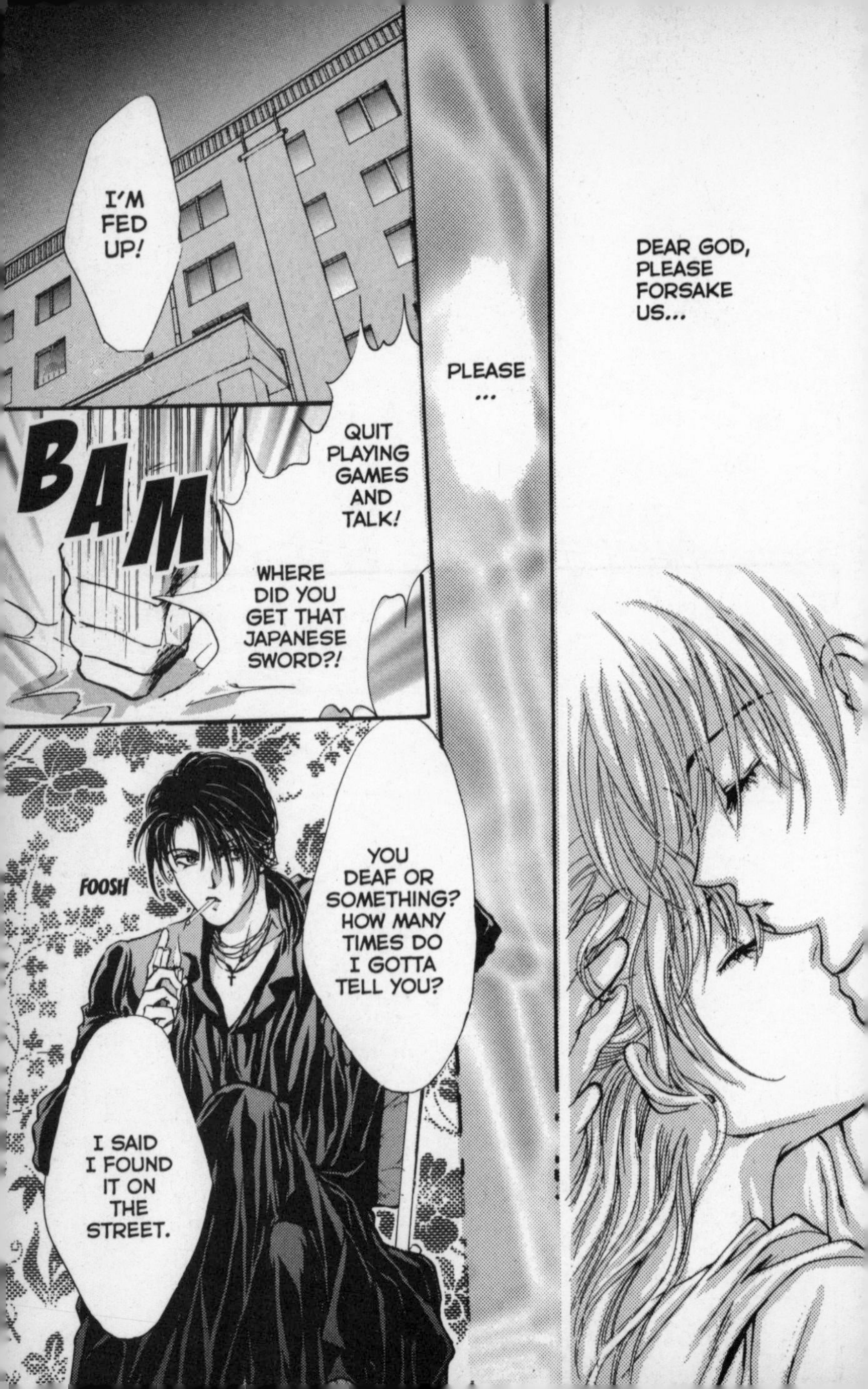
DEAR GOD, PLEASE FORSAKE US...
PLEASE ...
I'M FED UP!
QUIT PLAYING GAMES AND TALK!
WHERE DID YOU GET THAT JAPANESE SWORD?!
BAM
YOU DEAF OR SOMETHING? HOW MANY TIMES DO I GOTTA TELL YOU?
FOOSH
I SAID I FOUND IT ON THE STREET.

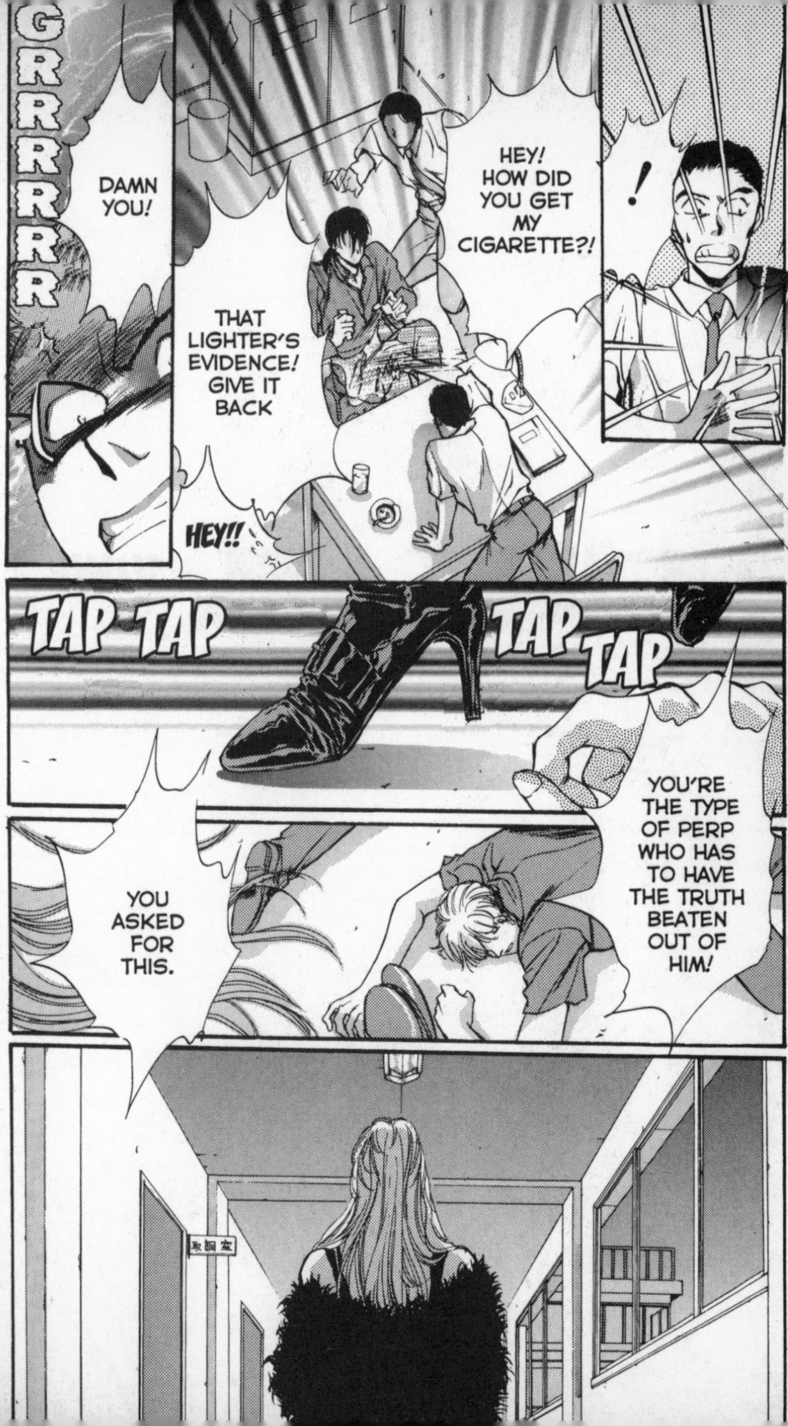
!
HEY! HOW DID YOU GET MY CIGARETTE?!
THAT LIGHTER'S EVIDENCE! GIVE IT BACK
HEY!!
GRRRRRRR
DAMN YOU!
TAP TAP TAP TAP
YOU'RE THE TYPE OF PERP WHO HAS TO HAVE THE TRUTH BEATEN OUT OF HIM!
YOU ASKED FOR THIS.

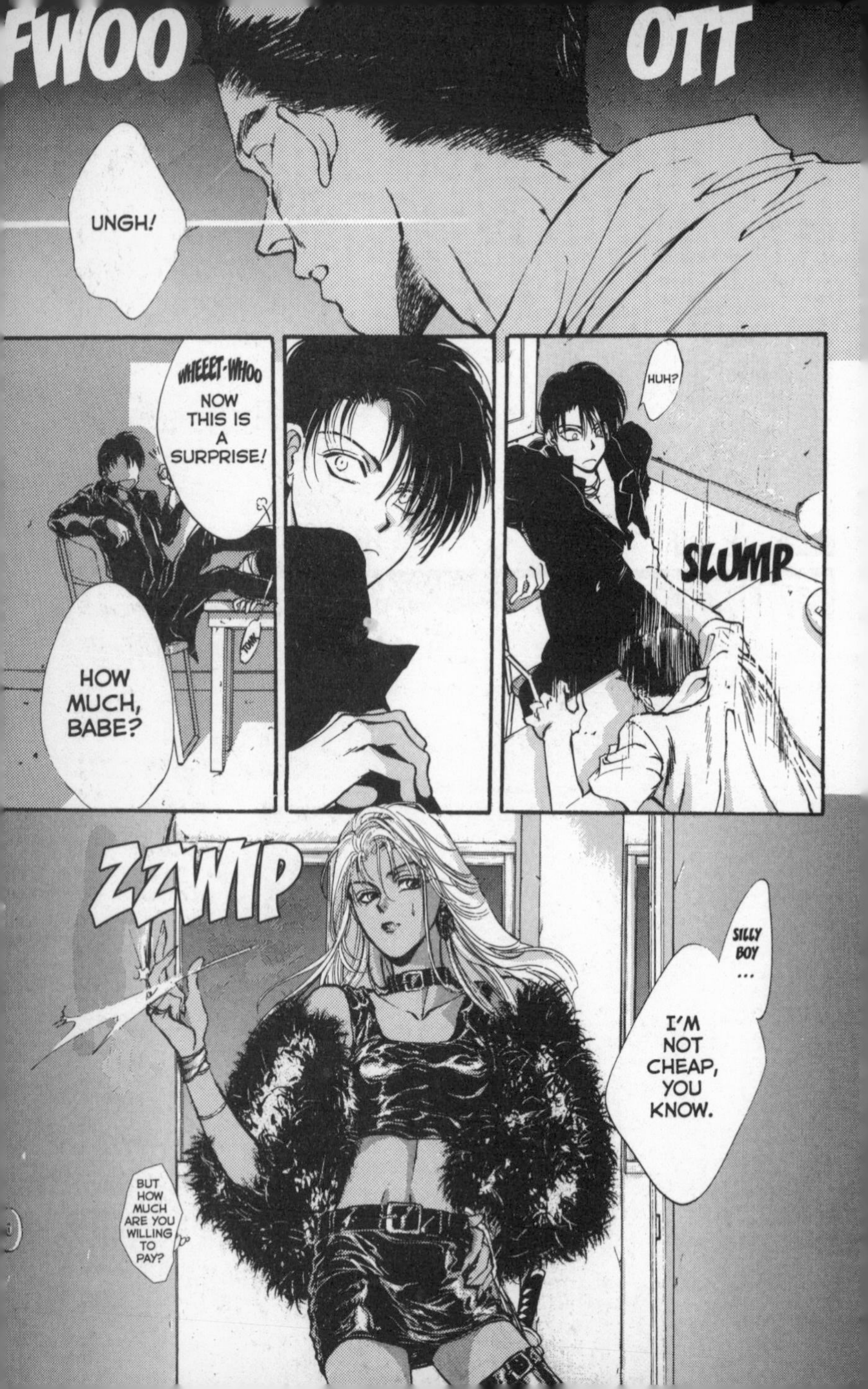
FWOO
OTT
UNGH!
HUH?
SLUMP
WHEEET-WHOO
NOW THIS IS A SURPRISE!
HOW MUCH, BABE?
ZZWIP
SILLY BOY ...
I'M NOT CHEAP, YOU KNOW.
BUT HOW MUCH ARE YOU WILLING TO PAY?

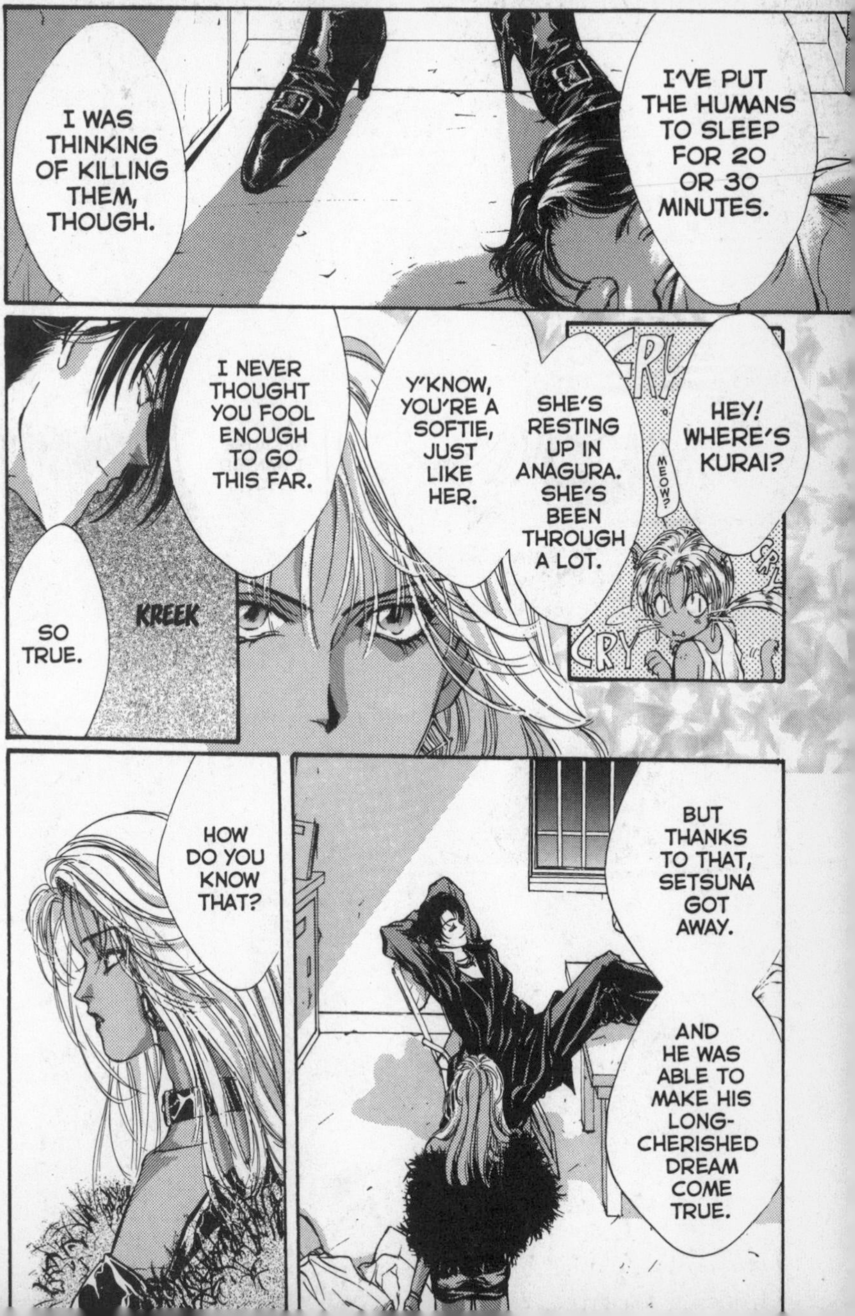
I'VE PUT THE HUMANS TO SLEEP FOR 20 OR 30 MINUTES.
I WAS THINKING OF KILLING THEM, THOUGH.
CRY
HEY! WHERE'S KURAI?
MEOW?
CRY
CRY
SHE'S RESTING UP IN ANAGURA. SHE'S BEEN THROUGH A LOT.
Y'KNOW, YOU'RE A SOFTIE, JUST LIKE HER.
I NEVER THOUGHT YOU FOOL ENOUGH TO GO THIS FAR.
KREEK
SO TRUE.
BUT THANKS TO THAT, SETSUNA GOT AWAY.
AND HE WAS ABLE TO MAKE HIS LONG-CHERISHED DREAM COME TRUE.
HOW DO YOU KNOW THAT?

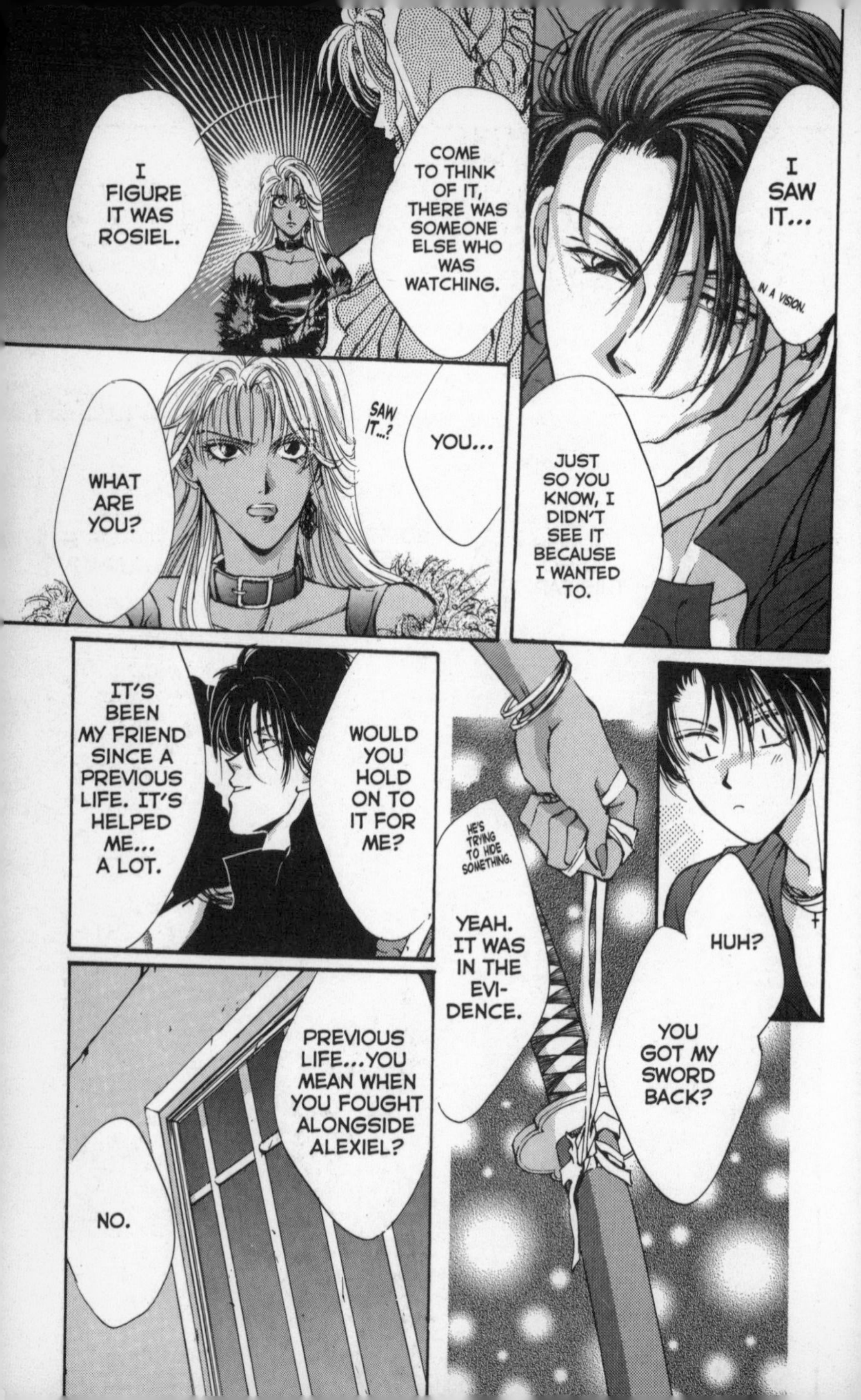
I SAW IT...
IN A VISION.
JUST SO YOU KNOW, I DIDN'T SEE IT BECAUSE I WANTED TO.
COME TO THINK OF IT, THERE WAS SOMEONE ELSE WHO WAS WATCHING.
I FIGURE IT WAS ROSIEL.
YOU...
SAW IT...?
WHAT ARE YOU?
HUH?
YOU GOT MY SWORD BACK?
YEAH. IT WAS IN THE EVIDENCE.
HE'S TRYING TO HIDE SOMETHING.
WOULD YOU HOLD ON TO IT FOR ME?
IT'S BEEN MY FRIEND SINCE A PREVIOUS LIFE. IT'S HELPED ME... A LOT.
PREVIOUS LIFE...YOU MEAN WHEN YOU FOUGHT ALONGSIDE ALEXIEL?
NO.

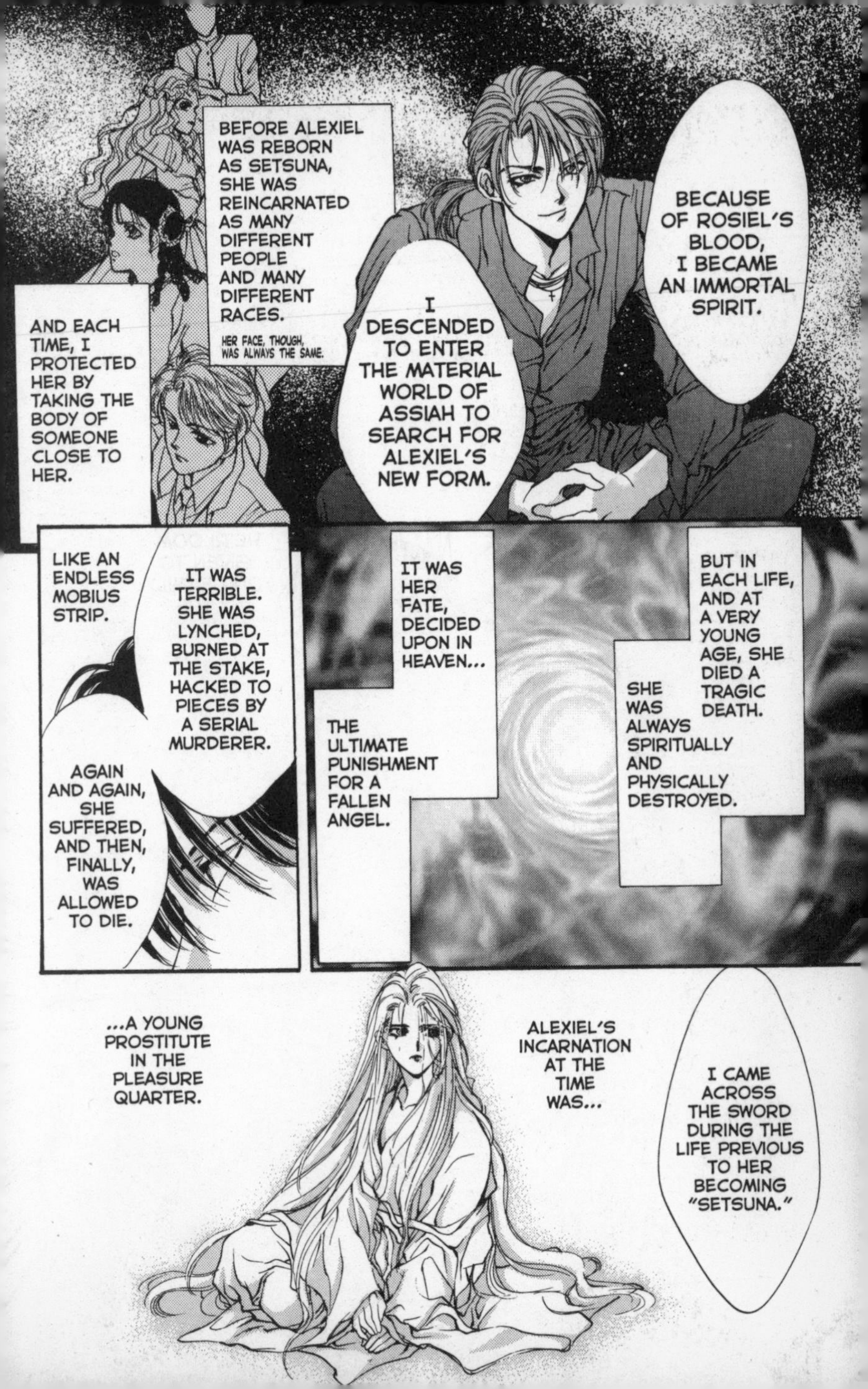
BECAUSE OF ROSIEL'S BLOOD, I BECAME AN IMMORTAL SPIRIT.
I DESCENDED TO ENTER THE MATERIAL WORLD OF ASSIAH TO SEARCH FOR ALEXIEL'S NEW FORM.
BEFORE ALEXIEL WAS REBORN AS SETSUNA, SHE WAS REINCARNATED AS MANY DIFFERENT PEOPLE AND MANY DIFFERENT RACES.
HER FACE, THOUGH, WAS ALWAYS THE SAME.
AND EACH TIME, I PROTECTED HER BY TAKING THE BODY OF SOMEONE CLOSE TO HER.
BUT IN EACH LIFE, AND AT A VERY YOUNG AGE, SHE DIED A TRAGIC DEATH.
SHE WAS ALWAYS SPIRITUALLY AND PHYSICALLY DESTROYED.
IT WAS HER FATE, DECIDED UPON IN HEAVEN...
THE ULTIMATE PUNISHMENT FOR A FALLEN ANGEL.
IT WAS TERRIBLE. SHE WAS LYNCHED, BURNED AT THE STAKE, HACKED TO PIECES BY A SERIAL MURDERER.
LIKE AN ENDLESS MOBIUS STRIP.
AGAIN AND AGAIN, SHE SUFFERED, AND THEN, FINALLY, WAS ALLOWED TO DIE.
I CAME ACROSS THE SWORD DURING THE LIFE PREVIOUS TO HER BECOMING "SETSUNA."
ALEXIEL'S INCARNATION AT THE TIME WAS...
...A YOUNG PROSTITUTE IN THE PLEASURE QUARTER.

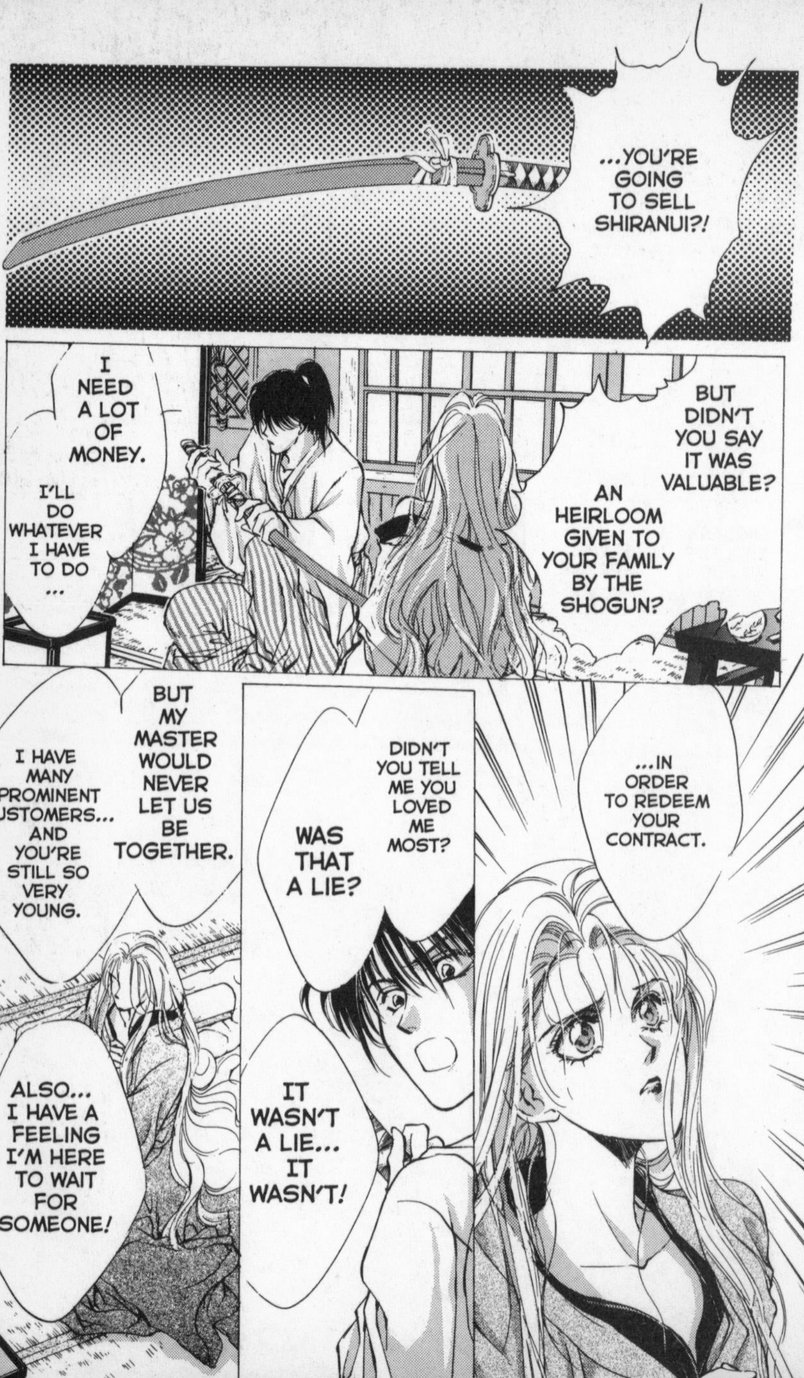
...YOU'RE GOING TO SELL SHIRANUI?!
BUT DIDN'T YOU SAY IT WAS VALUABLE?
AN HEIRLOOM GIVEN TO YOUR FAMILY BY THE SHOGUN?
I NEED A LOT OF MONEY.
I'LL DO WHATEVER I HAVE TO DO ...
...IN ORDER TO REDEEM YOUR CONTRACT.
DIDN'T YOU TELL ME YOU LOVED ME MOST?
WAS THAT A LIE?
IT WASN'T A LIE... IT WASN'T!
BUT MY MASTER WOULD NEVER LET US BE TOGETHER.
I HAVE MANY PROMINENT CUSTOMERS... AND YOU'RE STILL SO VERY YOUNG.
ALSO... I HAVE A FEELING I'M HERE TO WAIT FOR SOMEONE!

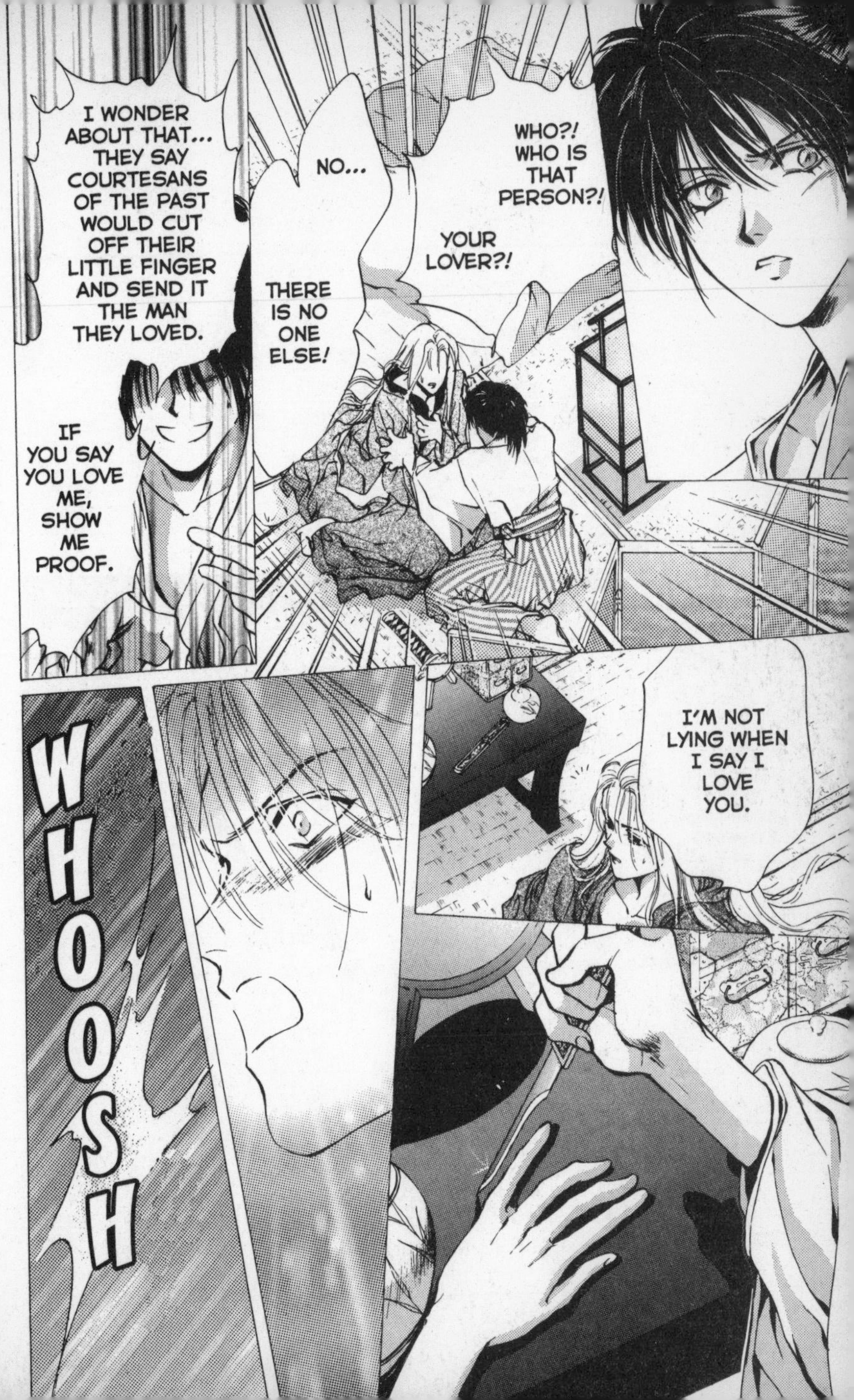
WHO?! WHO IS THAT PERSON?!
YOUR LOVER?!
NO...
THERE IS NO ONE ELSE!
I WONDER ABOUT THAT... THEY SAY COURTESANS OF THE PAST WOULD CUT OFF THEIR LITTLE FINGER AND SEND IT THE MAN THEY LOVED.
IF YOU SAY YOU LOVE ME, SHOW ME PROOF.
I'M NOT LYING WHEN I SAY I LOVE YOU.
WHOOSH

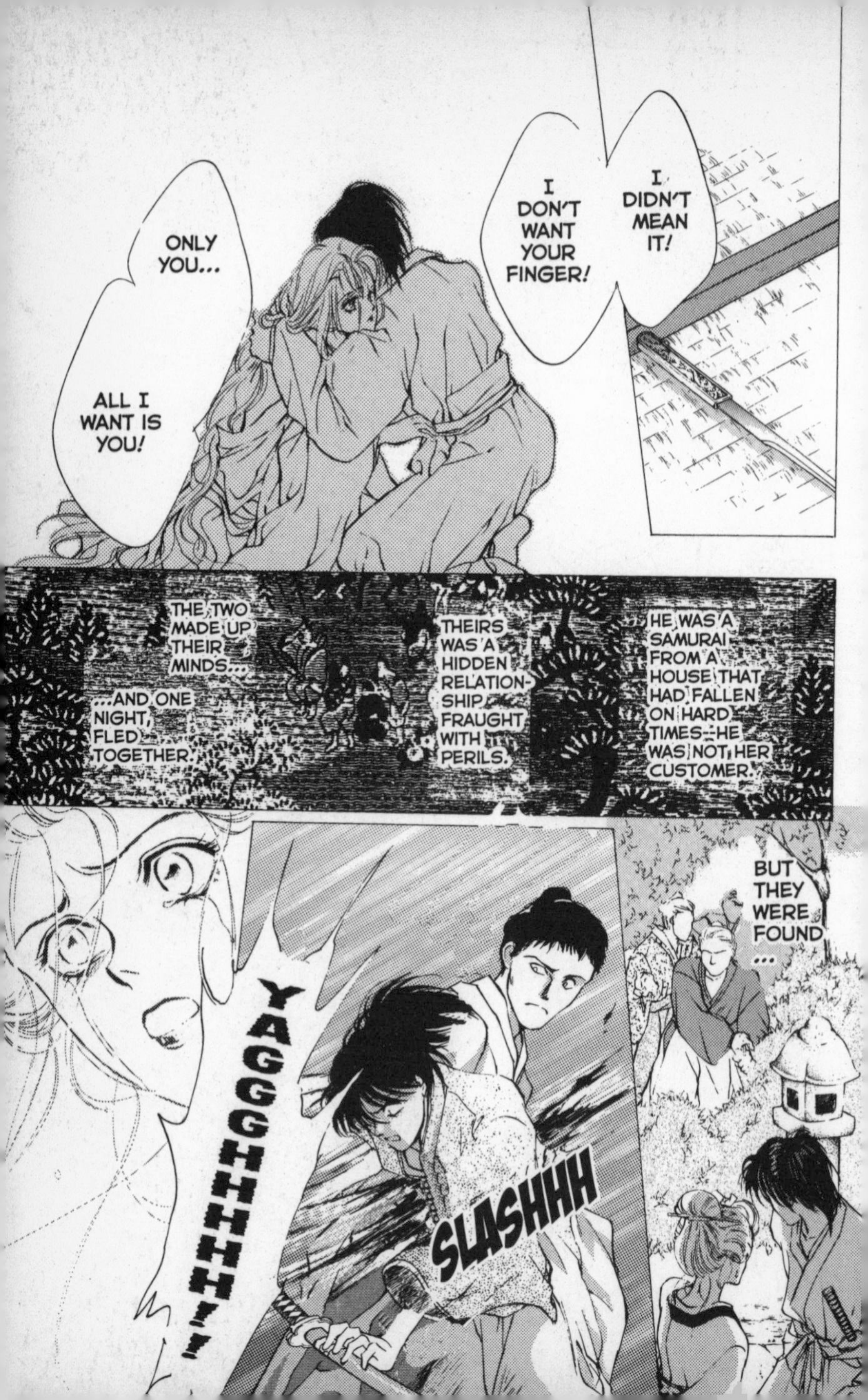

I DIDN'T MEAN IT!
I DON'T WANT YOUR FINGER!
ONLY YOU...
ALL I WANT IS YOU!
HE WAS A SAMURAI FROM A HOUSE THAT HAD FALLEN ON HARD TIMES--HE WAS NOT HER CUSTOMER.
THEIRS WAS A HIDDEN RELATIONSHIP FRAUGHT WITH PERILS.
THE TWO MADE UP THEIR MINDS...
...AND ONE NIGHT, FLED TOGETHER.
BUT THEY WERE FOUND ...
SLASHHH
YAGGGHHHHHHH!!!

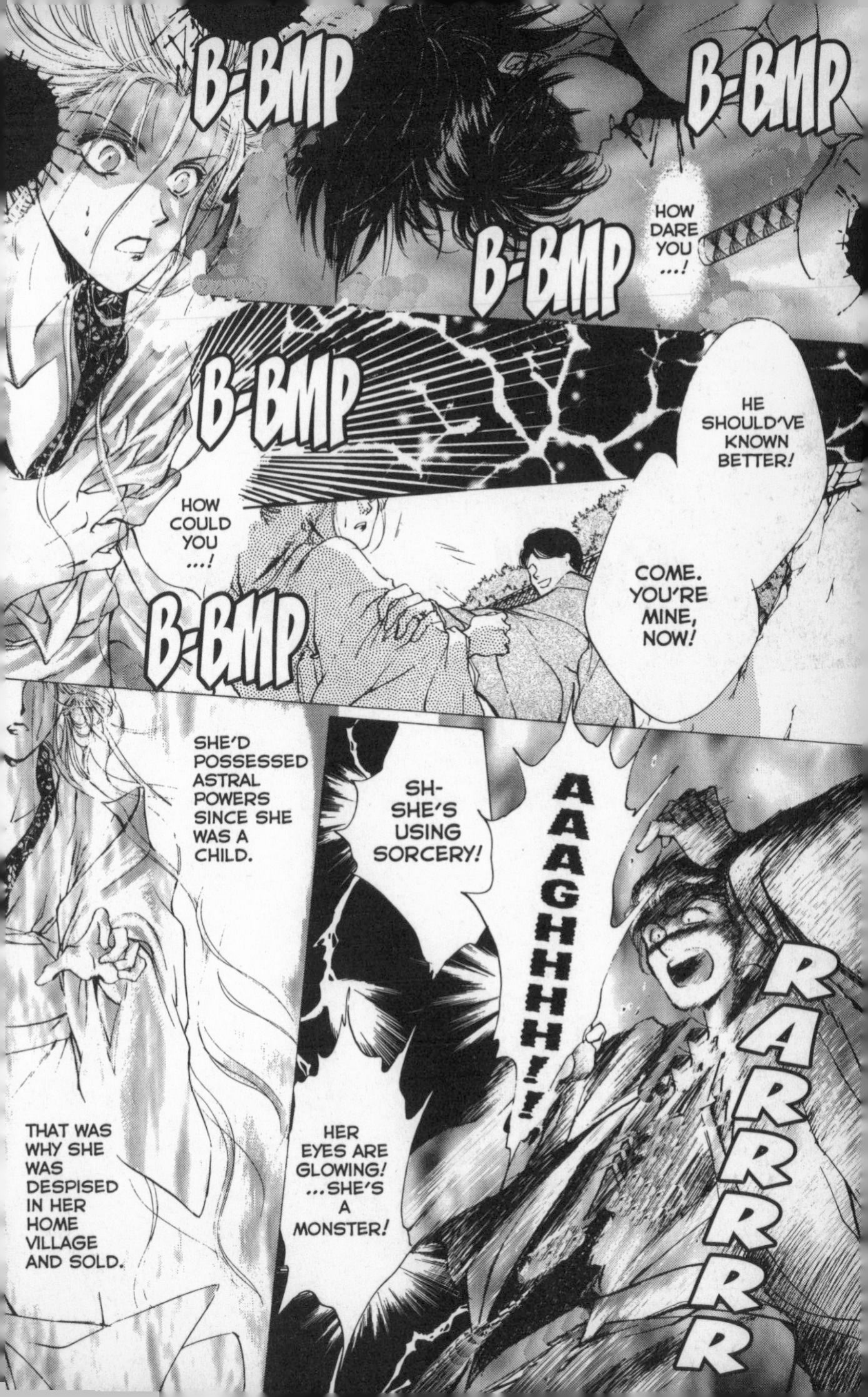
B-BMP
HOW DARE YOU ...!
B-BMP
B-BMP
HE SHOULD'VE KNOWN BETTER!
B-BMP
COME. YOU'RE MINE, NOW!
HOW COULD YOU ...!
B-BMP
RARRRRR
AAAGHHHH!!!
SH-SHE'S USING SORCERY!
HER EYES ARE GLOWING! ...SHE'S A MONSTER!
SHE'D POSSESSED ASTRAL POWERS SINCE SHE WAS A CHILD.
THAT WAS WHY SHE WAS DESPISED IN HER HOME VILLAGE AND SOLD.

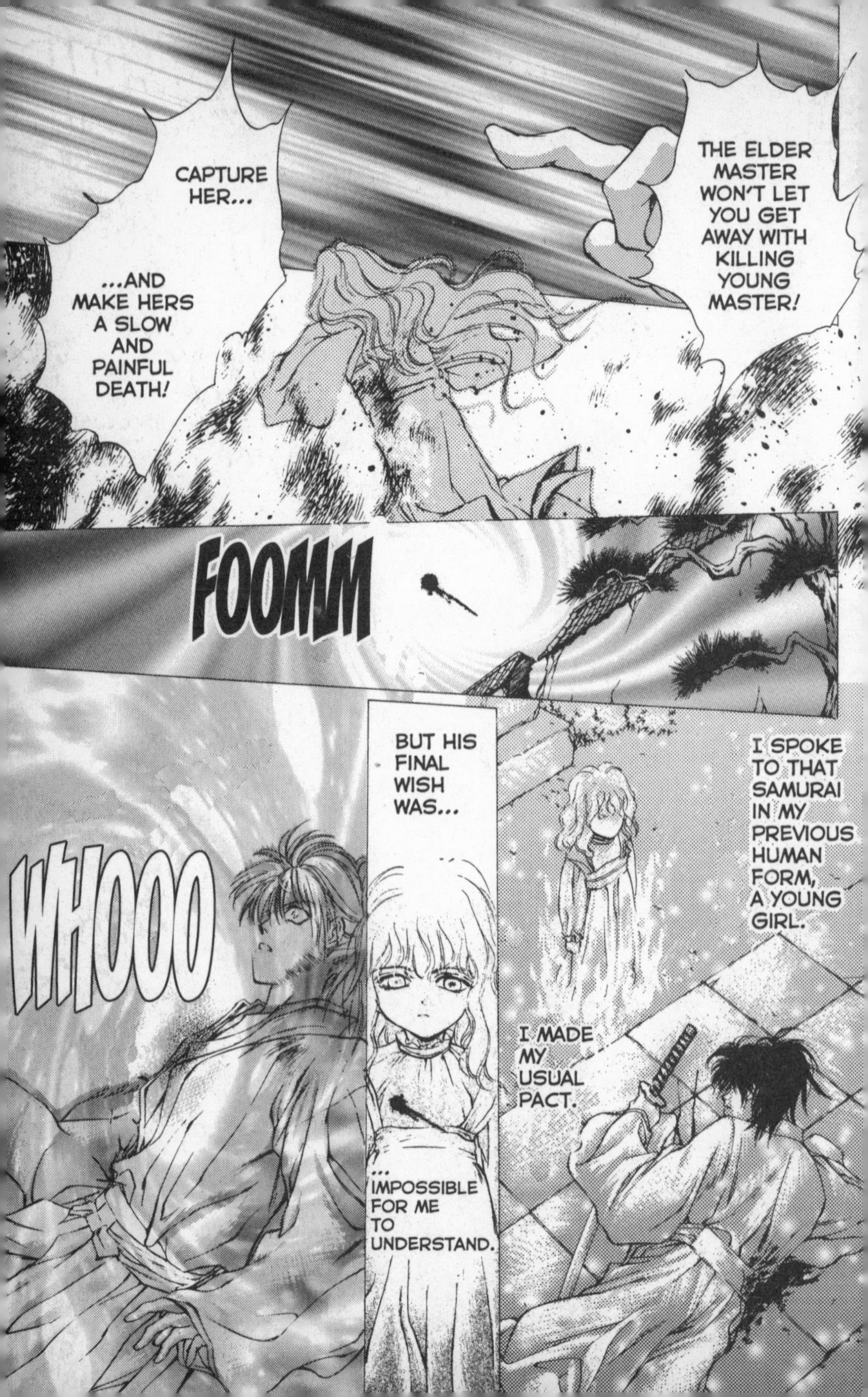
THE ELDER MASTER WON'T LET YOU GET AWAY WITH KILLING YOUNG MASTER!
CAPTURE HER...
...AND MAKE HERS A SLOW AND PAINFUL DEATH!
FOOMM
I SPOKE TO THAT SAMURAI IN MY PREVIOUS HUMAN FORM, A YOUNG GIRL.
I MADE MY USUAL PACT.
BUT HIS FINAL WISH WAS...
...IMPOSSIBLE FOR ME TO UNDERSTAND.
WHOOO

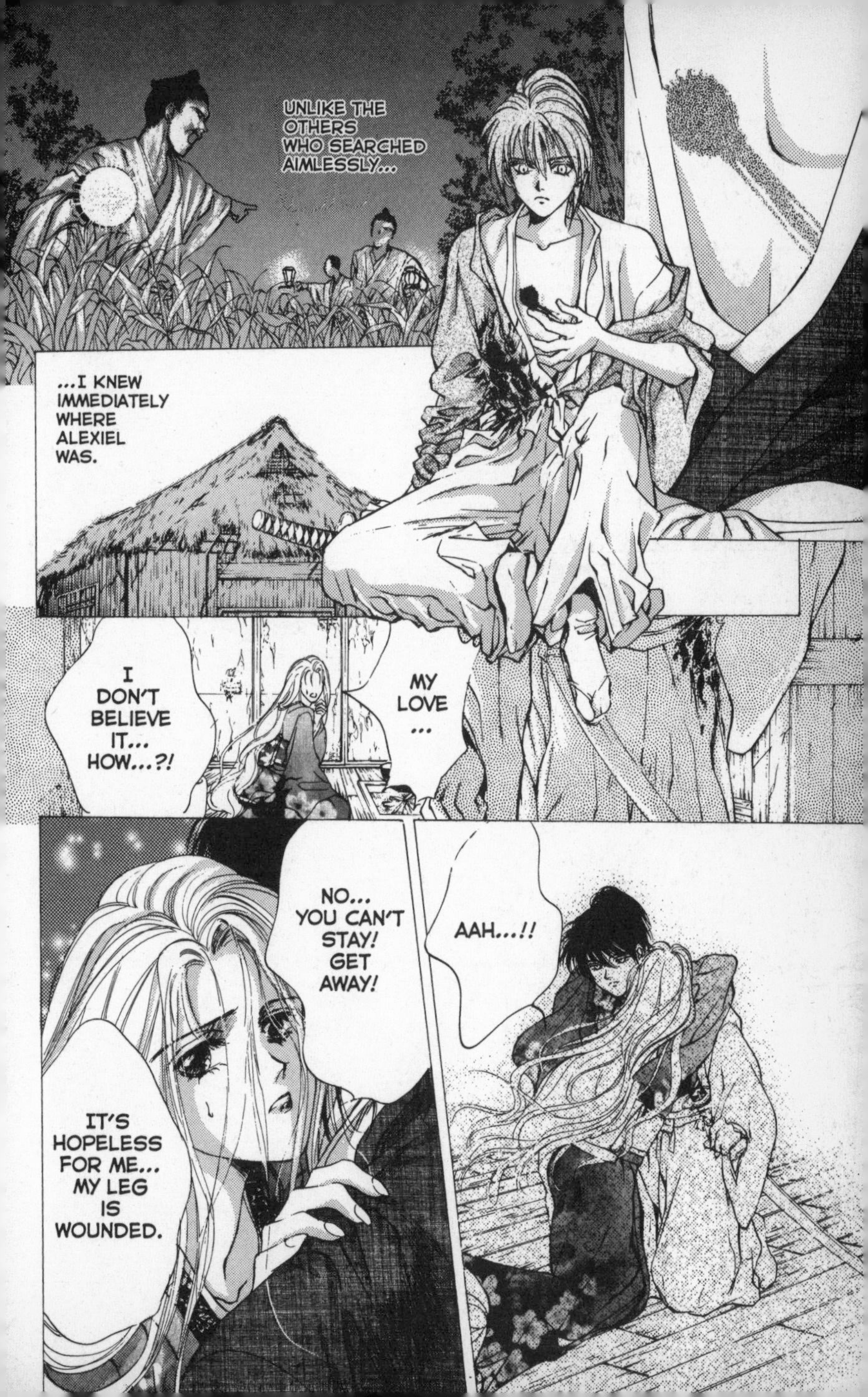
UNLIKE THE OTHERS WHO SEARCHED AIMLESSLY...
...I KNEW IMMEDIATELY WHERE ALEXIEL WAS.
MY LOVE ...
I DON'T BELIEVE IT... HOW...?!
AAH...!!
NO... YOU CAN'T STAY! GET AWAY!
IT'S HOPELESS FOR ME... MY LEG IS WOUNDED.

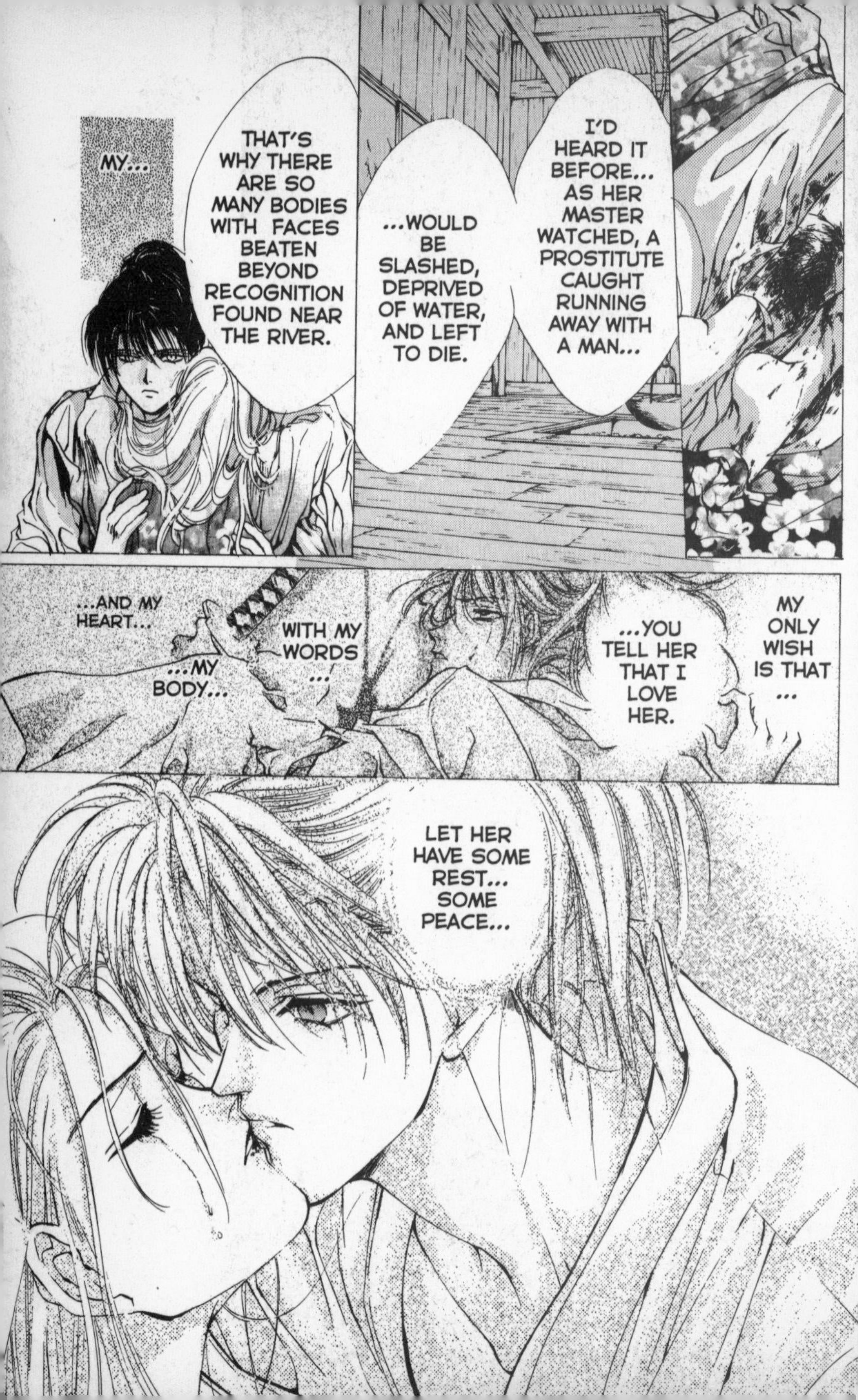
I'D HEARD IT BEFORE... AS HER MASTER WATCHED, A PROSTITUTE CAUGHT RUNNING AWAY WITH A MAN...
...WOULD BE SLASHED, DEPRIVED OF WATER, AND LEFT TO DIE.
THAT'S WHY THERE ARE SO MANY BODIES WITH FACES BEATEN BEYOND RECOGNITION FOUND NEAR THE RIVER.
MY...
MY ONLY WISH IS THAT ...
...YOU TELL HER THAT I LOVE HER.
WITH MY WORDS ...
...MY BODY...
...AND MY HEART...
LET HER HAVE SOME REST... SOME PEACE...

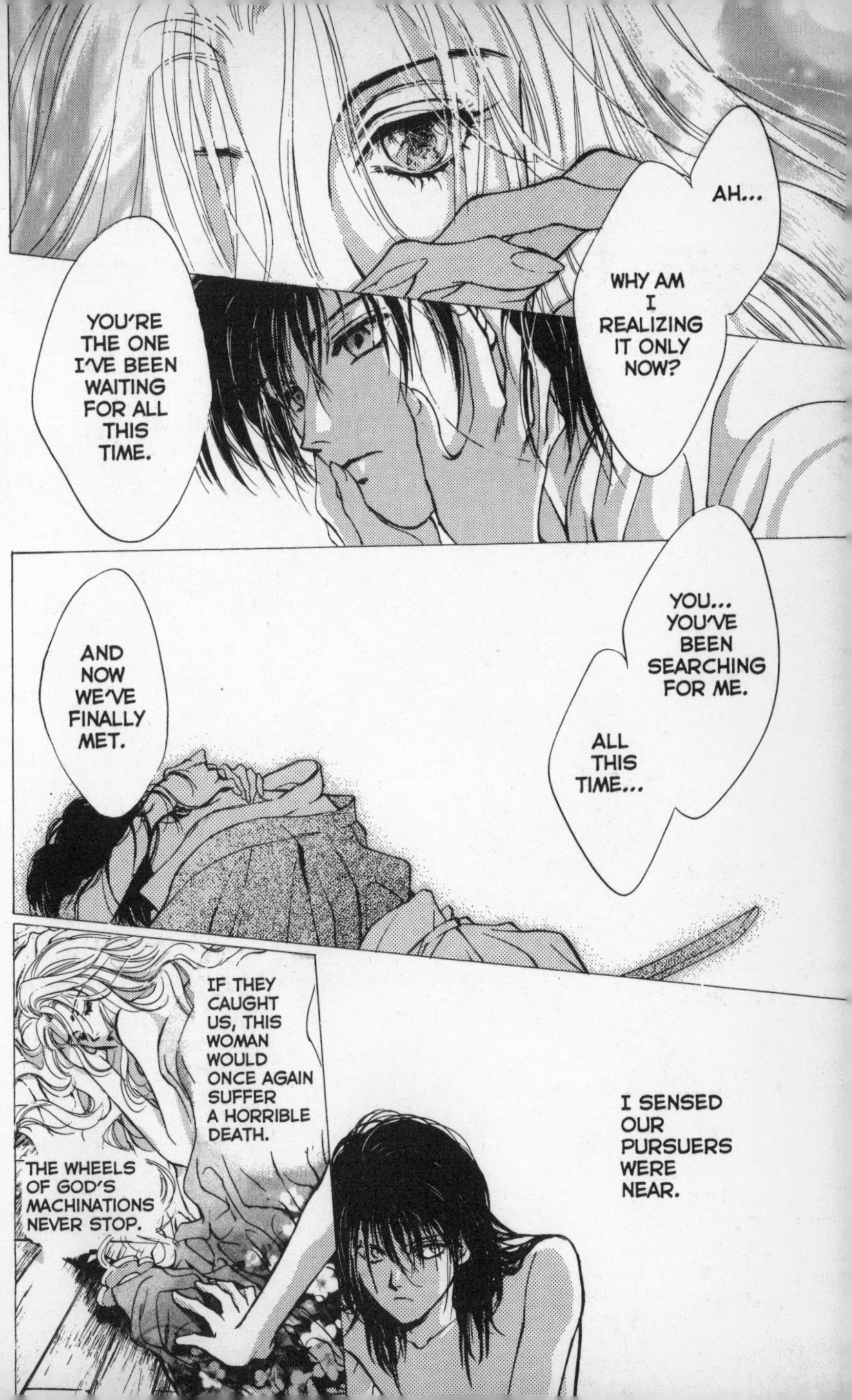
AH...
WHY AM I REALIZING IT ONLY NOW?
YOU'RE THE ONE I'VE BEEN WAITING FOR ALL THIS TIME.
YOU... YOU'VE BEEN SEARCHING FOR ME.
ALL THIS TIME...
AND NOW WE'VE FINALLY MET.
I SENSED OUR PURSUERS WERE NEAR.
IF THEY CAUGHT US, THIS WOMAN WOULD ONCE AGAIN SUFFER A HORRIBLE DEATH.
THE WHEELS OF GOD'S MACHINATIONS NEVER STOP.

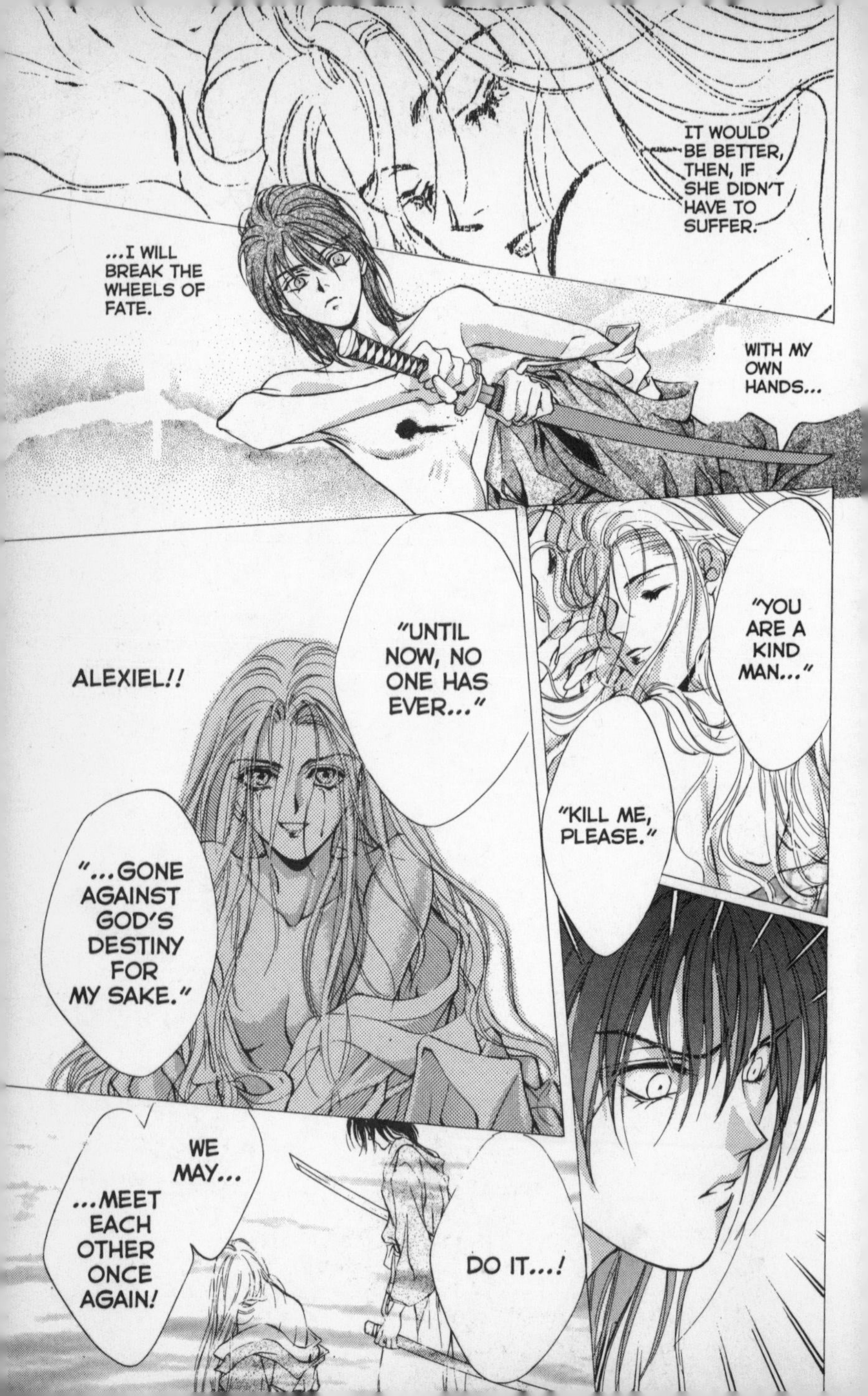
IT WOULD BE BETTER, THEN, IF SHE DIDN'T HAVE TO SUFFER.
WITH MY OWN HANDS...
...I WILL BREAK THE WHEELS OF FATE.
"YOU ARE A KIND MAN..."
"KILL ME, PLEASE."
DO IT...!
"UNTIL NOW, NO ONE HAS EVER..."
"...GONE AGAINST GOD'S DESTINY FOR MY SAKE."
ALEXIEL!!
WE MAY...
...MEET EACH OTHER ONCE AGAIN!

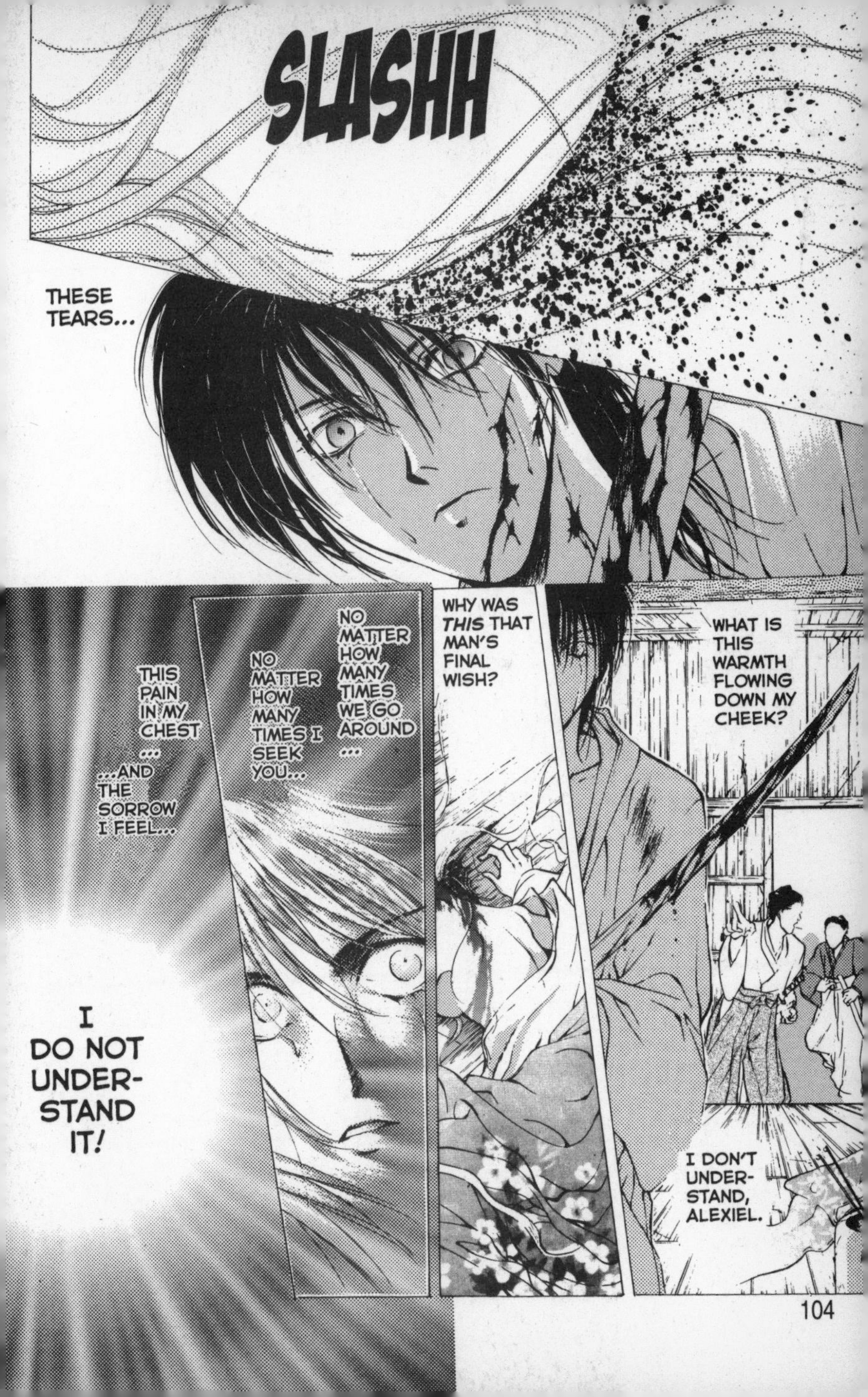
SLASHH
THESE TEARS...
WHAT IS THIS WARMTH FLOWING DOWN MY CHEEK?
I DON'T UNDERSTAND, ALEXIEL.
WHY WAS *THIS* THAT MAN'S FINAL WISH?
NO MATTER HOW MANY TIMES WE GO AROUND...
NO MATTER HOW MANY TIMES I SEEK YOU...
THIS PAIN IN MY CHEST...
...AND THE SORROW I FEEL...
I DO NOT UNDERSTAND IT!

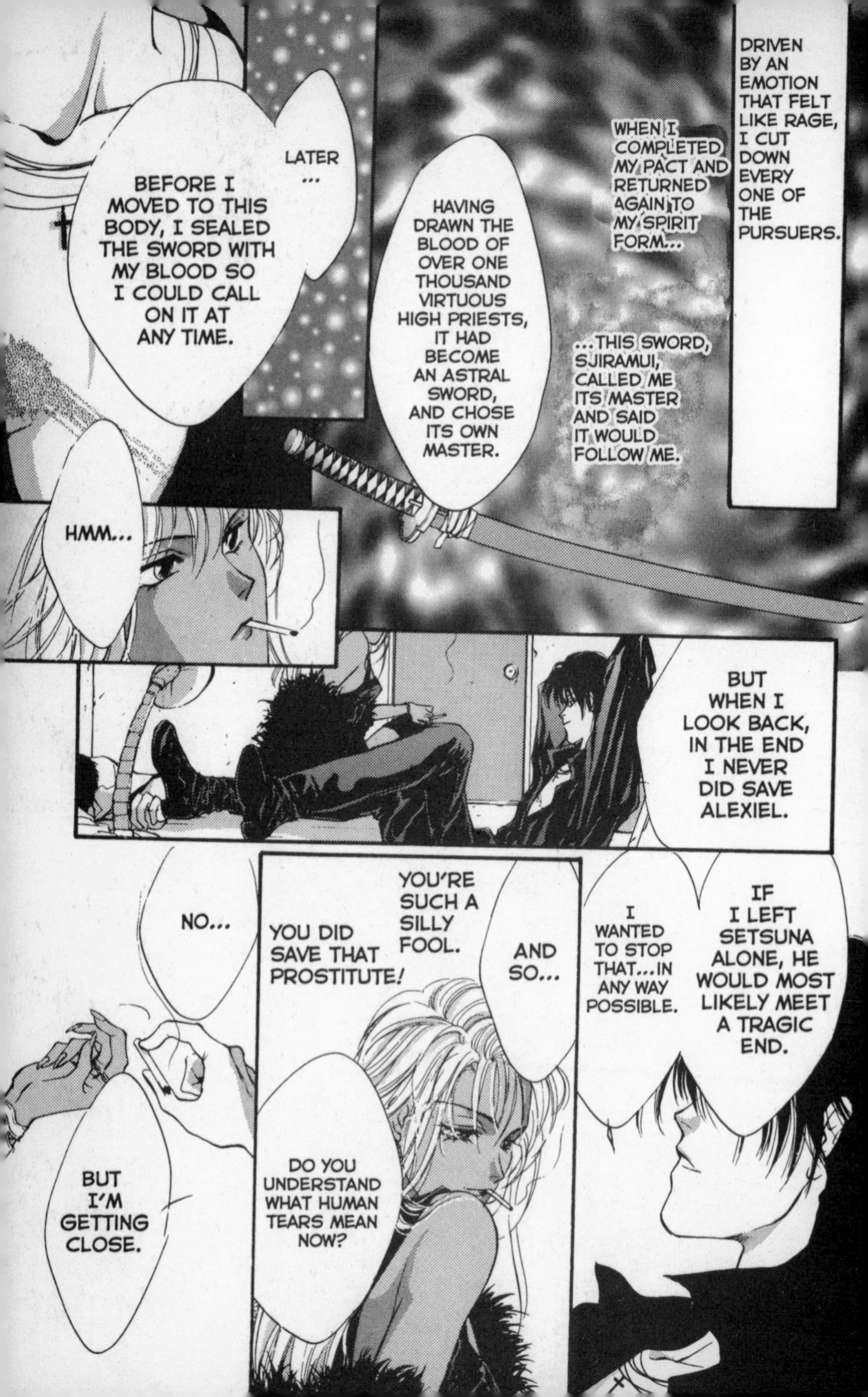
DRIVEN BY AN EMOTION THAT FELT LIKE RAGE, I CUT DOWN EVERY ONE OF THE PURSUERS.
WHEN I COMPLETED MY PACT AND RETURNED AGAIN TO MY SPIRIT FORM...
...THIS SWORD, SJIRAMUI, CALLED ME ITS MASTER AND SAID IT WOULD FOLLOW ME.
HAVING DRAWN THE BLOOD OF OVER ONE THOUSAND VIRTUOUS HIGH PRIESTS, IT HAD BECOME AN ASTRAL SWORD, AND CHOSE ITS OWN MASTER.
LATER ...
BEFORE I MOVED TO THIS BODY, I SEALED THE SWORD WITH MY BLOOD SO I COULD CALL ON IT AT ANY TIME.
HMM...
BUT WHEN I LOOK BACK, IN THE END I NEVER DID SAVE ALEXIEL.
IF I LEFT SETSUNA ALONE, HE WOULD MOST LIKELY MEET A TRAGIC END.
I WANTED TO STOP THAT...IN ANY WAY POSSIBLE.
AND SO...
YOU'RE SUCH A SILLY FOOL.
YOU DID SAVE THAT PROSTITUTE!
DO YOU UNDERSTAND WHAT HUMAN TEARS MEAN NOW?
NO...
BUT I'M GETTING CLOSE.

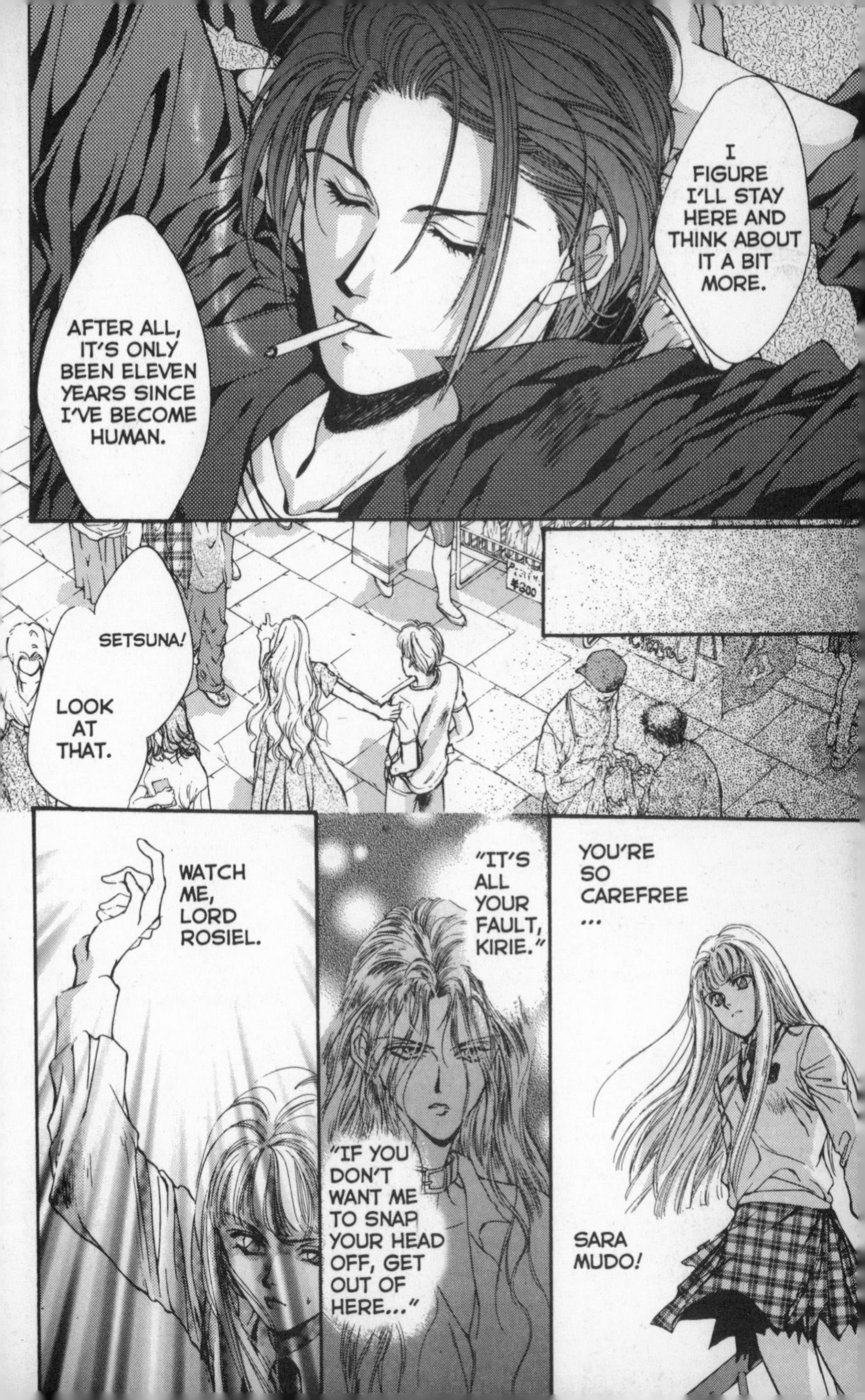
I FIGURE I'LL STAY HERE AND THINK ABOUT IT A BIT MORE.
AFTER ALL, IT'S ONLY BEEN ELEVEN YEARS SINCE I'VE BECOME HUMAN.
SETSUNA!
LOOK AT THAT.
YOU'RE SO CAREFREE ...
SARA MUDO!
"IT'S ALL YOUR FAULT, KIRIE."
"IF YOU DON'T WANT ME TO SNAP YOUR HEAD OFF, GET OUT OF HERE..."
WATCH ME, LORD ROSIEL.

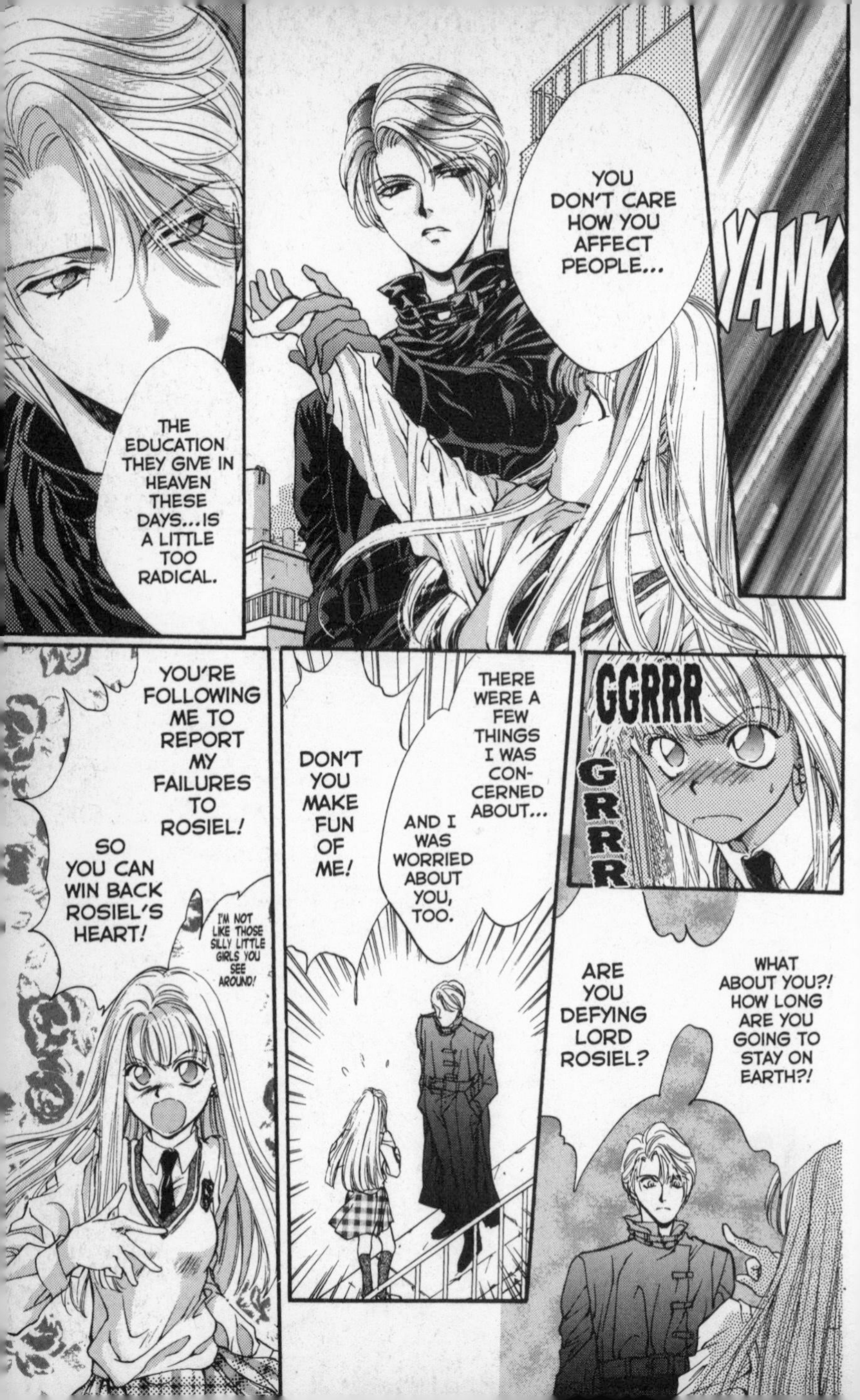
YANK
YOU DON'T CARE HOW YOU AFFECT PEOPLE...
THE EDUCATION THEY GIVE IN HEAVEN THESE DAYS...IS A LITTLE TOO RADICAL.
GGRRR
GRRR
WHAT ABOUT YOU?! HOW LONG ARE YOU GOING TO STAY ON EARTH?!
ARE YOU DEFYING LORD ROSIEL?
THERE WERE A FEW THINGS I WAS CON-CERNED ABOUT...
AND I WAS WORRIED ABOUT YOU, TOO.
DON'T YOU MAKE FUN OF ME!
YOU'RE FOLLOWING ME TO REPORT MY FAILURES TO ROSIEL!
SO YOU CAN WIN BACK ROSIEL'S HEART!
I'M NOT LIKE THOSE SILLY LITTLE GIRLS YOU SEE AROUND!

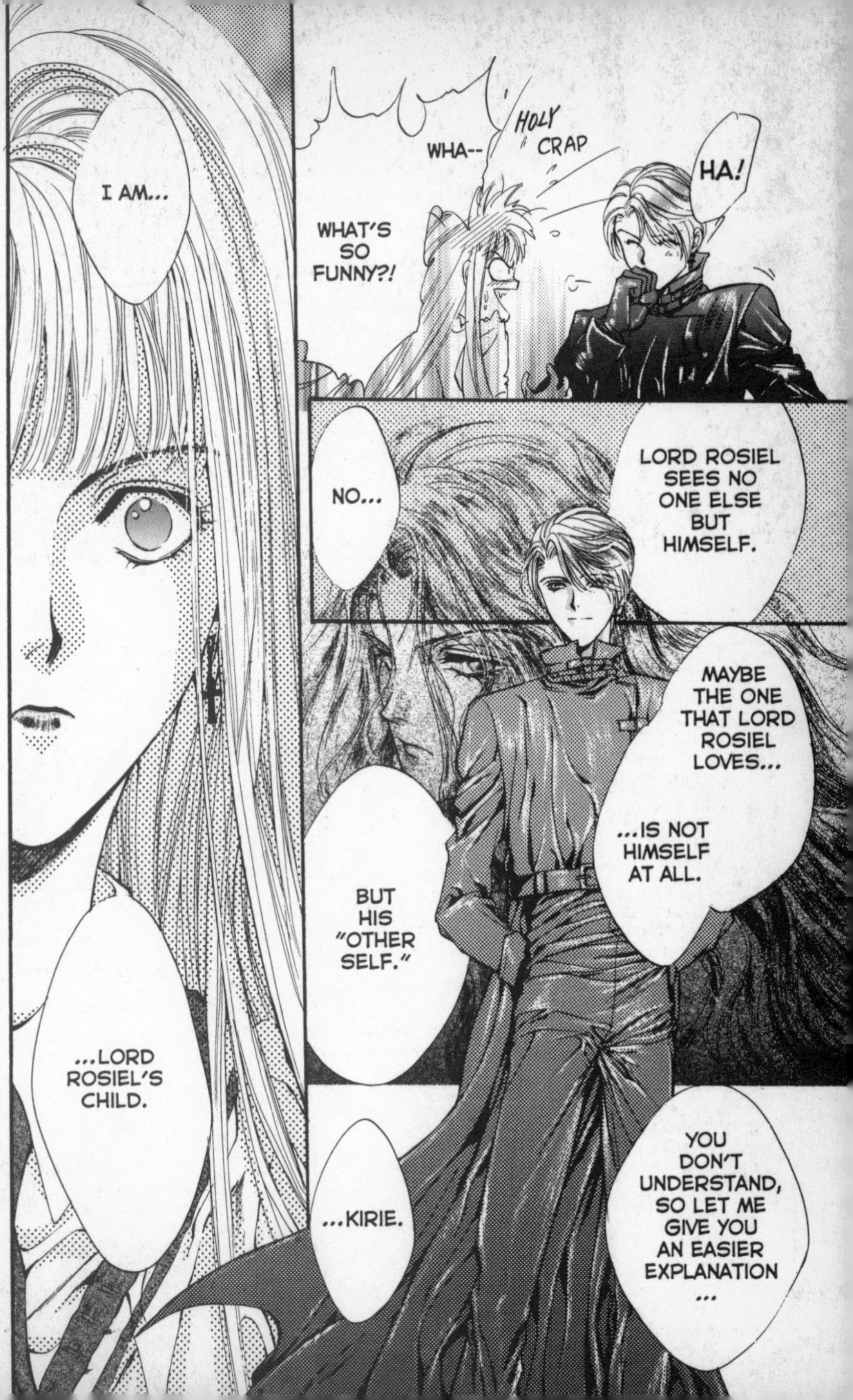
HA!
HOLY CRAP
WHA--
WHAT'S SO FUNNY?!
LORD ROSIEL SEES NO ONE ELSE BUT HIMSELF.
NO...
MAYBE THE ONE THAT LORD ROSIEL LOVES...
...IS NOT HIMSELF AT ALL.
BUT HIS "OTHER SELF."
YOU DON'T UNDERSTAND, SO LET ME GIVE YOU AN EASIER EXPLANATION ...
...KIRIE.
I AM...
...LORD ROSIEL'S CHILD.

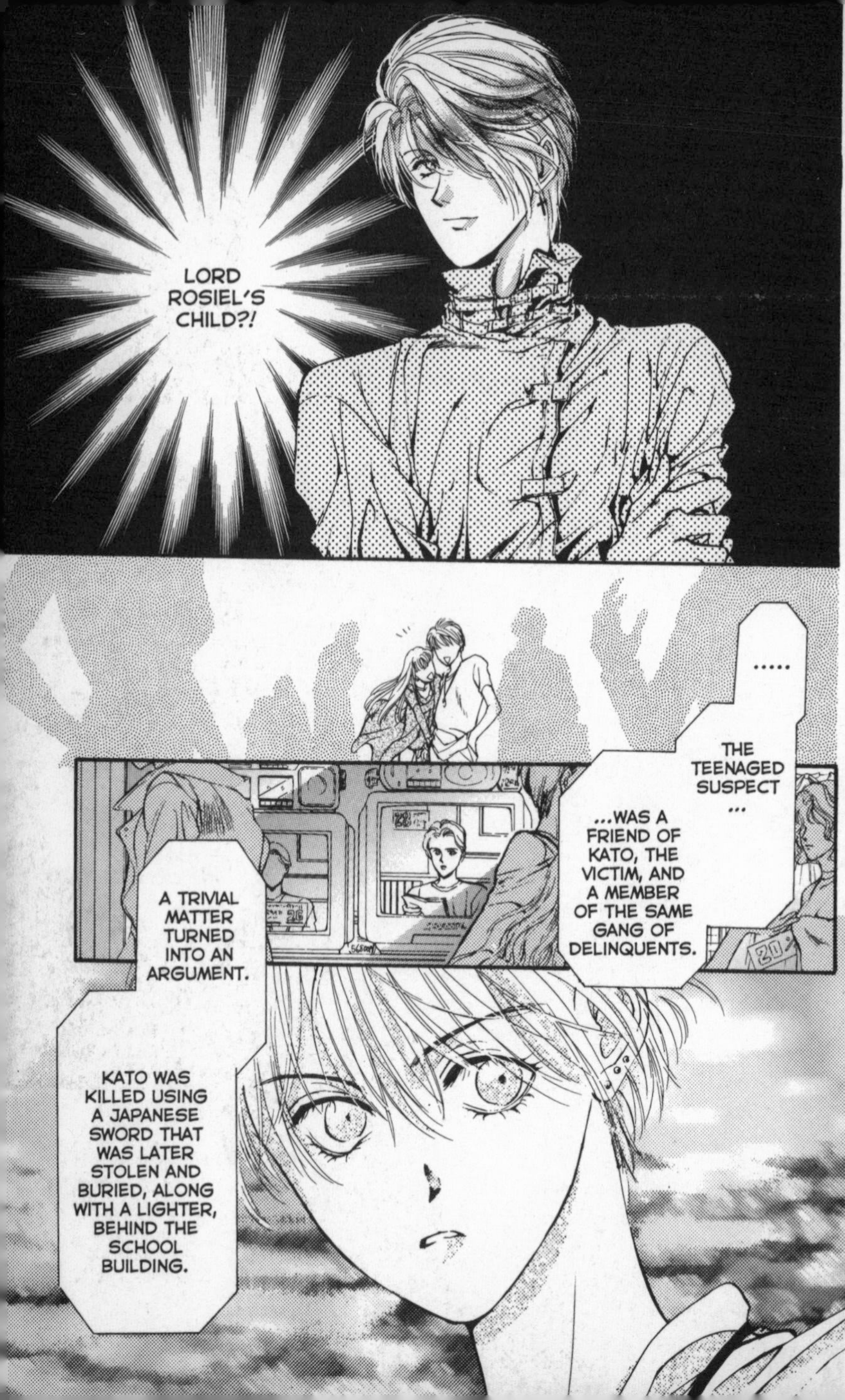
LORD ROSIEL'S CHILD?!
.....
THE TEENAGED SUSPECT ...
...WAS A FRIEND OF KATO, THE VICTIM, AND A MEMBER OF THE SAME GANG OF DELINQUENTS.
A TRIVIAL MATTER TURNED INTO AN ARGUMENT.
KATO WAS KILLED USING A JAPANESE SWORD THAT WAS LATER STOLEN AND BURIED, ALONG WITH A LIGHTER, BEHIND THE SCHOOL BUILDING.

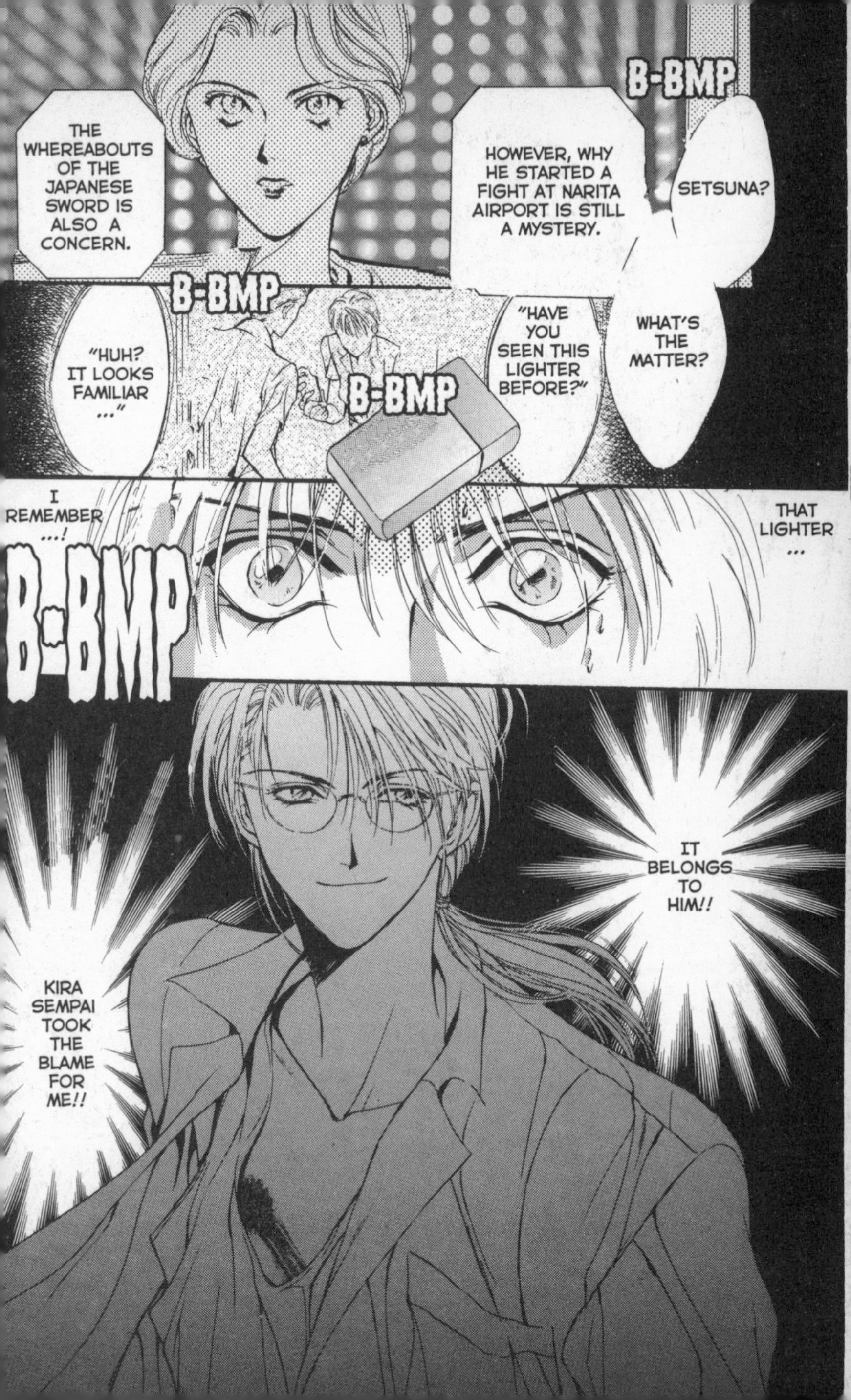

B-BMP
SETSUNA?
HOWEVER, WHY HE STARTED A FIGHT AT NARITA AIRPORT IS STILL A MYSTERY.
THE WHEREABOUTS OF THE JAPANESE SWORD IS ALSO A CONCERN.
B-BMP
WHAT'S THE MATTER?
"HAVE YOU SEEN THIS LIGHTER BEFORE?"
B-BMP
"HUH? IT LOOKS FAMILIAR ..."
THAT LIGHTER ...
I REMEMBER ...!
B-BMP
IT BELONGS TO HIM!!
KIRA SEMPAI TOOK THE BLAME FOR ME!!

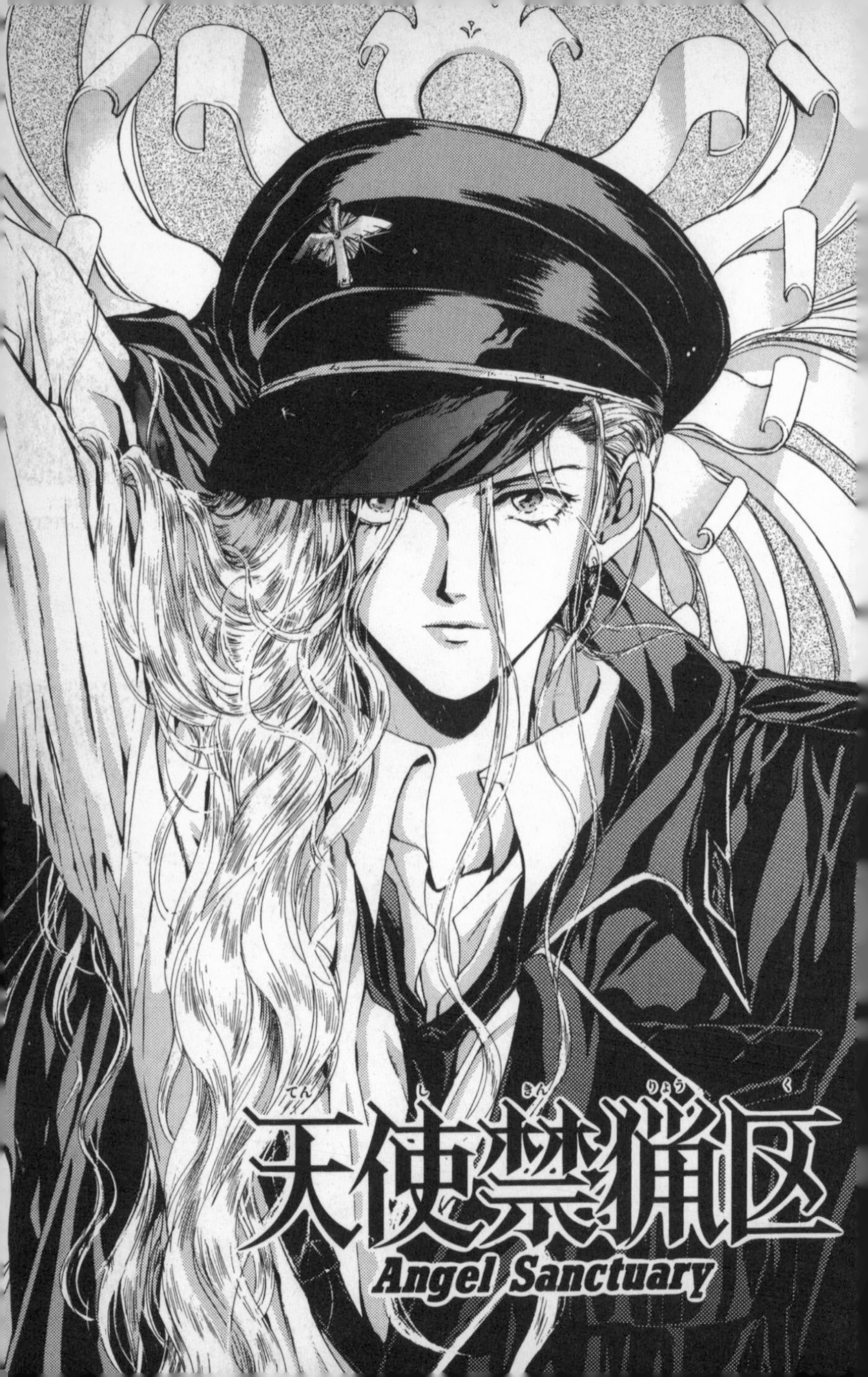
天使禁猟区
Angel Sanctuary

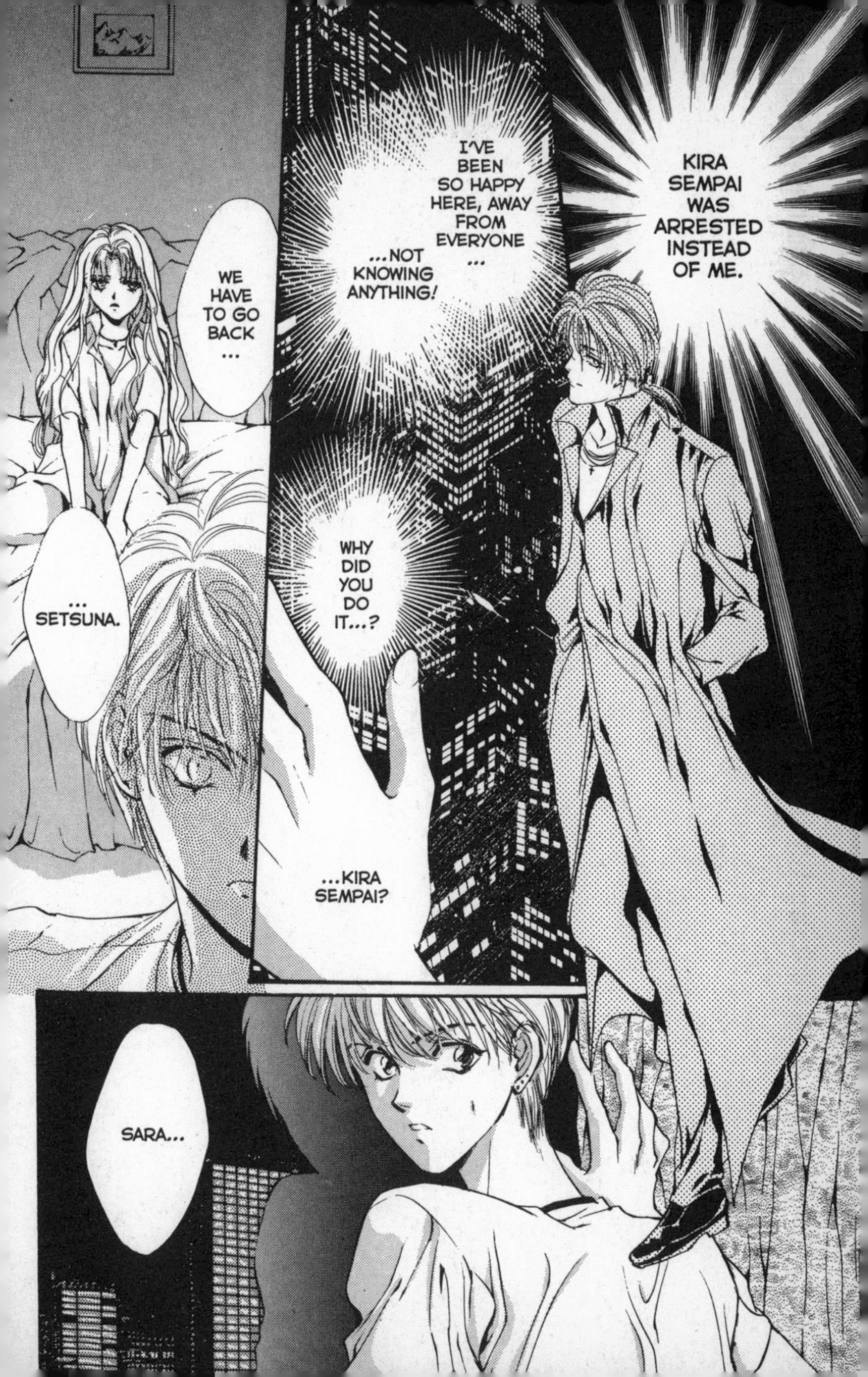
KIRA SEMPAI WAS ARRESTED INSTEAD OF ME.
I'VE BEEN SO HAPPY HERE, AWAY FROM EVERYONE ...
...NOT KNOWING ANYTHING!
WHY DID YOU DO IT...?
...KIRA SEMPAI?
WE HAVE TO GO BACK ...
... SETSUNA.
SARA...

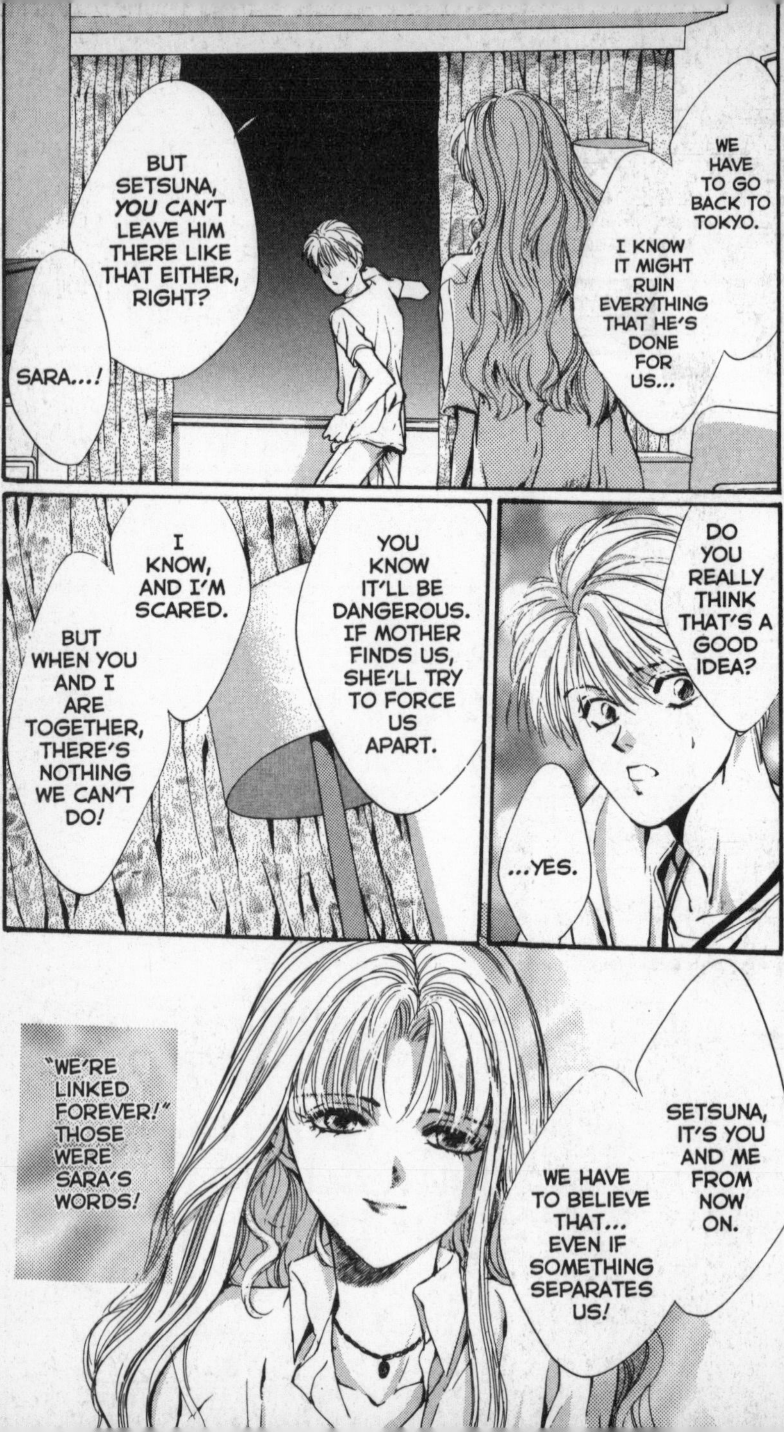
WE HAVE TO GO BACK TO TOKYO.
I KNOW IT MIGHT RUIN EVERYTHING THAT HE'S DONE FOR US...
BUT SETSUNA, *YOU* CAN'T LEAVE HIM THERE LIKE THAT EITHER, RIGHT?
SARA...!
DO YOU REALLY THINK THAT'S A GOOD IDEA?
...YES.
YOU KNOW IT'LL BE DANGEROUS. IF MOTHER FINDS US, SHE'LL TRY TO FORCE US APART.
I KNOW, AND I'M SCARED.
BUT WHEN YOU AND I ARE TOGETHER, THERE'S NOTHING WE CAN'T DO!
SETSUNA, IT'S YOU AND ME FROM NOW ON.
WE HAVE TO BELIEVE THAT... EVEN IF SOMETHING SEPARATES US!
"WE'RE LINKED FOREVER!" THOSE WERE SARA'S WORDS!

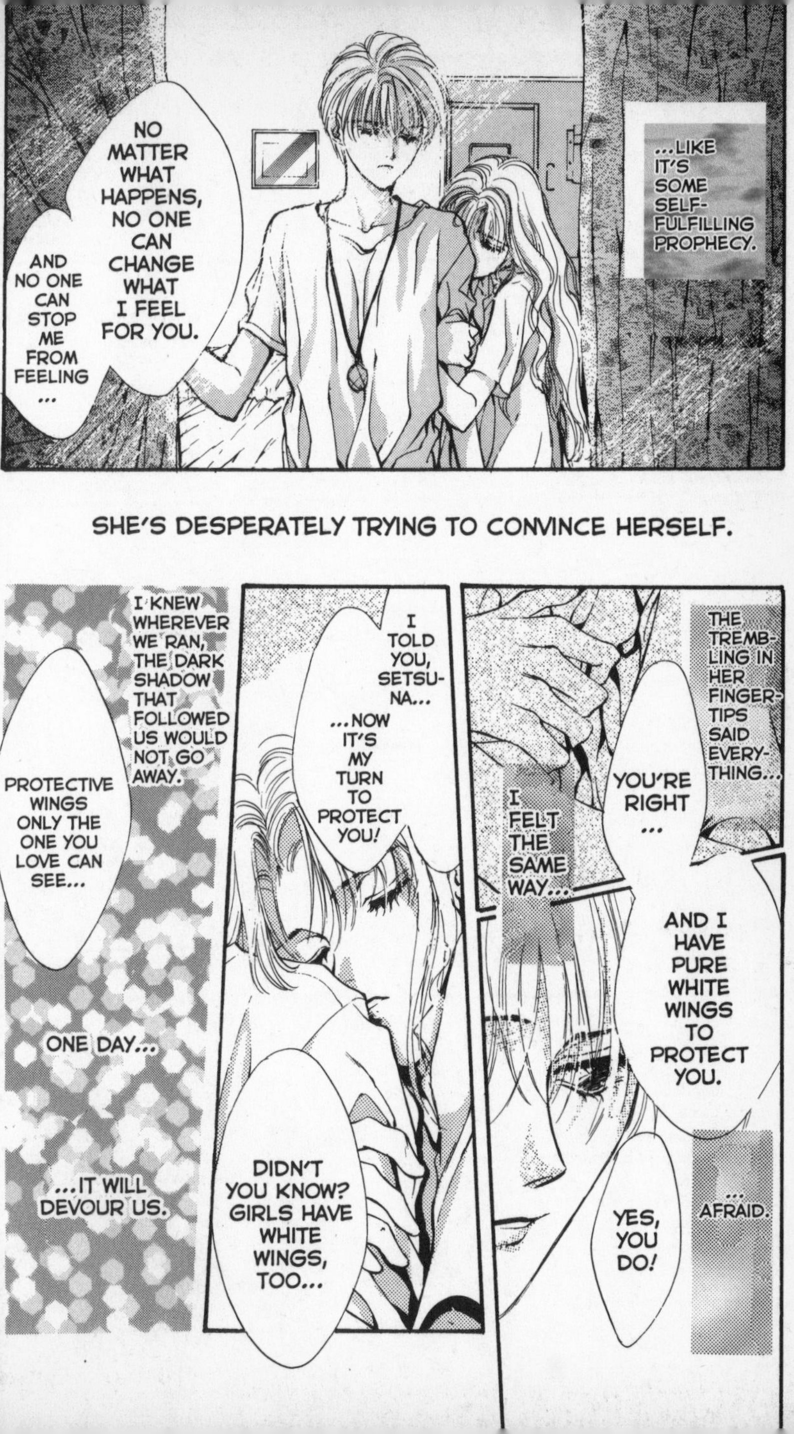
...LIKE IT'S SOME SELF-FULFILLING PROPHECY.
NO MATTER WHAT HAPPENS, NO ONE CAN CHANGE WHAT I FEEL FOR YOU.
AND NO ONE CAN STOP ME FROM FEELING ...
SHE'S DESPERATELY TRYING TO CONVINCE HERSELF.
THE TREMBLING IN HER FINGERTIPS SAID EVERYTHING...
YOU'RE RIGHT ...
I FELT THE SAME WAY...
AND I HAVE PURE WHITE WINGS TO PROTECT YOU.
... AFRAID.
YES, YOU DO!
I TOLD YOU, SETSUNA...
...NOW IT'S MY TURN TO PROTECT YOU!
DIDN'T YOU KNOW? GIRLS HAVE WHITE WINGS, TOO...
I KNEW WHEREVER WE RAN, THE DARK SHADOW THAT FOLLOWED US WOULD NOT GO AWAY.
PROTECTIVE WINGS ONLY THE ONE YOU LOVE CAN SEE...
ONE DAY...
...IT WILL DEVOUR US.

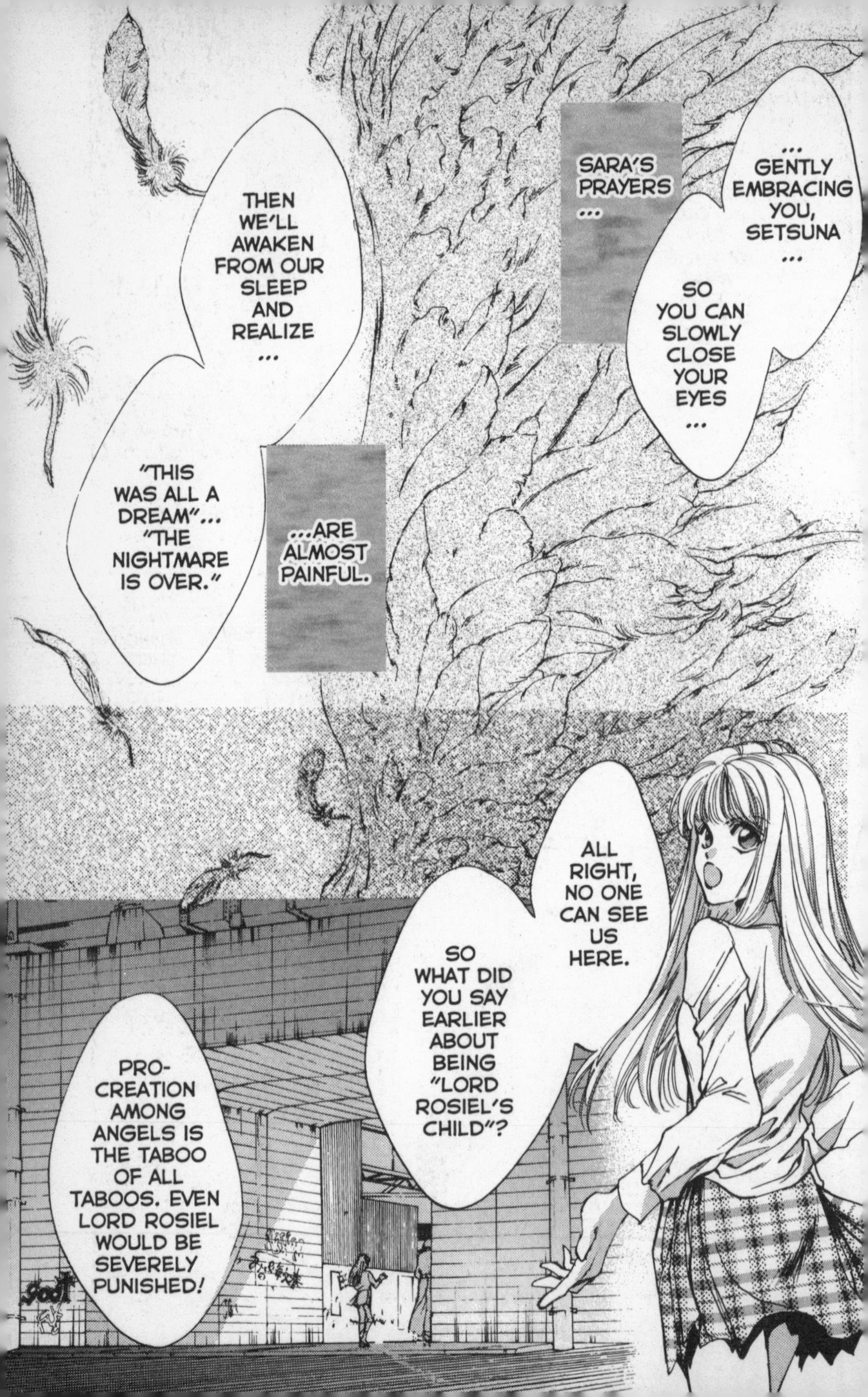
... GENTLY EMBRACING YOU, SETSUNA ...
SO YOU CAN SLOWLY CLOSE YOUR EYES ...
SARA'S PRAYERS ...
THEN WE'LL AWAKEN FROM OUR SLEEP AND REALIZE ...
"THIS WAS ALL A DREAM"... "THE NIGHTMARE IS OVER."
...ARE ALMOST PAINFUL.
ALL RIGHT, NO ONE CAN SEE US HERE.
SO WHAT DID YOU SAY EARLIER ABOUT BEING "LORD ROSIEL'S CHILD"?
PRO-CREATION AMONG ANGELS IS THE TABOO OF ALL TABOOS. EVEN LORD ROSIEL WOULD BE SEVERELY PUNISHED!

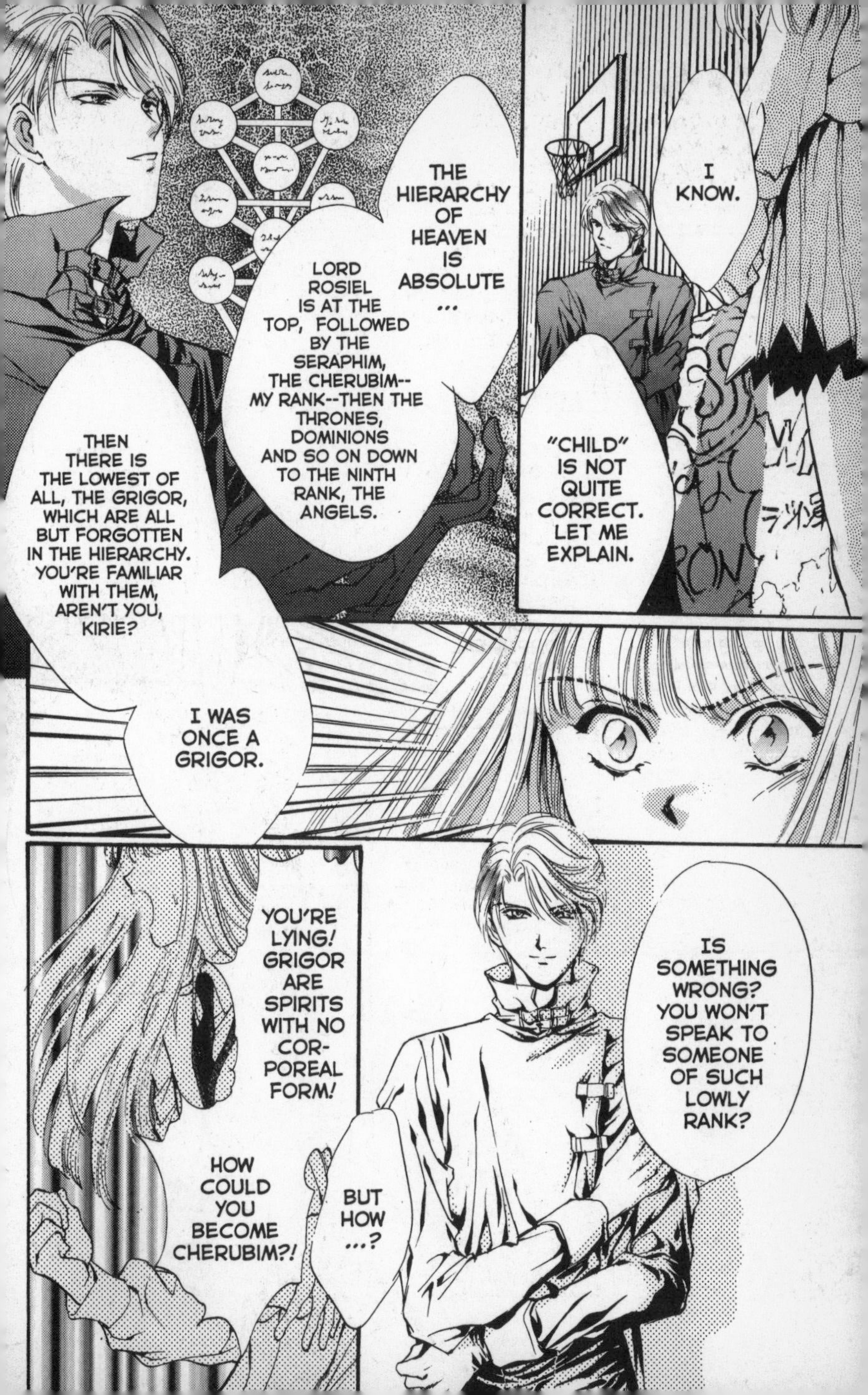
I KNOW.
"CHILD" IS NOT QUITE CORRECT. LET ME EXPLAIN.
THE HIERARCHY OF HEAVEN IS ABSOLUTE ...
LORD ROSIEL IS AT THE TOP, FOLLOWED BY THE SERAPHIM, THE CHERUBIM--MY RANK--THEN THE THRONES, DOMINIONS AND SO ON DOWN TO THE NINTH RANK, THE ANGELS.
THEN THERE IS THE LOWEST OF ALL, THE GRIGOR, WHICH ARE ALL BUT FORGOTTEN IN THE HIERARCHY. YOU'RE FAMILIAR WITH THEM, AREN'T YOU, KIRIE?
I WAS ONCE A GRIGOR.
IS SOMETHING WRONG? YOU WON'T SPEAK TO SOMEONE OF SUCH LOWLY RANK?
YOU'RE LYING! GRIGOR ARE SPIRITS WITH NO COR-POREAL FORM!
BUT HOW ...?
HOW COULD YOU BECOME CHERUBIM?!

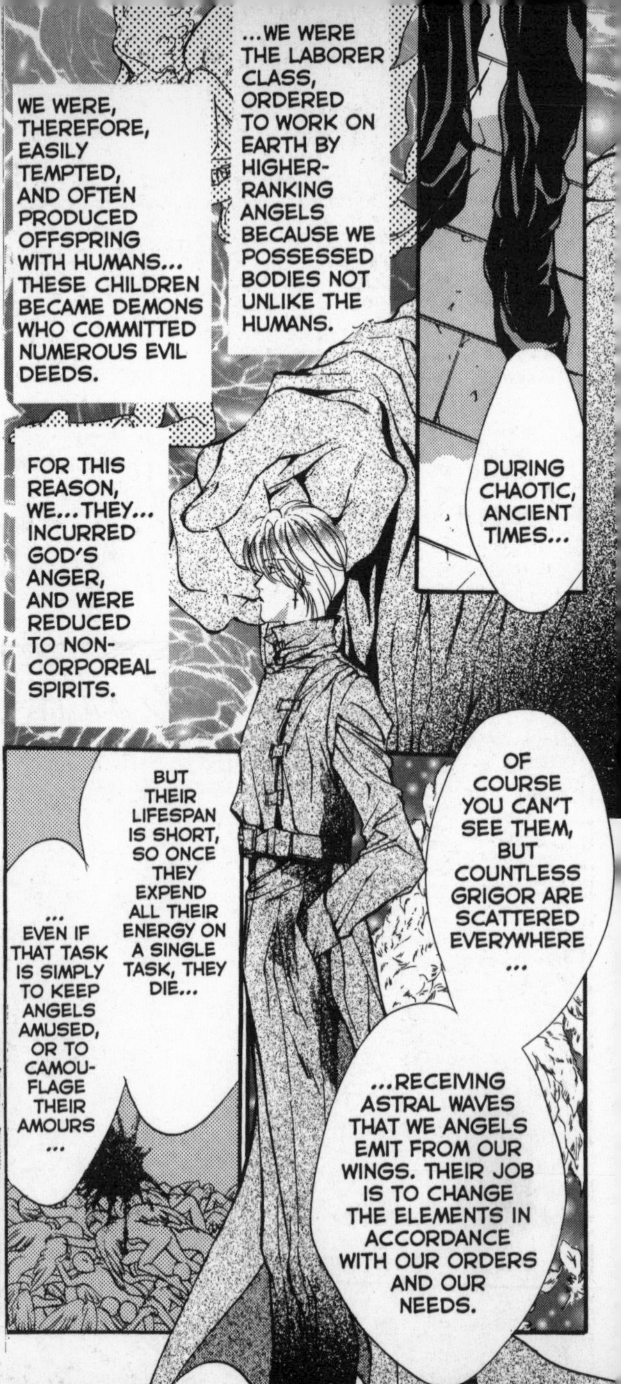
DURING CHAOTIC, ANCIENT TIMES...
...WE WERE THE LABORER CLASS, ORDERED TO WORK ON EARTH BY HIGHER-RANKING ANGELS BECAUSE WE POSSESSED BODIES NOT UNLIKE THE HUMANS.
WE WERE, THEREFORE, EASILY TEMPTED, AND OFTEN PRODUCED OFFSPRING WITH HUMANS... THESE CHILDREN BECAME DEMONS WHO COMMITTED NUMEROUS EVIL DEEDS.
FOR THIS REASON, WE...THEY... INCURRED GOD'S ANGER, AND WERE REDUCED TO NON-CORPOREAL SPIRITS.
OF COURSE YOU CAN'T SEE THEM, BUT COUNTLESS GRIGOR ARE SCATTERED EVERYWHERE ...
...RECEIVING ASTRAL WAVES THAT WE ANGELS EMIT FROM OUR WINGS. THEIR JOB IS TO CHANGE THE ELEMENTS IN ACCORDANCE WITH OUR ORDERS AND OUR NEEDS.
BUT THEIR LIFESPAN IS SHORT, SO ONCE THEY EXPEND ALL THEIR ENERGY ON A SINGLE TASK, THEY DIE...
... EVEN IF THAT TASK IS SIMPLY TO KEEP ANGELS AMUSED, OR TO CAMOU-FLAGE THEIR AMOURS ...

Kirie has been called "a child who doesn't listen to others." So very true.
Hmm D...
At this point, I wanted to show the "calm before the storm"; a sense of uneasiness. "Grigor" is more correctly "Grigori," but I chose a pronunciation that sounded better.
The story of how of young Katan first met Lord Rosiel was a very popular part of the story, but much of it was edited out.
waaah!
I'm not sure if I agree or disagree with the opinion of those who say they that while they like how Lord Rosiel was long ago, they prefer the present, mean-spirited Lord Rosiel better. When he was just born, Katan must surely have been smooth and shiny, like a boiled egg. I wonder what he would have turned out like if he had been a girl?

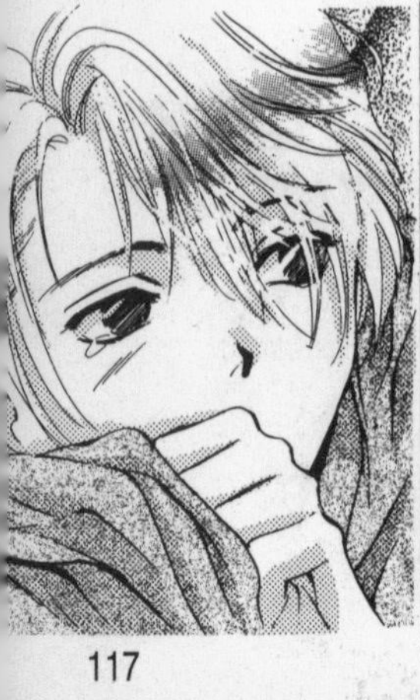

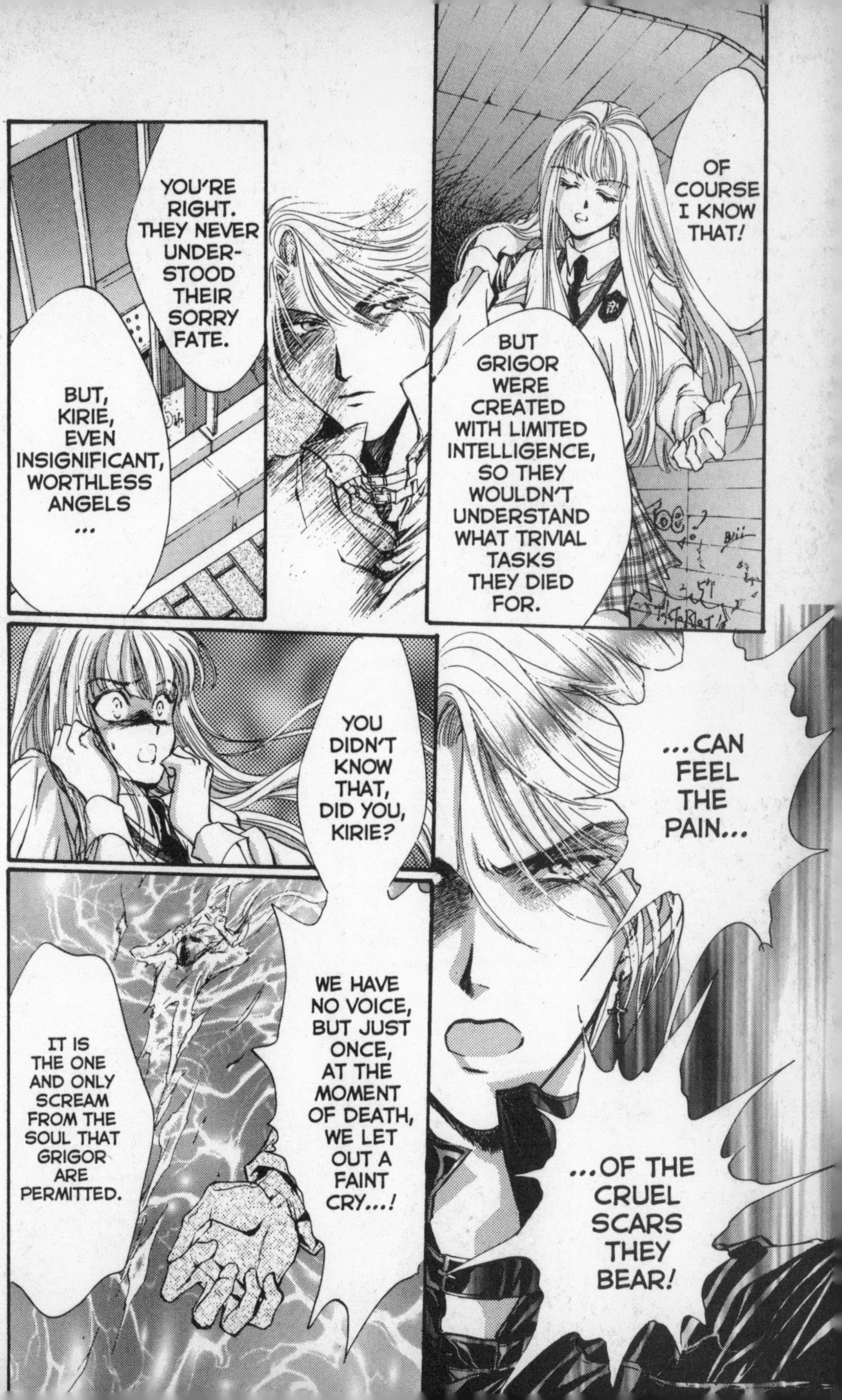
OF COURSE I KNOW THAT!
BUT GRIGOR WERE CREATED WITH LIMITED INTELLIGENCE, SO THEY WOULDN'T UNDERSTAND WHAT TRIVIAL TASKS THEY DIED FOR.
YOU'RE RIGHT. THEY NEVER UNDER-STOOD THEIR SORRY FATE.
BUT, KIRIE, EVEN INSIGNIFICANT, WORTHLESS ANGELS ...
...CAN FEEL THE PAIN...
...OF THE CRUEL SCARS THEY BEAR!
YOU DIDN'T KNOW THAT, DID YOU, KIRIE?
WE HAVE NO VOICE, BUT JUST ONCE, AT THE MOMENT OF DEATH, WE LET OUT A FAINT CRY...!
IT IS THE ONE AND ONLY SCREAM FROM THE SOUL THAT GRIGOR ARE PERMITTED.

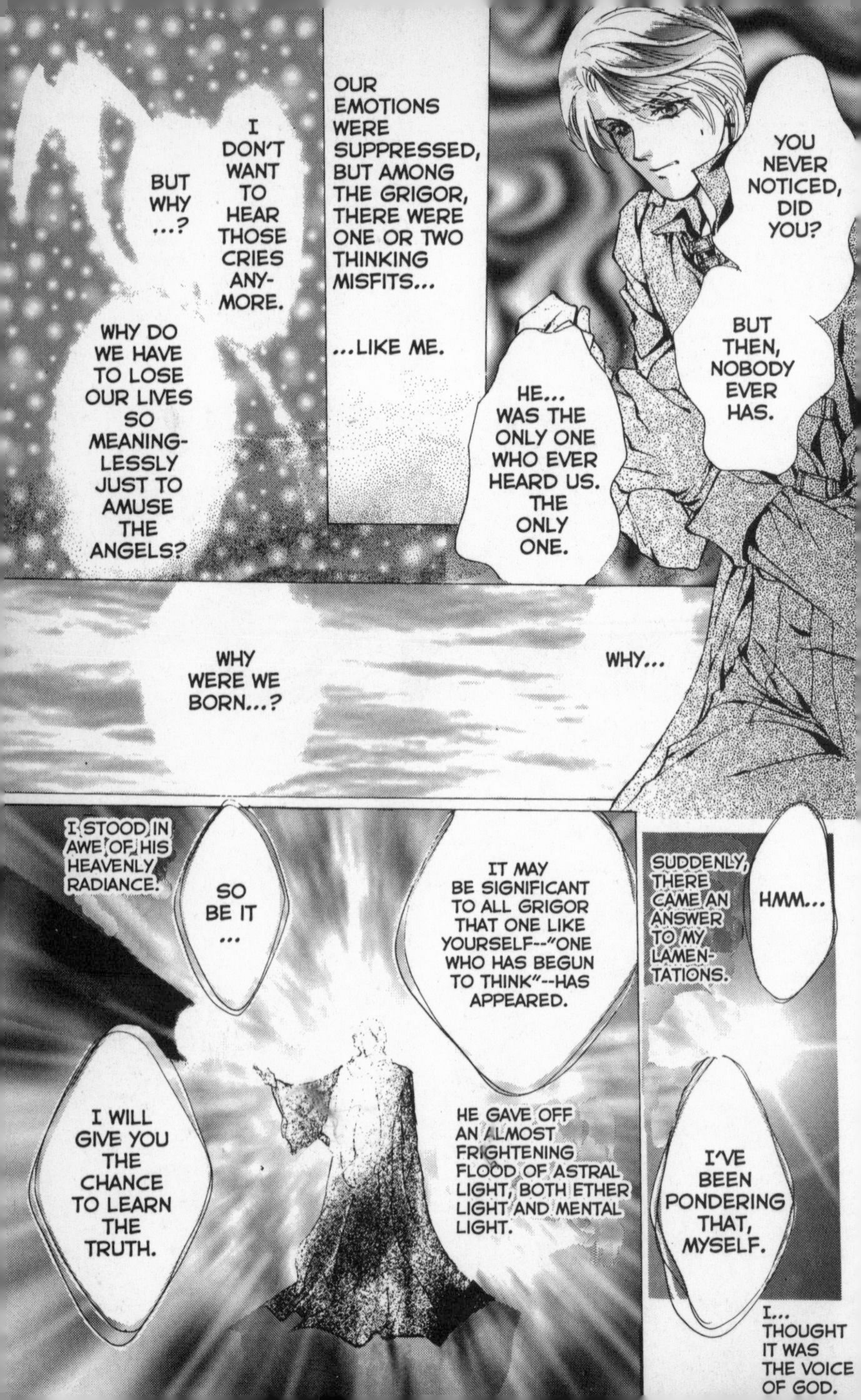
YOU NEVER NOTICED, DID YOU?
BUT THEN, NOBODY EVER HAS.
HE... WAS THE ONLY ONE WHO EVER HEARD US. THE ONLY ONE.
OUR EMOTIONS WERE SUPPRESSED, BUT AMONG THE GRIGOR, THERE WERE ONE OR TWO THINKING MISFITS...
...LIKE ME.
I DON'T WANT TO HEAR THOSE CRIES ANY-MORE.
BUT WHY ...?
WHY DO WE HAVE TO LOSE OUR LIVES SO MEANING-LESSLY JUST TO AMUSE THE ANGELS?
WHY...
WHY WERE WE BORN...?
SUDDENLY, THERE CAME AN ANSWER TO MY LAMEN-TATIONS.
HMM...
I'VE BEEN PONDERING THAT, MYSELF.
I... THOUGHT IT WAS THE VOICE OF GOD.
IT MAY BE SIGNIFICANT TO ALL GRIGOR THAT ONE LIKE YOURSELF--"ONE WHO HAS BEGUN TO THINK"--HAS APPEARED.
SO BE IT ...
I STOOD IN AWE OF HIS HEAVENLY RADIANCE.
HE GAVE OFF AN ALMOST FRIGHTENING FLOOD OF ASTRAL LIGHT, BOTH ETHER LIGHT AND MENTAL LIGHT.
I WILL GIVE YOU THE CHANCE TO LEARN THE TRUTH.

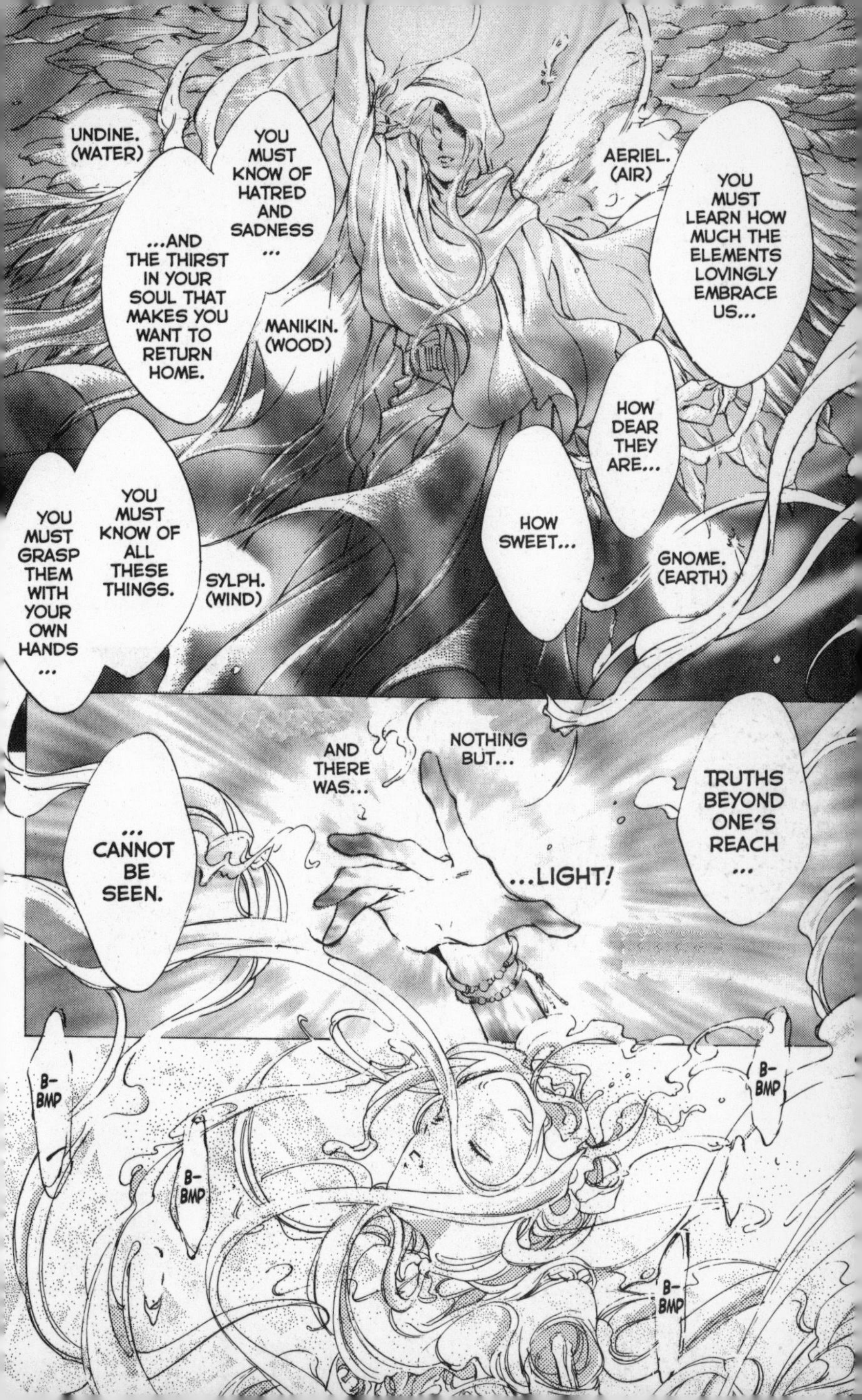
AERIEL. (AIR)
YOU MUST LEARN HOW MUCH THE ELEMENTS LOVINGLY EMBRACE US...
HOW DEAR THEY ARE...
YOU MUST KNOW OF HATRED AND SADNESS...
UNDINE. (WATER)
...AND THE THIRST IN YOUR SOUL THAT MAKES YOU WANT TO RETURN HOME.
MANIKIN. (WOOD)
HOW SWEET...
GNOME. (EARTH)
SYLPH. (WIND)
YOU MUST KNOW OF ALL THESE THINGS.
YOU MUST GRASP THEM WITH YOUR OWN HANDS...
TRUTHS BEYOND ONE'S REACH...
NOTHING BUT...
AND THERE WAS...
...LIGHT!
...CANNOT BE SEEN.
B-BMP
B-BMP
B-BMP
B-BMP

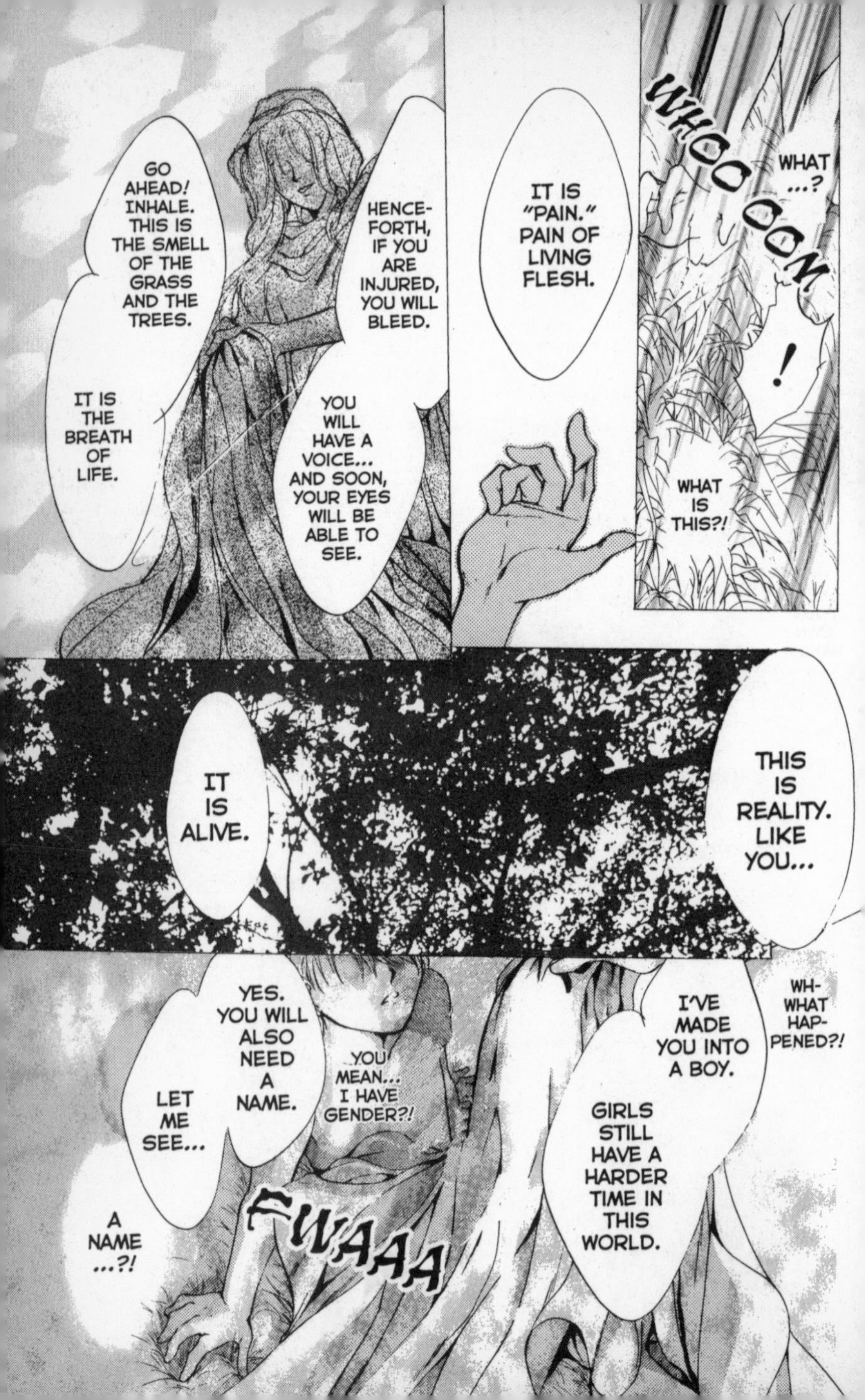
WHOOOOM
WHAT ...?
!
WHAT IS THIS?!
IT IS "PAIN." PAIN OF LIVING FLESH.
HENCE-FORTH, IF YOU ARE INJURED, YOU WILL BLEED.
GO AHEAD! INHALE. THIS IS THE SMELL OF THE GRASS AND THE TREES.
YOU WILL HAVE A VOICE... AND SOON, YOUR EYES WILL BE ABLE TO SEE.
IT IS THE BREATH OF LIFE.
THIS IS REALITY. LIKE YOU...
IT IS ALIVE.
WH-WHAT HAP-PENED?!
I'VE MADE YOU INTO A BOY.
GIRLS STILL HAVE A HARDER TIME IN THIS WORLD.
YOU MEAN... I HAVE GENDER?!
YES. YOU WILL ALSO NEED A NAME.
LET ME SEE...
FWAAA
A NAME ...?!

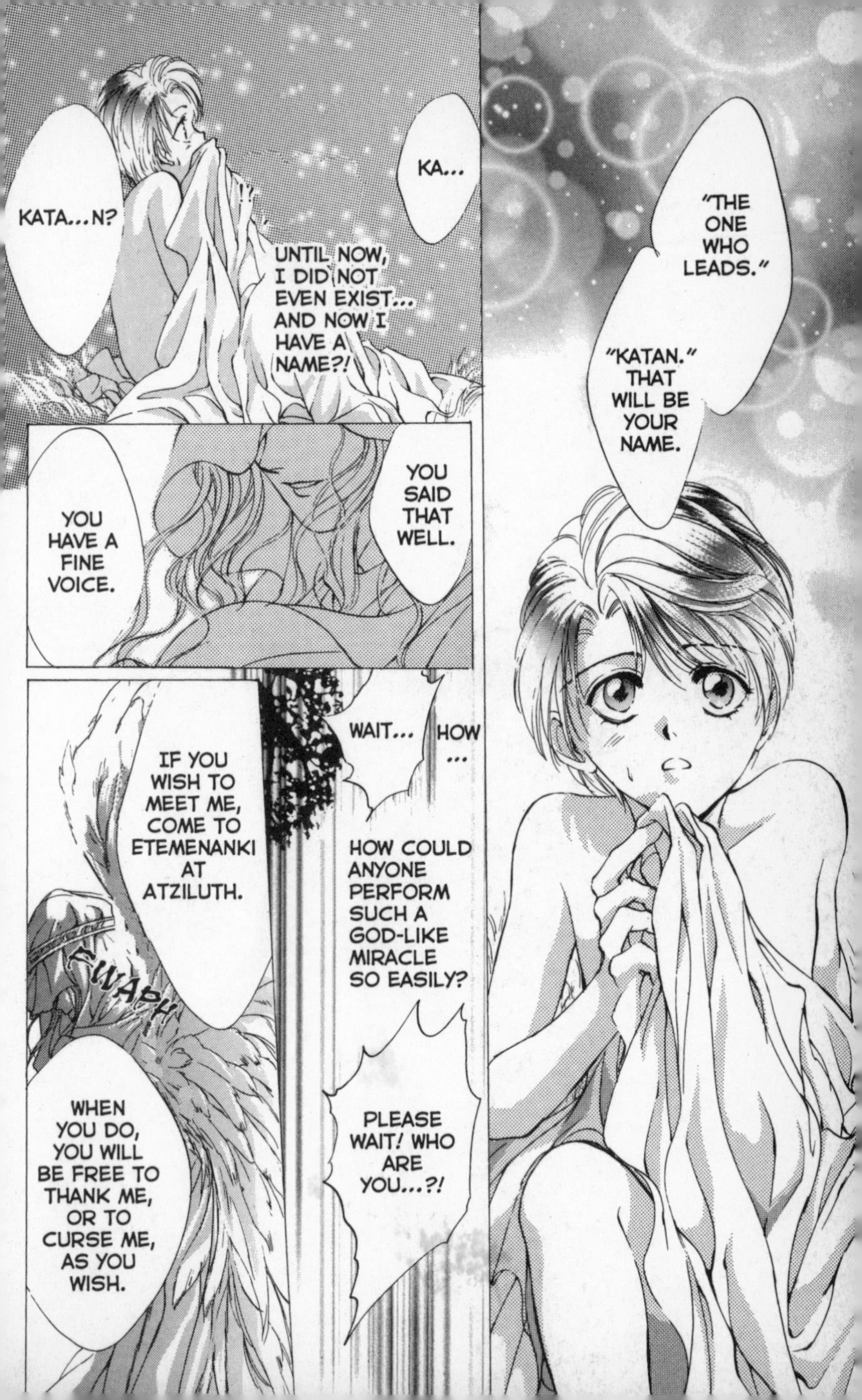
"THE ONE WHO LEADS."
"KATAN." THAT WILL BE YOUR NAME.
KA...
KATA...N?
UNTIL NOW, I DID NOT EVEN EXIST... AND NOW I HAVE A NAME?!
YOU SAID THAT WELL.
YOU HAVE A FINE VOICE.
WAIT... HOW ...
HOW COULD ANYONE PERFORM SUCH A GOD-LIKE MIRACLE SO EASILY?
IF YOU WISH TO MEET ME, COME TO ETEMENANKI AT ATZILUTH.
FWAPH
WHEN YOU DO, YOU WILL BE FREE TO THANK ME, OR TO CURSE ME, AS YOU WISH.
PLEASE WAIT! WHO ARE YOU...?!

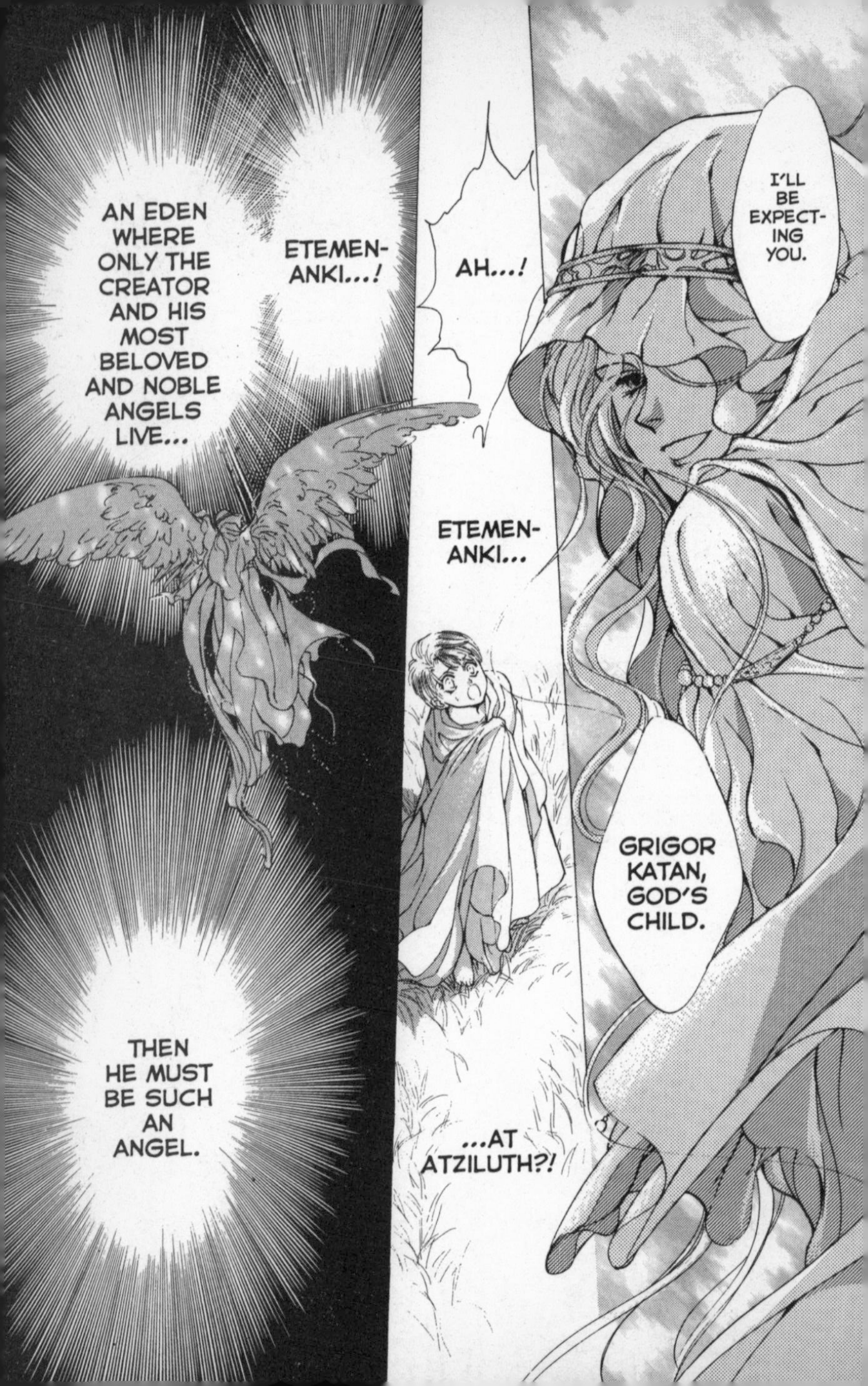
I'LL BE EXPECT-ING YOU.
GRIGOR KATAN, GOD'S CHILD.
AH...!
ETEMEN-ANKI...
...AT ATZILUTH?!
ETEMEN-ANKI...!
AN EDEN WHERE ONLY THE CREATOR AND HIS MOST BELOVED AND NOBLE ANGELS LIVE...
THEN HE MUST BE SUCH AN ANGEL.

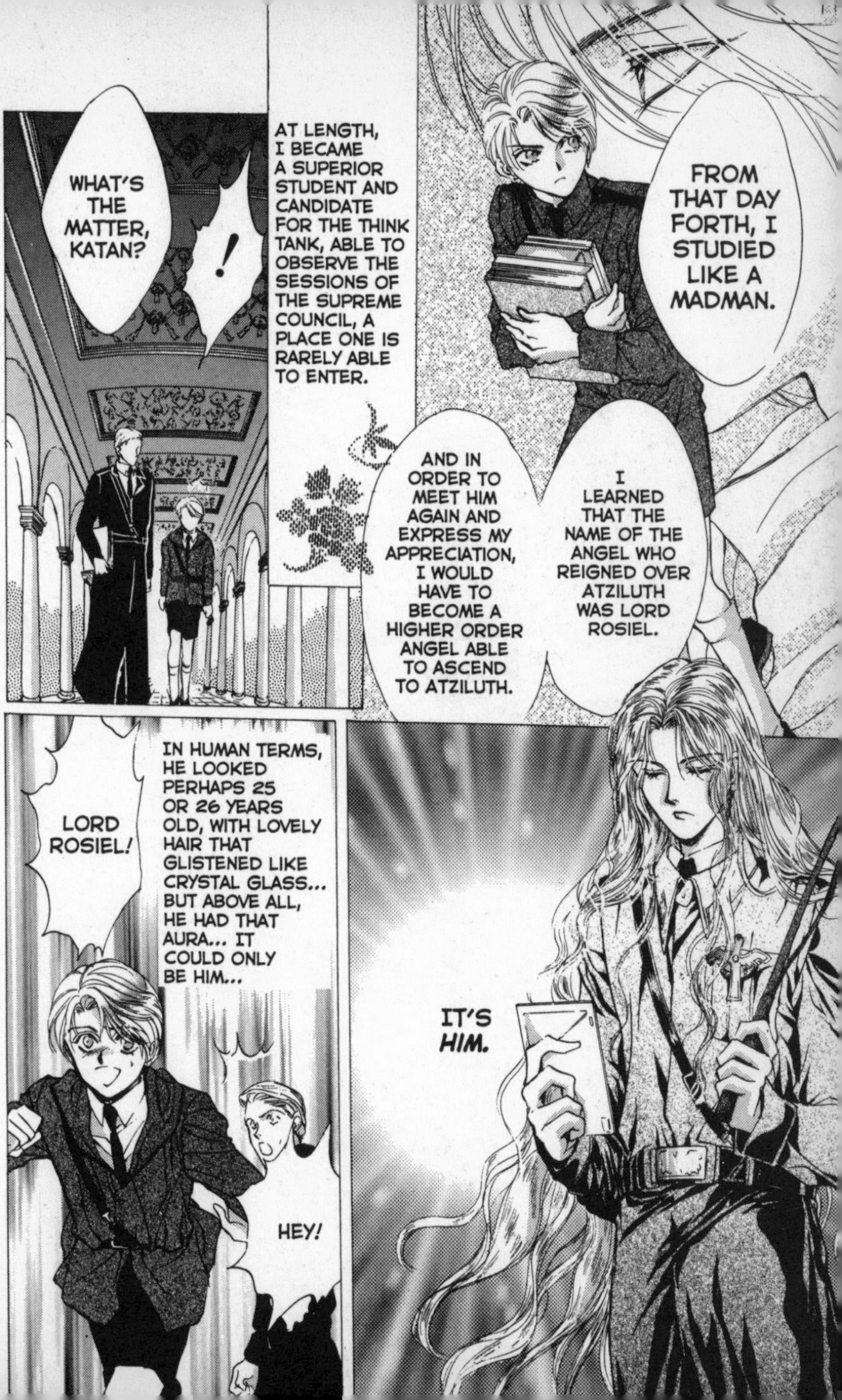
FROM THAT DAY FORTH, I STUDIED LIKE A MADMAN.
I LEARNED THAT THE NAME OF THE ANGEL WHO REIGNED OVER ATZILUTH WAS LORD ROSIEL.
AND IN ORDER TO MEET HIM AGAIN AND EXPRESS MY APPRECIATION, I WOULD HAVE TO BECOME A HIGHER ORDER ANGEL ABLE TO ASCEND TO ATZILUTH.
AT LENGTH, I BECAME A SUPERIOR STUDENT AND CANDIDATE FOR THE THINK TANK, ABLE TO OBSERVE THE SESSIONS OF THE SUPREME COUNCIL, A PLACE ONE IS RARELY ABLE TO ENTER.
WHAT'S THE MATTER, KATAN?
!
IT'S *HIM.*
IN HUMAN TERMS, HE LOOKED PERHAPS 25 OR 26 YEARS OLD, WITH LOVELY HAIR THAT GLISTENED LIKE CRYSTAL GLASS... BUT ABOVE ALL, HE HAD THAT AURA... IT COULD ONLY BE HIM...
LORD ROSIEL!
HEY!

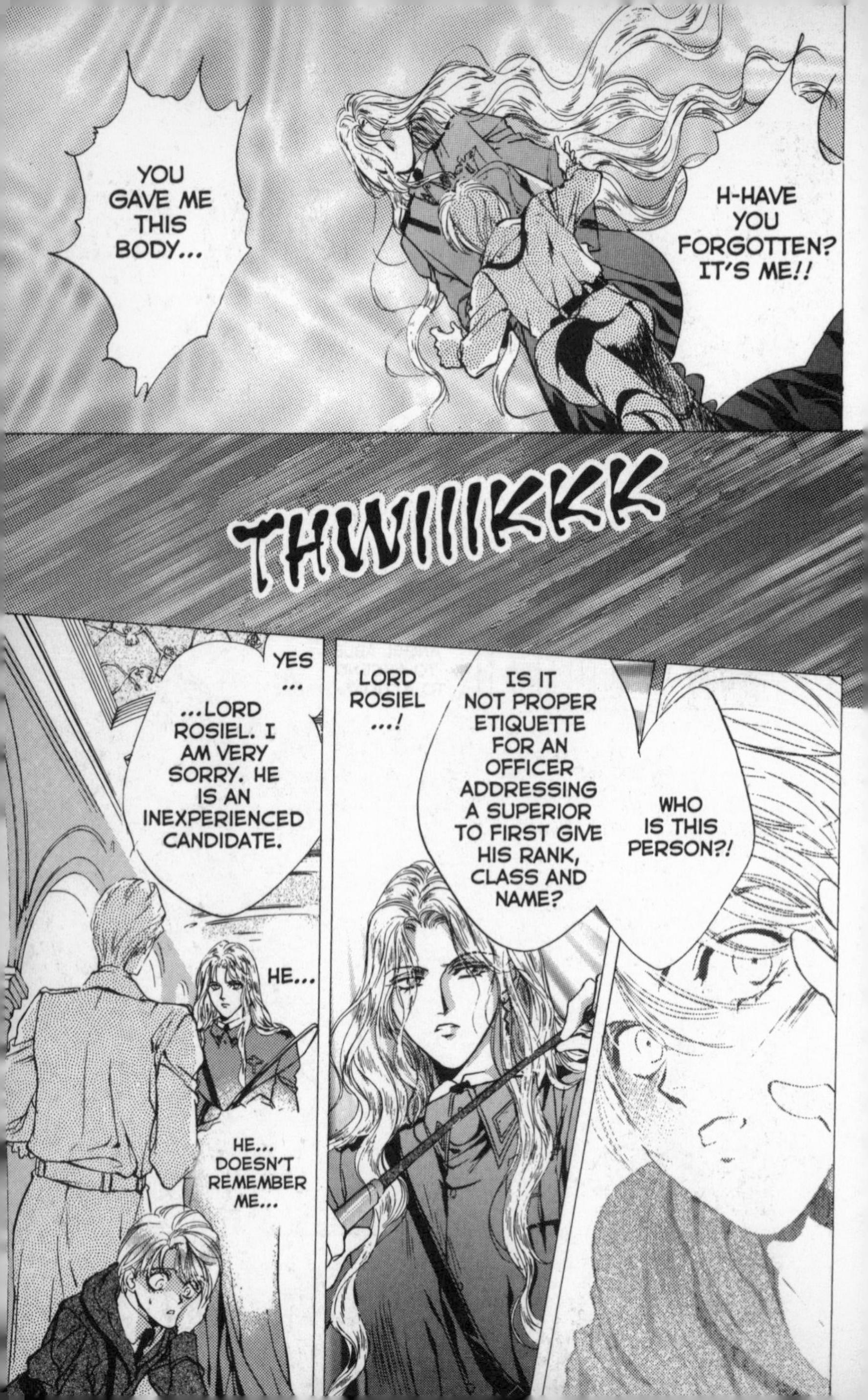
H-HAVE YOU FORGOTTEN? IT'S ME!!
YOU GAVE ME THIS BODY...
THWIIIKKK
WHO IS THIS PERSON?!
IS IT NOT PROPER ETIQUETTE FOR AN OFFICER ADDRESSING A SUPERIOR TO FIRST GIVE HIS RANK, CLASS AND NAME?
LORD ROSIEL ...!
YES ...
...LORD ROSIEL. I AM VERY SORRY. HE IS AN INEXPERIENCED CANDIDATE.
HE...
HE... DOESN'T REMEMBER ME...

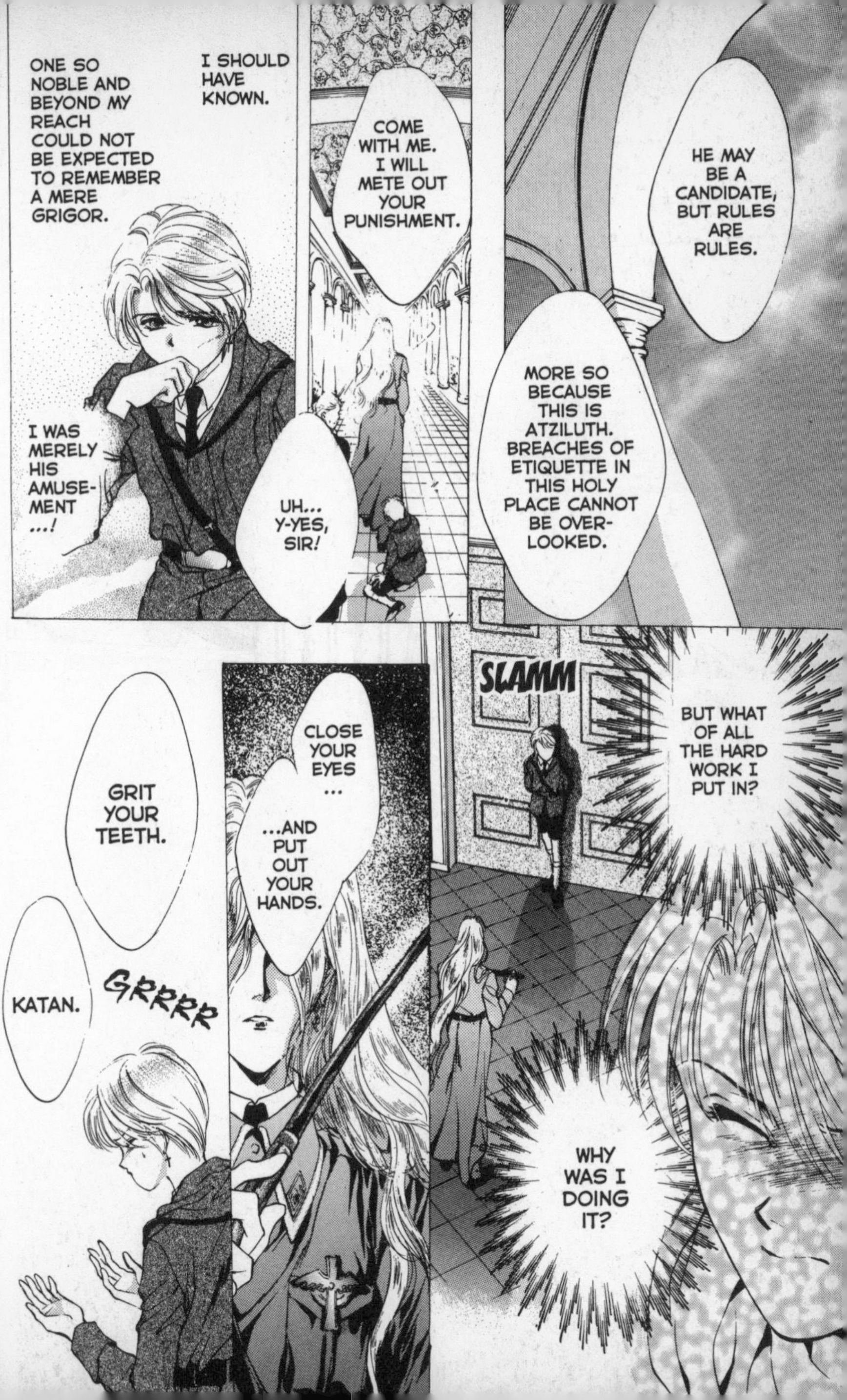
HE MAY BE A CANDIDATE, BUT RULES ARE RULES.
MORE SO BECAUSE THIS IS ATZILUTH. BREACHES OF ETIQUETTE IN THIS HOLY PLACE CANNOT BE OVER-LOOKED.
COME WITH ME. I WILL METE OUT YOUR PUNISHMENT.
UH... Y-YES, SIR!
I SHOULD HAVE KNOWN.
ONE SO NOBLE AND BEYOND MY REACH COULD NOT BE EXPECTED TO REMEMBER A MERE GRIGOR.
I WAS MERELY HIS AMUSE-MENT ...!
SLAMM
BUT WHAT OF ALL THE HARD WORK I PUT IN?
WHY WAS I DOING IT?
CLOSE YOUR EYES ...
...AND PUT OUT YOUR HANDS.
GRIT YOUR TEETH.
GRRRRR
KATAN.

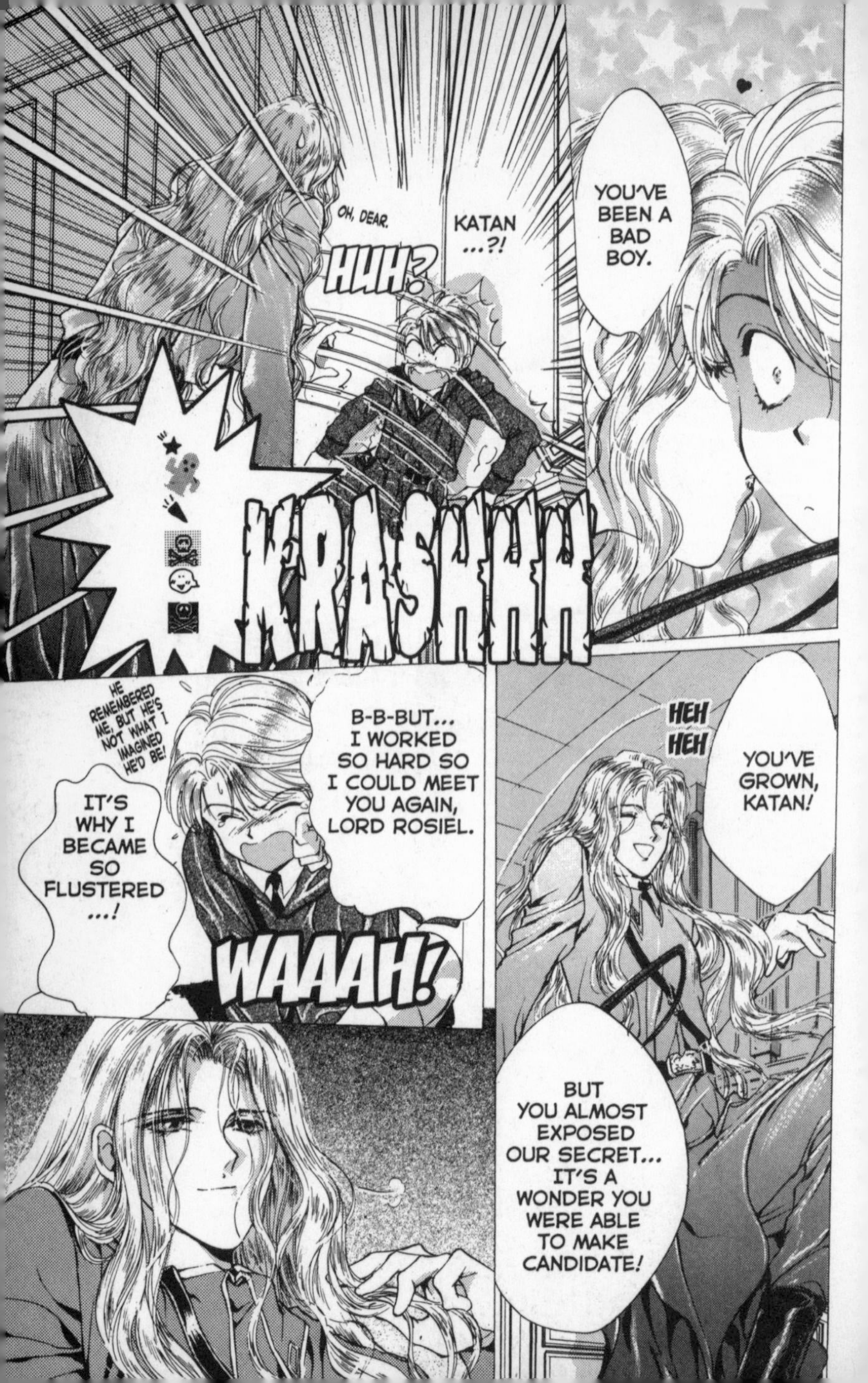
YOU'VE BEEN A BAD BOY.
KATAN ...?!
OH, DEAR.
HUH?
KRASHHH
HEH HEH
YOU'VE GROWN, KATAN!
B-B-BUT... I WORKED SO HARD SO I COULD MEET YOU AGAIN, LORD ROSIEL.
HE REMEMBERED ME, BUT HE'S NOT WHAT I IMAGINED HE'D BE!
IT'S WHY I BECAME SO FLUSTERED ...!
WAAAH!
BUT YOU ALMOST EXPOSED OUR SECRET... IT'S A WONDER YOU WERE ABLE TO MAKE CANDIDATE!

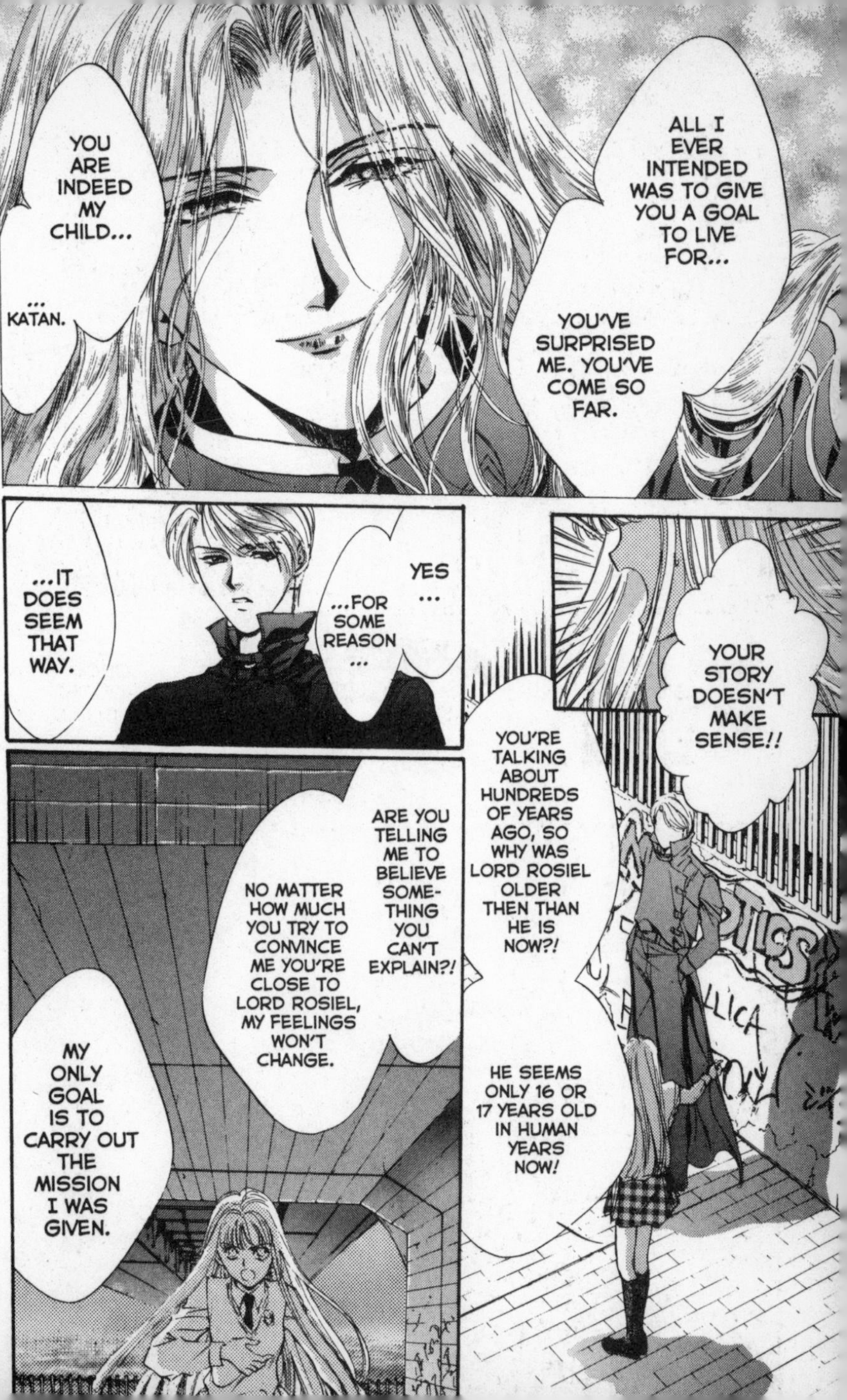
ALL I EVER INTENDED WAS TO GIVE YOU A GOAL TO LIVE FOR...
YOU'VE SURPRISED ME. YOU'VE COME SO FAR.
YOU ARE INDEED MY CHILD...
... KATAN.
YOUR STORY DOESN'T MAKE SENSE!!
YOU'RE TALKING ABOUT HUNDREDS OF YEARS AGO, SO WHY WAS LORD ROSIEL OLDER THEN THAN HE IS NOW?!
HE SEEMS ONLY 16 OR 17 YEARS OLD IN HUMAN YEARS NOW!
YES ...
...FOR SOME REASON ...
...IT DOES SEEM THAT WAY.
ARE YOU TELLING ME TO BELIEVE SOME-THING YOU CAN'T EXPLAIN?!
NO MATTER HOW MUCH YOU TRY TO CONVINCE ME YOU'RE CLOSE TO LORD ROSIEL, MY FEELINGS WON'T CHANGE.
MY ONLY GOAL IS TO CARRY OUT THE MISSION I WAS GIVEN.

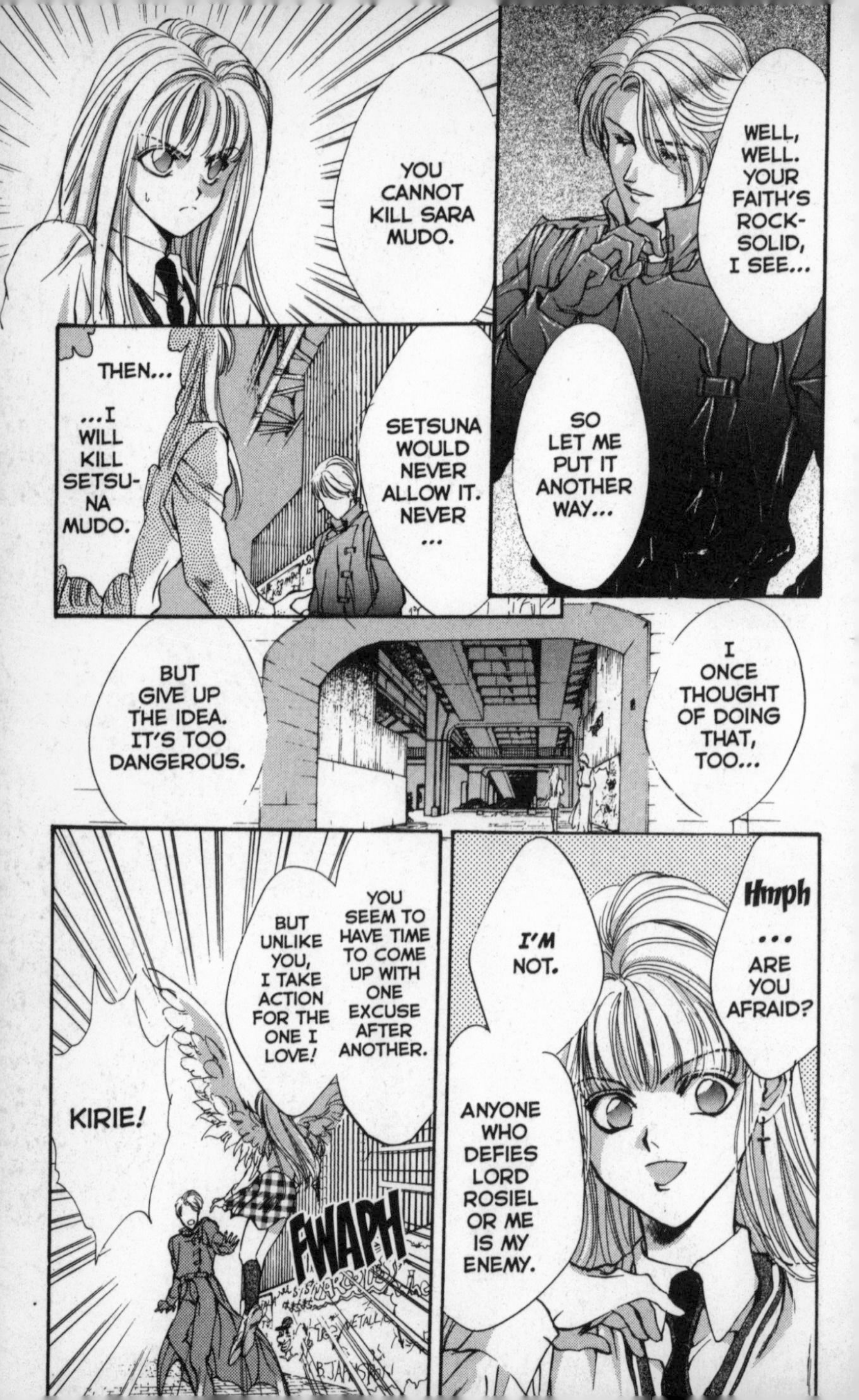
WELL, WELL. YOUR FAITH'S ROCK-SOLID, I SEE...
SO LET ME PUT IT ANOTHER WAY...
YOU CANNOT KILL SARA MUDO.
THEN...
...I WILL KILL SETSU-NA MUDO.
SETSUNA WOULD NEVER ALLOW IT. NEVER ...
I ONCE THOUGHT OF DOING THAT, TOO...
BUT GIVE UP THE IDEA. IT'S TOO DANGEROUS.
Hmph
... ARE YOU AFRAID?
I'M NOT.
ANYONE WHO DEFIES LORD ROSIEL OR ME IS MY ENEMY.
YOU SEEM TO HAVE TIME TO COME UP WITH ONE EXCUSE AFTER ANOTHER.
BUT UNLIKE YOU, I TAKE ACTION FOR THE ONE I LOVE!
KIRIE!
FWAPH

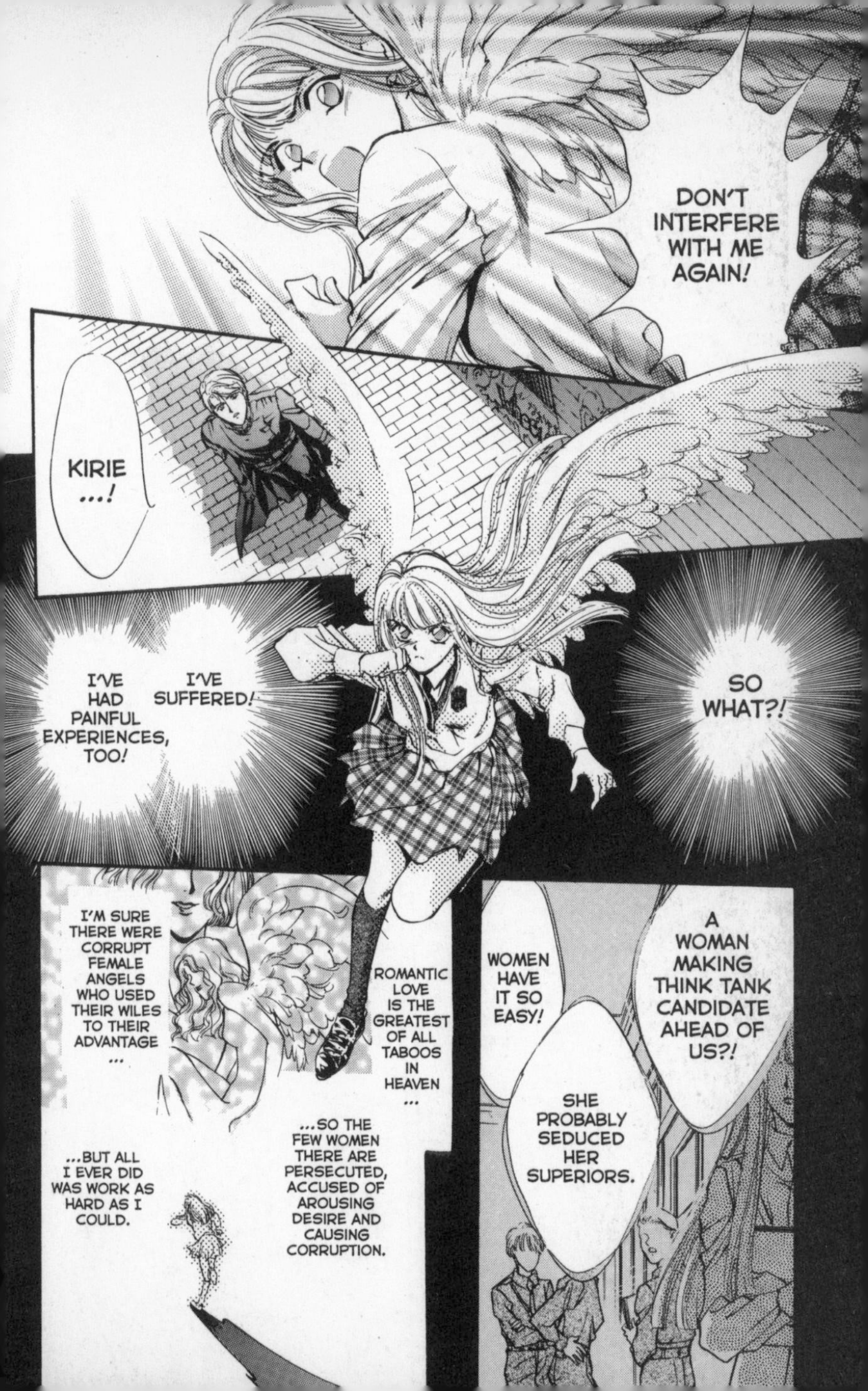
DON'T INTERFERE WITH ME AGAIN!
KIRIE ...!
SO WHAT?!
I'VE SUFFERED!
I'VE HAD PAINFUL EXPERIENCES, TOO!
A WOMAN MAKING THINK TANK CANDIDATE AHEAD OF US?!
WOMEN HAVE IT SO EASY!
SHE PROBABLY SEDUCED HER SUPERIORS.
ROMANTIC LOVE IS THE GREATEST OF ALL TABOOS IN HEAVEN ...
I'M SURE THERE WERE CORRUPT FEMALE ANGELS WHO USED THEIR WILES TO THEIR ADVANTAGE ...
...SO THE FEW WOMEN THERE ARE PERSECUTED, ACCUSED OF AROUSING DESIRE AND CAUSING CORRUPTION.
...BUT ALL I EVER DID WAS WORK AS HARD AS I COULD.

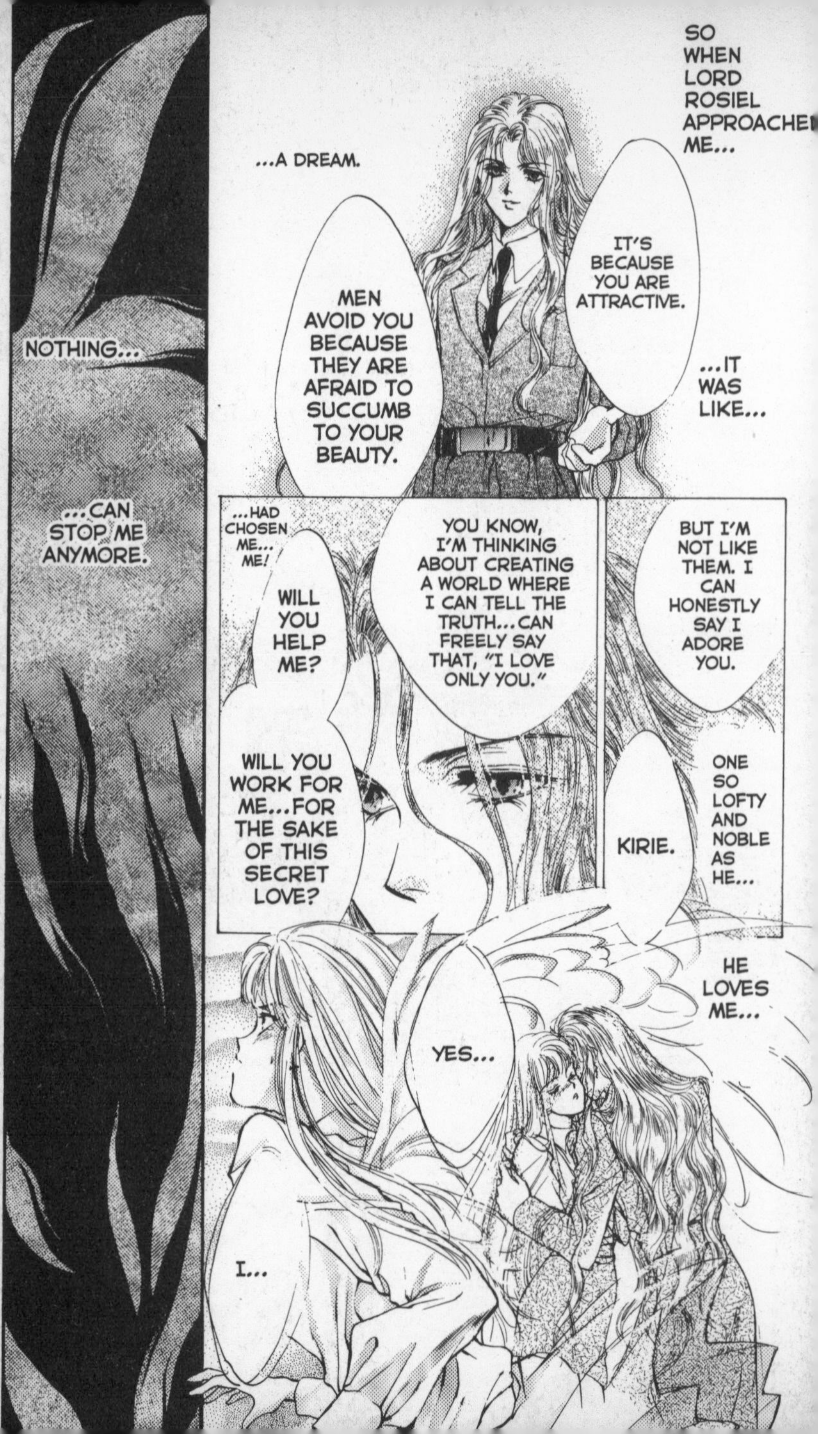
SO WHEN LORD ROSIEL APPROACHE ME...
IT'S BECAUSE YOU ARE ATTRACTIVE.
MEN AVOID YOU BECAUSE THEY ARE AFRAID TO SUCCUMB TO YOUR BEAUTY.
...IT WAS LIKE...
...A DREAM.
BUT I'M NOT LIKE THEM. I CAN HONESTLY SAY I ADORE YOU.
ONE SO LOFTY AND NOBLE AS HE...
KIRIE.
YOU KNOW, I'M THINKING ABOUT CREATING A WORLD WHERE I CAN TELL THE TRUTH...CAN FREELY SAY THAT, "I LOVE ONLY YOU."
...HAD CHOSEN ME... ME!
WILL YOU HELP ME?
WILL YOU WORK FOR ME...FOR THE SAKE OF THIS SECRET LOVE?
HE LOVES ME...
YES...
I...
NOTHING...
...CAN STOP ME ANYMORE.

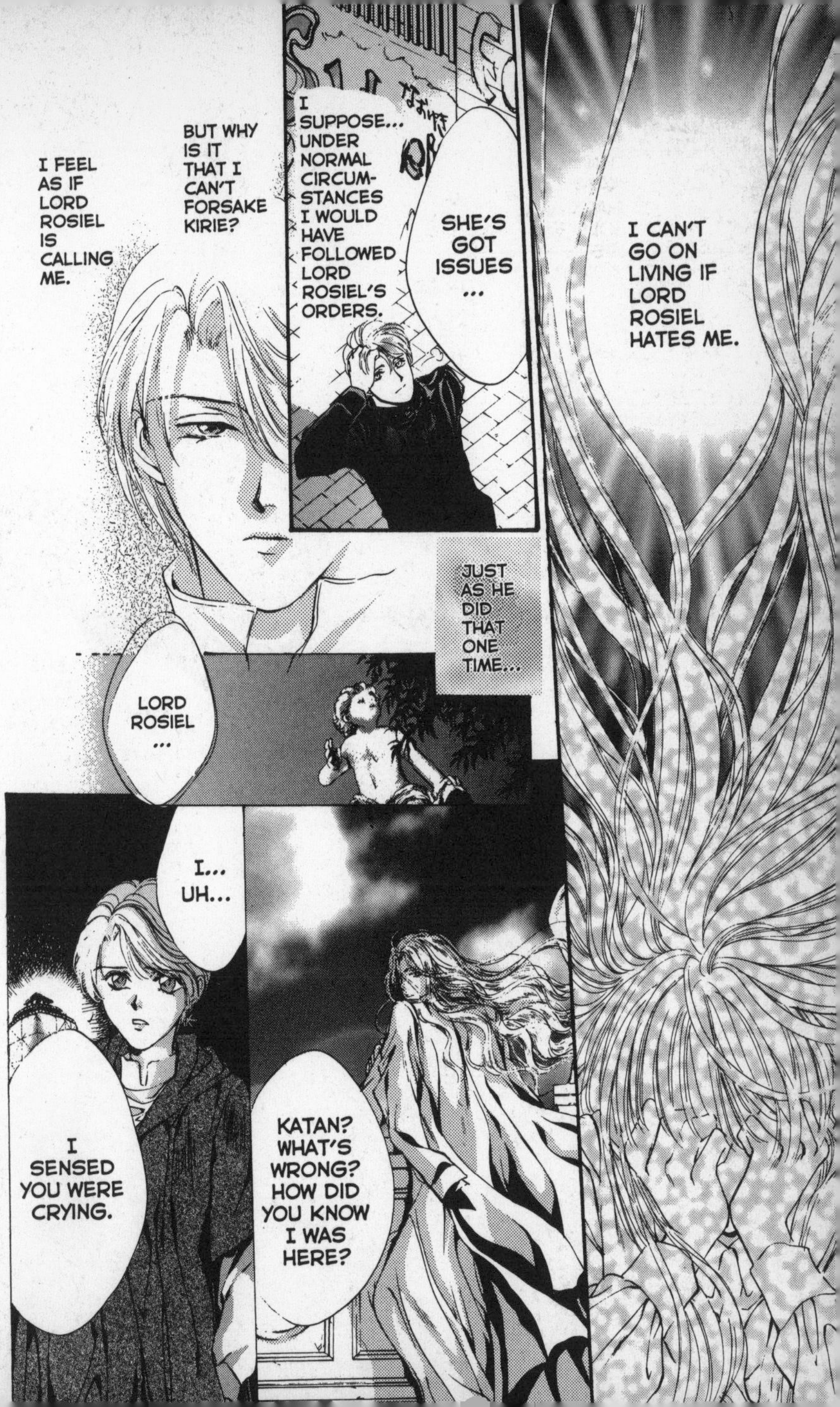

I CAN'T GO ON LIVING IF LORD ROSIEL HATES ME.
SHE'S GOT ISSUES ...
I SUPPOSE... UNDER NORMAL CIRCUMSTANCES I WOULD HAVE FOLLOWED LORD ROSIEL'S ORDERS.
BUT WHY IS IT THAT I CAN'T FORSAKE KIRIE?
I FEEL AS IF LORD ROSIEL IS CALLING ME.
JUST AS HE DID THAT ONE TIME...
LORD ROSIEL ...
KATAN? WHAT'S WRONG? HOW DID YOU KNOW I WAS HERE?
I... UH...
I SENSED YOU WERE CRYING.

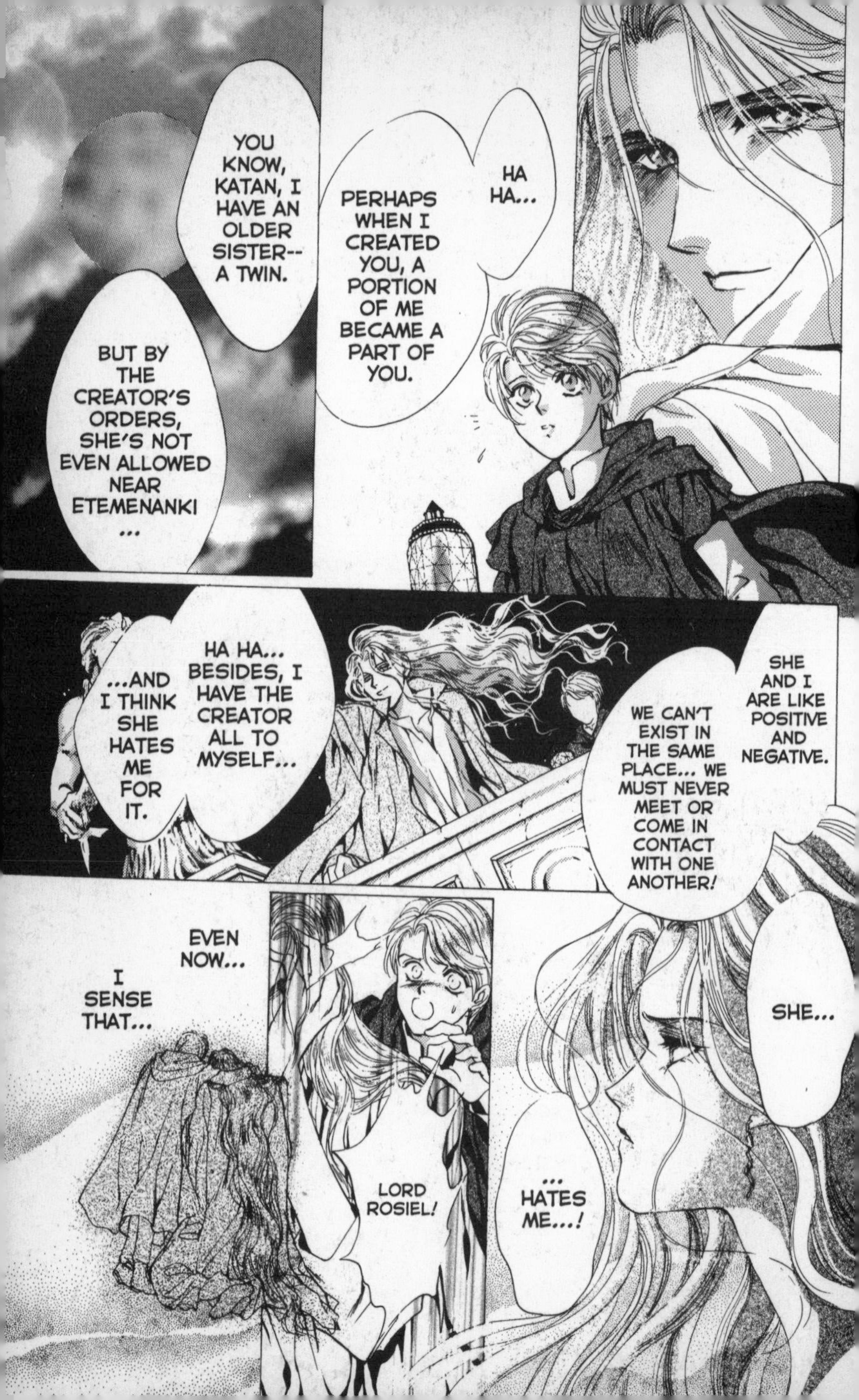
HA HA...
PERHAPS WHEN I CREATED YOU, A PORTION OF ME BECAME A PART OF YOU.
YOU KNOW, KATAN, I HAVE AN OLDER SISTER-- A TWIN.
BUT BY THE CREATOR'S ORDERS, SHE'S NOT EVEN ALLOWED NEAR ETEMENANKI ...
SHE AND I ARE LIKE POSITIVE AND NEGATIVE.
WE CAN'T EXIST IN THE SAME PLACE... WE MUST NEVER MEET OR COME IN CONTACT WITH ONE ANOTHER!
HA HA... BESIDES, I HAVE THE CREATOR ALL TO MYSELF...
...AND I THINK SHE HATES ME FOR IT.
SHE...
... HATES ME...!
LORD ROSIEL!
EVEN NOW...
I SENSE THAT...

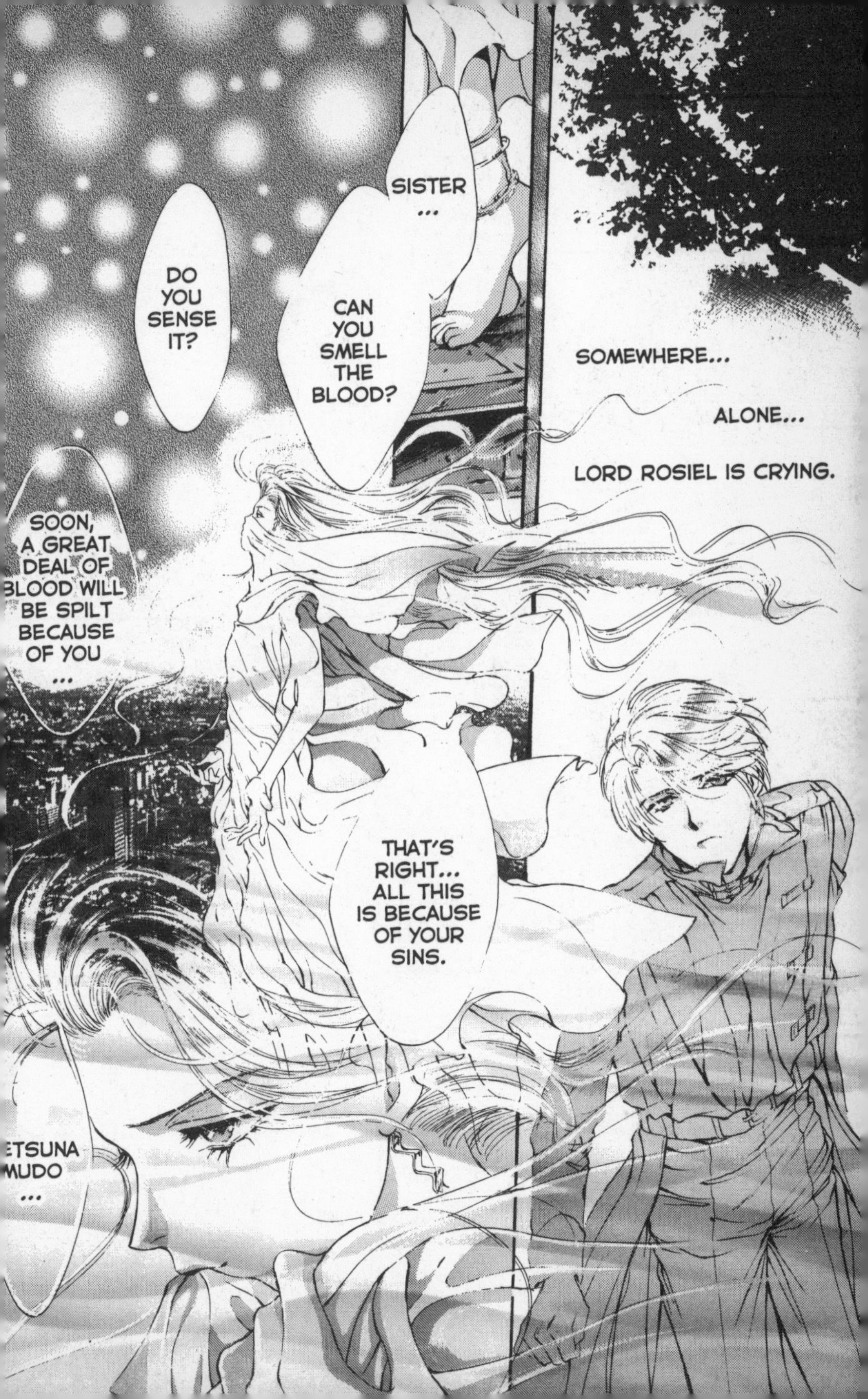
SOMEWHERE...
ALONE...
LORD ROSIEL IS CRYING.
SISTER ...
CAN YOU SMELL THE BLOOD?
DO YOU SENSE IT?
SOON, A GREAT DEAL OF BLOOD WILL BE SPILT BECAUSE OF YOU ...
THAT'S RIGHT... ALL THIS IS BECAUSE OF YOUR SINS.
ETSUNA MUDO ...

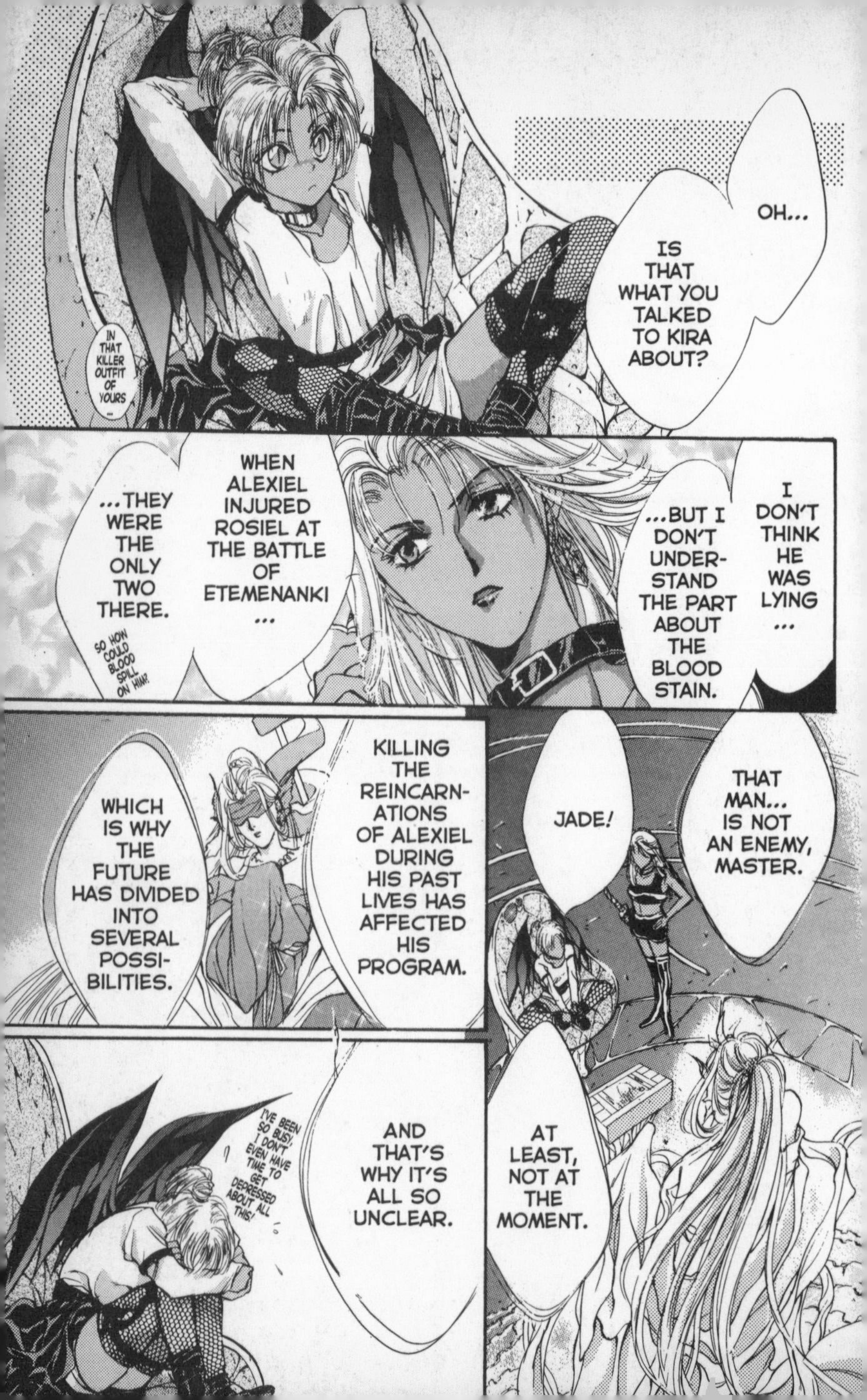
OH...
IS THAT WHAT YOU TALKED TO KIRA ABOUT?
IN THAT KILLER OUTFIT OF YOURS...
I DON'T THINK HE WAS LYING...
...BUT I DON'T UNDER-STAND THE PART ABOUT THE BLOOD STAIN.
WHEN ALEXIEL INJURED ROSIEL AT THE BATTLE OF ETEMENANKI...
...THEY WERE THE ONLY TWO THERE.
SO HOW COULD BLOOD SPILL ON HIM?
THAT MAN... IS NOT AN ENEMY, MASTER.
JADE!
AT LEAST, NOT AT THE MOMENT.
KILLING THE REINCARN-ATIONS OF ALEXIEL DURING HIS PAST LIVES HAS AFFECTED HIS PROGRAM.
WHICH IS WHY THE FUTURE HAS DIVIDED INTO SEVERAL POSSI-BILITIES.
AND THAT'S WHY IT'S ALL SO UNCLEAR.
I'VE BEEN SO BUSY, I DON'T EVEN HAVE TIME TO GET DEPRESSED ABOUT ALL THIS!

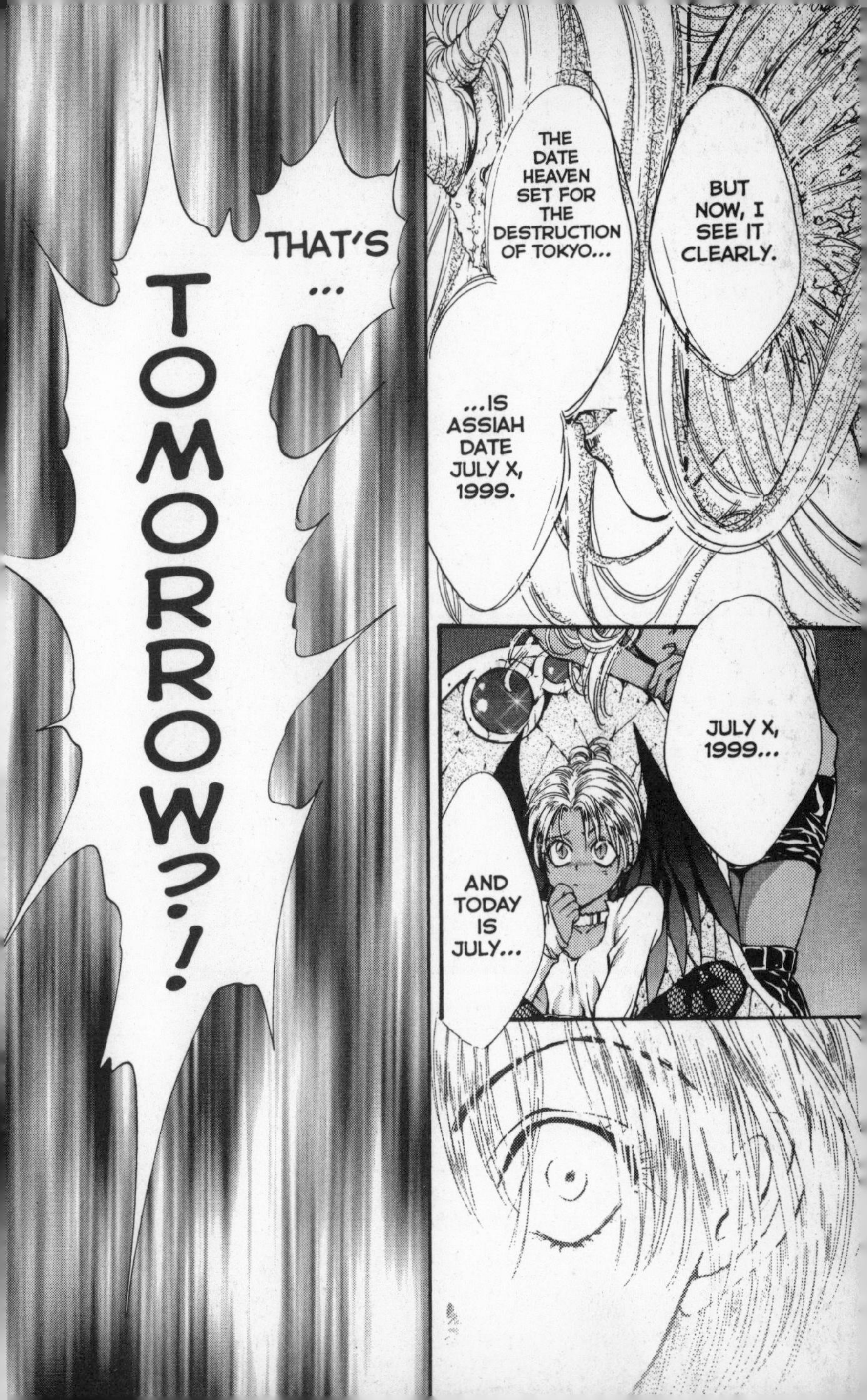
BUT NOW, I SEE IT CLEARLY.
THE DATE HEAVEN SET FOR THE DESTRUCTION OF TOKYO...
...IS ASSIAH DATE JULY X, 1999.
JULY X, 1999...
AND TODAY IS JULY...
THAT'S ...
TOMORROW?!

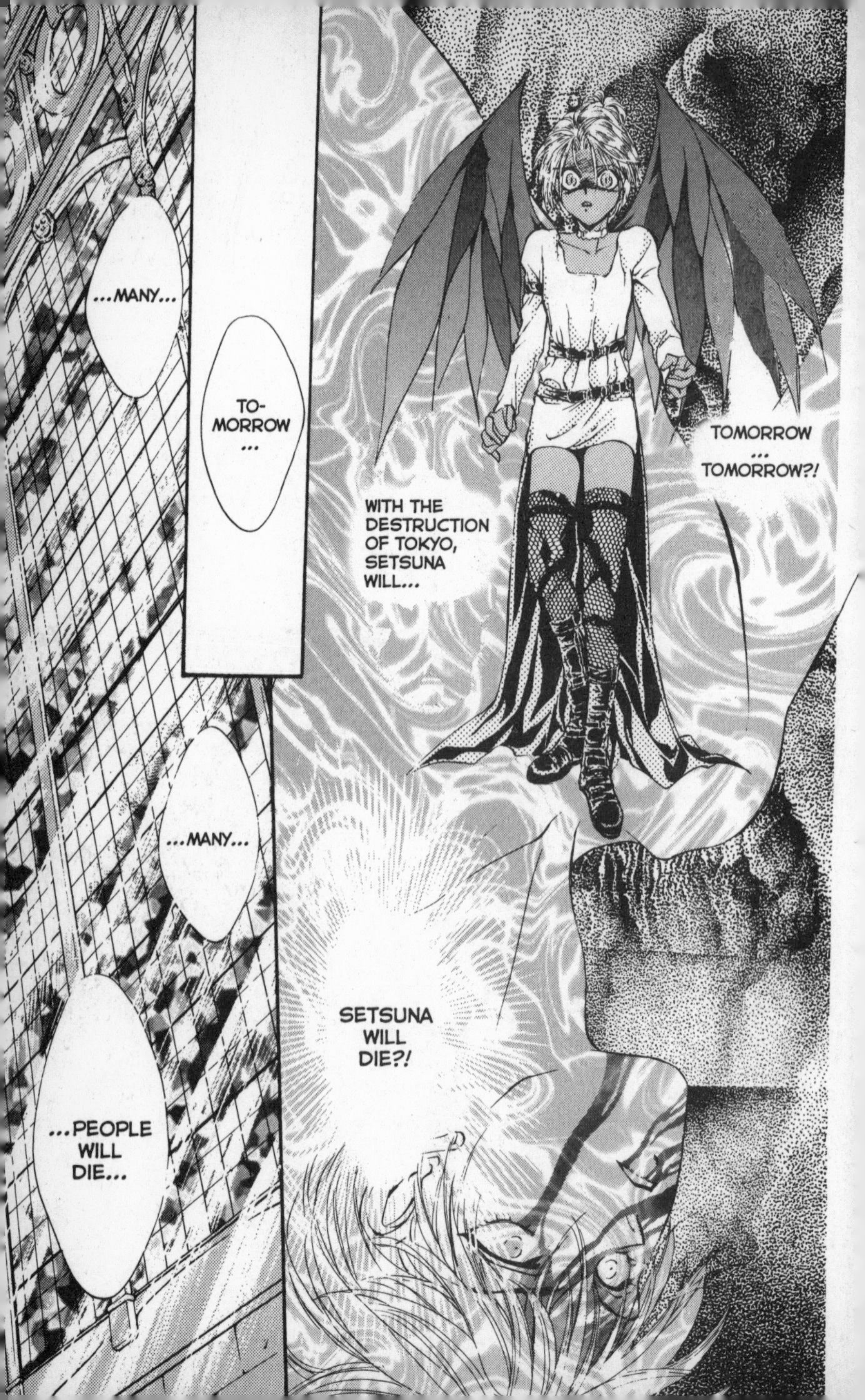
TOMORROW ... TOMORROW?!
WITH THE DESTRUCTION OF TOKYO, SETSUNA WILL...
SETSUNA WILL DIE?!
TO-MORROW ...
...MANY...
...MANY...
...PEOPLE WILL DIE...

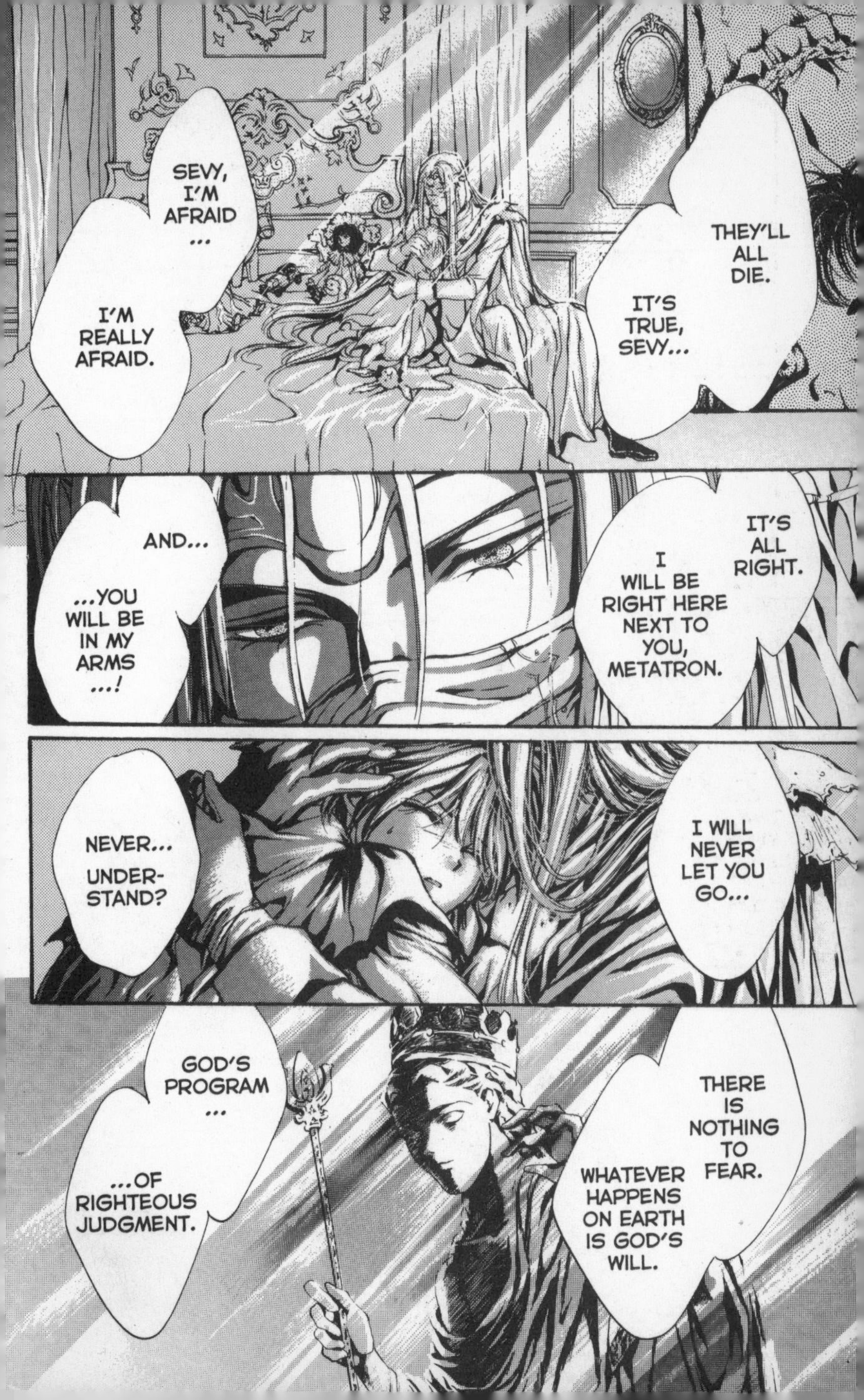
THEY'LL ALL DIE.
IT'S TRUE, SEVY...
SEVY, I'M AFRAID ...
I'M REALLY AFRAID.
IT'S ALL RIGHT.
I WILL BE RIGHT HERE NEXT TO YOU, METATRON.
AND...
...YOU WILL BE IN MY ARMS ...!
I WILL NEVER LET YOU GO...
NEVER...
UNDER-STAND?
THERE IS NOTHING TO FEAR.
WHATEVER HAPPENS ON EARTH IS GOD'S WILL.
GOD'S PROGRAM ...
...OF RIGHTEOUS JUDGMENT.

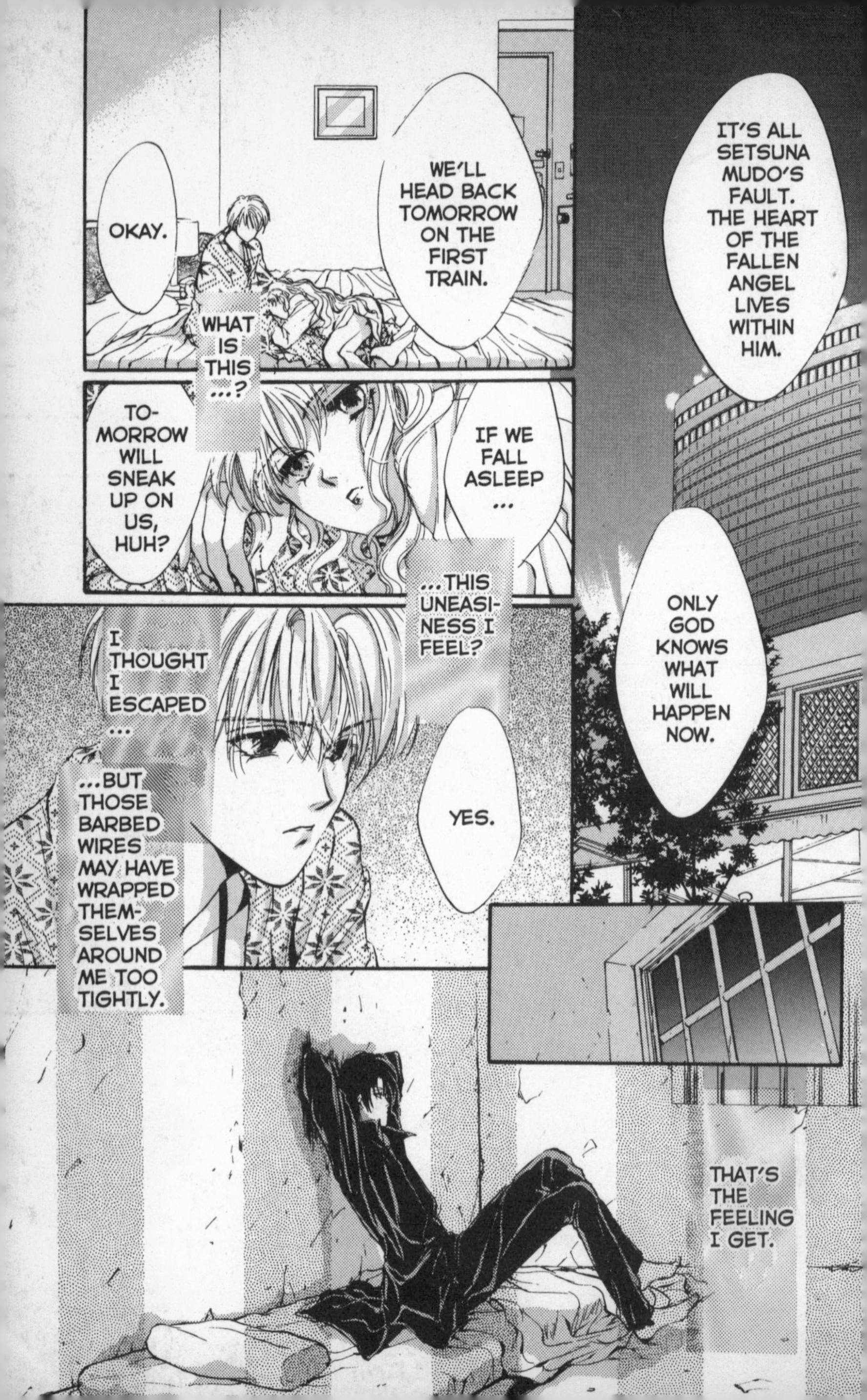
IT'S ALL SETSUNA MUDO'S FAULT. THE HEART OF THE FALLEN ANGEL LIVES WITHIN HIM.
ONLY GOD KNOWS WHAT WILL HAPPEN NOW.
WE'LL HEAD BACK TOMORROW ON THE FIRST TRAIN.
OKAY.
WHAT IS THIS ...?
IF WE FALL ASLEEP ...
TO-MORROW WILL SNEAK UP ON US, HUH?
...THIS UNEASI-NESS I FEEL?
YES.
I THOUGHT I ESCAPED ...
...BUT THOSE BARBED WIRES MAY HAVE WRAPPED THEM-SELVES AROUND ME TOO TIGHTLY.
THAT'S THE FEELING I GET.

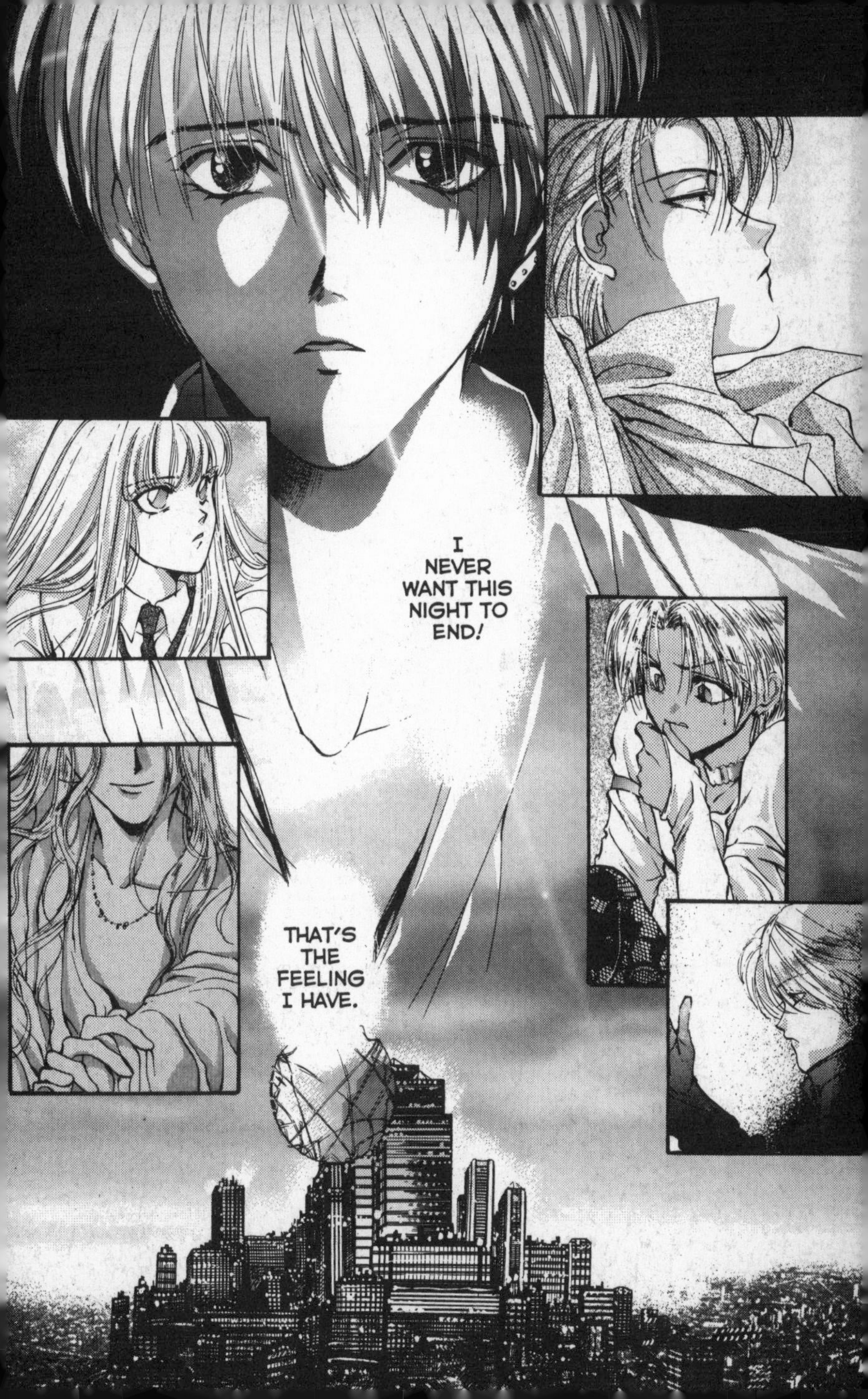
I NEVER WANT THIS NIGHT TO END!
THAT'S THE FEELING I HAVE.

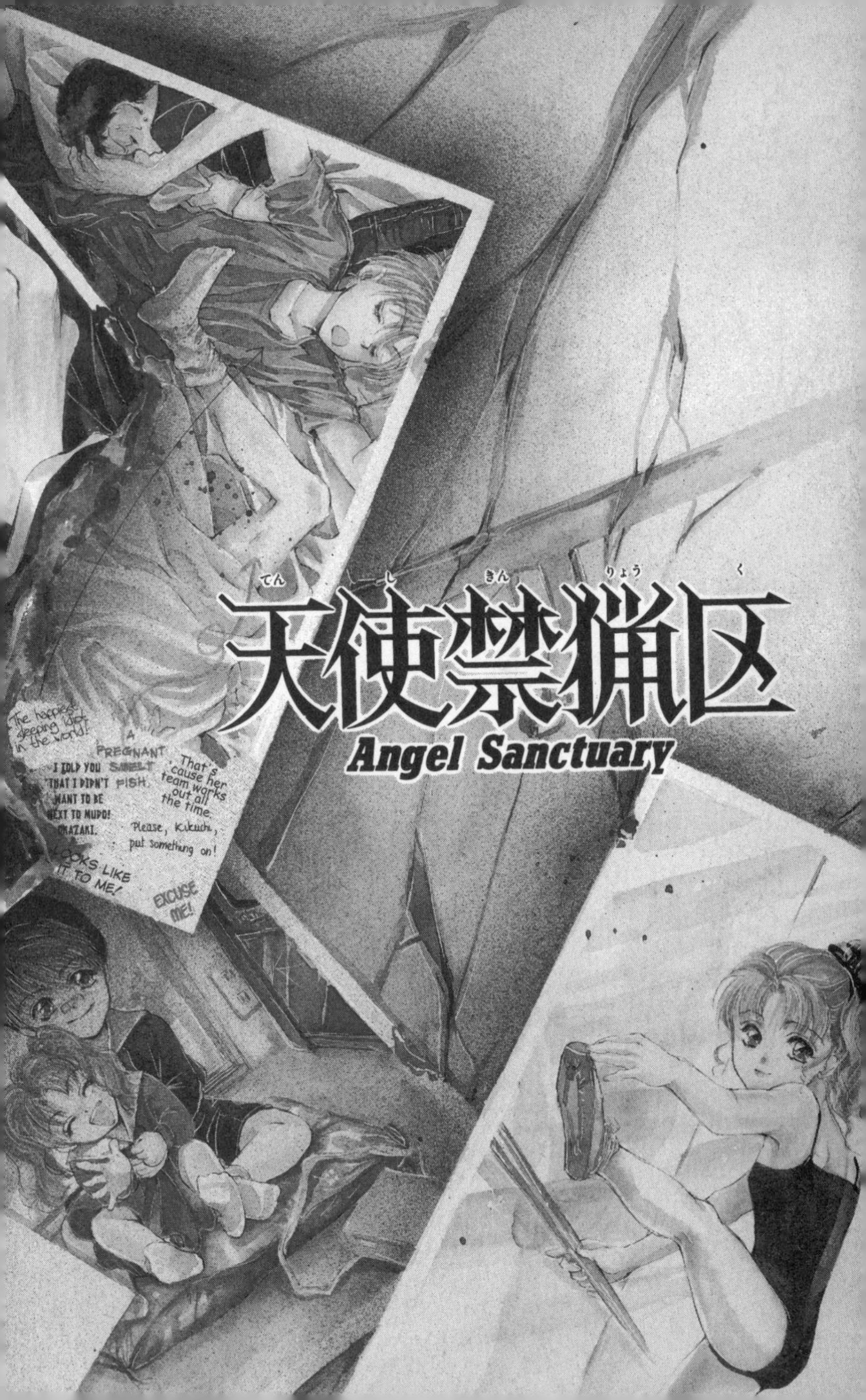
てん し きん りょう く
天使禁猟区
Angel Sanctuary
That's 'cause her team works out all the time.
Please, Kikuchi, put something on!
EXCUSE ME!
A PREGNANT SMELT FISH.
LOOKS LIKE IT TO ME!
The happiest sleeping idiot in the world!
I TOLD YOU THAT I DIDN'T WANT TO BE NEXT TO MUDO! OKAZAKI.

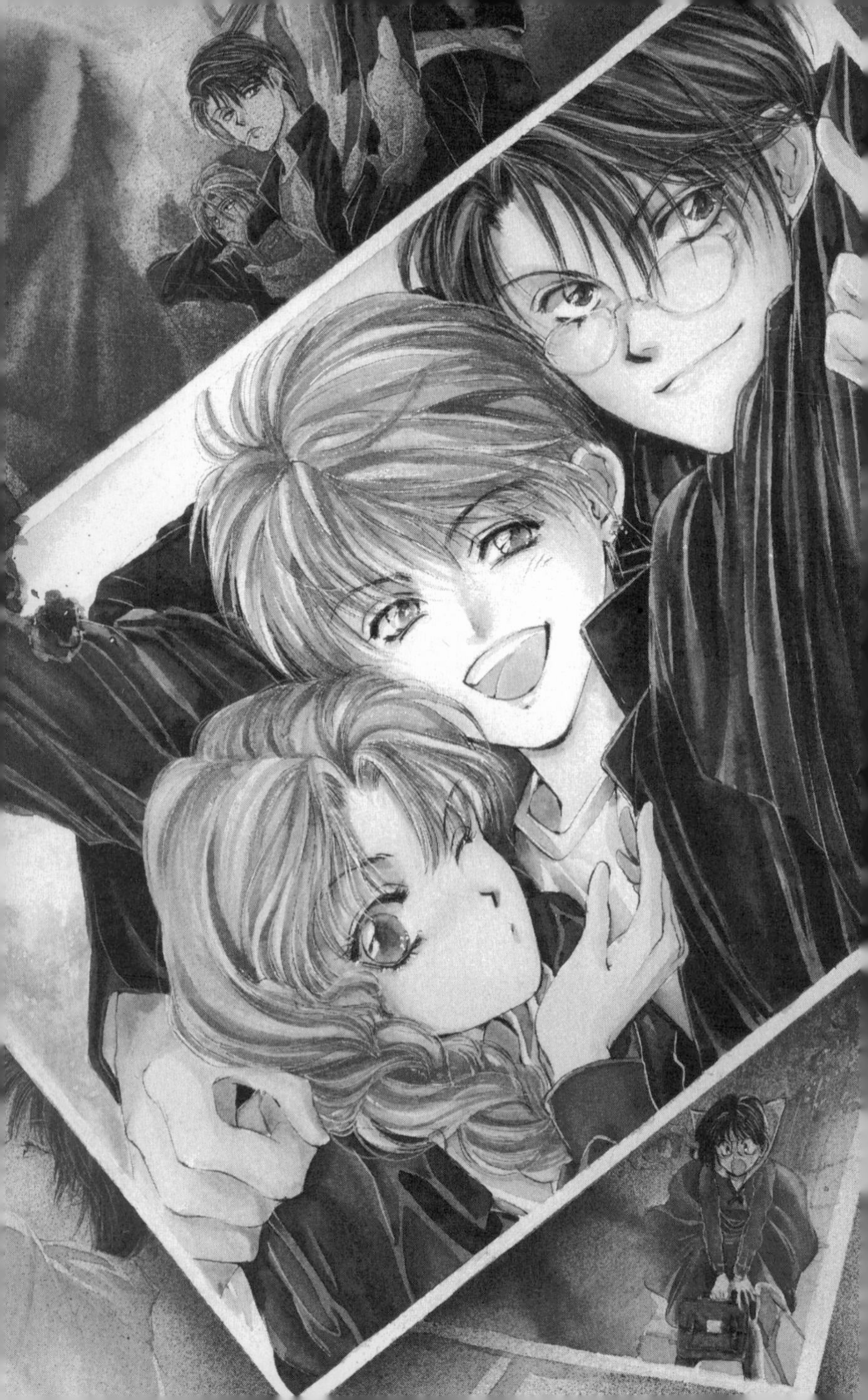

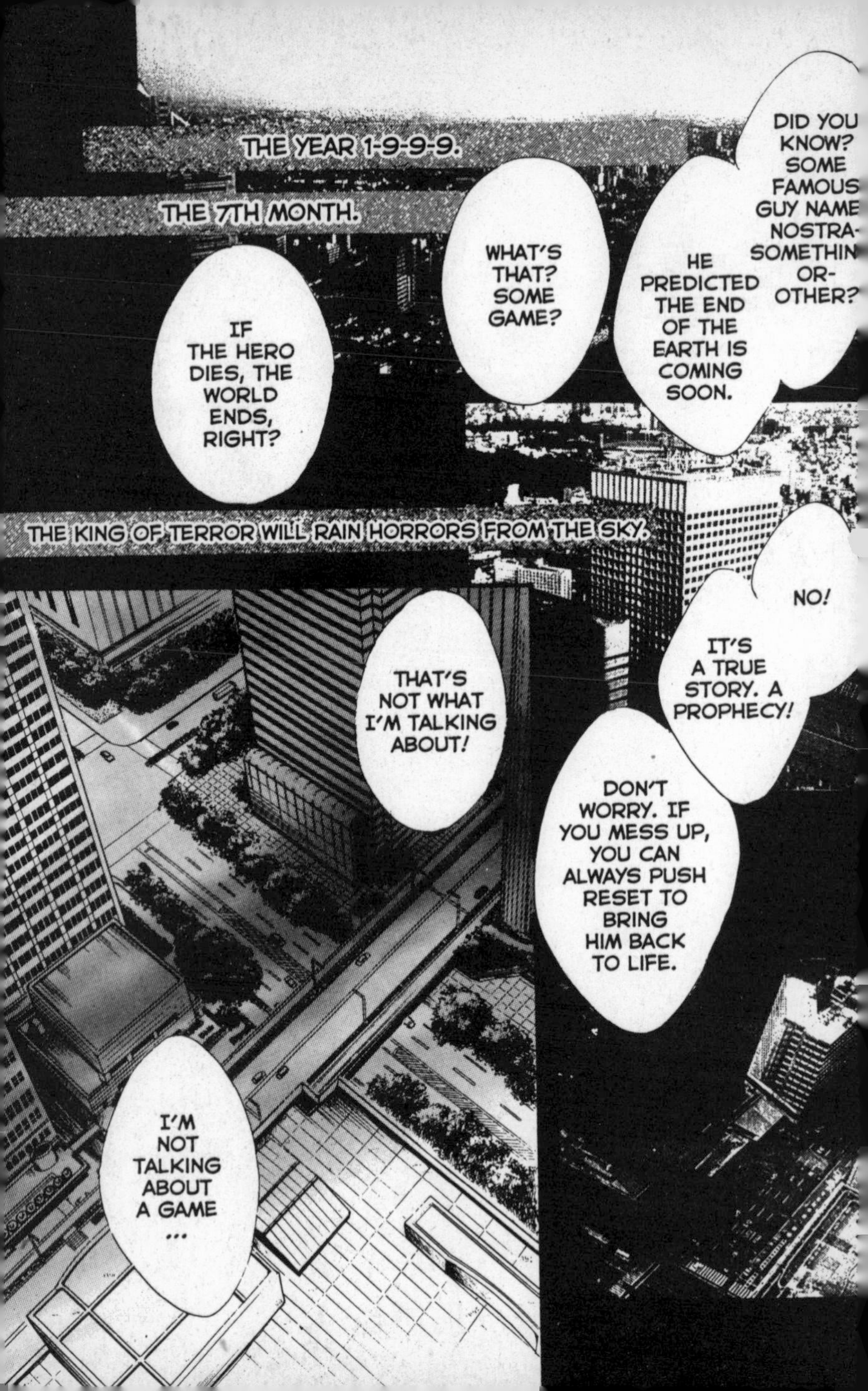
DID YOU KNOW? SOME FAMOUS GUY NAME NOSTRA-SOMETHIN OR-OTHER?
HE PREDICTED THE END OF THE EARTH IS COMING SOON.
WHAT'S THAT? SOME GAME?
IF THE HERO DIES, THE WORLD ENDS, RIGHT?
THE YEAR 1-9-9-9.
THE 7TH MONTH.
THE KING OF TERROR WILL RAIN HORRORS FROM THE SKY.
NO!
IT'S A TRUE STORY. A PROPHECY!
THAT'S NOT WHAT I'M TALKING ABOUT!
DON'T WORRY. IF YOU MESS UP, YOU CAN ALWAYS PUSH RESET TO BRING HIM BACK TO LIFE.
I'M NOT TALKING ABOUT A GAME ...

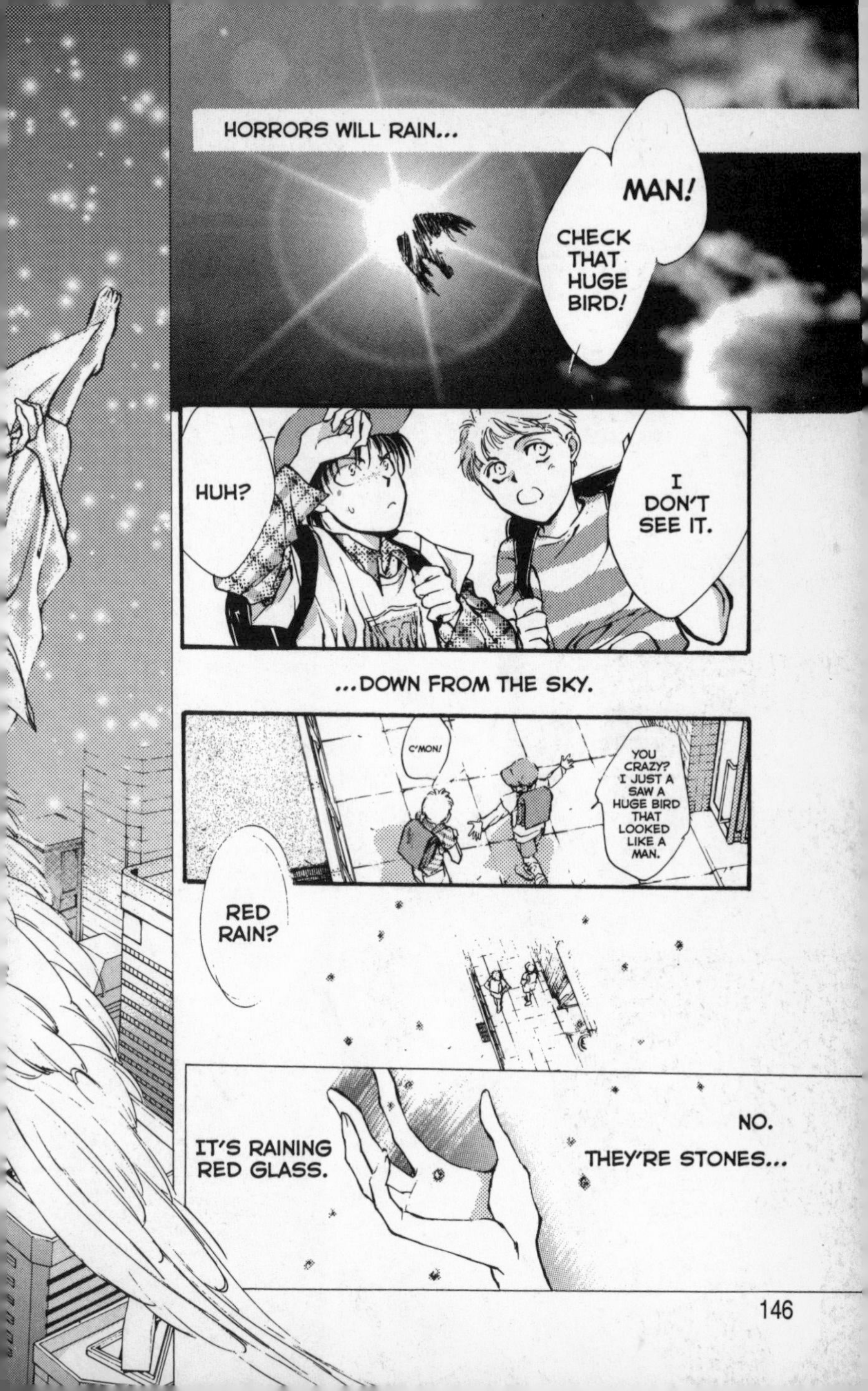
HORRORS WILL RAIN...
MAN!
CHECK THAT HUGE BIRD!
I DON'T SEE IT.
HUH?
...DOWN FROM THE SKY.
YOU CRAZY? I JUST A SAW A HUGE BIRD THAT LOOKED LIKE A MAN.
C'MON!
RED RAIN?
NO.
THEY'RE STONES...
IT'S RAINING RED GLASS.

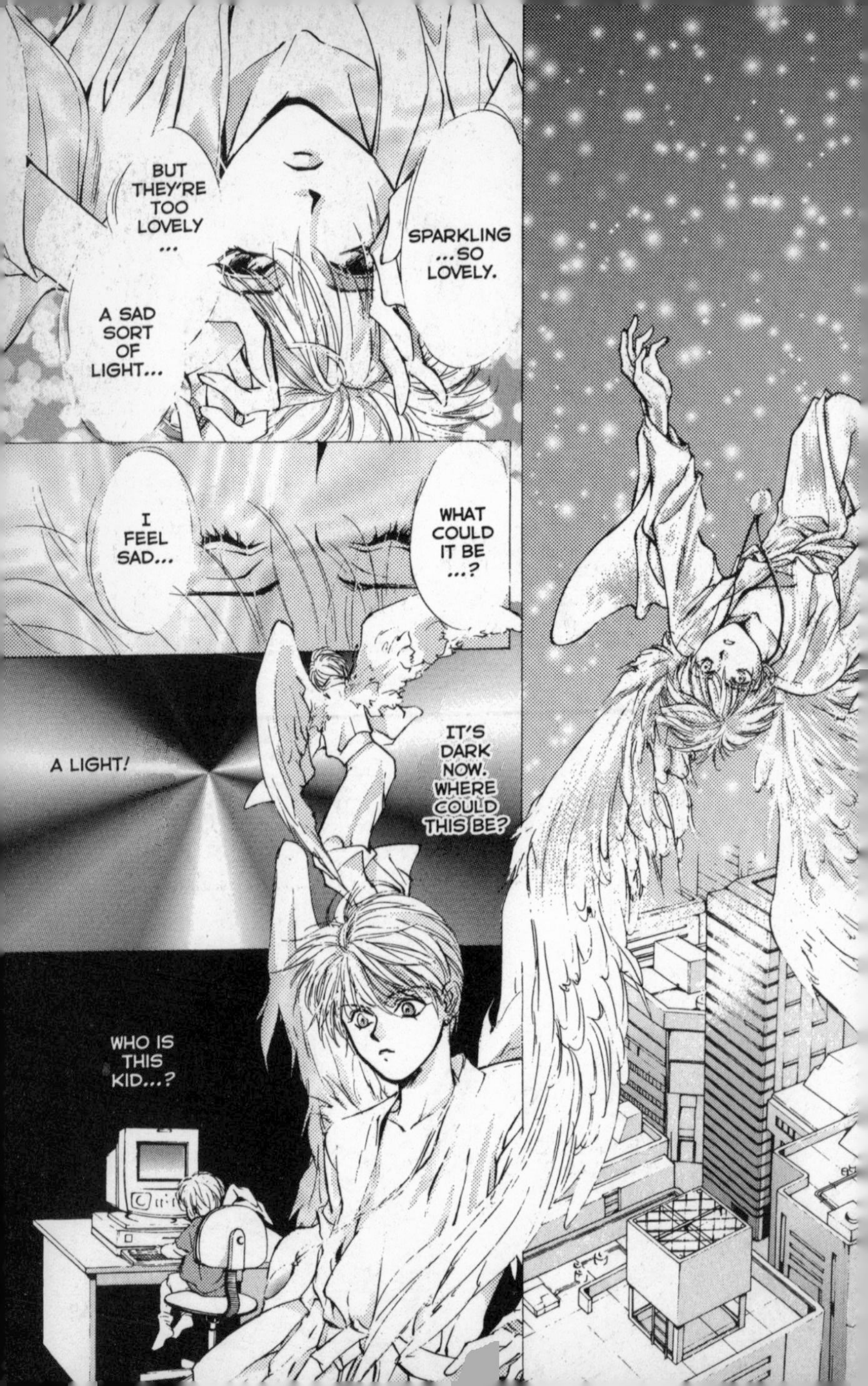
SPARKLING ...SO LOVELY.
BUT THEY'RE TOO LOVELY ...
A SAD SORT OF LIGHT...
WHAT COULD IT BE ...?
I FEEL SAD...
IT'S DARK NOW. WHERE COULD THIS BE?
A LIGHT!
WHO IS THIS KID...?

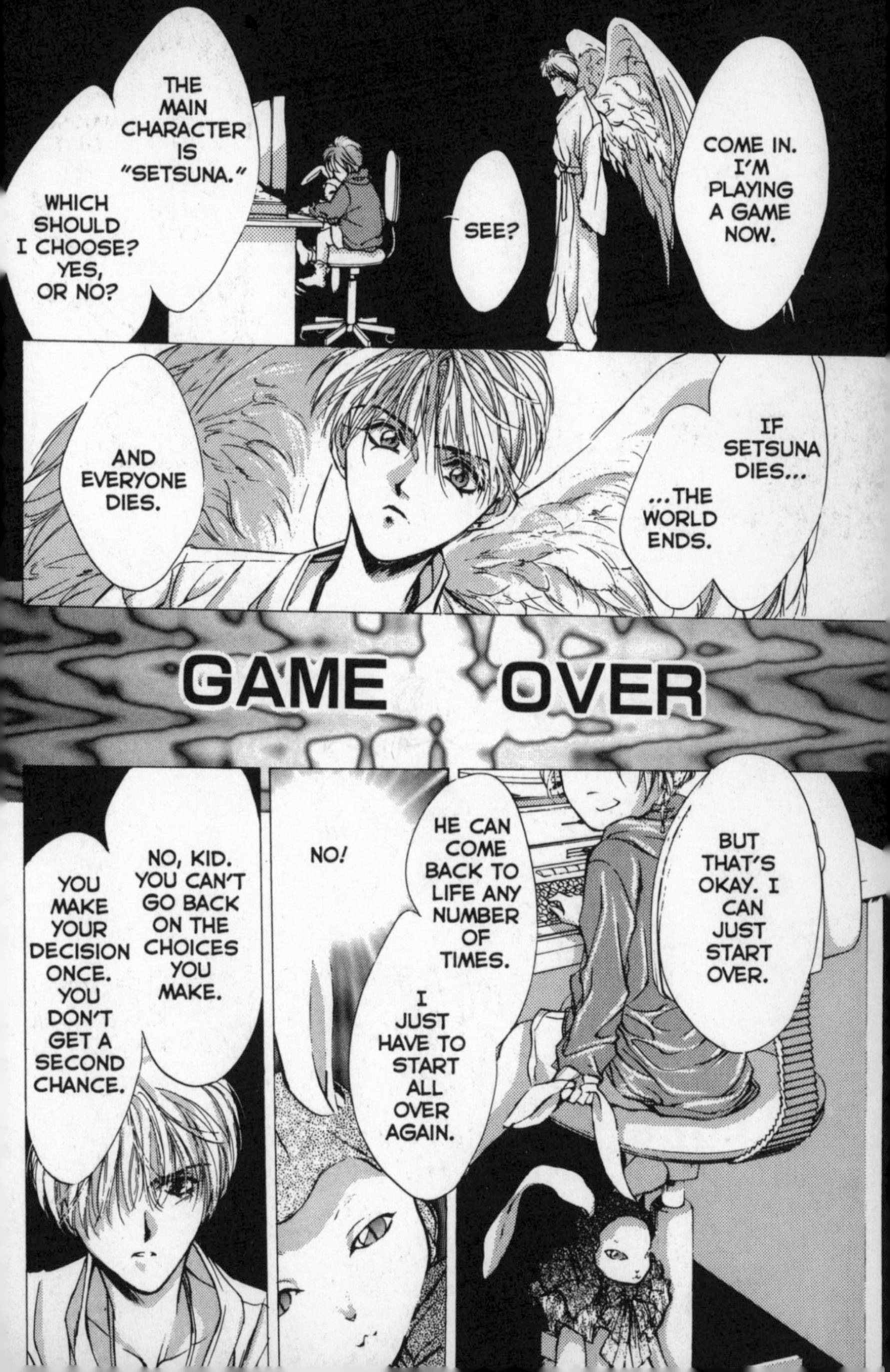
COME IN. I'M PLAYING A GAME NOW.
SEE?
THE MAIN CHARACTER IS "SETSUNA."
WHICH SHOULD I CHOOSE? YES, OR NO?
IF SETSUNA DIES...
...THE WORLD ENDS.
AND EVERYONE DIES.
GAME OVER
BUT THAT'S OKAY. I CAN JUST START OVER.
HE CAN COME BACK TO LIFE ANY NUMBER OF TIMES.
I JUST HAVE TO START ALL OVER AGAIN.
NO!
NO, KID. YOU CAN'T GO BACK ON THE CHOICES YOU MAKE.
YOU MAKE YOUR DECISION ONCE. YOU DON'T GET A SECOND CHANCE.

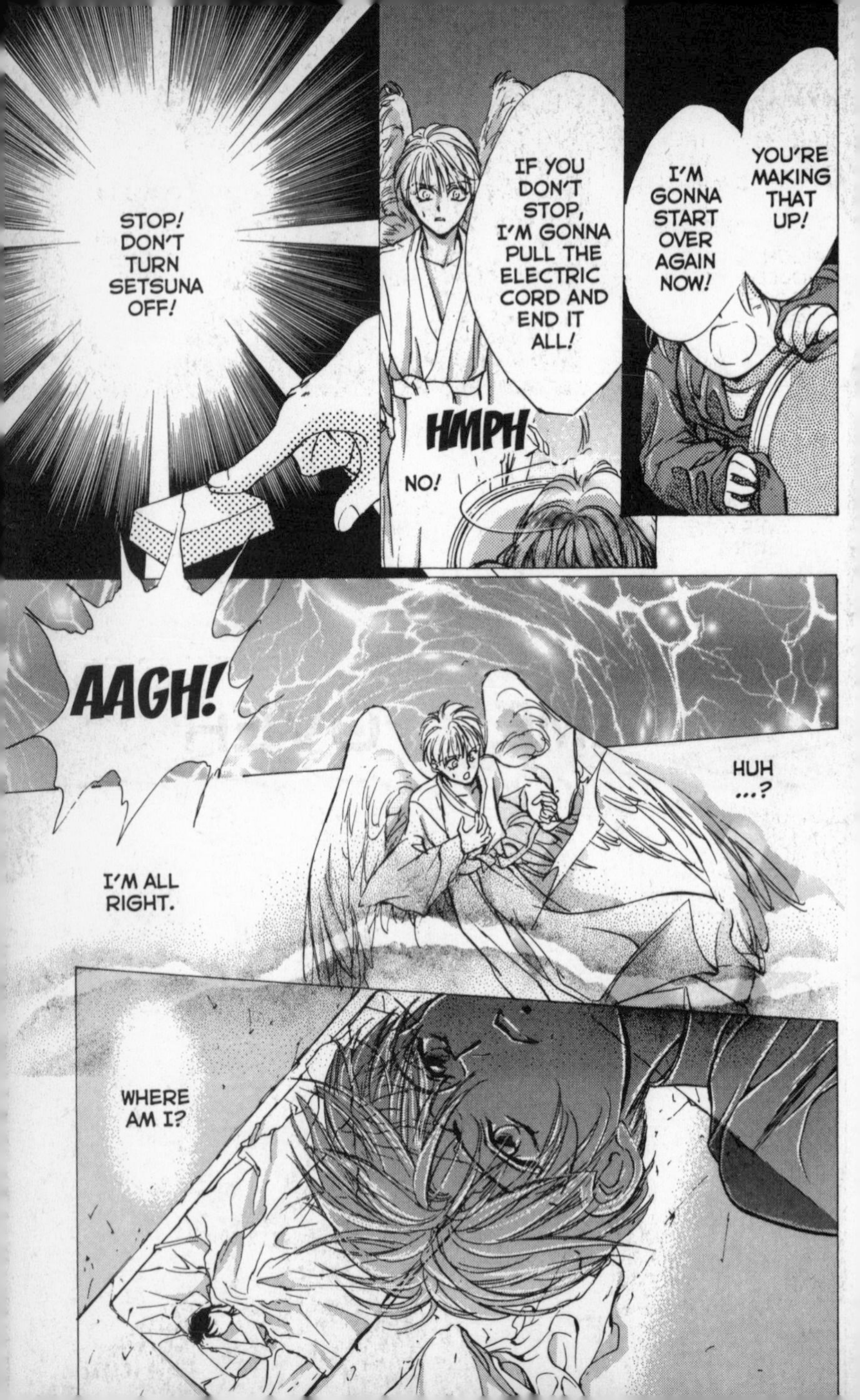
YOU'RE MAKING THAT UP!
I'M GONNA START OVER AGAIN NOW!
IF YOU DON'T STOP, I'M GONNA PULL THE ELECTRIC CORD AND END IT ALL!
HMPH
NO!
STOP! DON'T TURN SETSUNA OFF!
AAGH!
HUH ...?
I'M ALL RIGHT.
WHERE AM I?

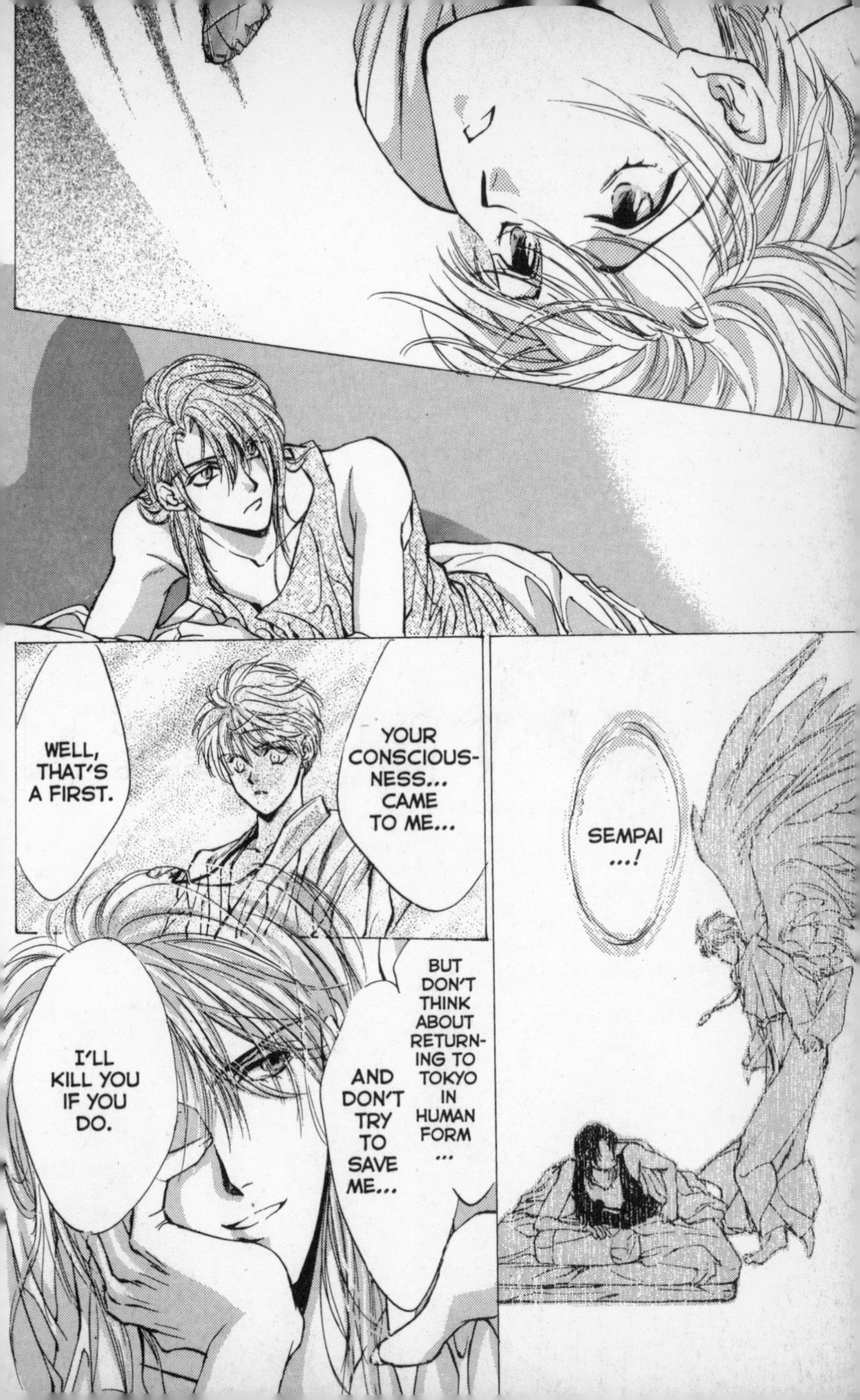
SEMPAI ...!
YOUR CONSCIOUS-NESS... CAME TO ME...
WELL, THAT'S A FIRST.
BUT DON'T THINK ABOUT RETURN-ING TO TOKYO IN HUMAN FORM ...
AND DON'T TRY TO SAVE ME...
I'LL KILL YOU IF YOU DO.

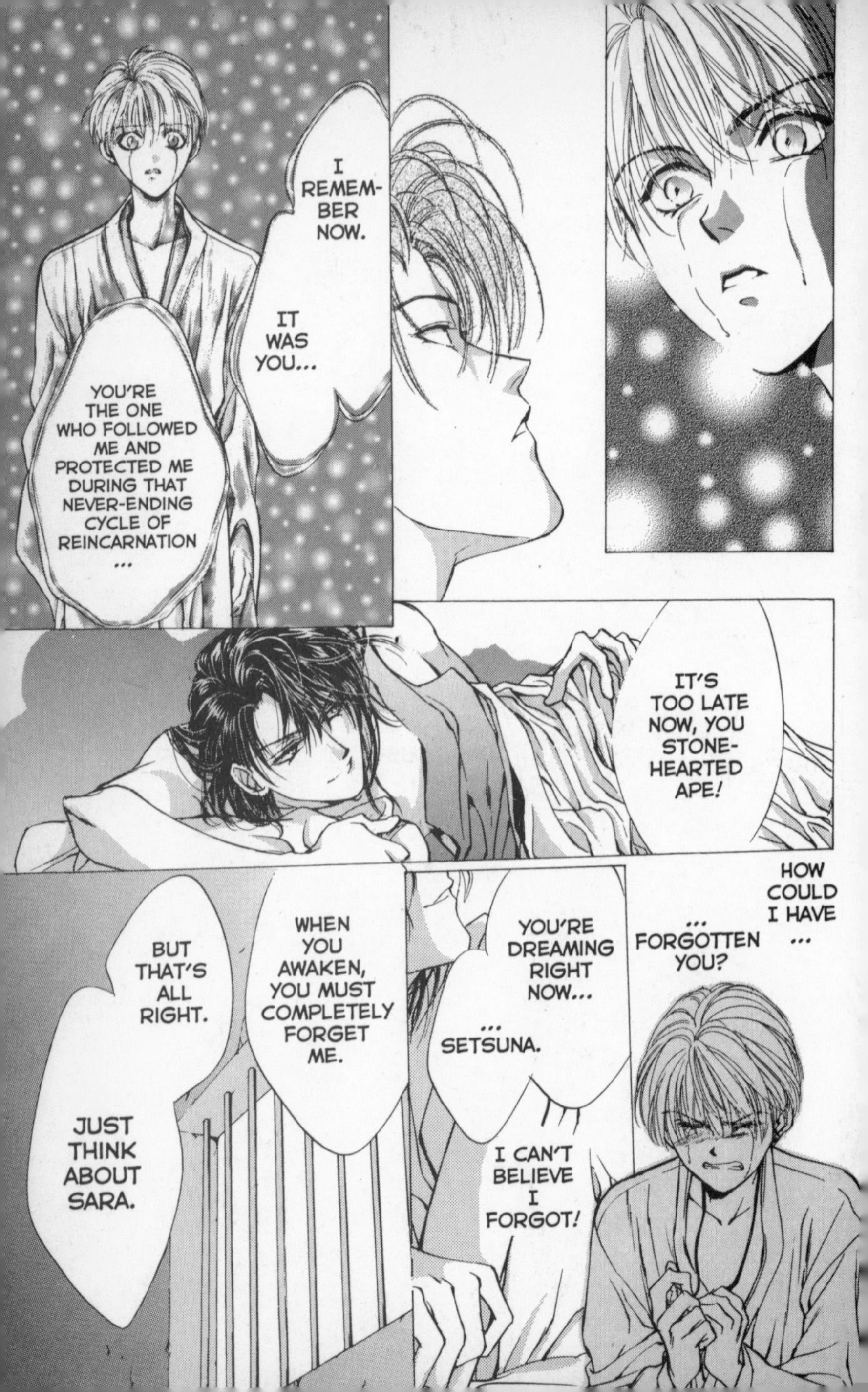
I REMEMBER NOW.
IT WAS YOU...
YOU'RE THE ONE WHO FOLLOWED ME AND PROTECTED ME DURING THAT NEVER-ENDING CYCLE OF REINCARNATION ...
IT'S TOO LATE NOW, YOU STONE-HEARTED APE!
HOW COULD I HAVE ...
... FORGOTTEN YOU?
I CAN'T BELIEVE I FORGOT!
YOU'RE DREAMING RIGHT NOW...
... SETSUNA.
WHEN YOU AWAKEN, YOU MUST COMPLETELY FORGET ME.
BUT THAT'S ALL RIGHT.
JUST THINK ABOUT SARA.

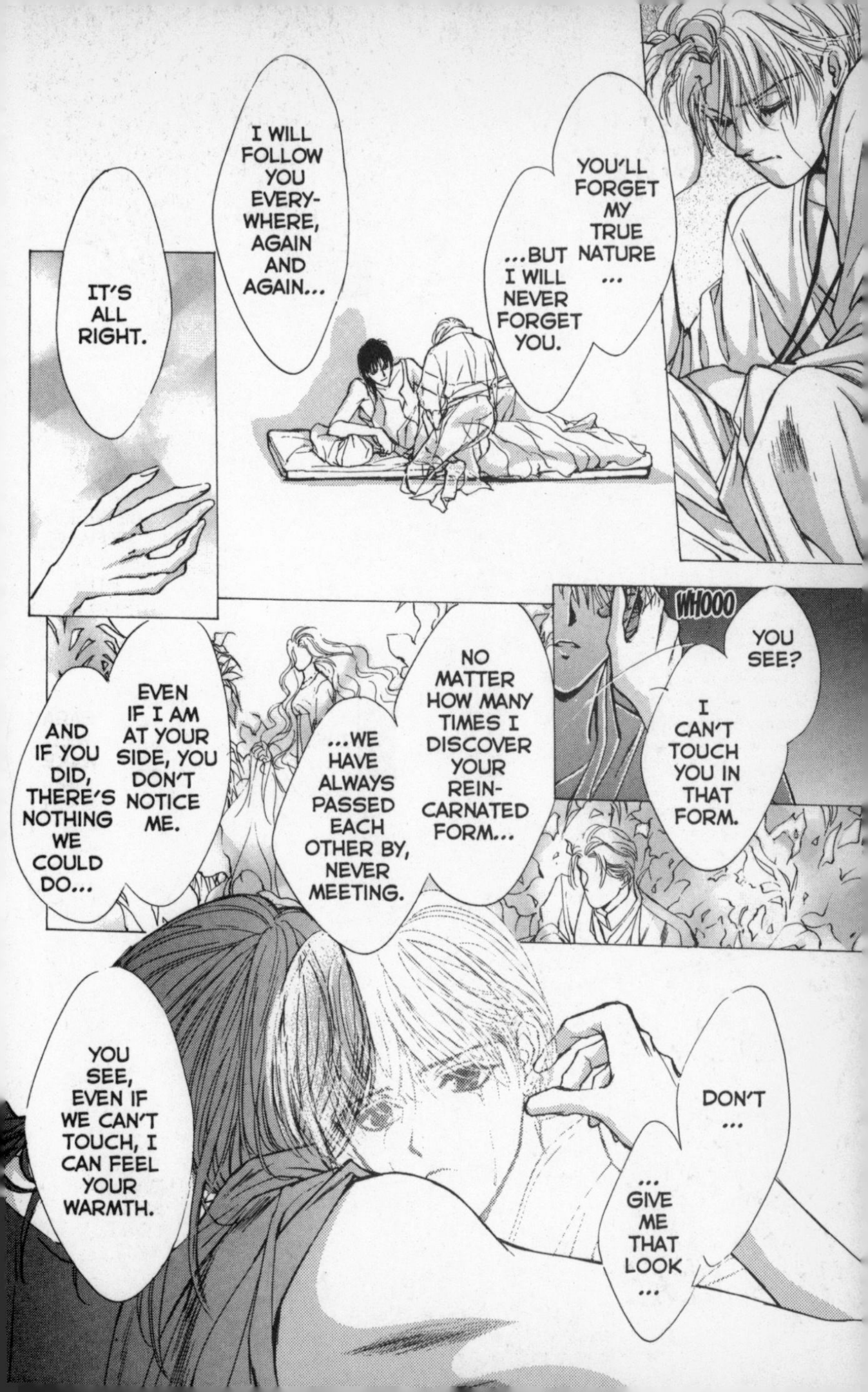
YOU'LL FORGET MY TRUE NATURE...
...BUT I WILL NEVER FORGET YOU.
I WILL FOLLOW YOU EVERY-WHERE, AGAIN AND AGAIN...
IT'S ALL RIGHT.
WHOOO
YOU SEE?
I CAN'T TOUCH YOU IN THAT FORM.
NO MATTER HOW MANY TIMES I DISCOVER YOUR REIN-CARNATED FORM...
...WE HAVE ALWAYS PASSED EACH OTHER BY, NEVER MEETING.
EVEN IF I AM AT YOUR SIDE, YOU DON'T NOTICE ME.
AND IF YOU DID, THERE'S NOTHING WE COULD DO...
DON'T...
...GIVE ME THAT LOOK...
YOU SEE, EVEN IF WE CAN'T TOUCH, I CAN FEEL YOUR WARMTH.

Someone asked me, "Does anyone use such old expressions like 'In the 7th month of the year 1999' anymore?" Well, excuse me! I thought it sounded nice and archaic, and it seemed appropriate for describing the coming of end of the world. Besides, it wouldn't have made much sense to use an expression no one has ever heard of. I wanted to make the picture on the opening page of this chapter one that was suggestive of something very sad, but only if you give it a lot of thought

At first glance, it may appear very cheerful, but old albums and music boxes seem to convey a very sad image because they contain lost memories that can never be retrieved. By the way, just thought you might be interested to know that drawing Kira's old man is very difficult. But I like troubled middle-aged men.

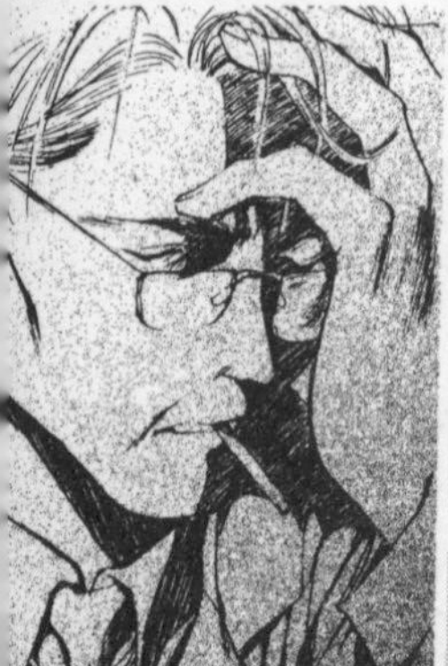

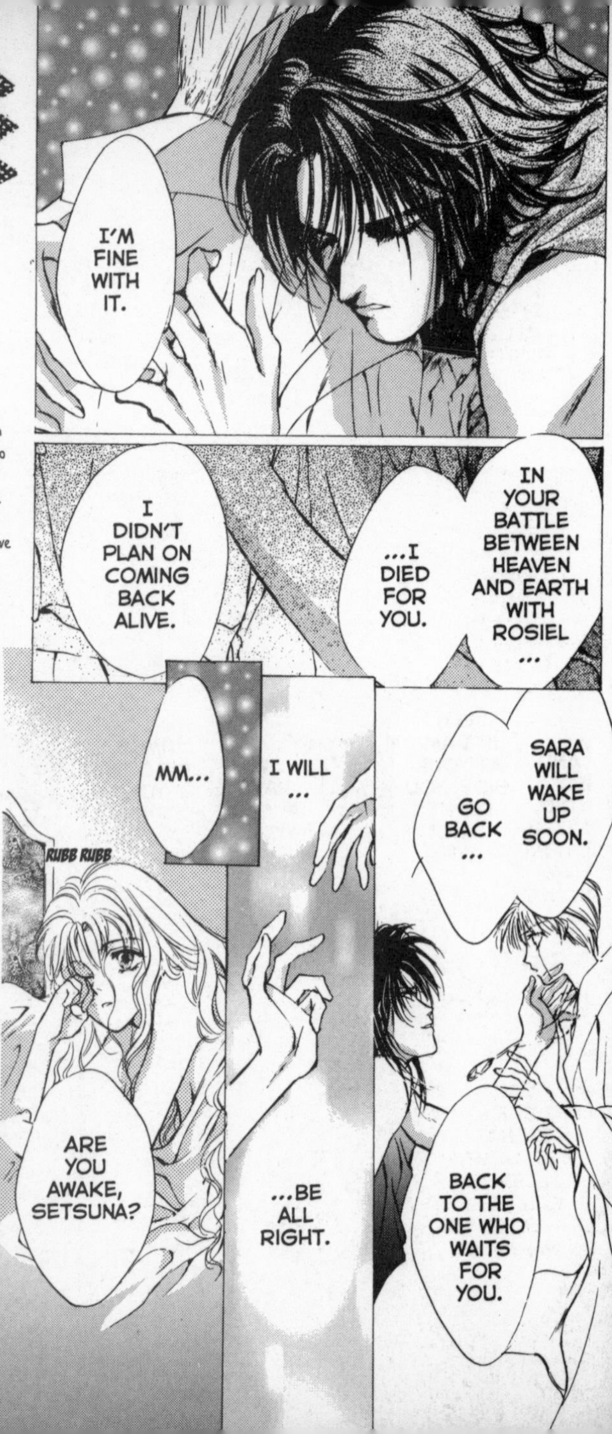
I'M FINE WITH IT.
IN YOUR BATTLE BETWEEN HEAVEN AND EARTH WITH ROSIEL...
...I DIED FOR YOU.
I DIDN'T PLAN ON COMING BACK ALIVE.
SARA WILL WAKE UP SOON.
GO BACK...
BACK TO THE ONE WHO WAITS FOR YOU.
I WILL...
...BE ALL RIGHT.
MM...
RUBB RUBB
ARE YOU AWAKE, SETSUNA?

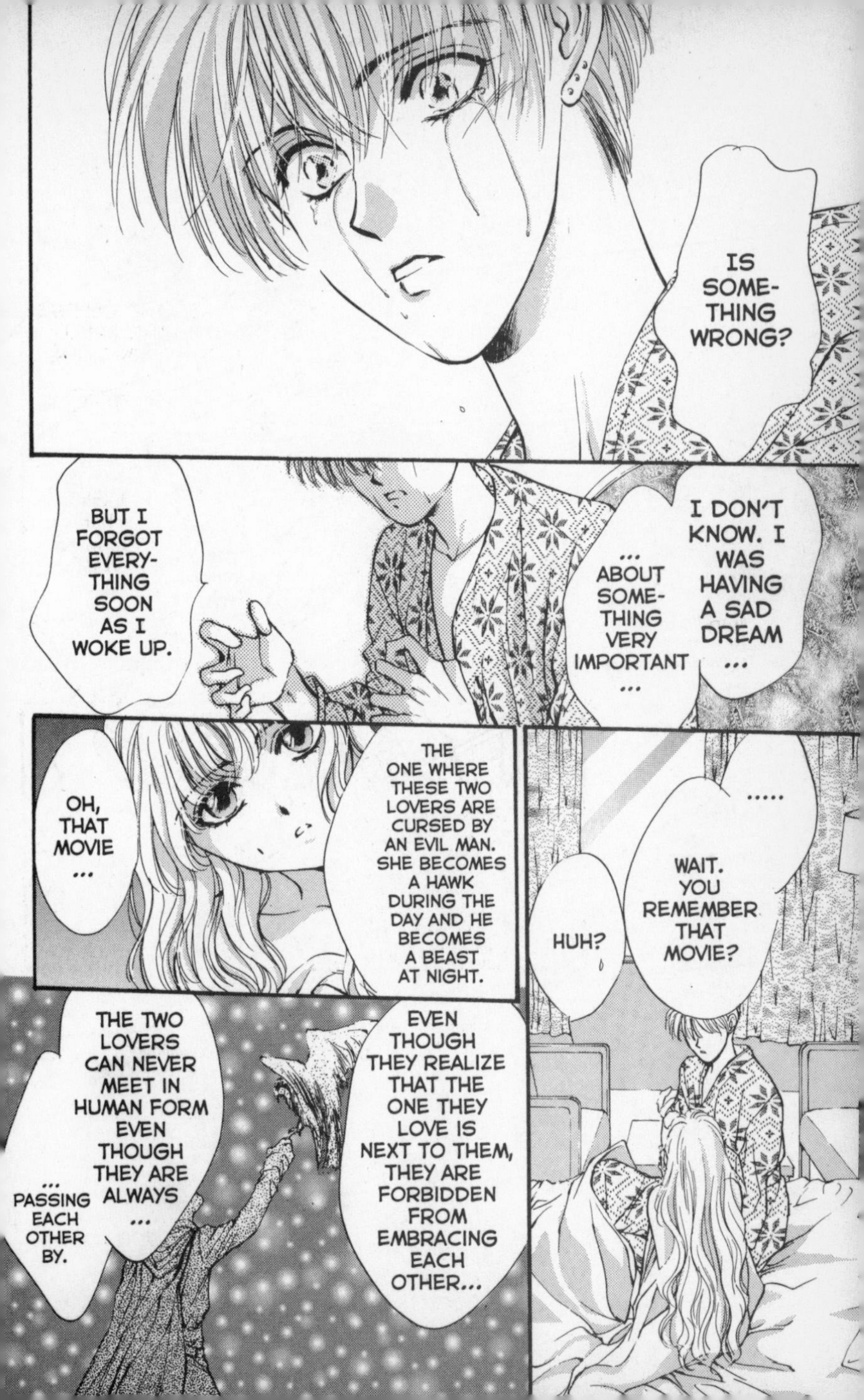
IS SOMETHING WRONG?
I DON'T KNOW. I WAS HAVING A SAD DREAM ...
... ABOUT SOMETHING VERY IMPORTANT ...
BUT I FORGOT EVERYTHING SOON AS I WOKE UP.
.....
WAIT. YOU REMEMBER THAT MOVIE?
HUH?
THE ONE WHERE THESE TWO LOVERS ARE CURSED BY AN EVIL MAN. SHE BECOMES A HAWK DURING THE DAY AND HE BECOMES A BEAST AT NIGHT.
OH, THAT MOVIE ...
EVEN THOUGH THEY REALIZE THAT THE ONE THEY LOVE IS NEXT TO THEM, THEY ARE FORBIDDEN FROM EMBRACING EACH OTHER...
THE TWO LOVERS CAN NEVER MEET IN HUMAN FORM EVEN THOUGH THEY ARE ALWAYS ...
... PASSING EACH OTHER BY.

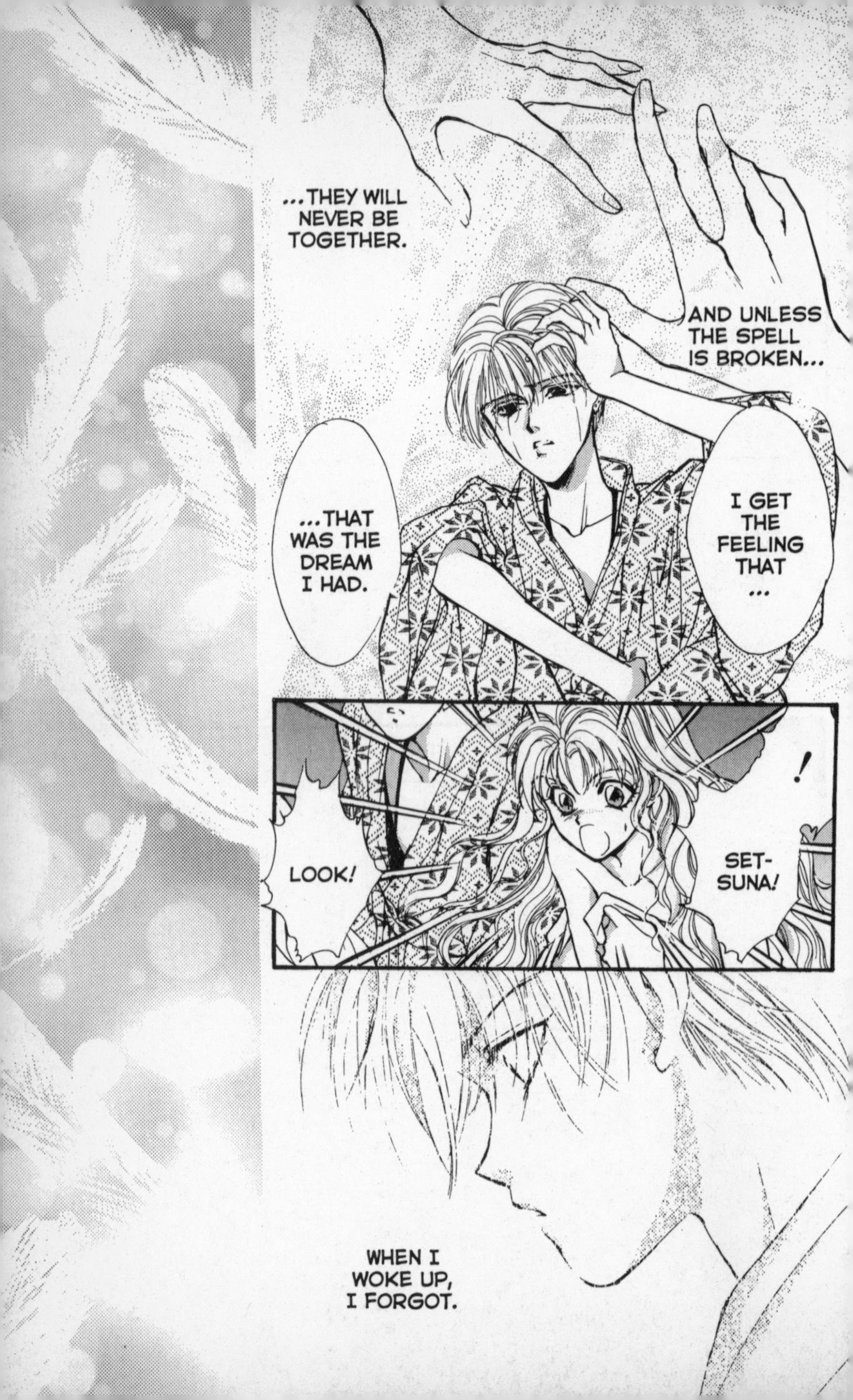
AND UNLESS THE SPELL IS BROKEN...
...THEY WILL NEVER BE TOGETHER.
I GET THE FEELING THAT ...
...THAT WAS THE DREAM I HAD.
!
SET-SUNA!
LOOK!
WHEN I WOKE UP, I FORGOT.

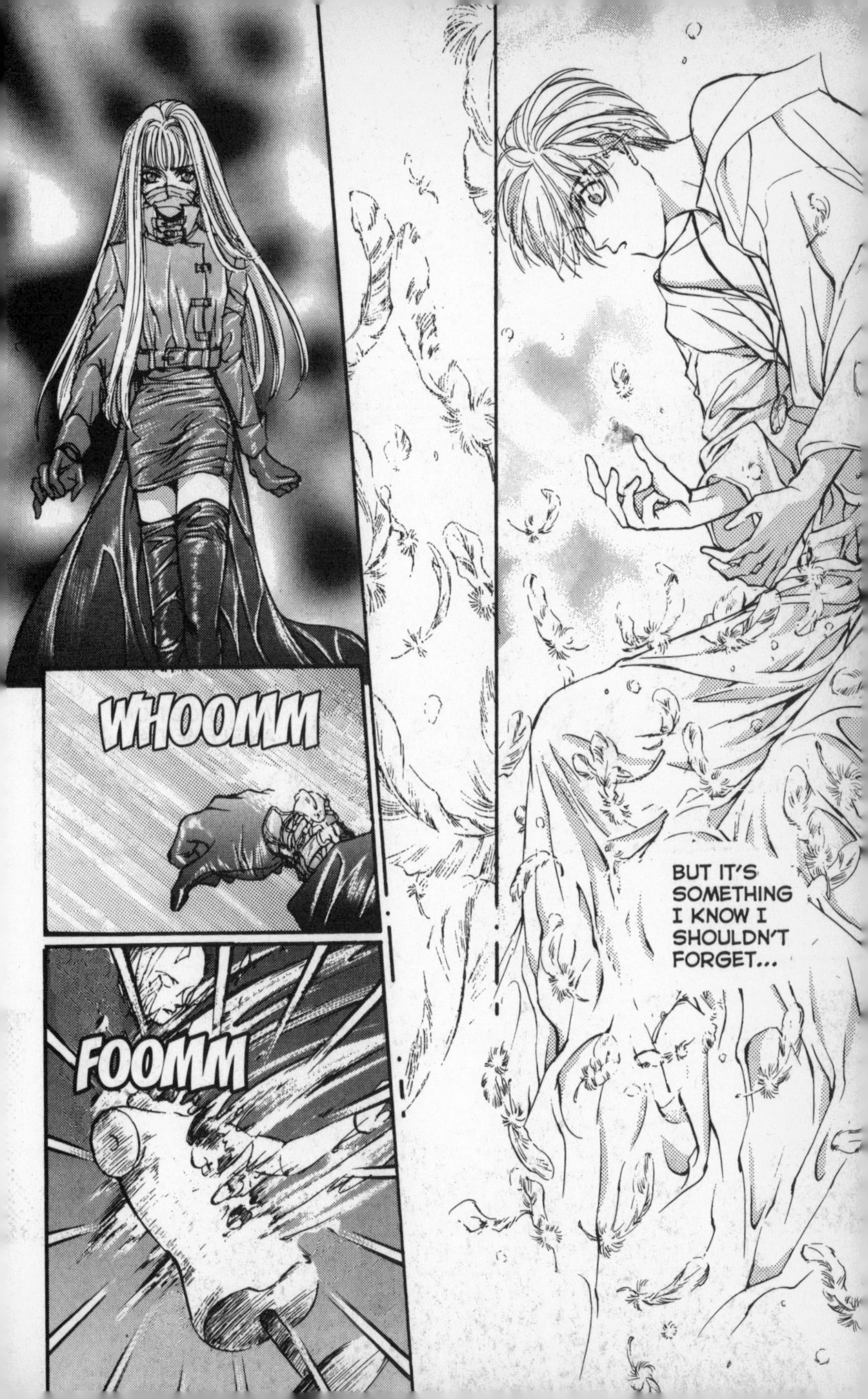
BUT IT'S SOMETHING I KNOW I SHOULDN'T FORGET...
WHOOMM
FOOMM

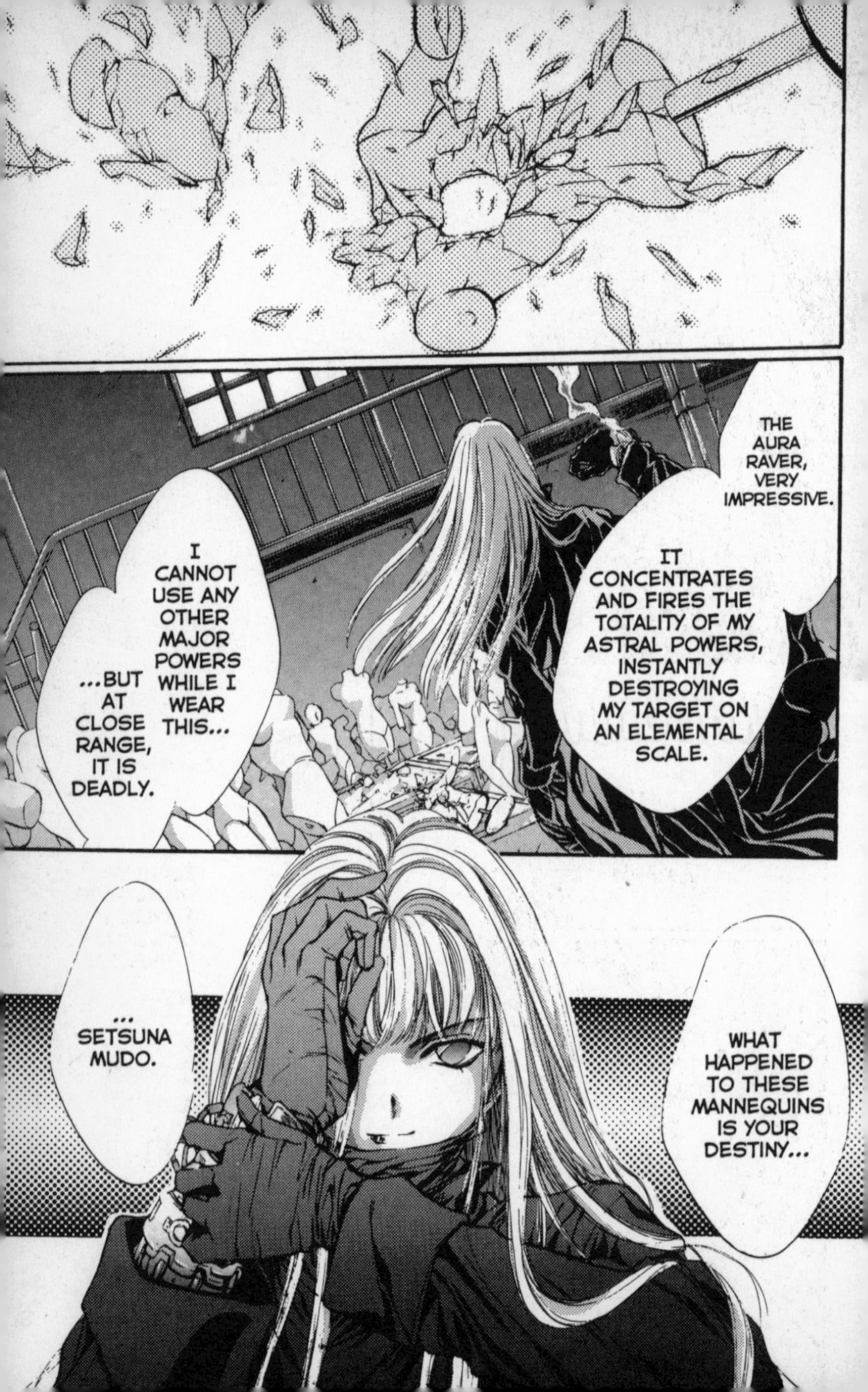
THE AURA RAVER, VERY IMPRESSIVE.
IT CONCENTRATES AND FIRES THE TOTALITY OF MY ASTRAL POWERS, INSTANTLY DESTROYING MY TARGET ON AN ELEMENTAL SCALE.
I CANNOT USE ANY OTHER MAJOR POWERS WHILE I WEAR THIS...
...BUT AT CLOSE RANGE, IT IS DEADLY.
WHAT HAPPENED TO THESE MANNEQUINS IS YOUR DESTINY...
... SETSUNA MUDO.

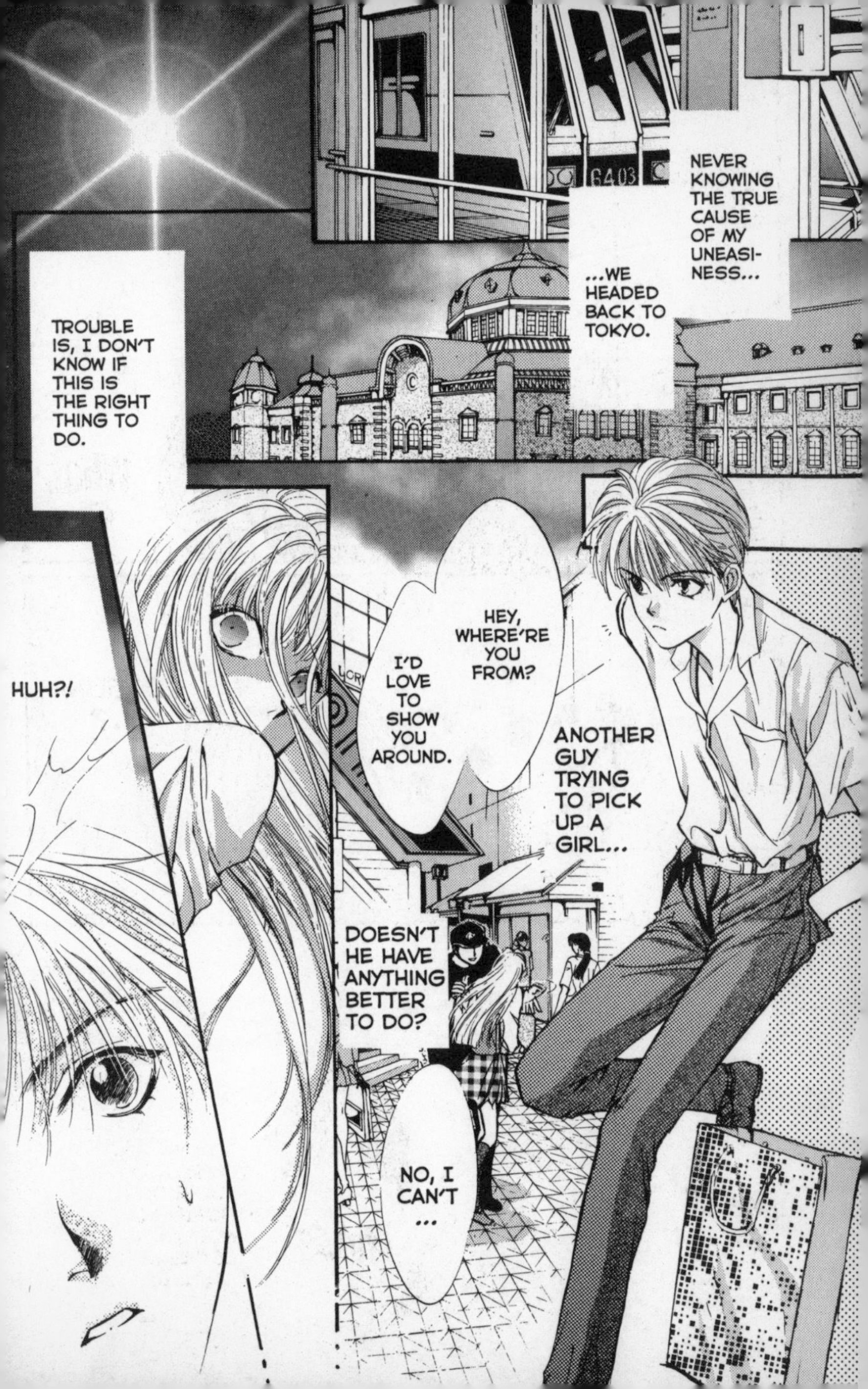
NEVER KNOWING THE TRUE CAUSE OF MY UNEASINESS...
...WE HEADED BACK TO TOKYO.
TROUBLE IS, I DON'T KNOW IF THIS IS THE RIGHT THING TO DO.
HEY, WHERE'RE YOU FROM?
I'D LOVE TO SHOW YOU AROUND.
ANOTHER GUY TRYING TO PICK UP A GIRL...
DOESN'T HE HAVE ANYTHING BETTER TO DO?
NO, I CAN'T ...
HUH?!

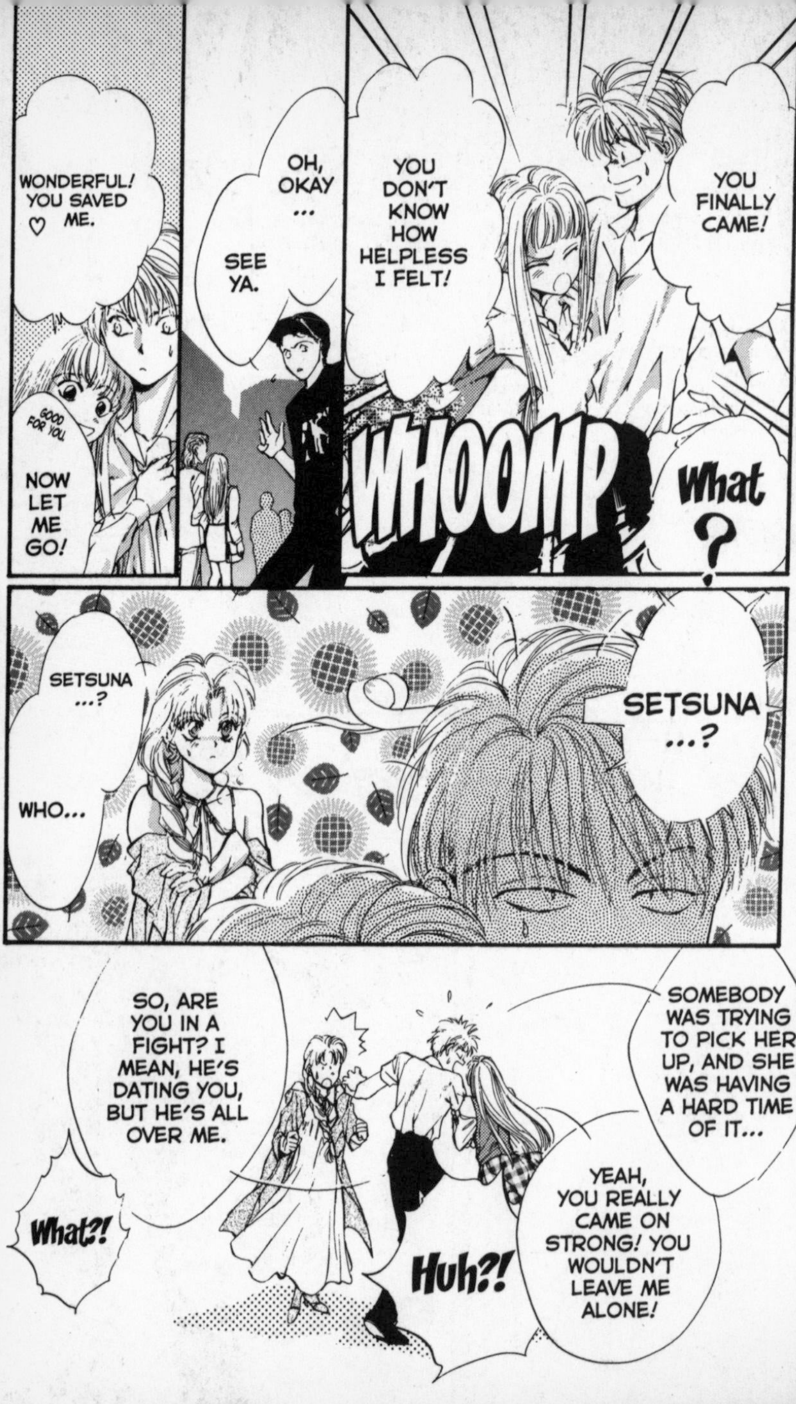
YOU FINALLY CAME!
YOU DON'T KNOW HOW HELPLESS I FELT!
What ?
WHOOMP
OH, OKAY ...
SEE YA.
WONDERFUL! YOU SAVED ME. ♡
GOOD FOR YOU.
NOW LET ME GO!
SETSUNA ...?
SETSUNA ...?
WHO...
SOMEBODY WAS TRYING TO PICK HER UP, AND SHE WAS HAVING A HARD TIME OF IT...
SO, ARE YOU IN A FIGHT? I MEAN, HE'S DATING YOU, BUT HE'S ALL OVER ME.
YEAH, YOU REALLY CAME ON STRONG! YOU WOULDN'T LEAVE ME ALONE!
Huh?!
What?!

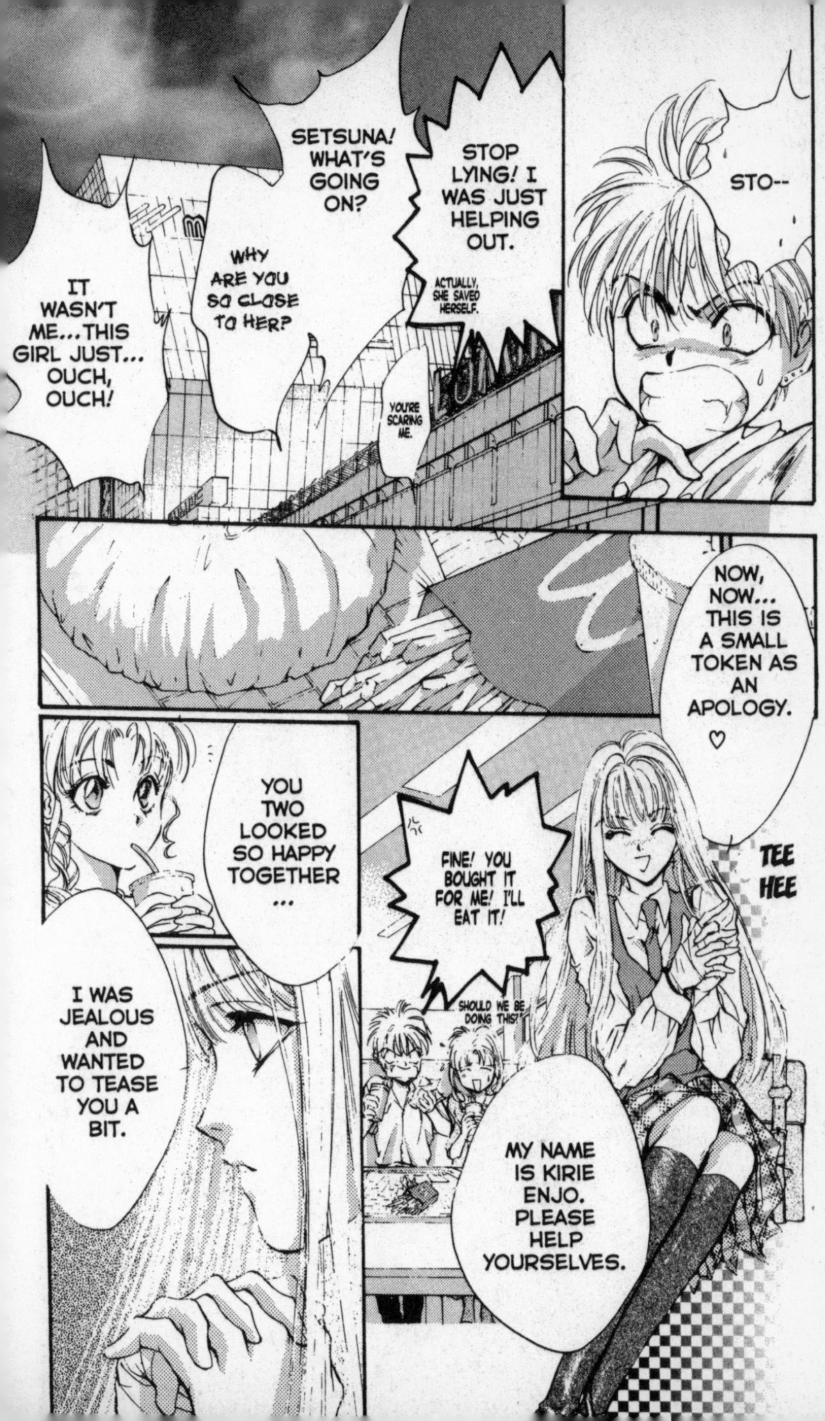
STO--
SETSUNA! WHAT'S GOING ON?
STOP LYING! I WAS JUST HELPING OUT.
ACTUALLY, SHE SAVED HERSELF.
WHY ARE YOU SO CLOSE TO HER?
YOU'RE SCARING ME.
IT WASN'T ME...THIS GIRL JUST... OUCH, OUCH!
NOW, NOW... THIS IS A SMALL TOKEN AS AN APOLOGY. ♡
TEE HEE
FINE! YOU BOUGHT IT FOR ME! I'LL EAT IT!
SHOULD WE BE DOING THIS?
MY NAME IS KIRIE ENJO. PLEASE HELP YOURSELVES.
YOU TWO LOOKED SO HAPPY TOGETHER ...
I WAS JEALOUS AND WANTED TO TEASE YOU A BIT.

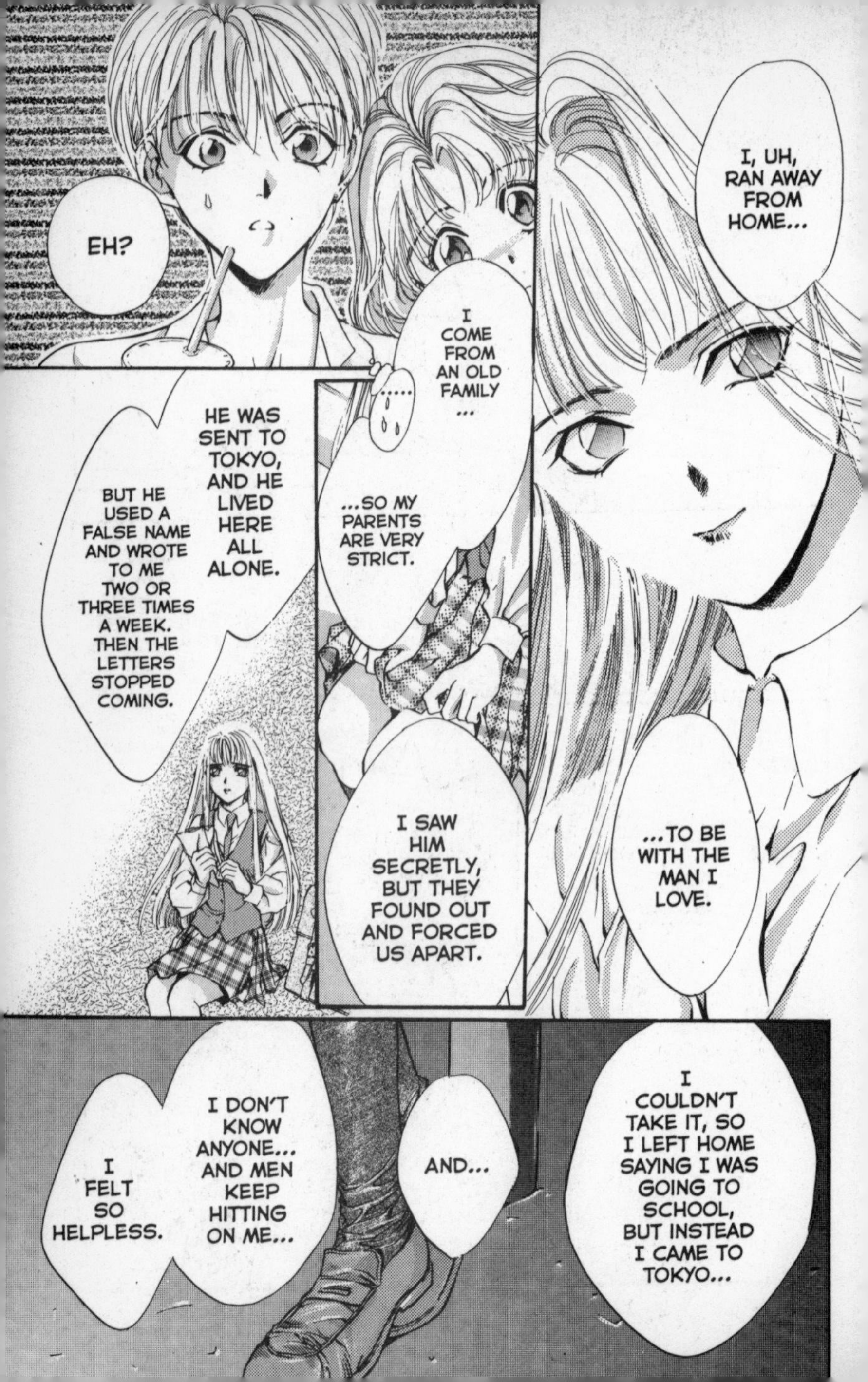

I, UH, RAN AWAY FROM HOME...
EH?
.....
...TO BE WITH THE MAN I LOVE.
I COME FROM AN OLD FAMILY ...
...SO MY PARENTS ARE VERY STRICT.
I SAW HIM SECRETLY, BUT THEY FOUND OUT AND FORCED US APART.
HE WAS SENT TO TOKYO, AND HE LIVED HERE ALL ALONE.
BUT HE USED A FALSE NAME AND WROTE TO ME TWO OR THREE TIMES A WEEK. THEN THE LETTERS STOPPED COMING.
I COULDN'T TAKE IT, SO I LEFT HOME SAYING I WAS GOING TO SCHOOL, BUT INSTEAD I CAME TO TOKYO...
AND...
I DON'T KNOW ANYONE... AND MEN KEEP HITTING ON ME...
I FELT SO HELPLESS.

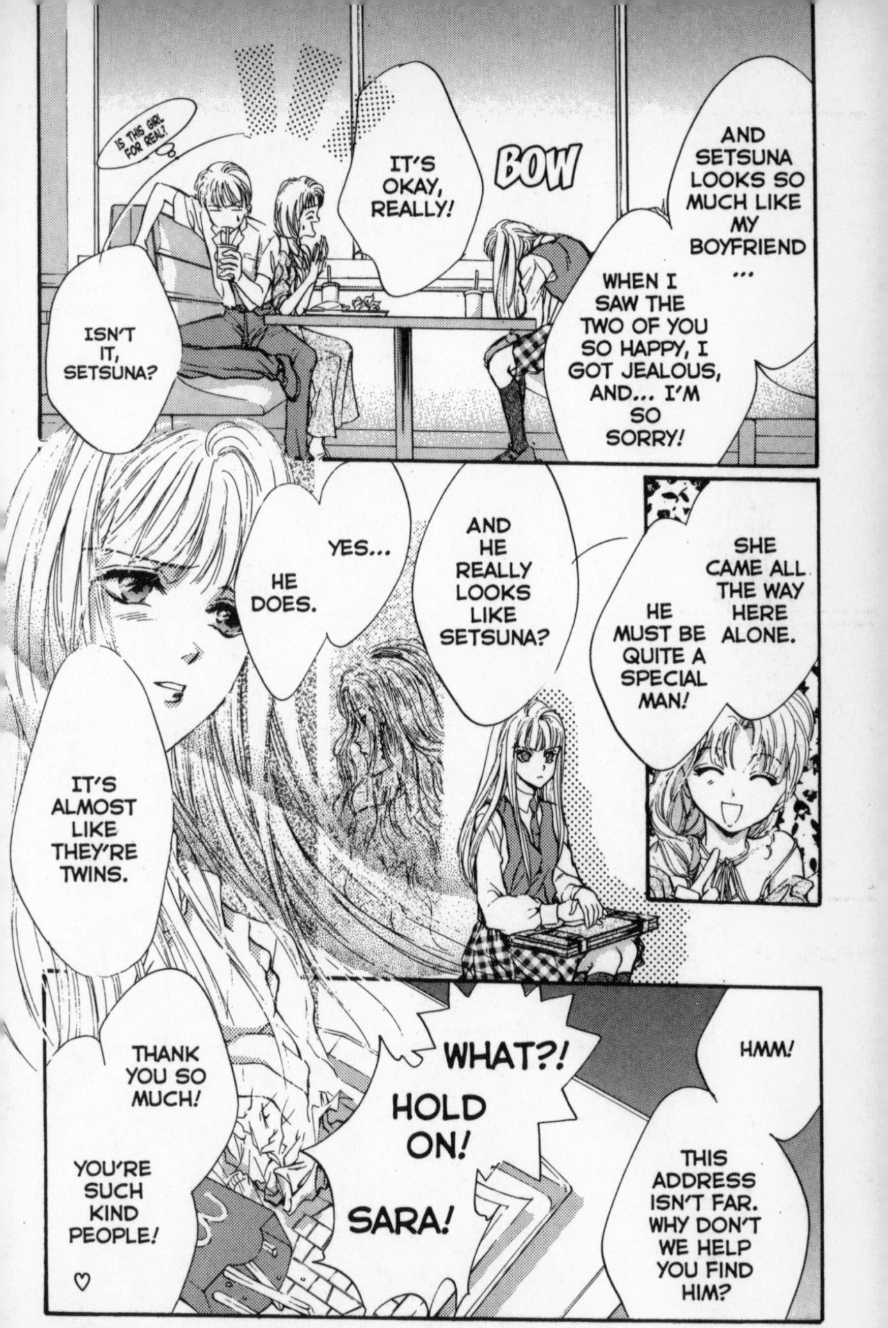
AND SETSUNA LOOKS SO MUCH LIKE MY BOYFRIEND...
WHEN I SAW THE TWO OF YOU SO HAPPY, I GOT JEALOUS, AND... I'M SO SORRY!
BOW
IT'S OKAY, REALLY!
IS THIS GIRL FOR REAL?
ISN'T IT, SETSUNA?
SHE CAME ALL THE WAY HERE ALONE.
HE MUST BE QUITE A SPECIAL MAN!
AND HE REALLY LOOKS LIKE SETSUNA?
YES...
HE DOES.
IT'S ALMOST LIKE THEY'RE TWINS.
HMM!
THIS ADDRESS ISN'T FAR. WHY DON'T WE HELP YOU FIND HIM?
WHAT?!
HOLD ON!
SARA!
THANK YOU SO MUCH!
YOU'RE SUCH KIND PEOPLE! ♡

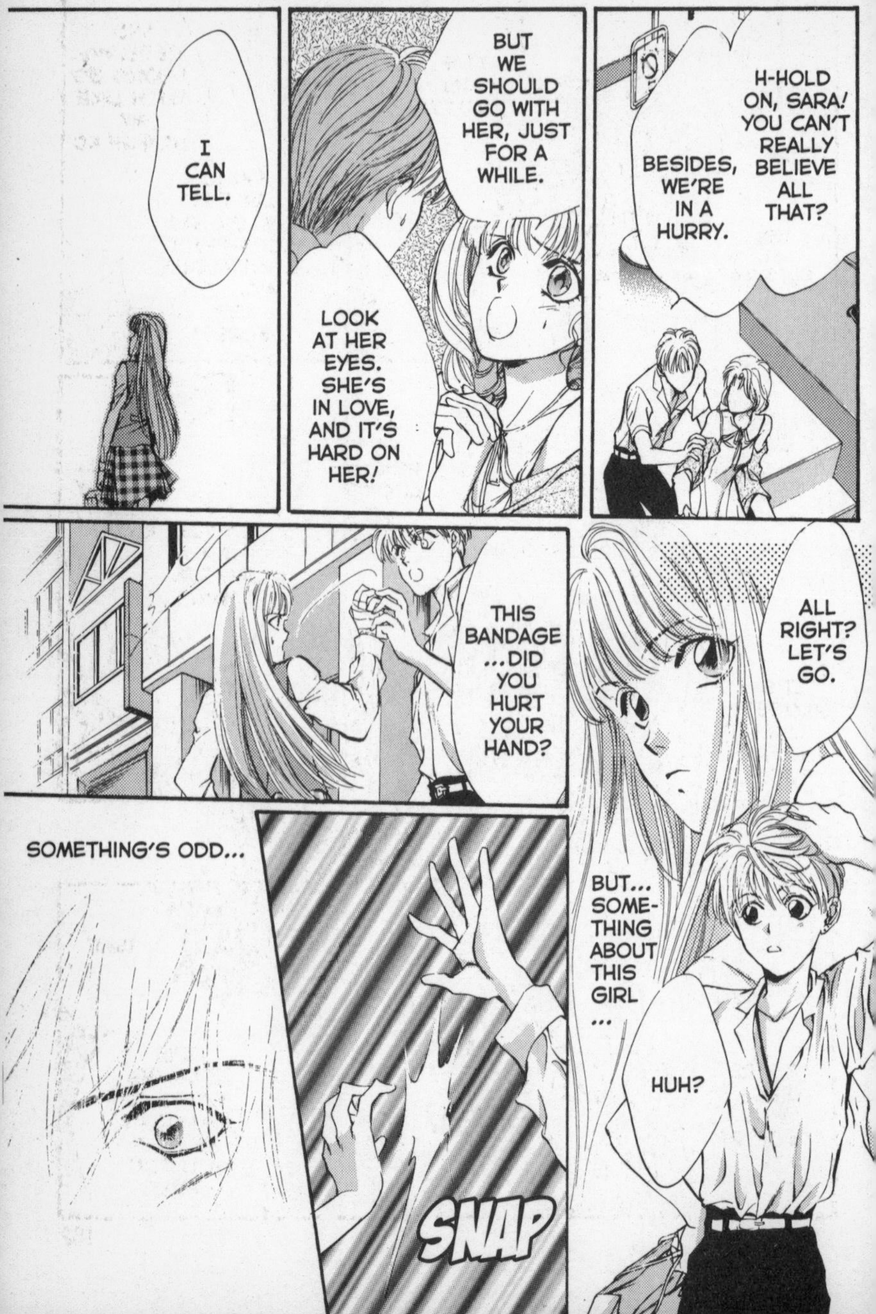
H-HOLD ON, SARA! YOU CAN'T REALLY BELIEVE ALL THAT?
BESIDES, WE'RE IN A HURRY.
BUT WE SHOULD GO WITH HER, JUST FOR A WHILE.
LOOK AT HER EYES. SHE'S IN LOVE, AND IT'S HARD ON HER!
I CAN TELL.
ALL RIGHT? LET'S GO.
BUT... SOMETHING ABOUT THIS GIRL ...
HUH?
THIS BANDAGE ...DID YOU HURT YOUR HAND?
SNAP
SOMETHING'S ODD...

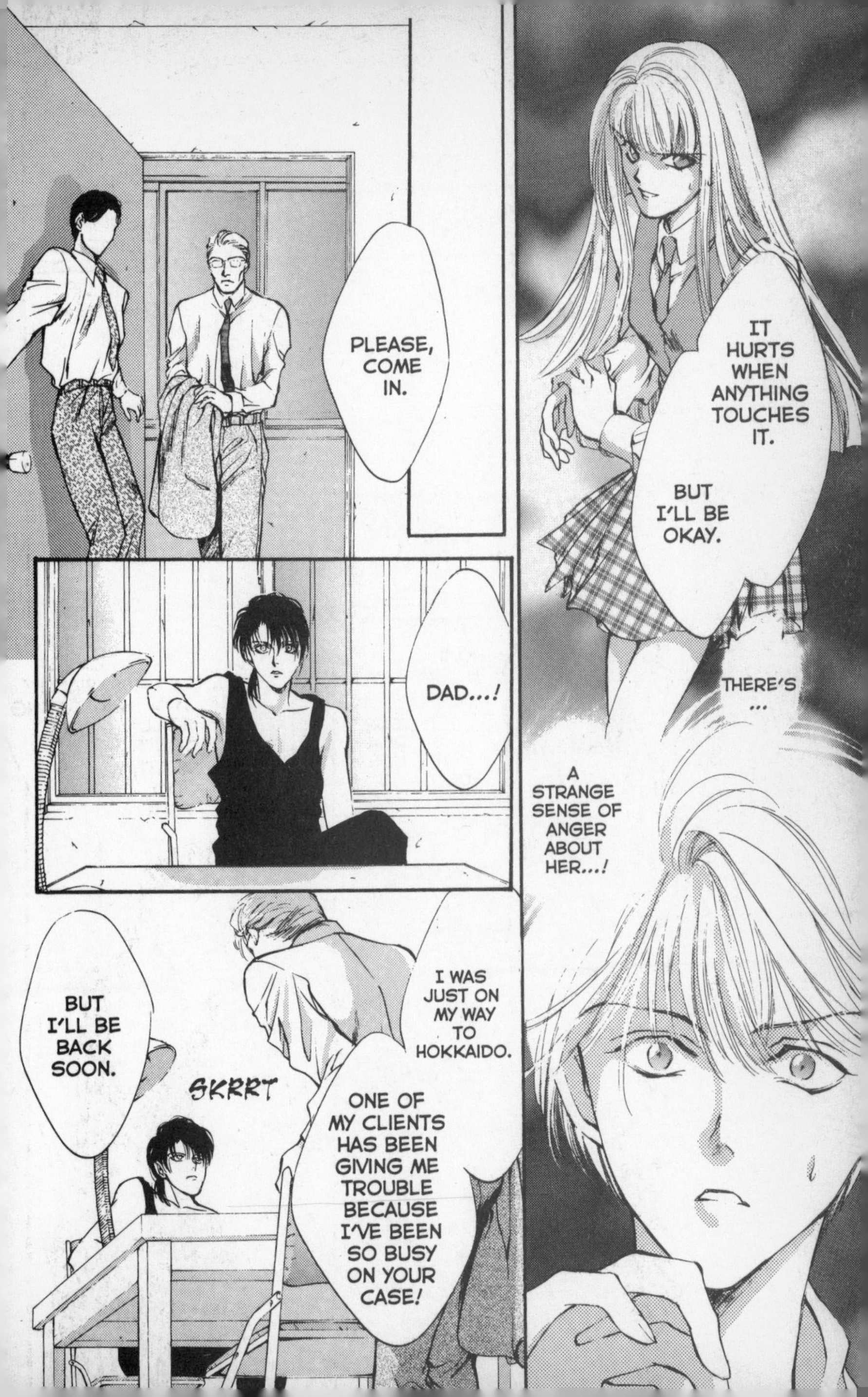
IT HURTS WHEN ANYTHING TOUCHES IT.
BUT I'LL BE OKAY.
THERE'S ...
A STRANGE SENSE OF ANGER ABOUT HER...!
PLEASE, COME IN.
DAD...!
I WAS JUST ON MY WAY TO HOKKAIDO.
ONE OF MY CLIENTS HAS BEEN GIVING ME TROUBLE BECAUSE I'VE BEEN SO BUSY ON YOUR CASE!
SKRRT
BUT I'LL BE BACK SOON.

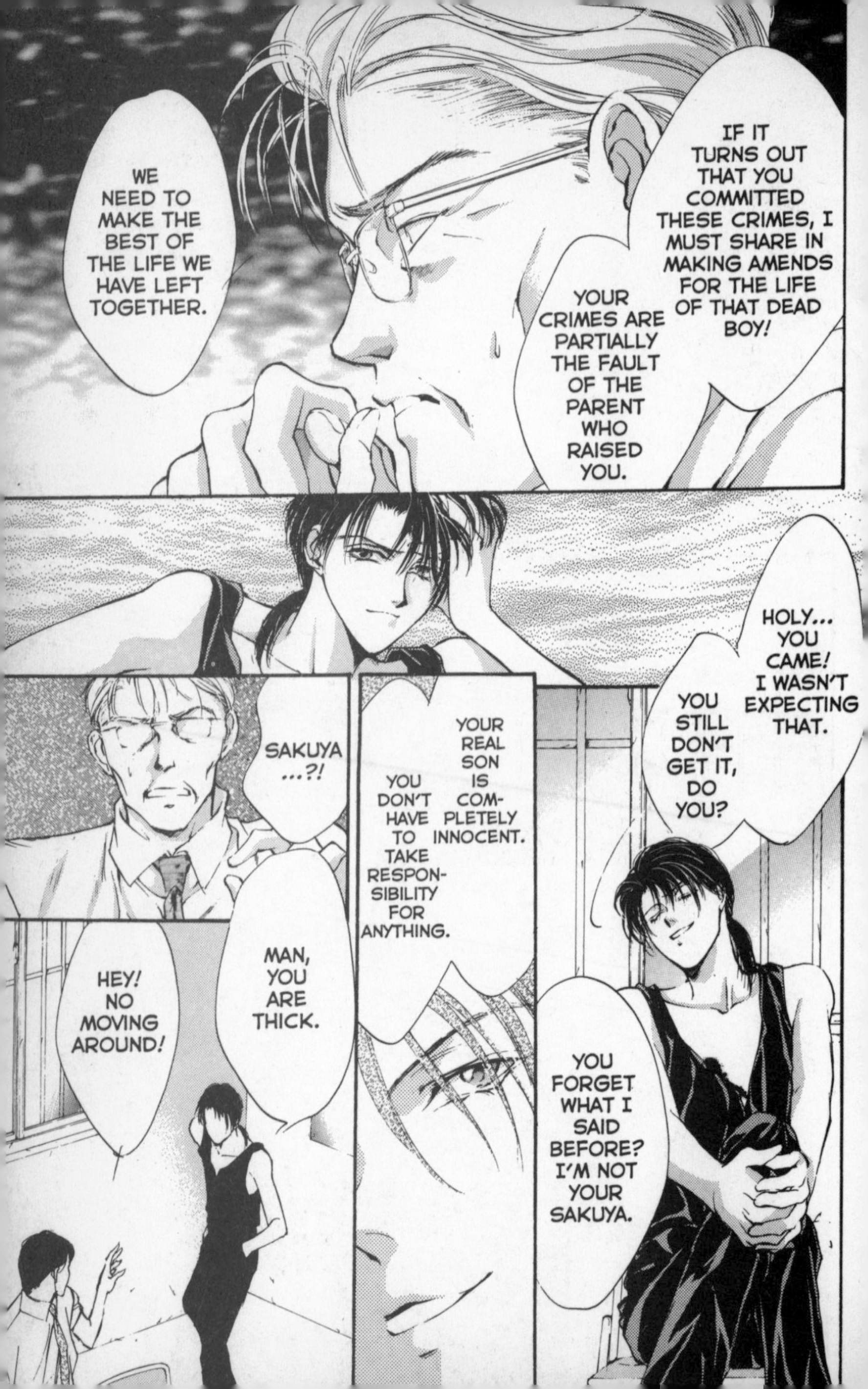
IF IT TURNS OUT THAT YOU COMMITTED THESE CRIMES, I MUST SHARE IN MAKING AMENDS FOR THE LIFE OF THAT DEAD BOY!
YOUR CRIMES ARE PARTIALLY THE FAULT OF THE PARENT WHO RAISED YOU.
WE NEED TO MAKE THE BEST OF THE LIFE WE HAVE LEFT TOGETHER.
HOLY... YOU CAME! I WASN'T EXPECTING THAT.
YOU STILL DON'T GET IT, DO YOU?
YOU FORGET WHAT I SAID BEFORE? I'M NOT YOUR SAKUYA.
YOUR REAL SON IS COM-PLETELY INNOCENT.
YOU DON'T HAVE TO TAKE RESPON-SIBILITY FOR ANYTHING.
SAKUYA ...?!
MAN, YOU ARE THICK.
HEY! NO MOVING AROUND!

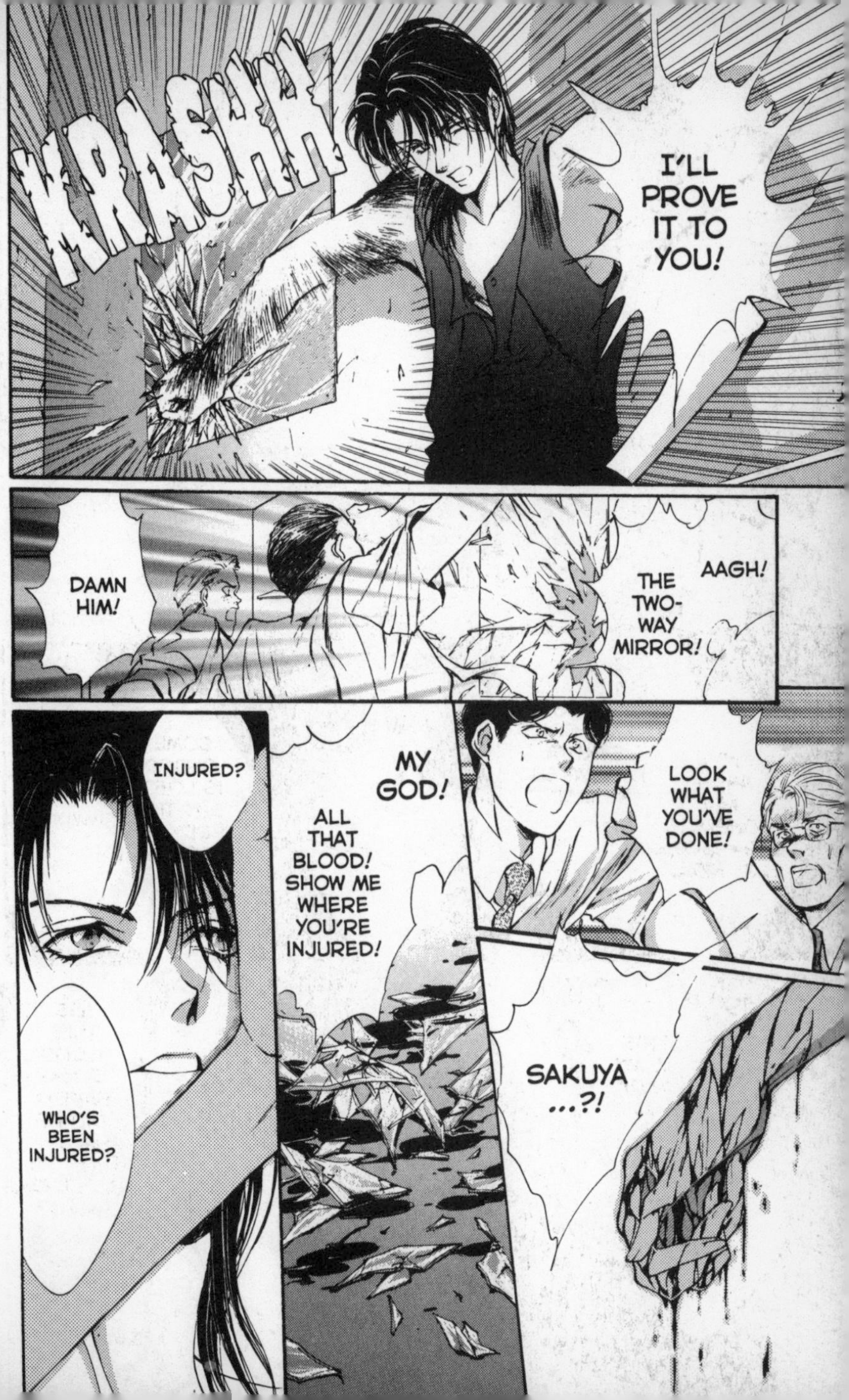
I'LL PROVE IT TO YOU!
KRASHH
AAGH!
THE TWO-WAY MIRROR!
DAMN HIM!
LOOK WHAT YOU'VE DONE!
MY GOD!
ALL THAT BLOOD! SHOW ME WHERE YOU'RE INJURED!
SAKUYA ...?!
INJURED?
WHO'S BEEN INJURED?

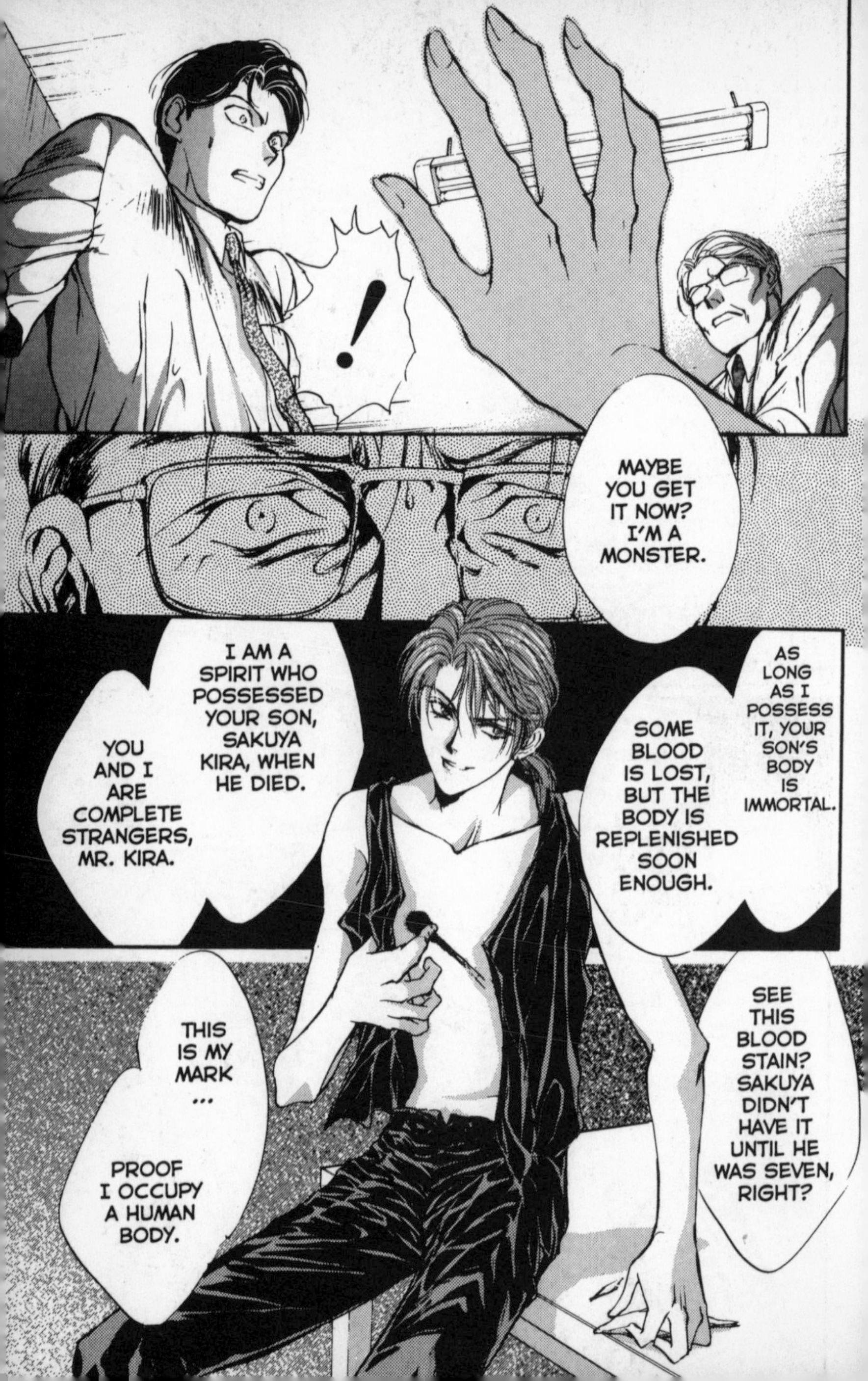
!
MAYBE YOU GET IT NOW? I'M A MONSTER.
AS LONG AS I POSSESS IT, YOUR SON'S BODY IS IMMORTAL.
SOME BLOOD IS LOST, BUT THE BODY IS REPLENISHED SOON ENOUGH.
I AM A SPIRIT WHO POSSESSED YOUR SON, SAKUYA KIRA, WHEN HE DIED.
YOU AND I ARE COMPLETE STRANGERS, MR. KIRA.
SEE THIS BLOOD STAIN? SAKUYA DIDN'T HAVE IT UNTIL HE WAS SEVEN, RIGHT?
THIS IS MY MARK ...
PROOF I OCCUPY A HUMAN BODY.

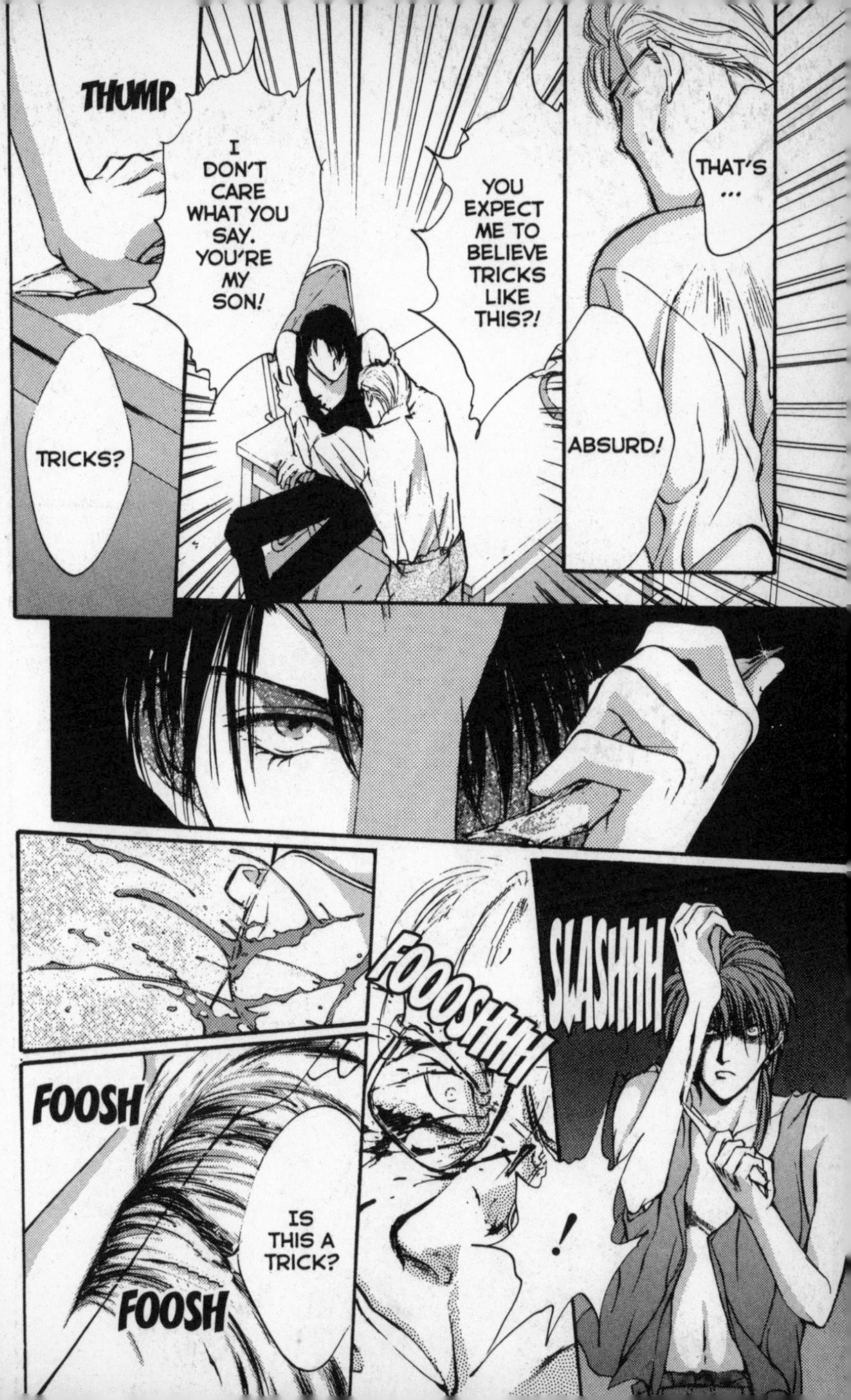
THAT'S...
ABSURD!
YOU EXPECT ME TO BELIEVE TRICKS LIKE THIS?!
I DON'T CARE WHAT YOU SAY. YOU'RE MY SON!
THUMP
TRICKS?
SLASHHH
FOOOSHHH
!
FOOSH
IS THIS A TRICK?
FOOSH

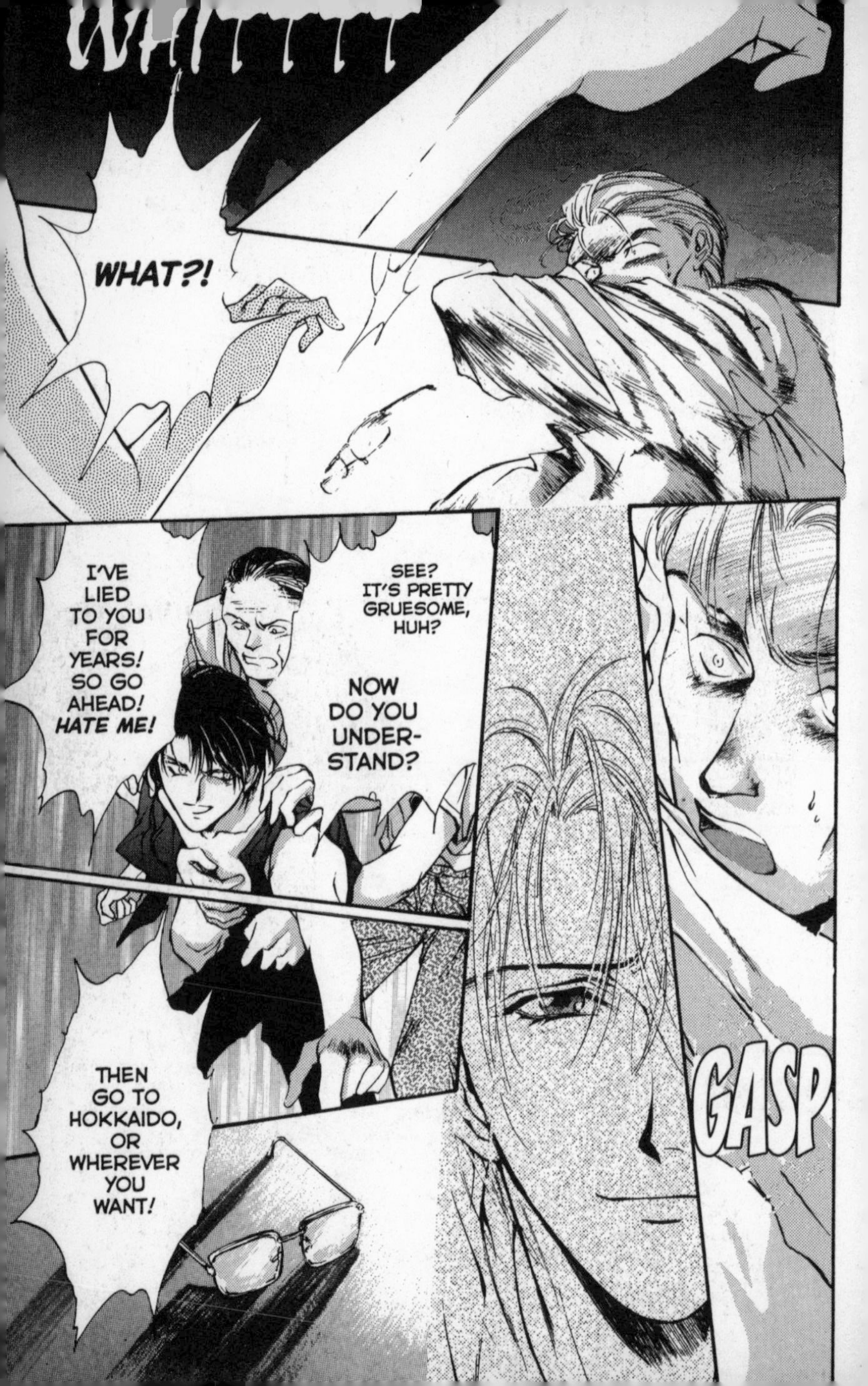
WHAT?!
GASP
SEE? IT'S PRETTY GRUESOME, HUH?
NOW DO YOU UNDER-STAND?
I'VE LIED TO YOU FOR YEARS! SO GO AHEAD! *HATE ME!*
THEN GO TO HOKKAIDO, OR WHEREVER YOU WANT!

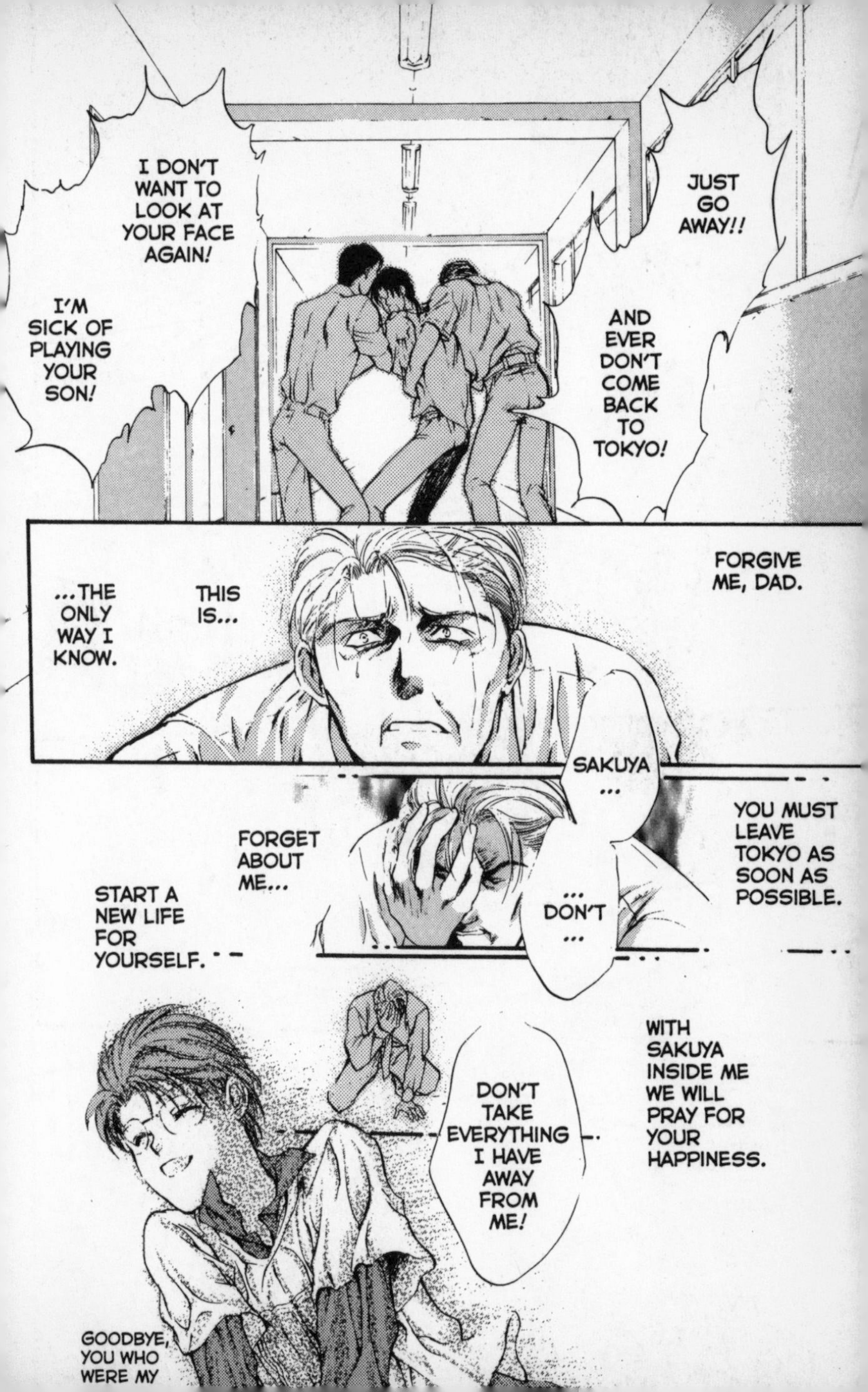
JUST GO AWAY!!
AND EVER DON'T COME BACK TO TOKYO!
I DON'T WANT TO LOOK AT YOUR FACE AGAIN!
I'M SICK OF PLAYING YOUR SON!
FORGIVE ME, DAD.
THIS IS...
...THE ONLY WAY I KNOW.
SAKUYA ...
YOU MUST LEAVE TOKYO AS SOON AS POSSIBLE.
... DON'T ...
FORGET ABOUT ME...
START A NEW LIFE FOR YOURSELF.
WITH SAKUYA INSIDE ME WE WILL PRAY FOR YOUR HAPPINESS.
DON'T TAKE EVERYTHING I HAVE AWAY FROM ME!
GOODBYE, YOU WHO WERE MY

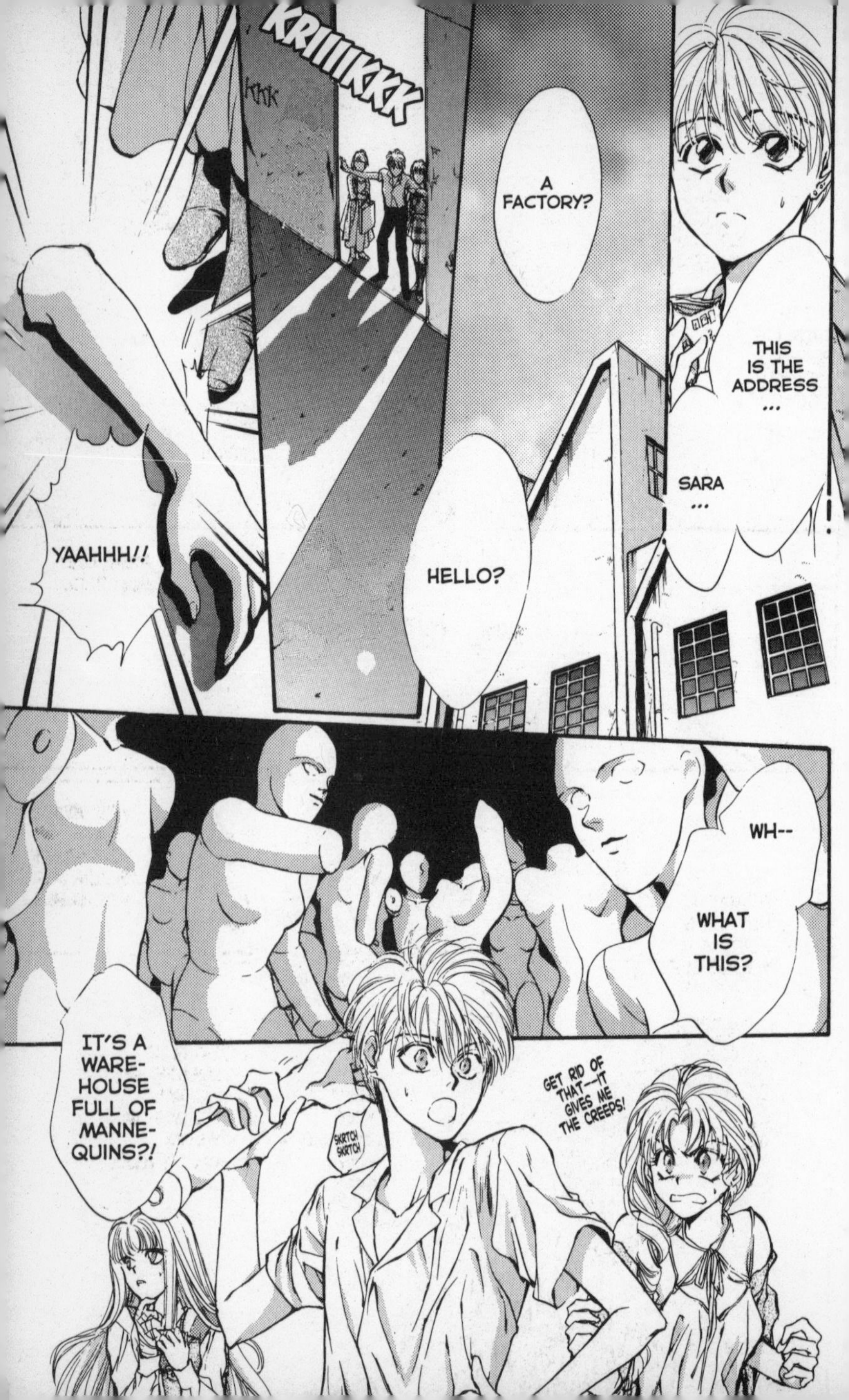

A FACTORY?
THIS IS THE ADDRESS ...
SARA ...
HELLO?
KRIIIIKKK
KKK
YAAHHH!!
WH--
WHAT IS THIS?
GET RID OF THAT--IT GIVES ME THE CREEPS!
SKRTCH SKRTCH
IT'S A WARE-HOUSE FULL OF MANNE-QUINS?!

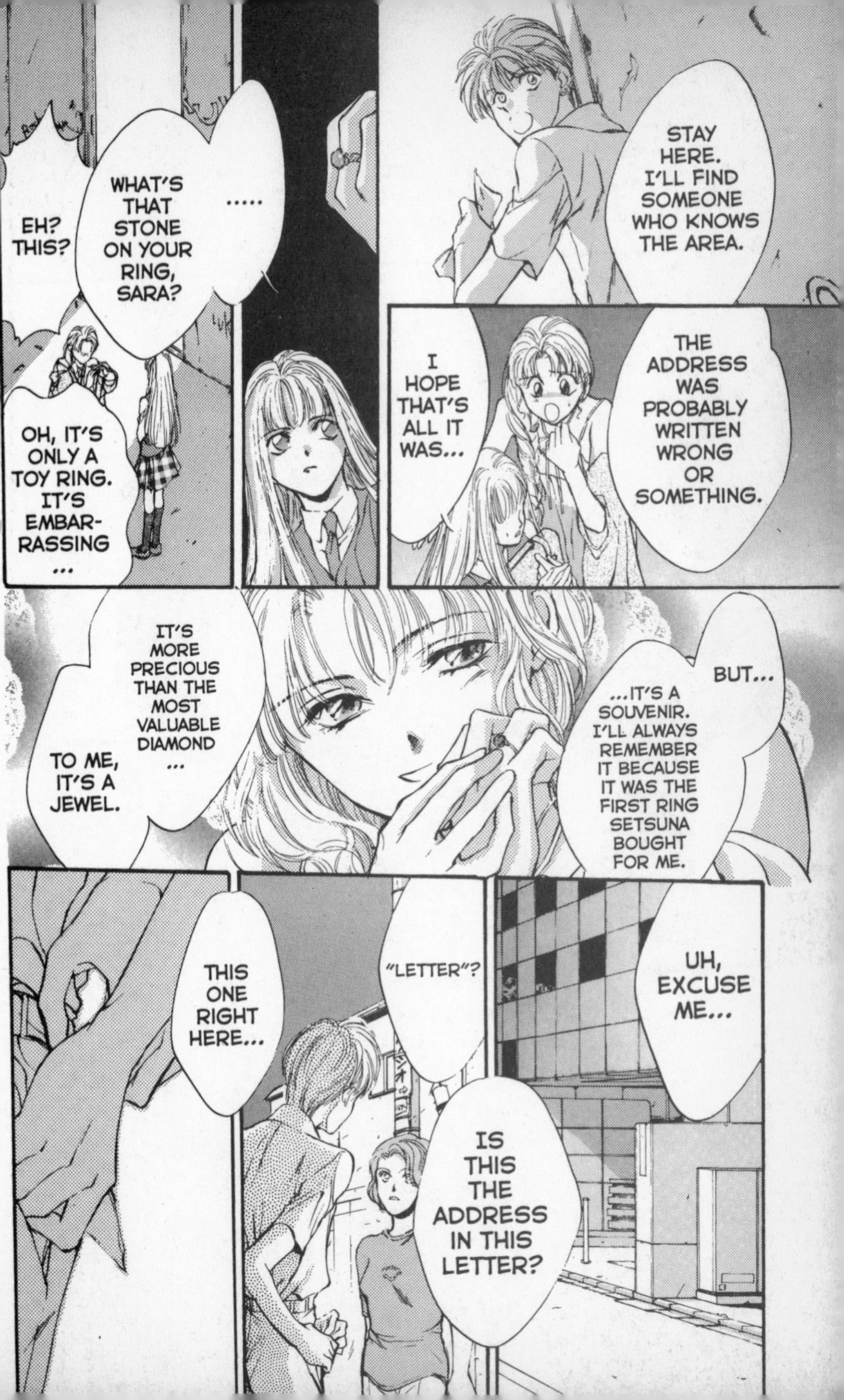
STAY HERE. I'LL FIND SOMEONE WHO KNOWS THE AREA.
THE ADDRESS WAS PROBABLY WRITTEN WRONG OR SOMETHING.
I HOPE THAT'S ALL IT WAS...
.....
WHAT'S THAT STONE ON YOUR RING, SARA?
EH? THIS?
OH, IT'S ONLY A TOY RING. IT'S EMBARRASSING...
BUT...
...IT'S A SOUVENIR. I'LL ALWAYS REMEMBER IT BECAUSE IT WAS THE FIRST RING SETSUNA BOUGHT FOR ME.
IT'S MORE PRECIOUS THAN THE MOST VALUABLE DIAMOND...
TO ME, IT'S A JEWEL.
UH, EXCUSE ME...
IS THIS THE ADDRESS IN THIS LETTER?
"LETTER"?
THIS ONE RIGHT HERE...

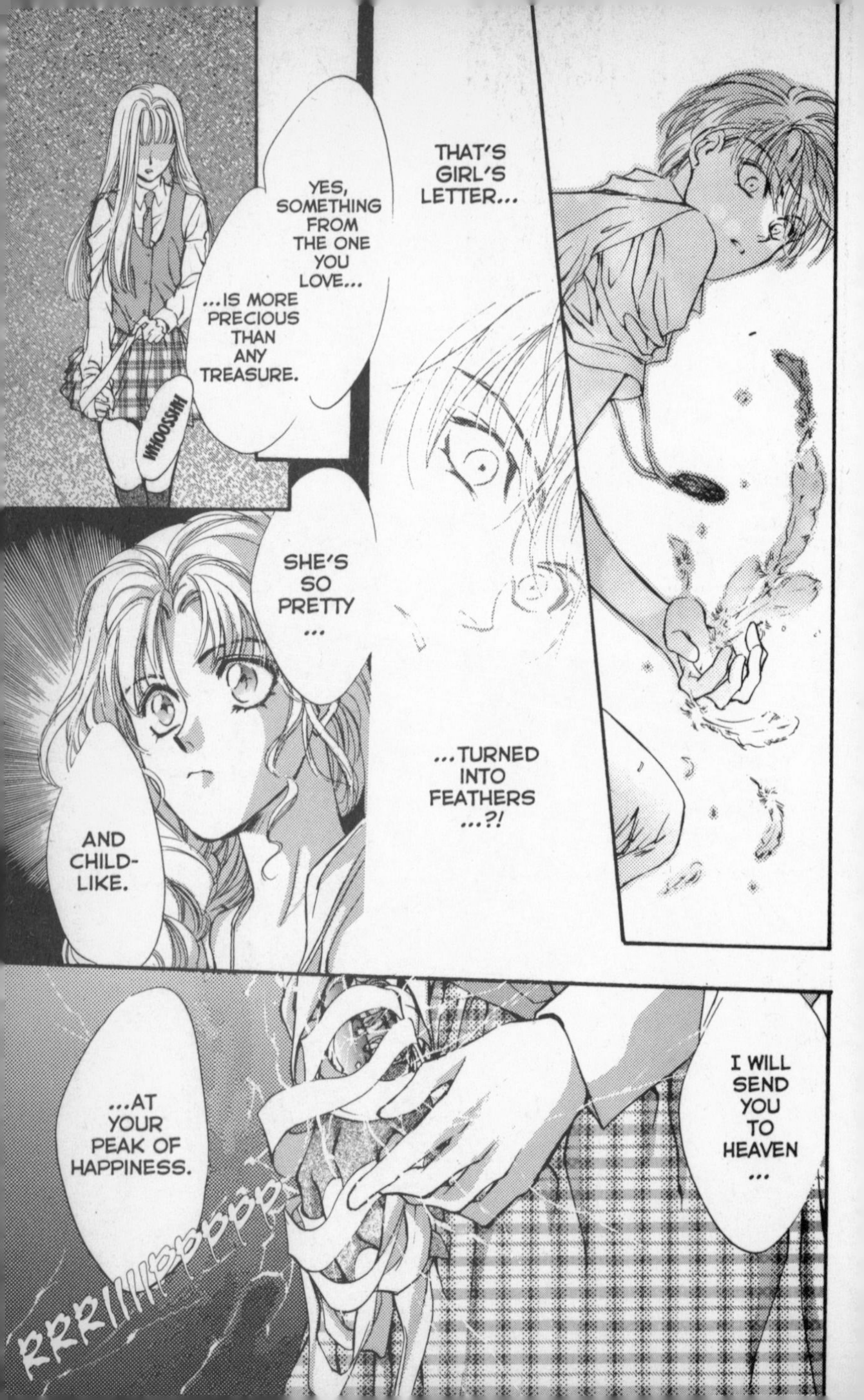
THAT'S GIRL'S LETTER...
...TURNED INTO FEATHERS...?!
YES, SOMETHING FROM THE ONE YOU LOVE...
...IS MORE PRECIOUS THAN ANY TREASURE.
WHOOSSH
SHE'S SO PRETTY...
AND CHILD-LIKE.
I WILL SEND YOU TO HEAVEN...
...AT YOUR PEAK OF HAPPINESS.
RRRIIIIPPPPP

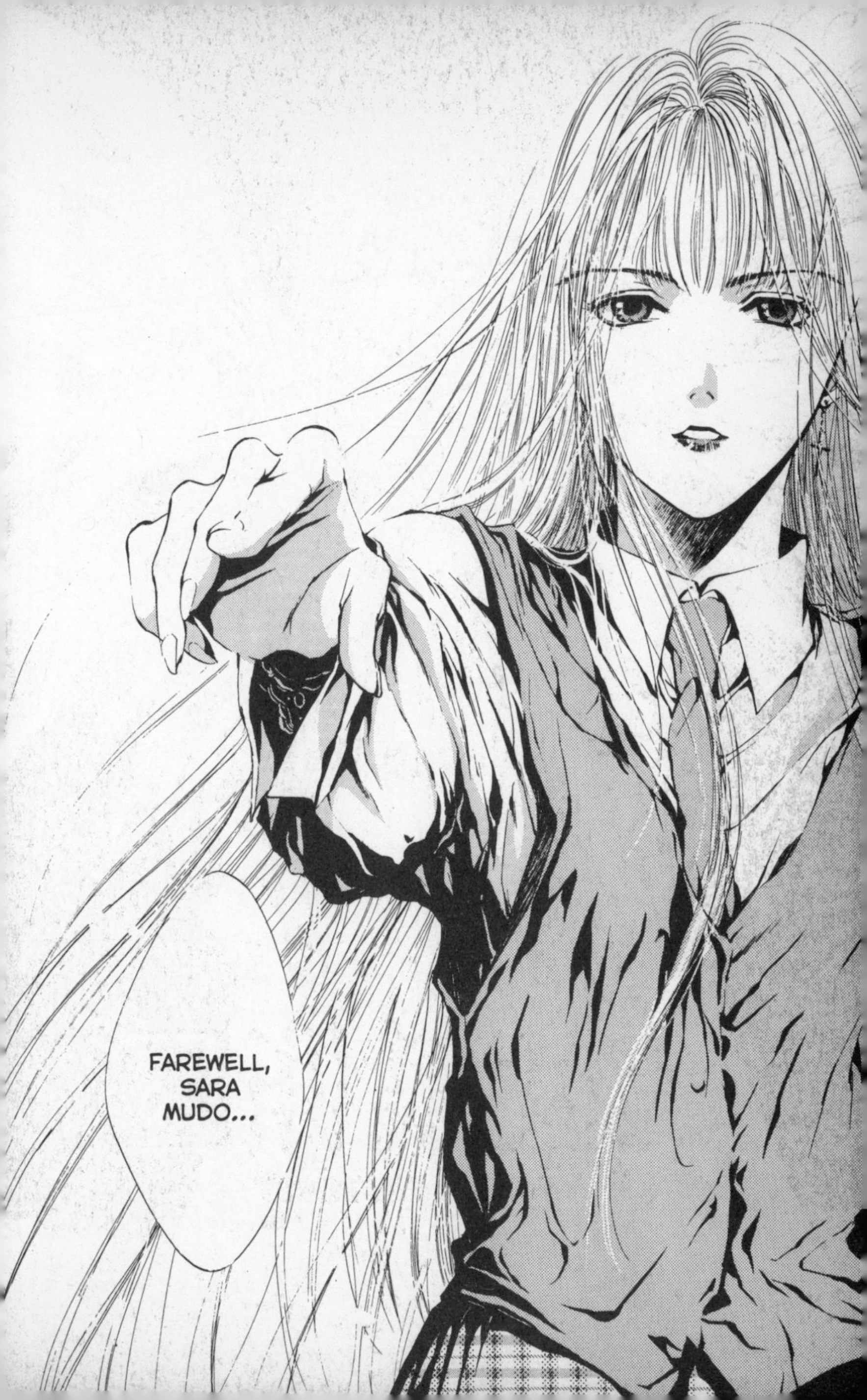
FAREWELL, SARA MUDO...

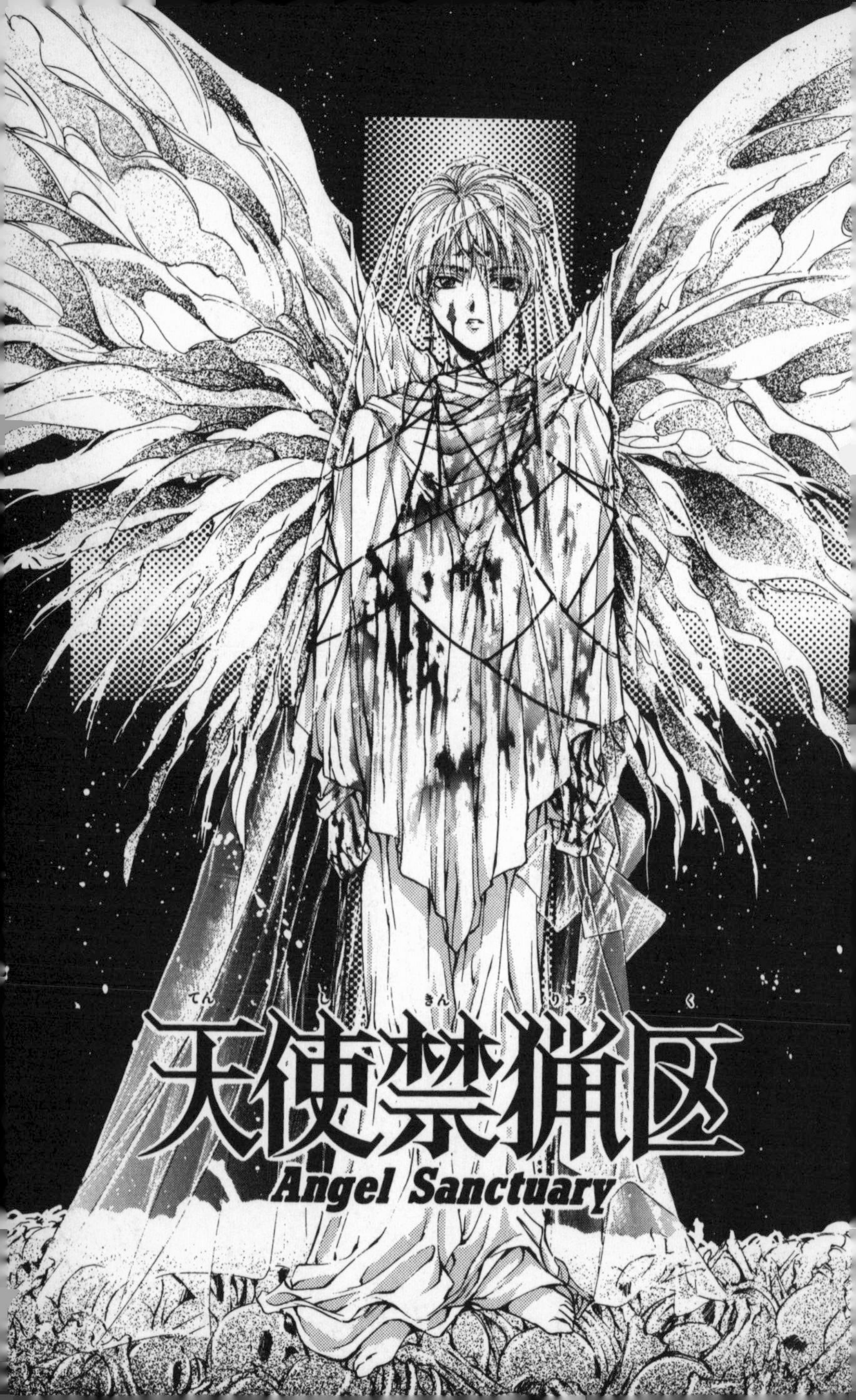
天使禁猟区
Angel Sanctuary

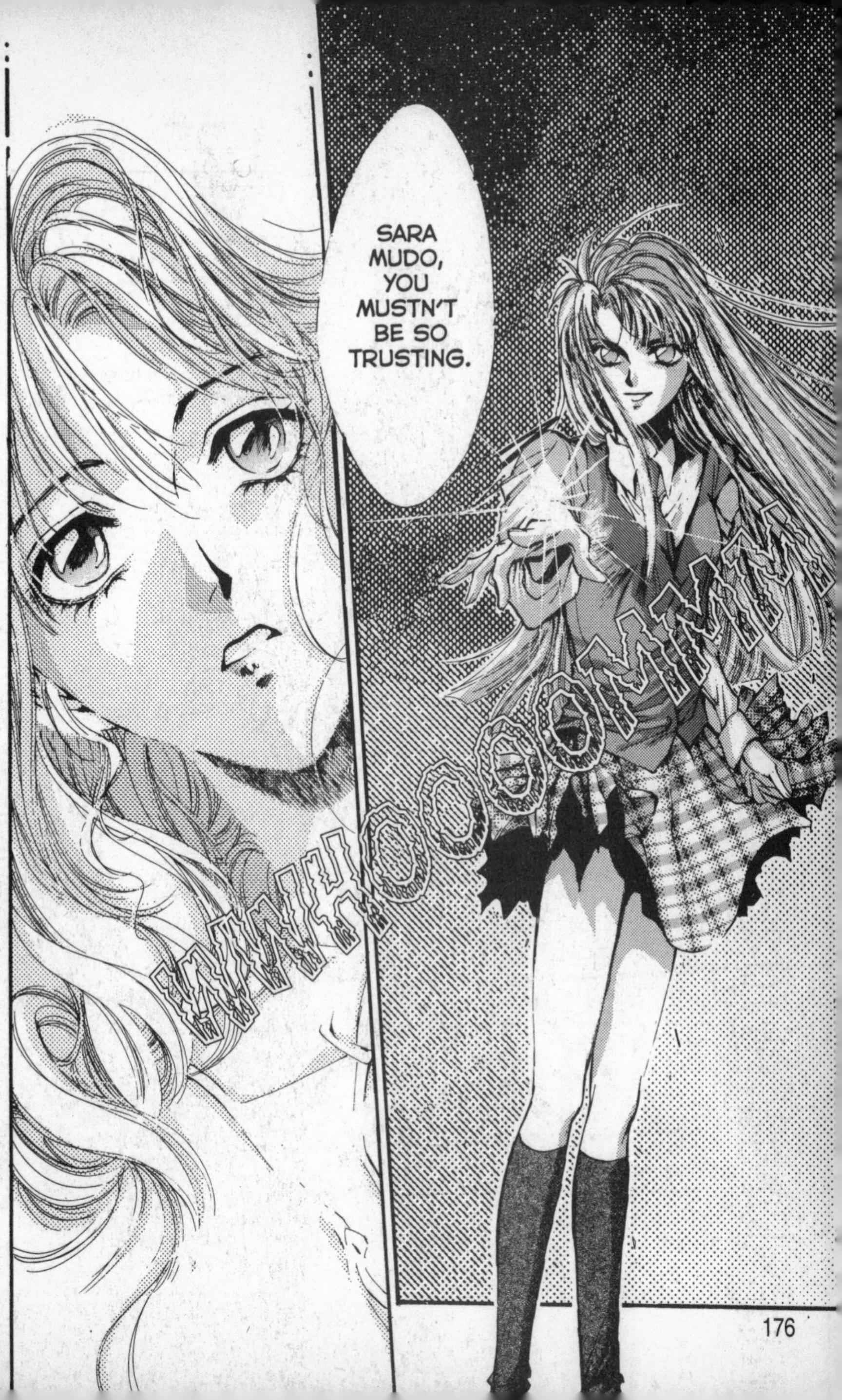
SARA MUDO, YOU MUSTN'T BE SO TRUSTING.
WWWHOOOOOOMMMM

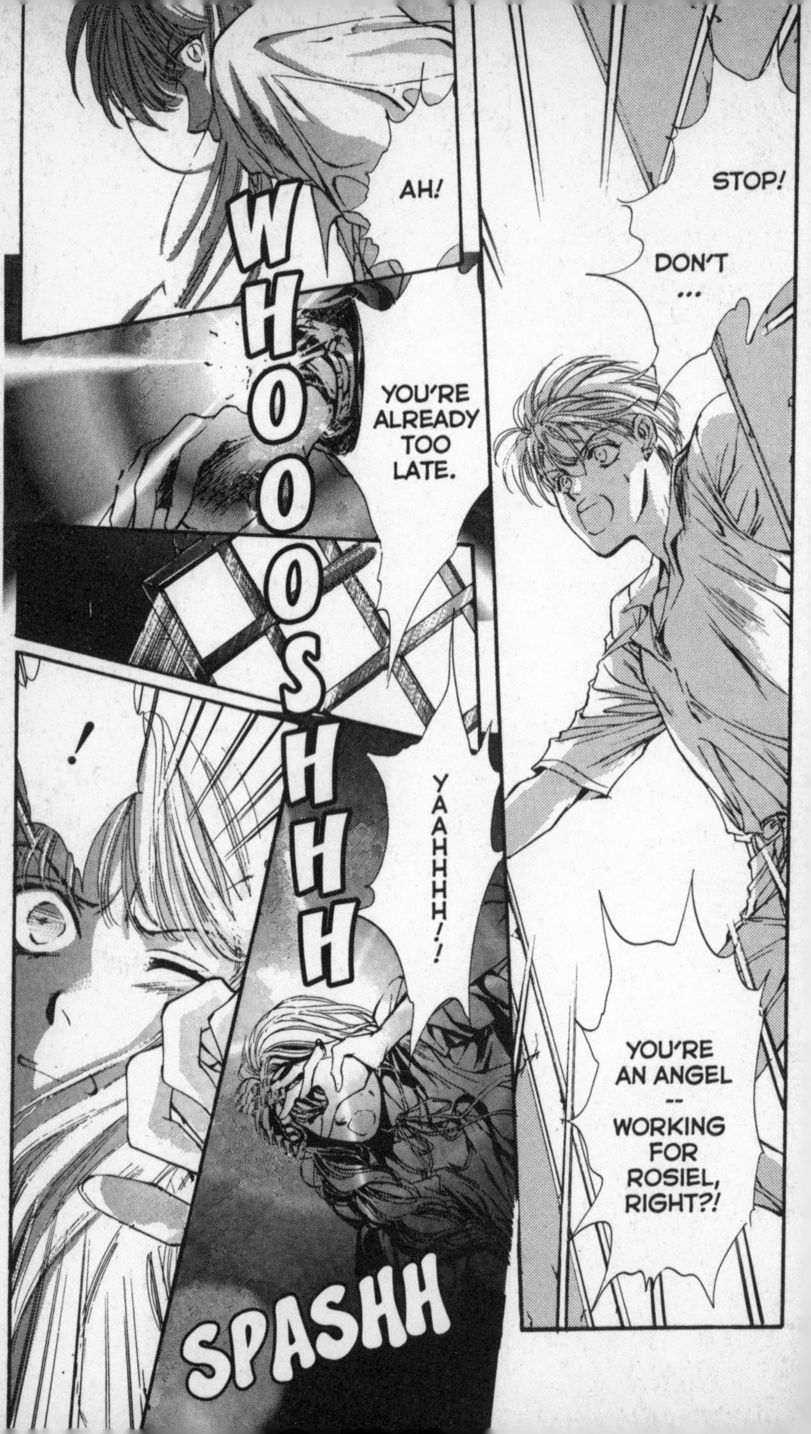
STOP!
DON'T ...
YOU'RE AN ANGEL -- WORKING FOR ROSIEL, RIGHT?!
AH!
WHOOOOSHHHH
YOU'RE ALREADY TOO LATE.
YAAHHHH!!
!
SPASHH

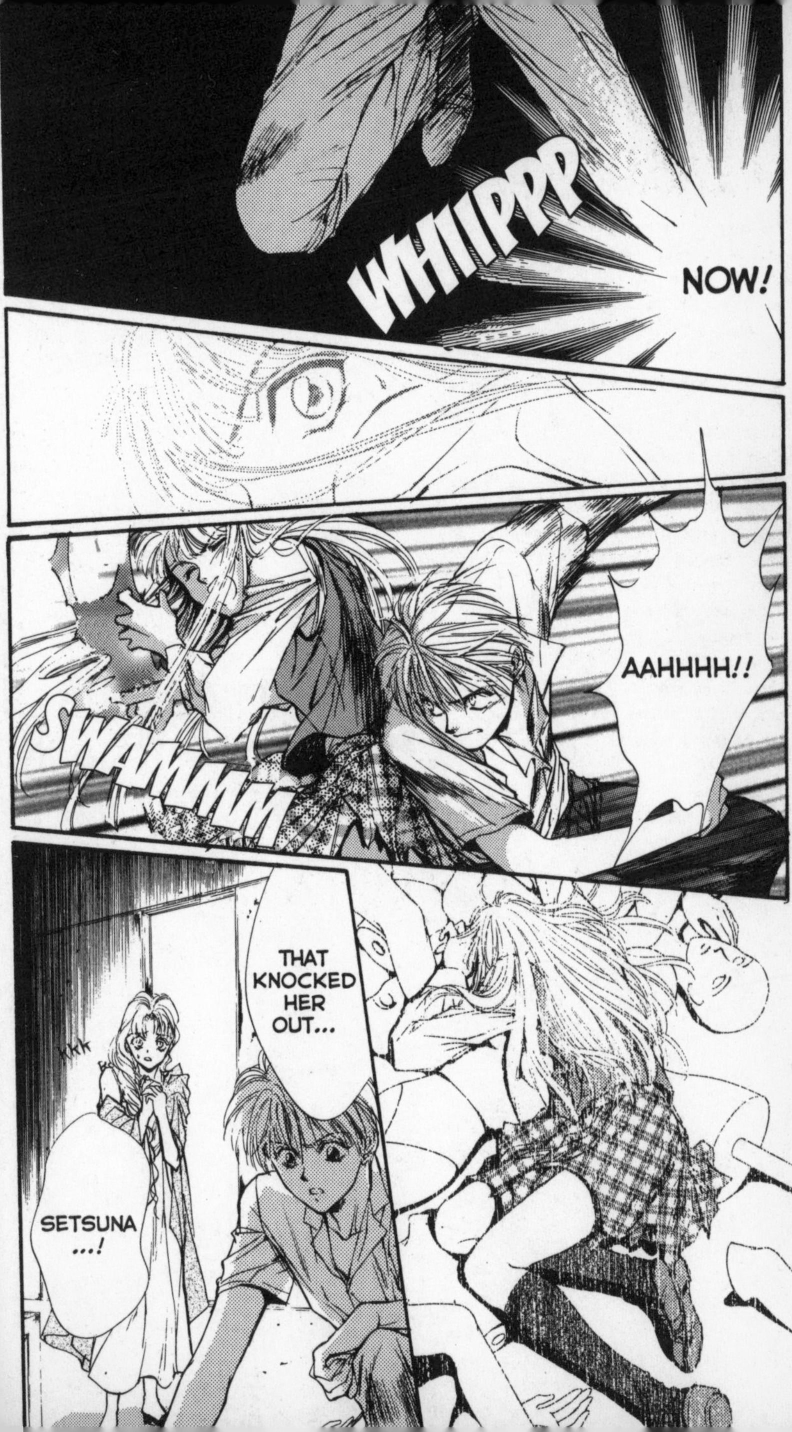
WHIIPPP
NOW!
AAHHHH!!
SWAMMMM
THAT KNOCKED HER OUT...
kkk
SETSUNA ...!

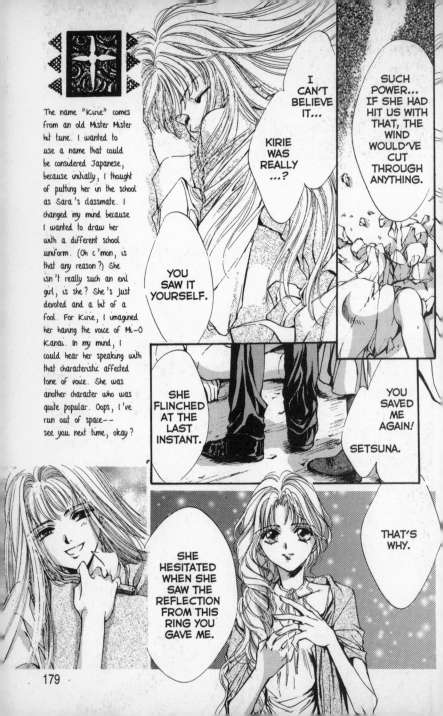

The name "Kirie" comes from an old Mister Mister hit tune. I wanted to use a name that could be considered Japanese, because initially, I thought of putting her in the school as Sara's classmate. I changed my mind because I wanted to draw her with a different school uniform. (Oh c'mon, is that any reason?) She isn't really such an evil girl, is she? She's just devoted and a bit of a fool. For Kirie, I imagined her having the voice of Mi-O Kanai. In my mind, I could hear her speaking with that characteristic affected tone of voice. She was another character who was quite popular. Oops, I've run out of space--
see you next time, okay?

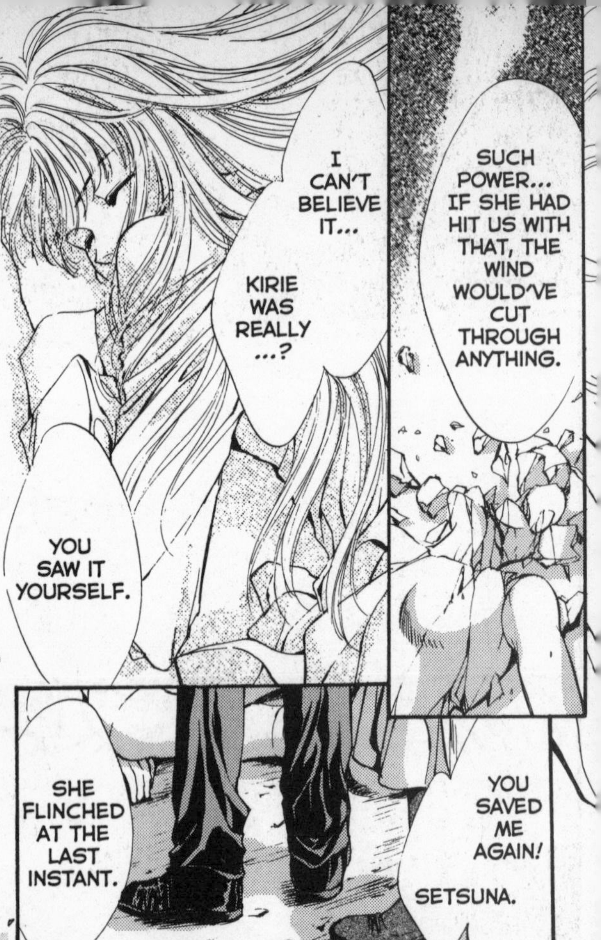
SUCH POWER... IF SHE HAD HIT US WITH THAT, THE WIND WOULD'VE CUT THROUGH ANYTHING.
I CAN'T BELIEVE IT...
KIRIE WAS REALLY ...?
YOU SAW IT YOURSELF.
YOU SAVED ME AGAIN!
SETSUNA.
SHE FLINCHED AT THE LAST INSTANT.

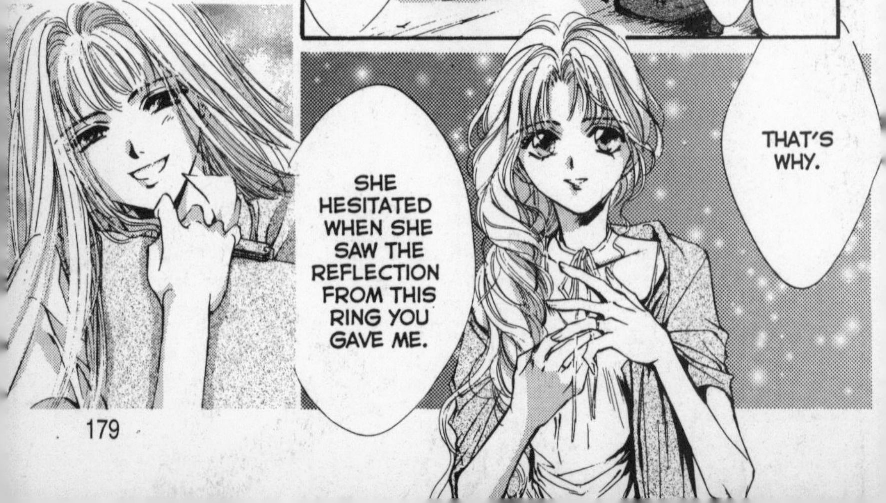
THAT'S WHY.
SHE HESITATED WHEN SHE SAW THE REFLECTION FROM THIS RING YOU GAVE ME.

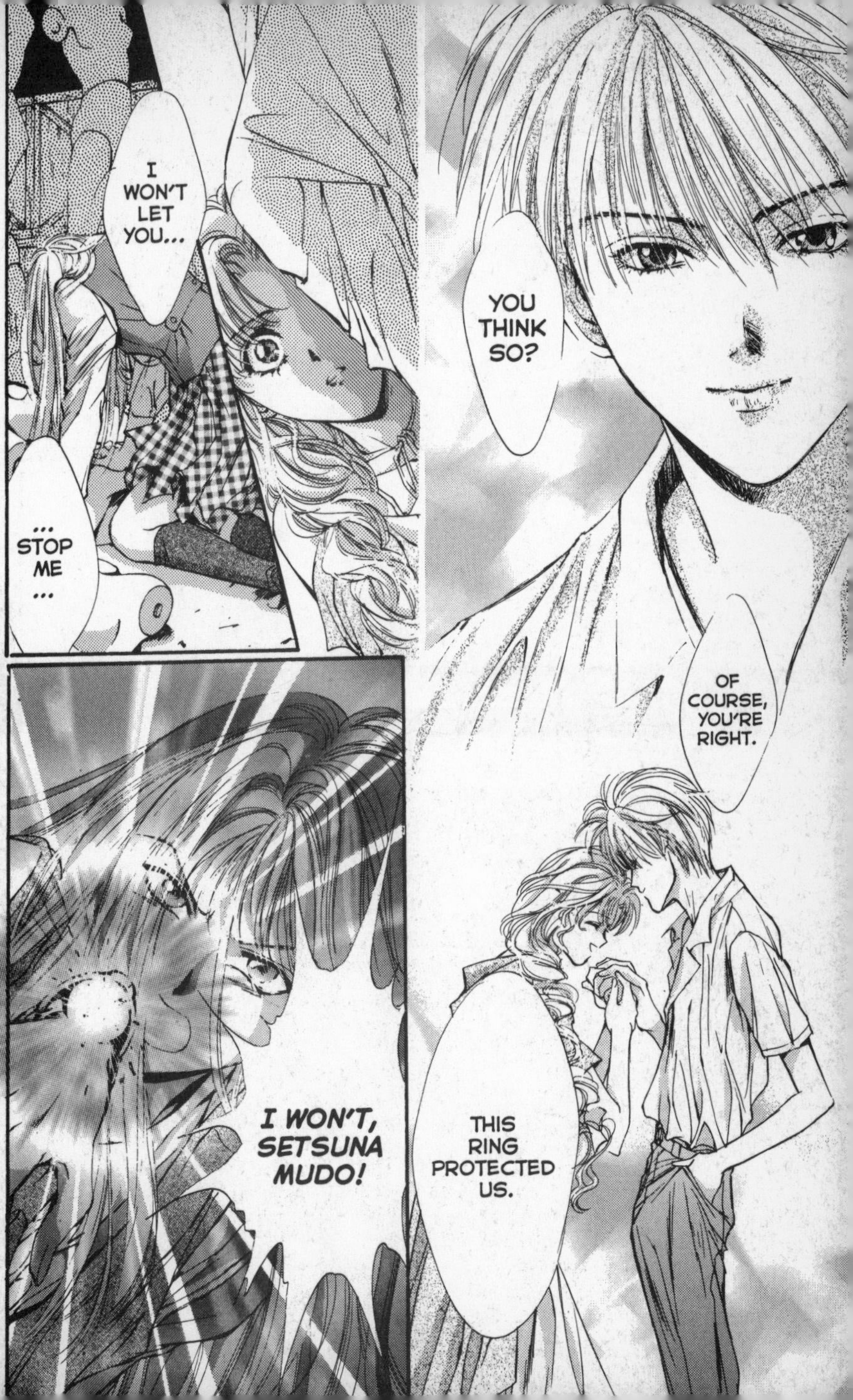
YOU THINK SO?
OF COURSE, YOU'RE RIGHT.
THIS RING PROTECTED US.
I WON'T LET YOU...
...STOP ME...
I WON'T, SETSUNA MUDO!

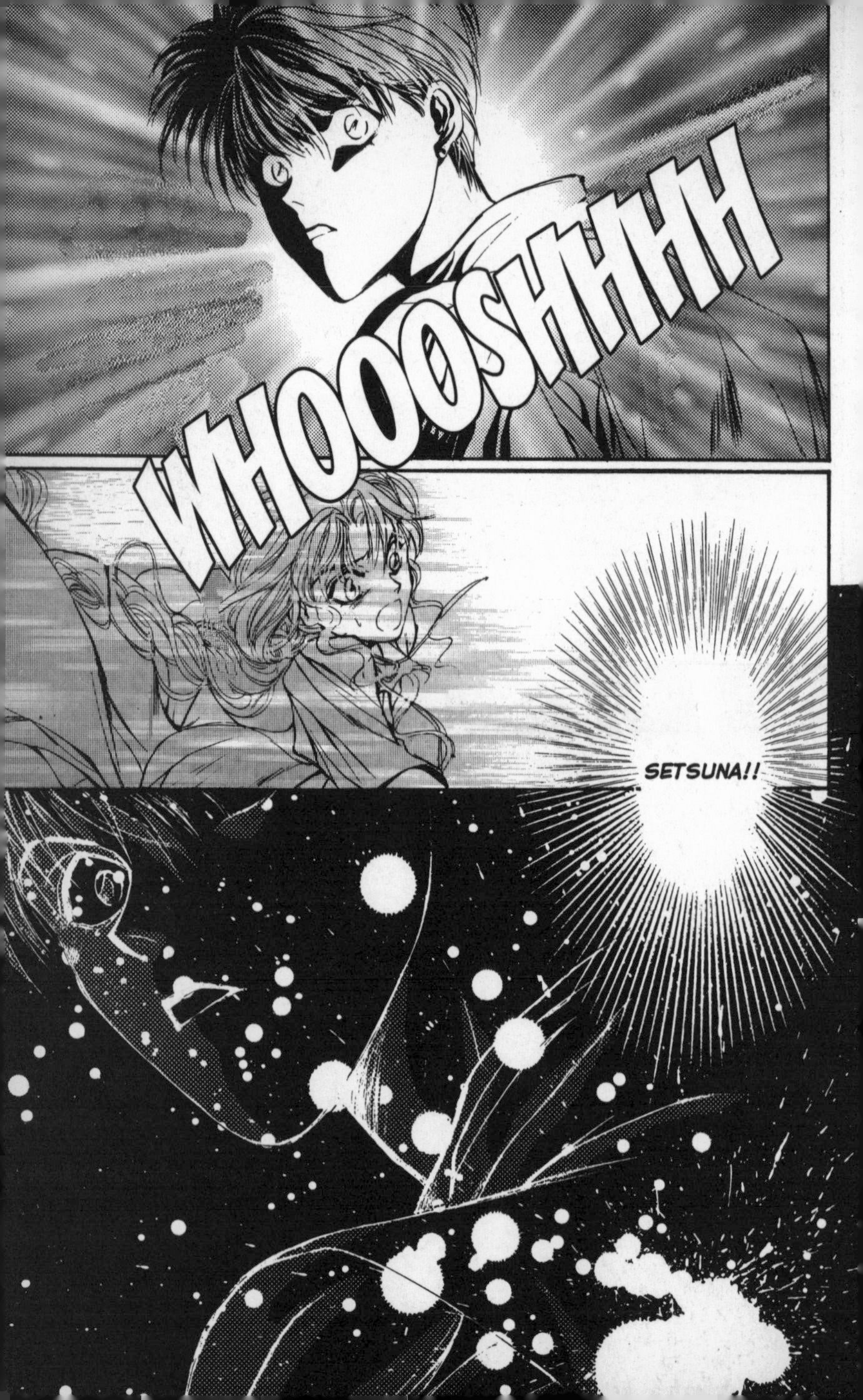
WHOOOSHHHH
SETSUNA!!

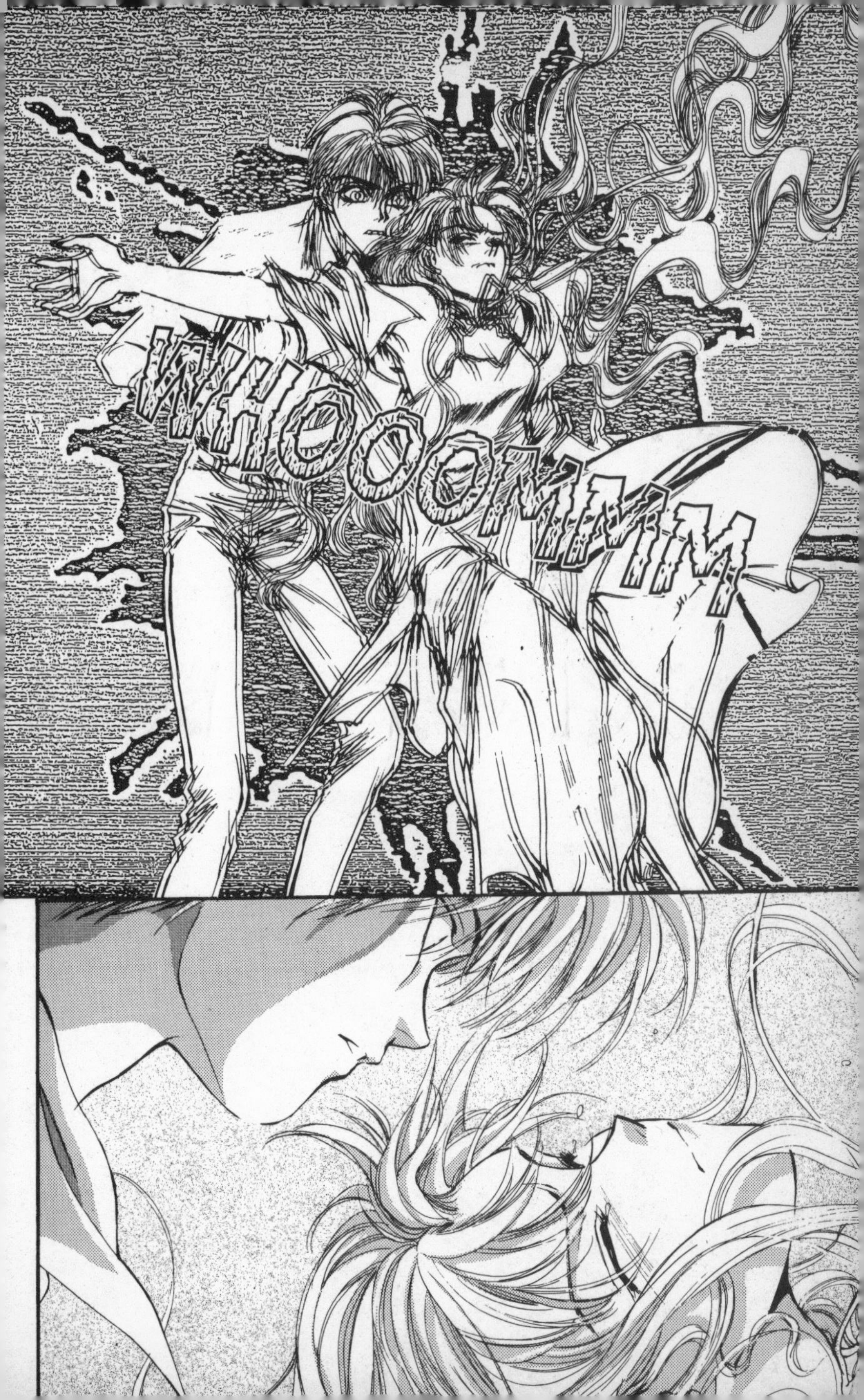
WHOOOOMMM

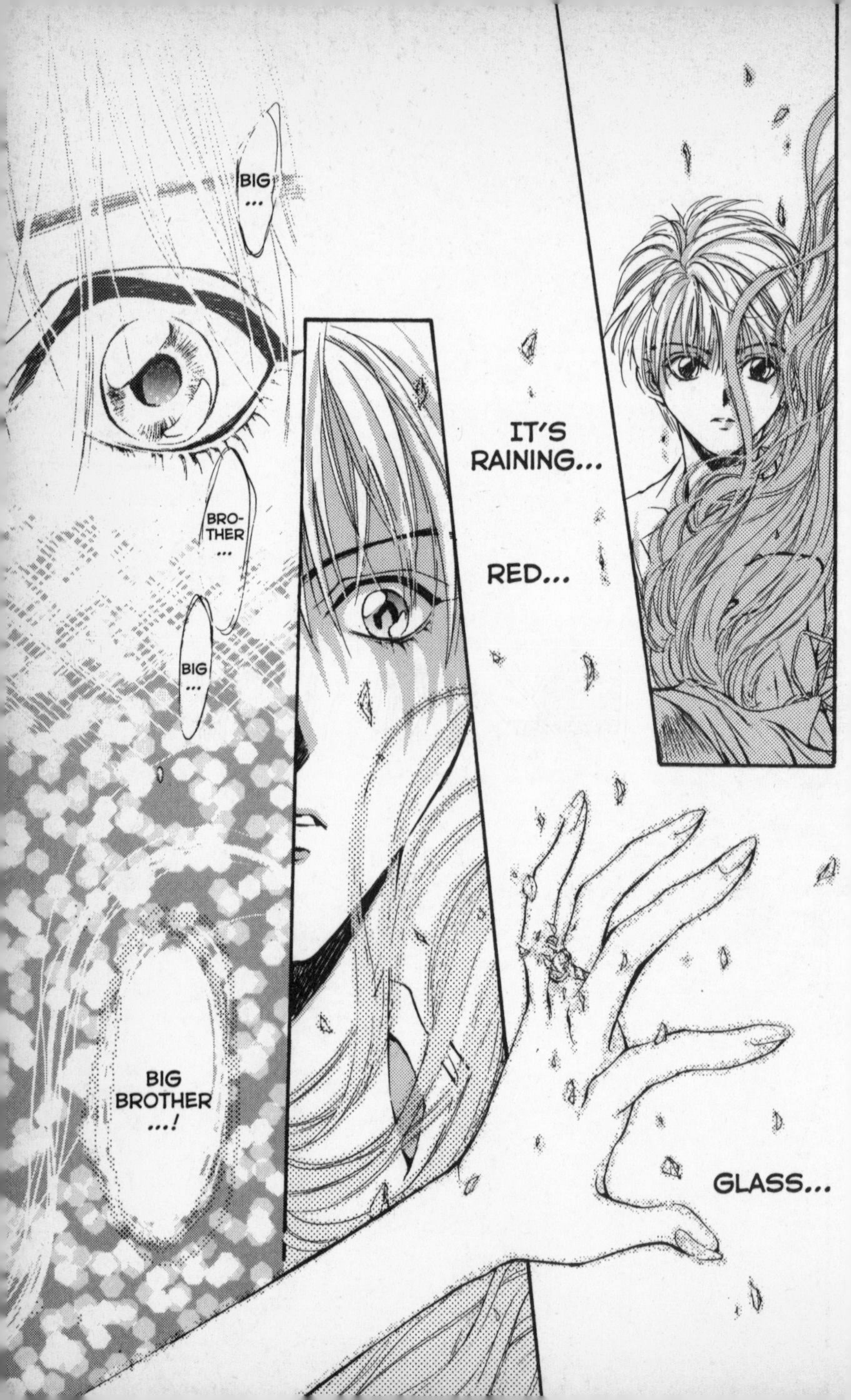
IT'S RAINING...
RED...
GLASS...
BIG ...
BROTHER ...
BIG ...
BIG BROTHER ...!

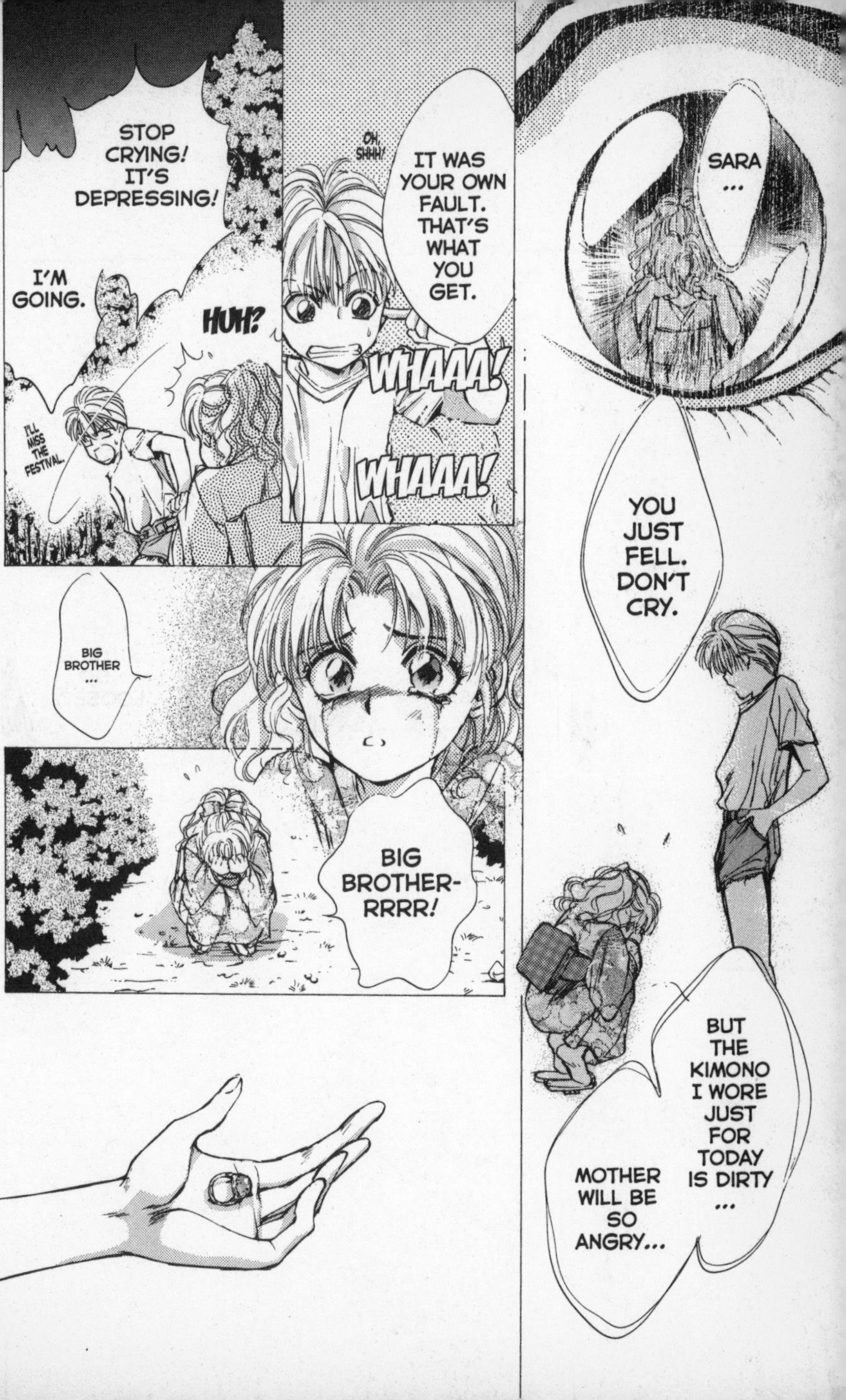
SARA ...
YOU JUST FELL. DON'T CRY.
BUT THE KIMONO I WORE JUST FOR TODAY IS DIRTY ...
MOTHER WILL BE SO ANGRY...
IT WAS YOUR OWN FAULT. THAT'S WHAT YOU GET.
OH, SHHH!
WHAAA!
WHAAA!
STOP CRYING! IT'S DEPRESSING!
I'M GOING.
HUH?
I'LL MISS THE FESTIVAL.
BIG BROTHER ...
BIG BROTHER-RRRR!

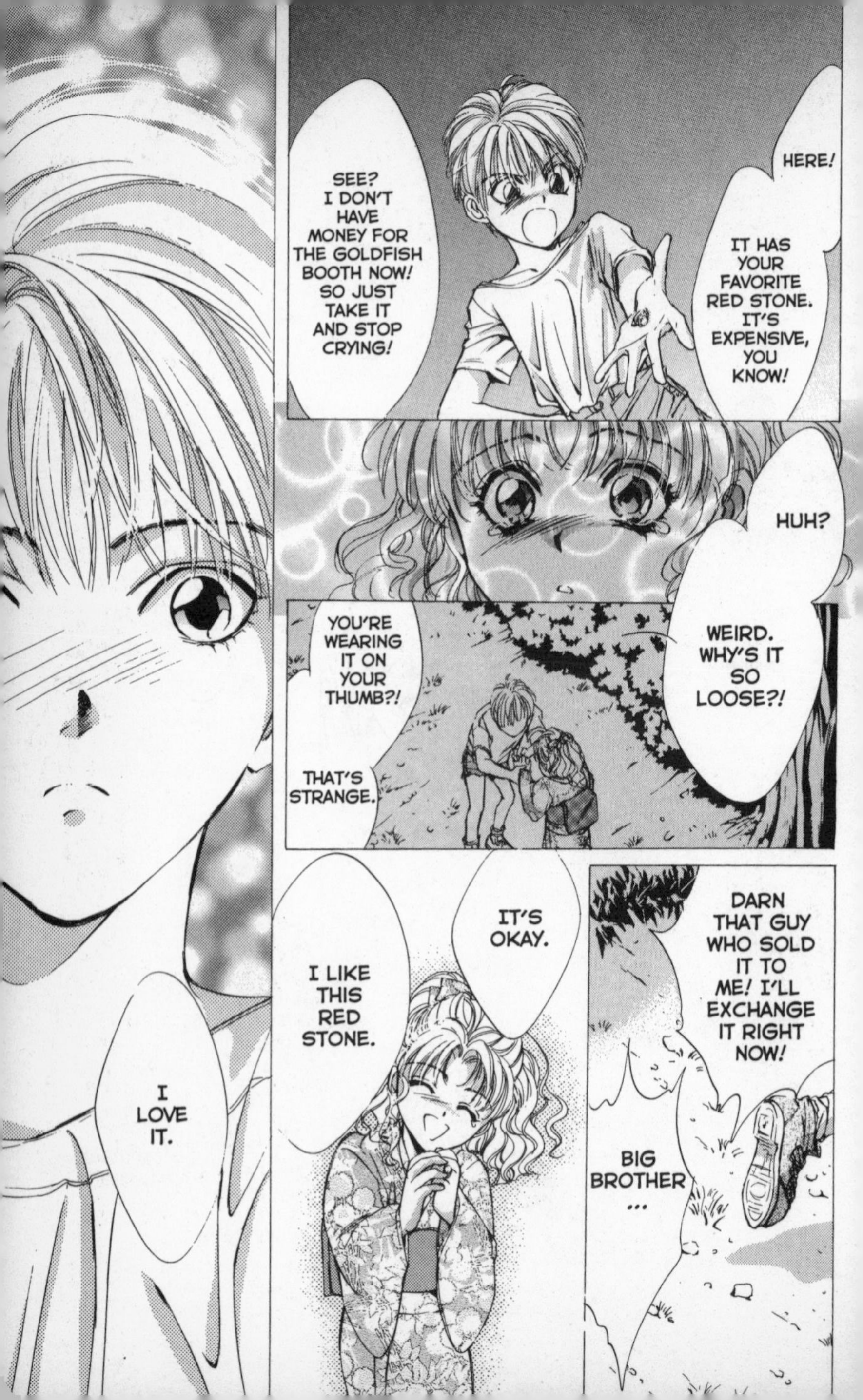
HERE!
IT HAS YOUR FAVORITE RED STONE. IT'S EXPENSIVE, YOU KNOW!
SEE? I DON'T HAVE MONEY FOR THE GOLDFISH BOOTH NOW! SO JUST TAKE IT AND STOP CRYING!
HUH?
WEIRD. WHY'S IT SO LOOSE?!
YOU'RE WEARING IT ON YOUR THUMB?!
THAT'S STRANGE.
DARN THAT GUY WHO SOLD IT TO ME! I'LL EXCHANGE IT RIGHT NOW!
BIG BROTHER ...
IT'S OKAY.
I LIKE THIS RED STONE.
I LOVE IT.

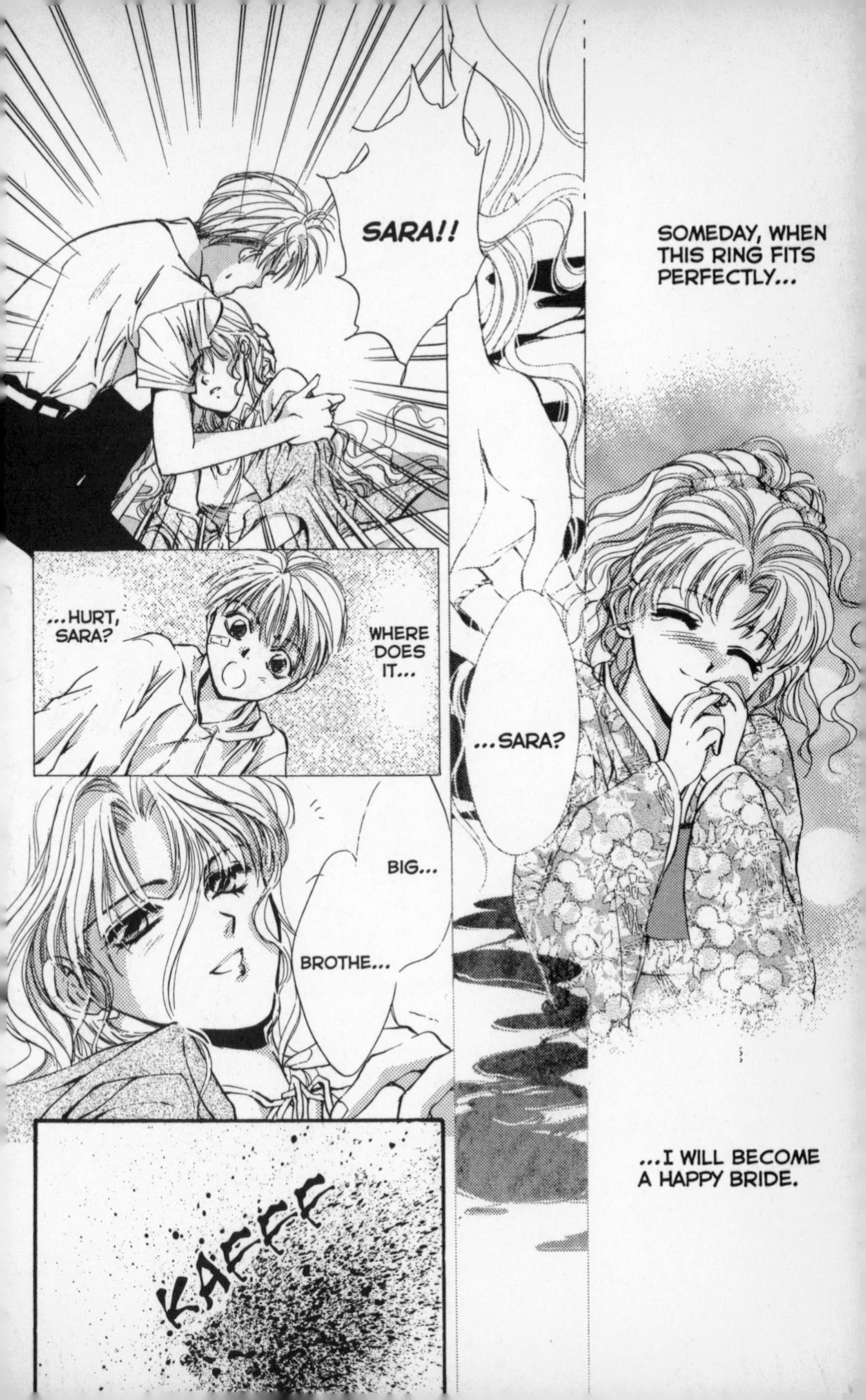
SOMEDAY, WHEN THIS RING FITS PERFECTLY...
...I WILL BECOME A HAPPY BRIDE.
...SARA?
SARA!!
WHERE DOES IT...
...HURT, SARA?
BIG...
BROTHE...
KAFFF

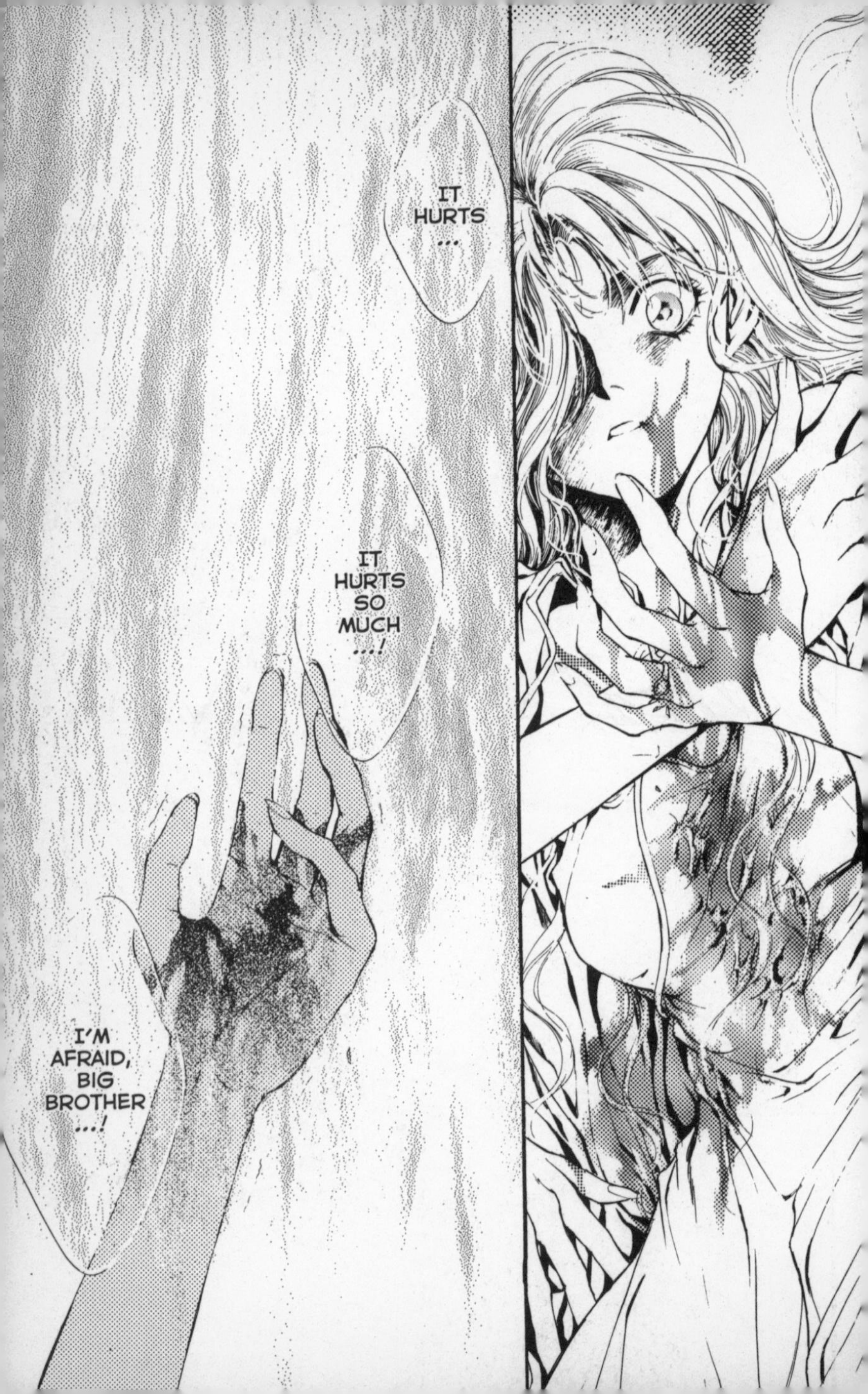
IT HURTS ...
IT HURTS SO MUCH ...!
I'M AFRAID, BIG BROTHER ...!

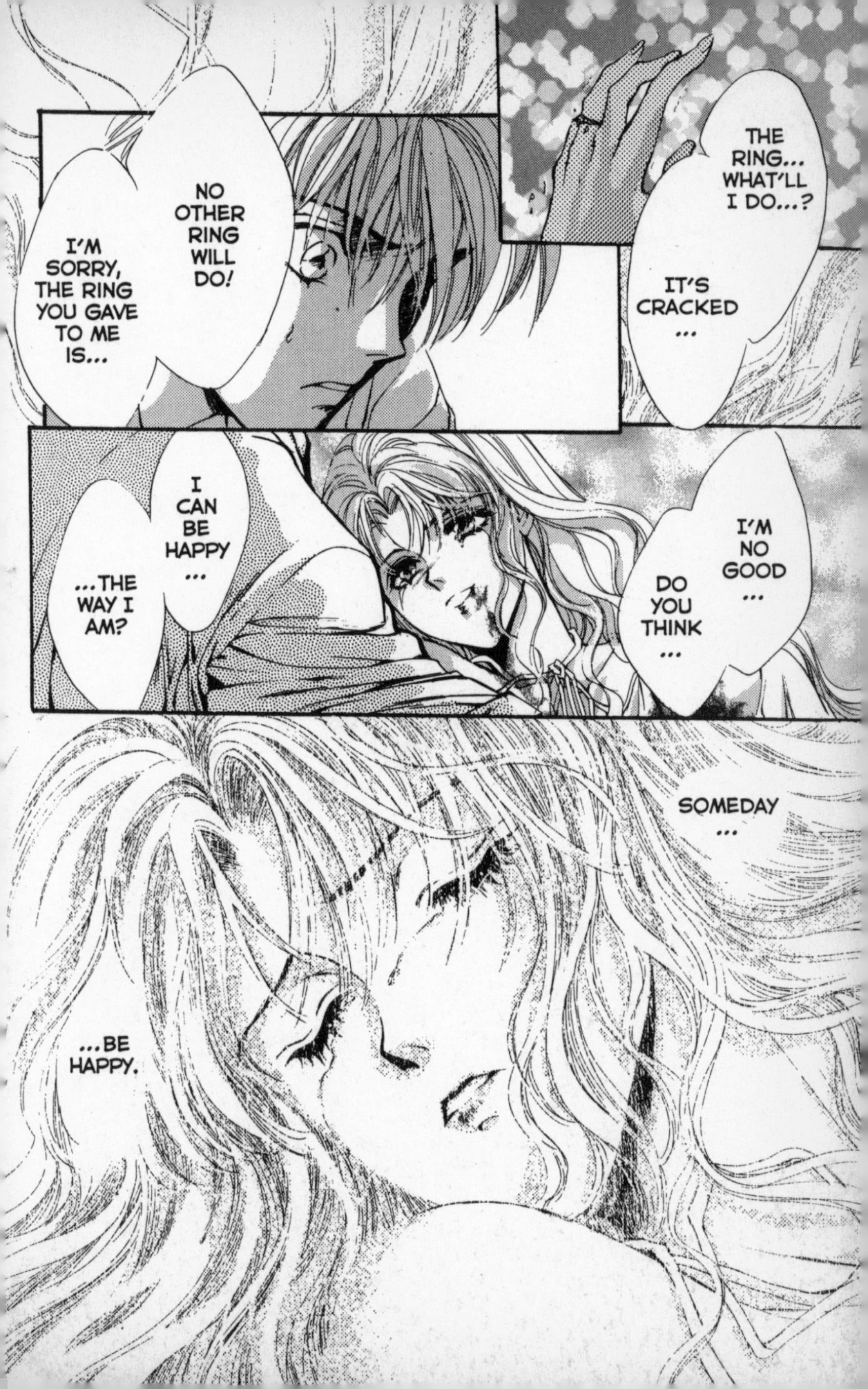
THE RING... WHAT'LL I DO...?
IT'S CRACKED ...
NO OTHER RING WILL DO!
I'M SORRY, THE RING YOU GAVE TO ME IS...
I'M NO GOOD ...
DO YOU THINK ...
I CAN BE HAPPY ...
...THE WAY I AM?
SOMEDAY ...
...BE HAPPY.

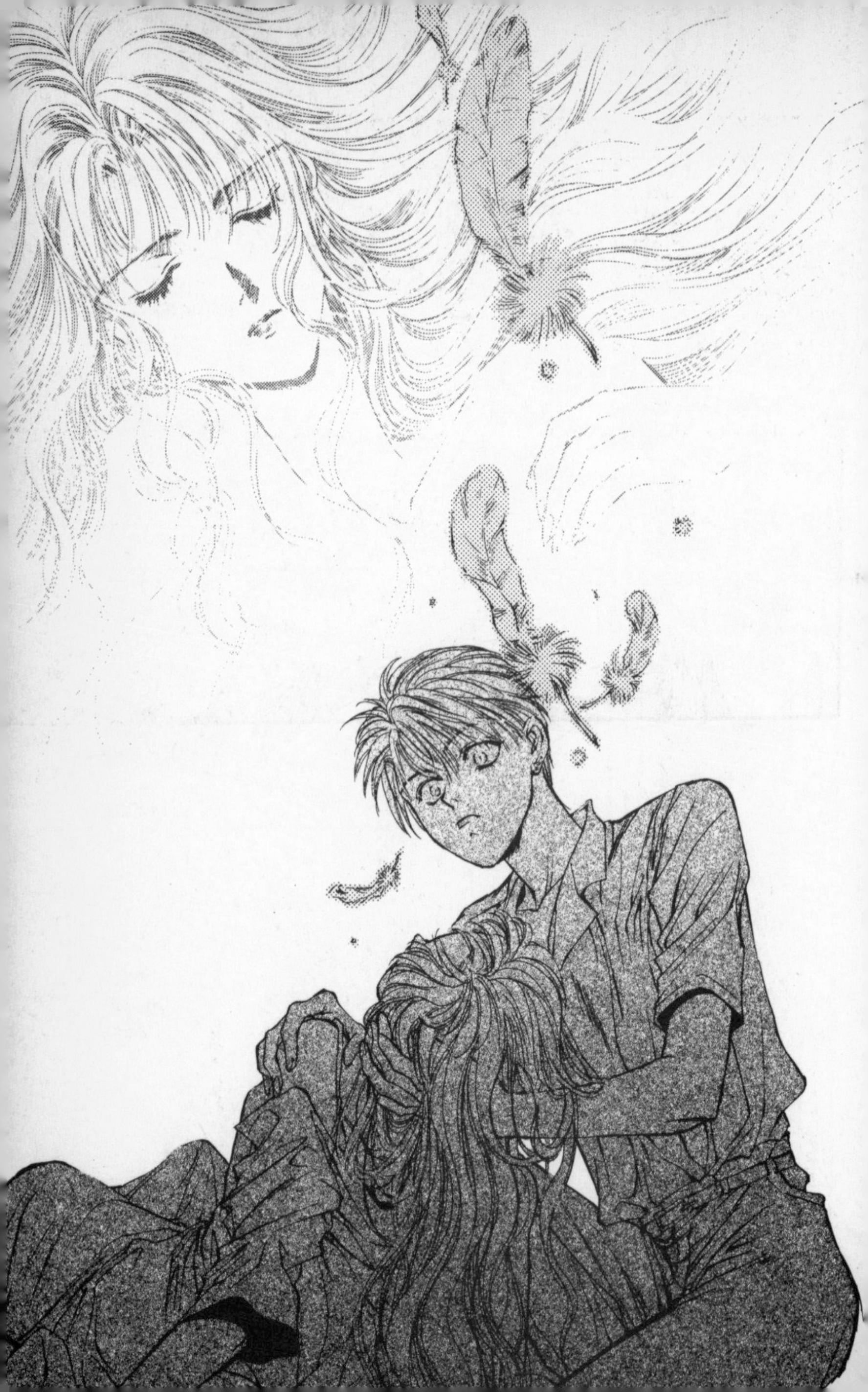

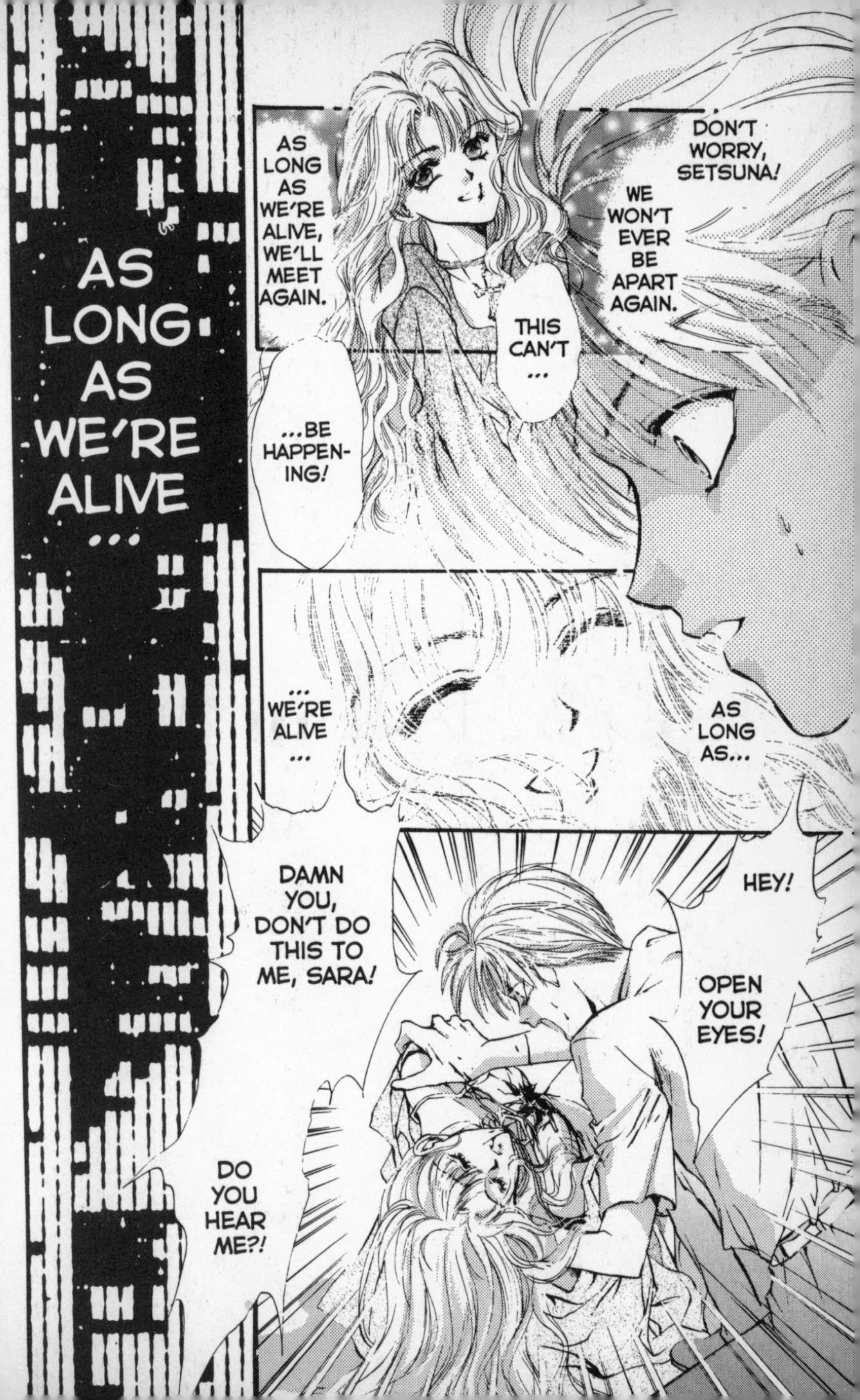
DON'T WORRY, SETSUNA!
WE WON'T EVER BE APART AGAIN.
AS LONG AS WE'RE ALIVE, WE'LL MEET AGAIN.
THIS CAN'T ...
...BE HAPPEN-ING!
AS LONG AS...
... WE'RE ALIVE ...
HEY!
OPEN YOUR EYES!
DAMN YOU, DON'T DO THIS TO ME, SARA!
DO YOU HEAR ME?!
AS LONG AS WE'RE ALIVE ...

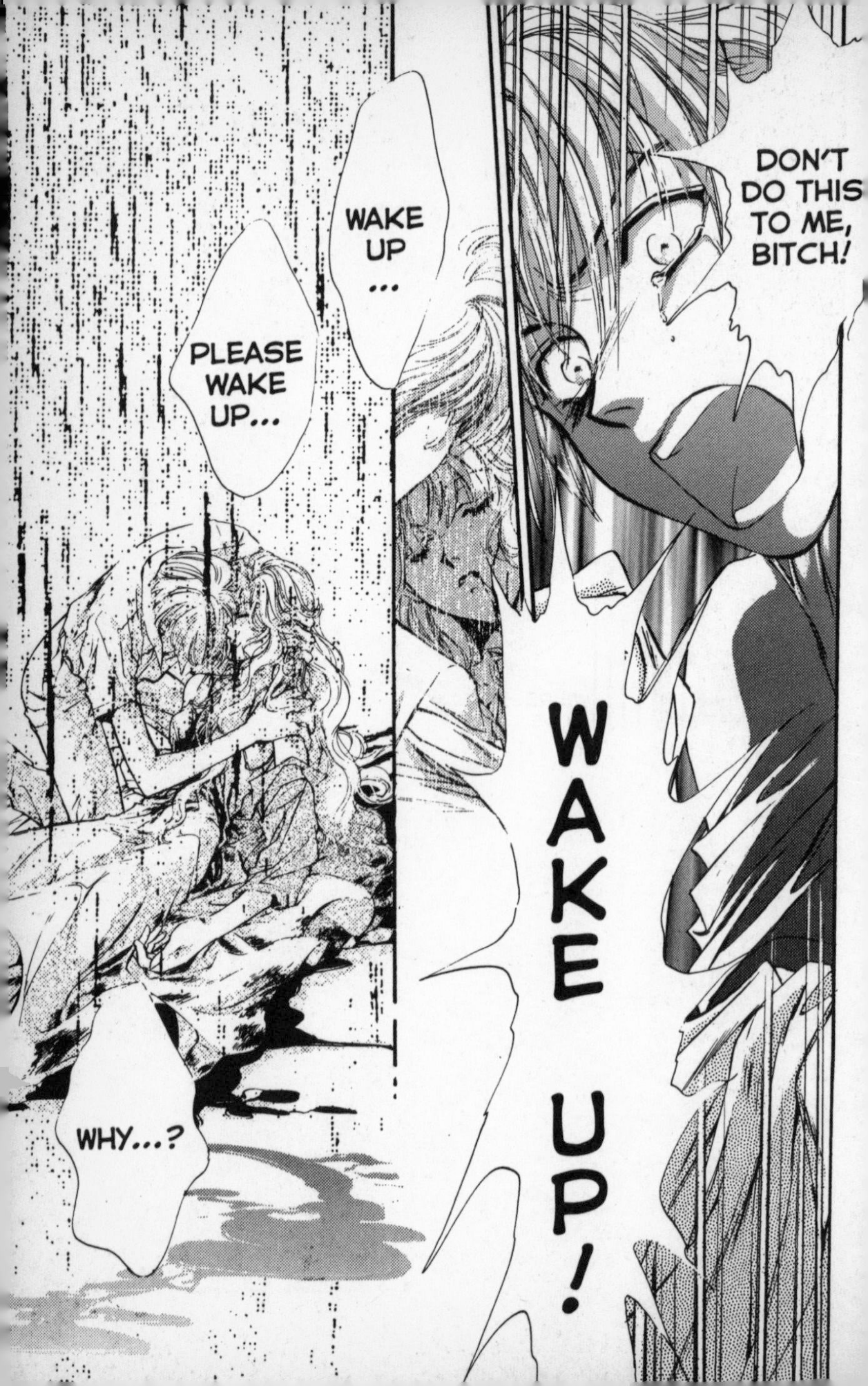
DON'T DO THIS TO ME, BITCH!
WAKE UP!
WAKE UP ...
PLEASE WAKE UP...
WHY...?

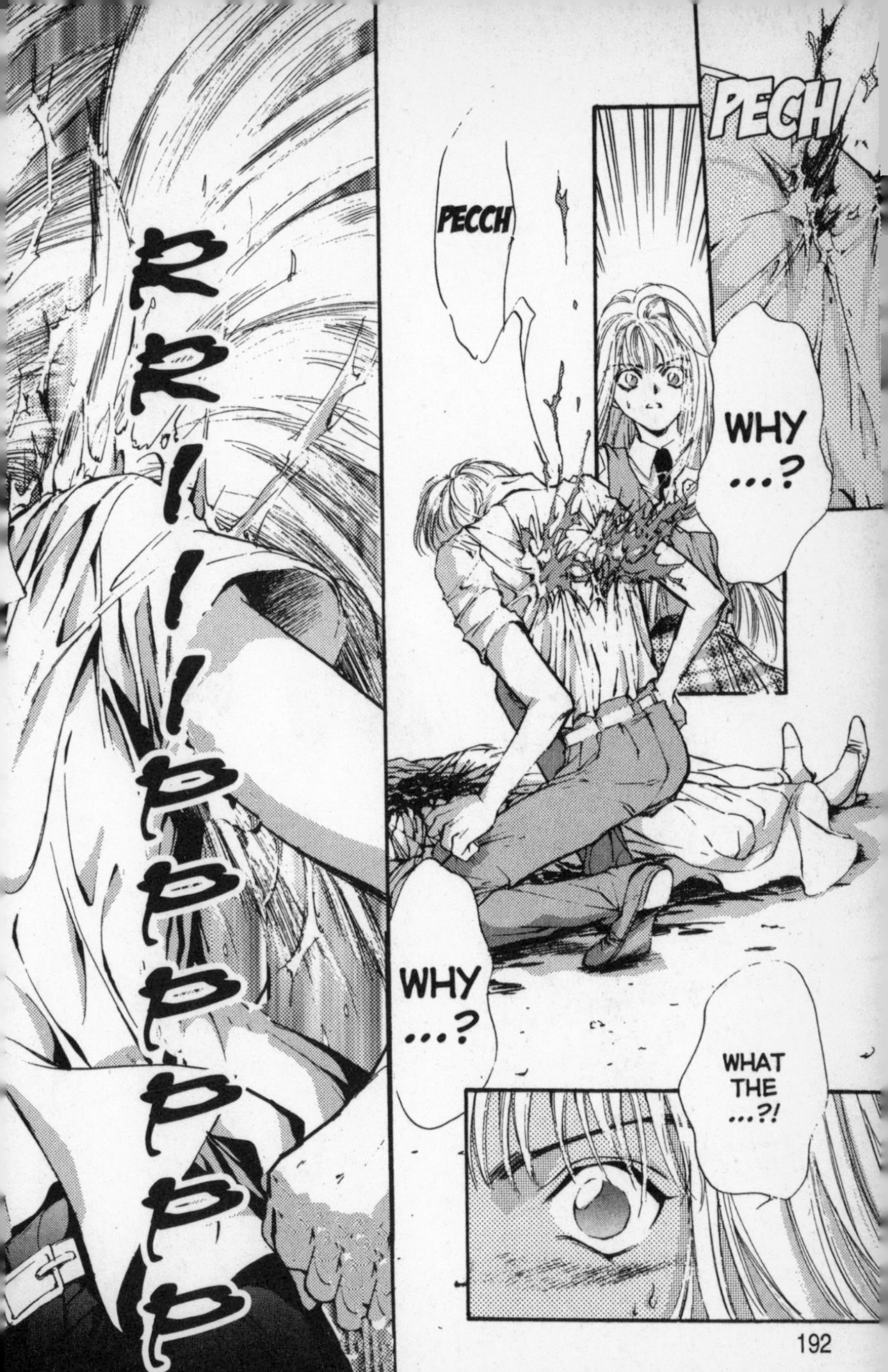
PECH
WHY ...?
PECCH
WHY ...?
WHAT THE ...?!
RRIIIPPPPPP

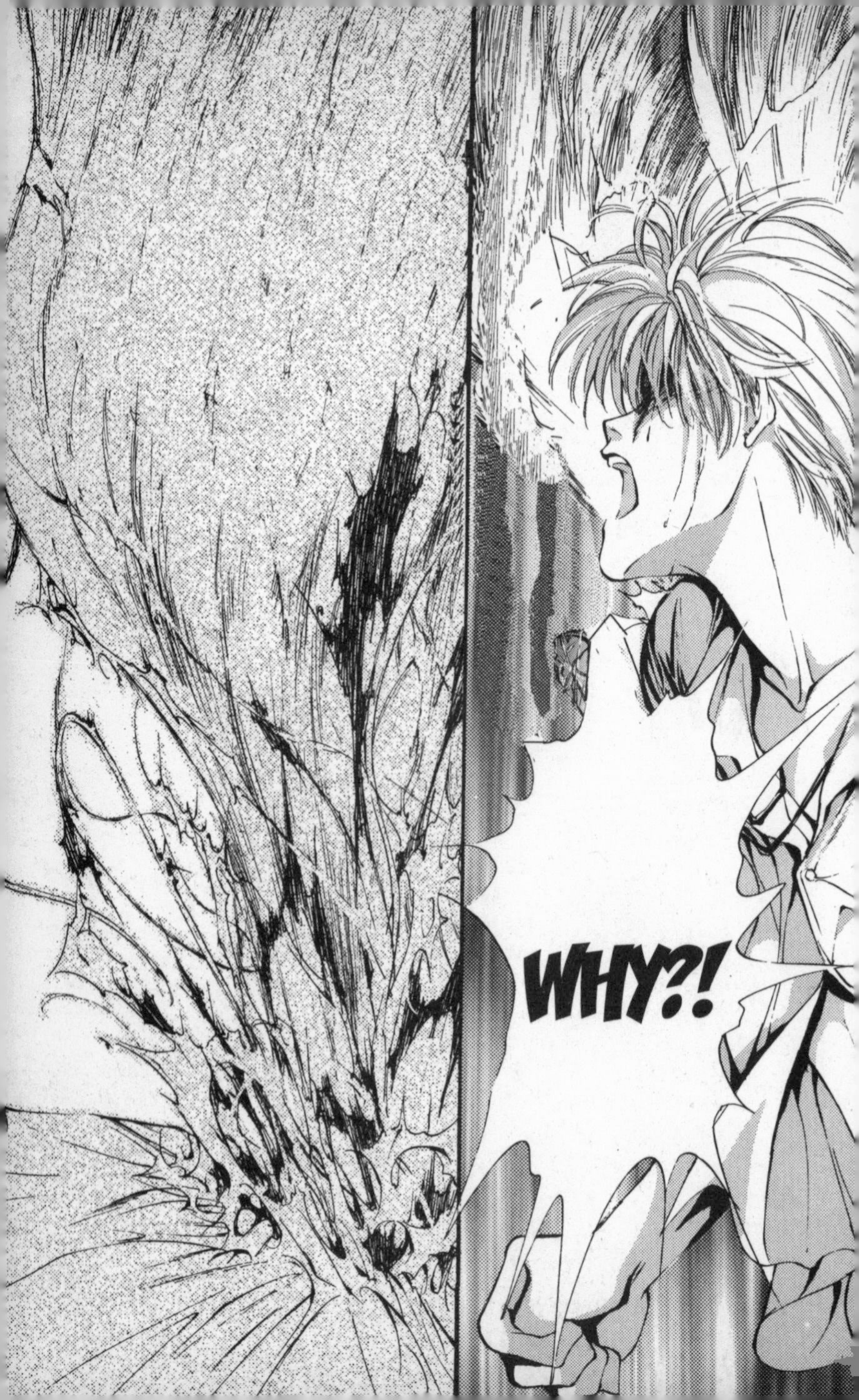
WHY?!

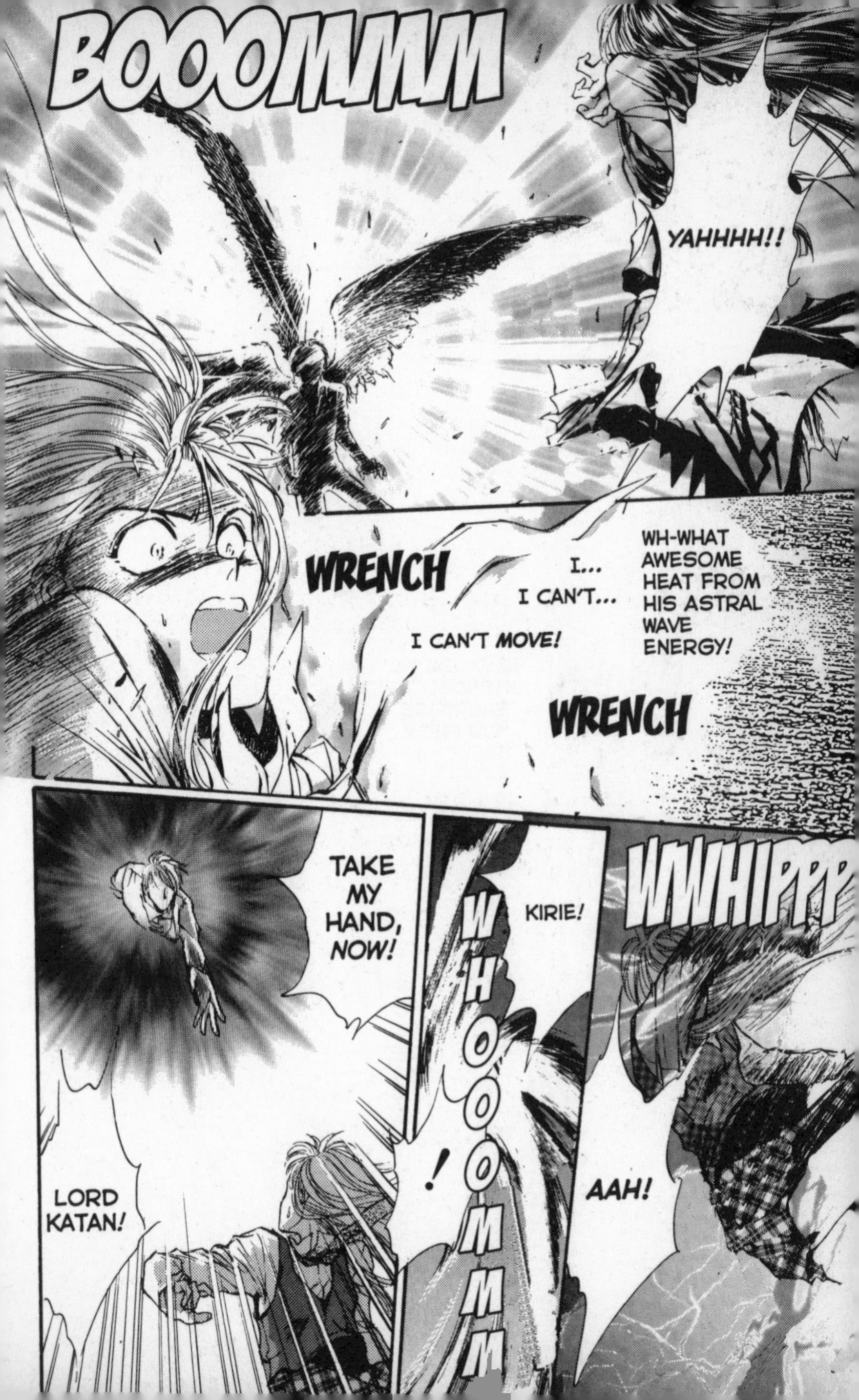
BOOOMMMM
YAHHHH!!
WH-WHAT AWESOME HEAT FROM HIS ASTRAL WAVE ENERGY!
I... I CAN'T...
WRENCH
I CAN'T *MOVE!*
WRENCH
WWHIPPP
AAH!
KIRIE!
WHOOOOMMMM
!
TAKE MY HAND, *NOW!*
LORD KATAN!

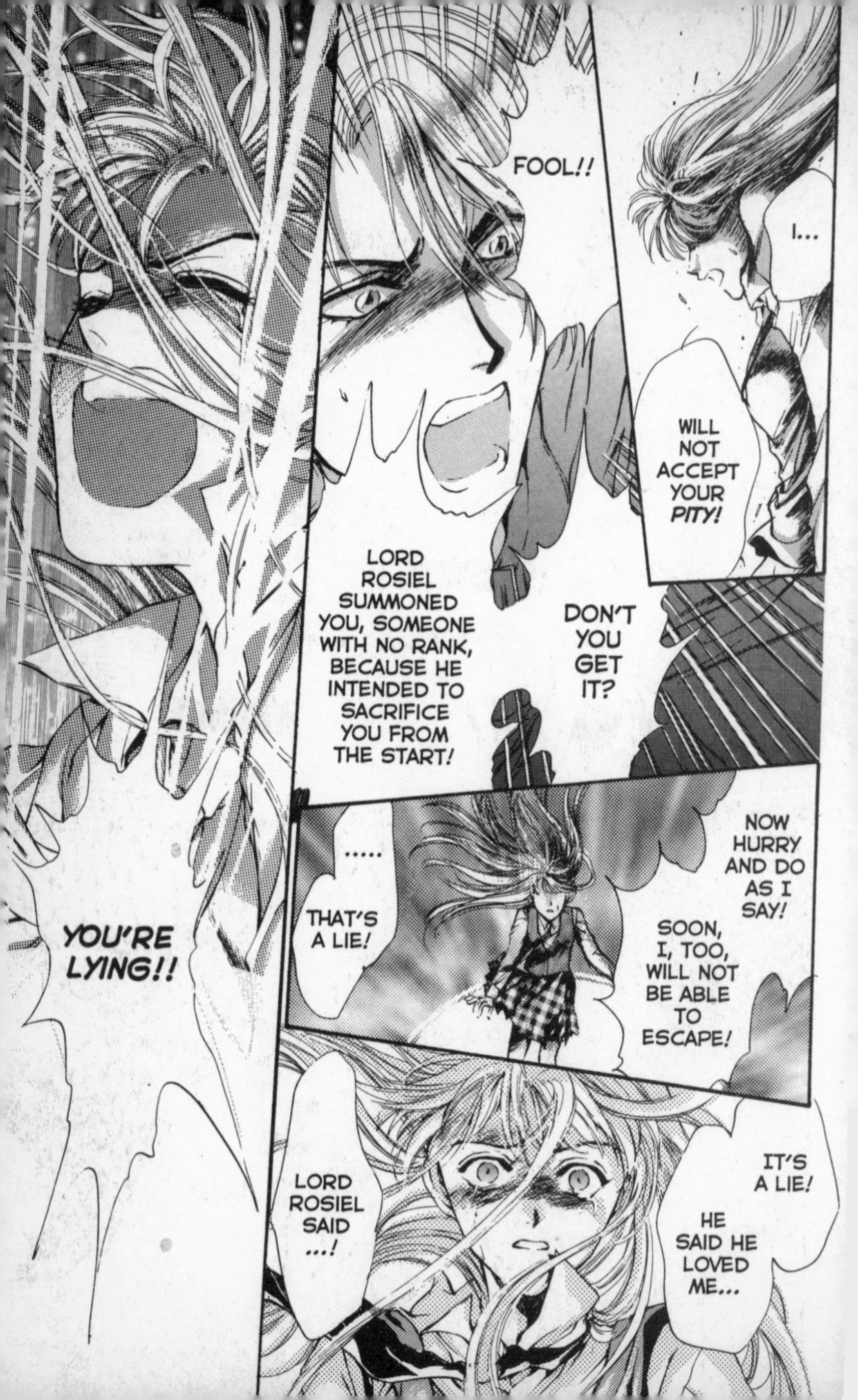
I...
WILL NOT ACCEPT YOUR *PITY!*
FOOL!!
DON'T YOU GET IT?
LORD ROSIEL SUMMONED YOU, SOMEONE WITH NO RANK, BECAUSE HE INTENDED TO SACRIFICE YOU FROM THE START!
NOW HURRY AND DO AS I SAY!
SOON, I, TOO, WILL NOT BE ABLE TO ESCAPE!
.....
THAT'S A LIE!
IT'S A LIE!
HE SAID HE LOVED ME...
LORD ROSIEL SAID ...!
YOU'RE LYING!!

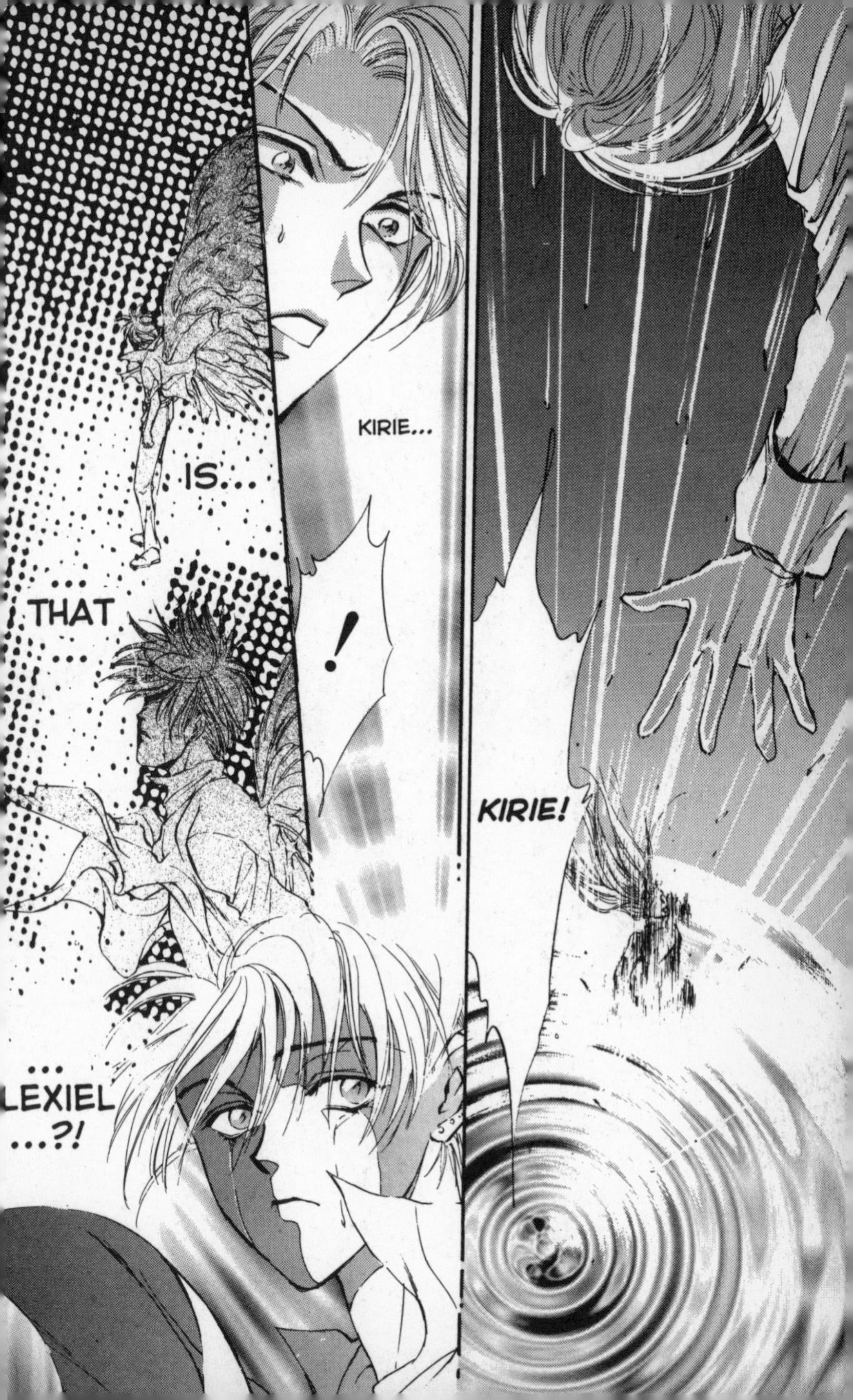
KIRIE!
KIRIE...
!
IS...
...THAT...
...LEXIEL
...?!

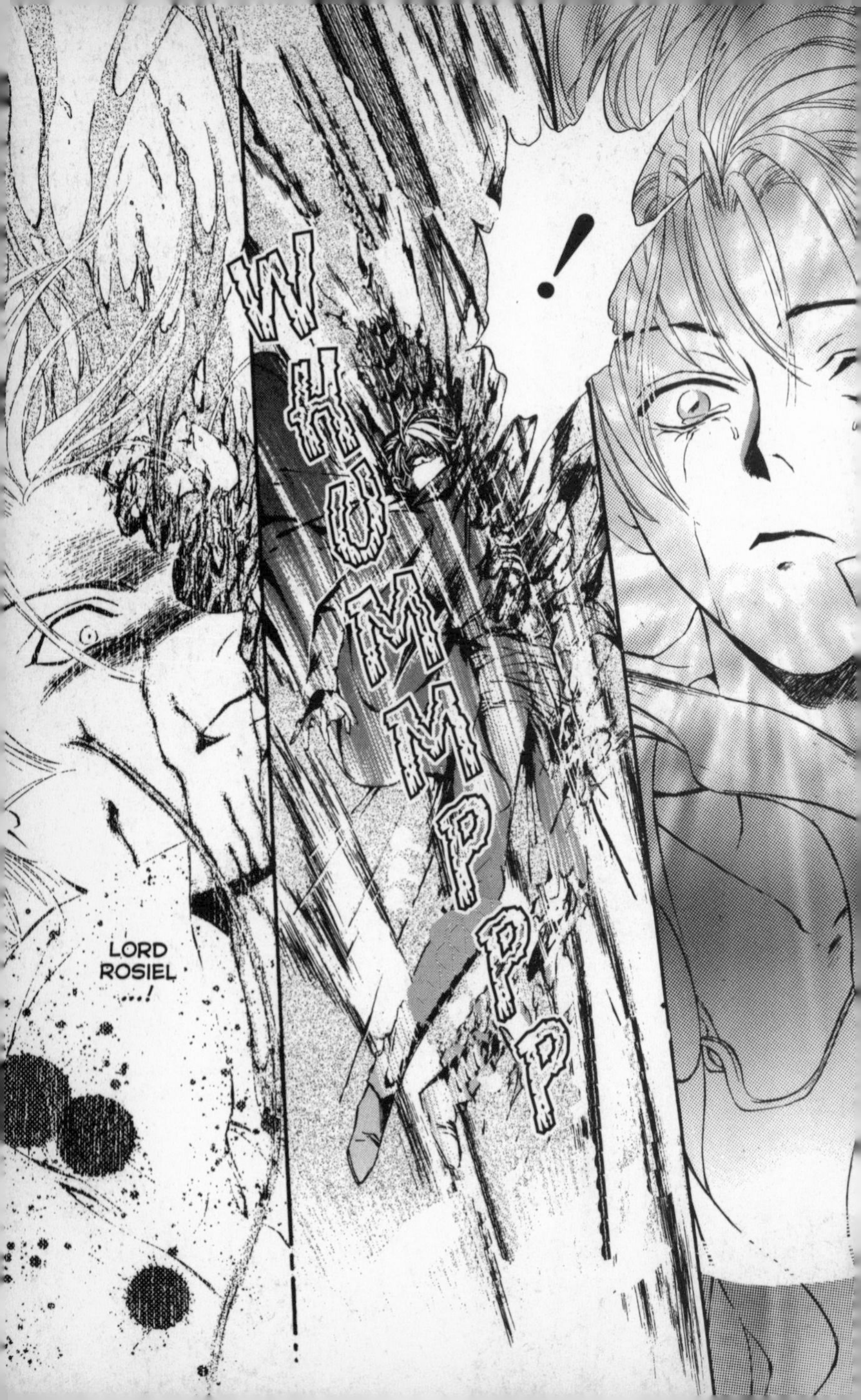
!
WHUMPPPP
LORD ROSIEL ...!

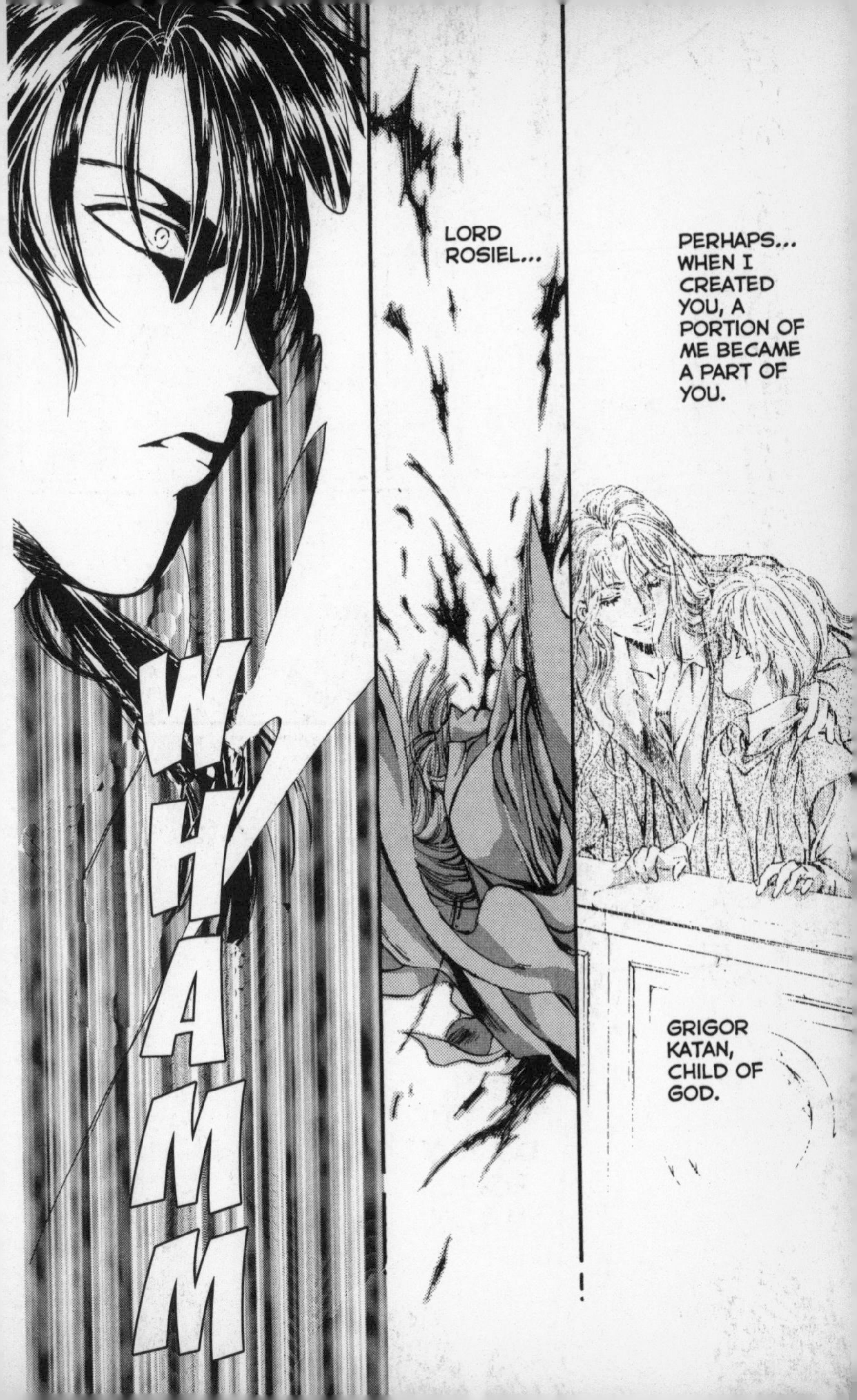
PERHAPS... WHEN I CREATED YOU, A PORTION OF ME BECAME A PART OF YOU.
GRIGOR KATAN, CHILD OF GOD.
LORD ROSIEL...
WHAMM

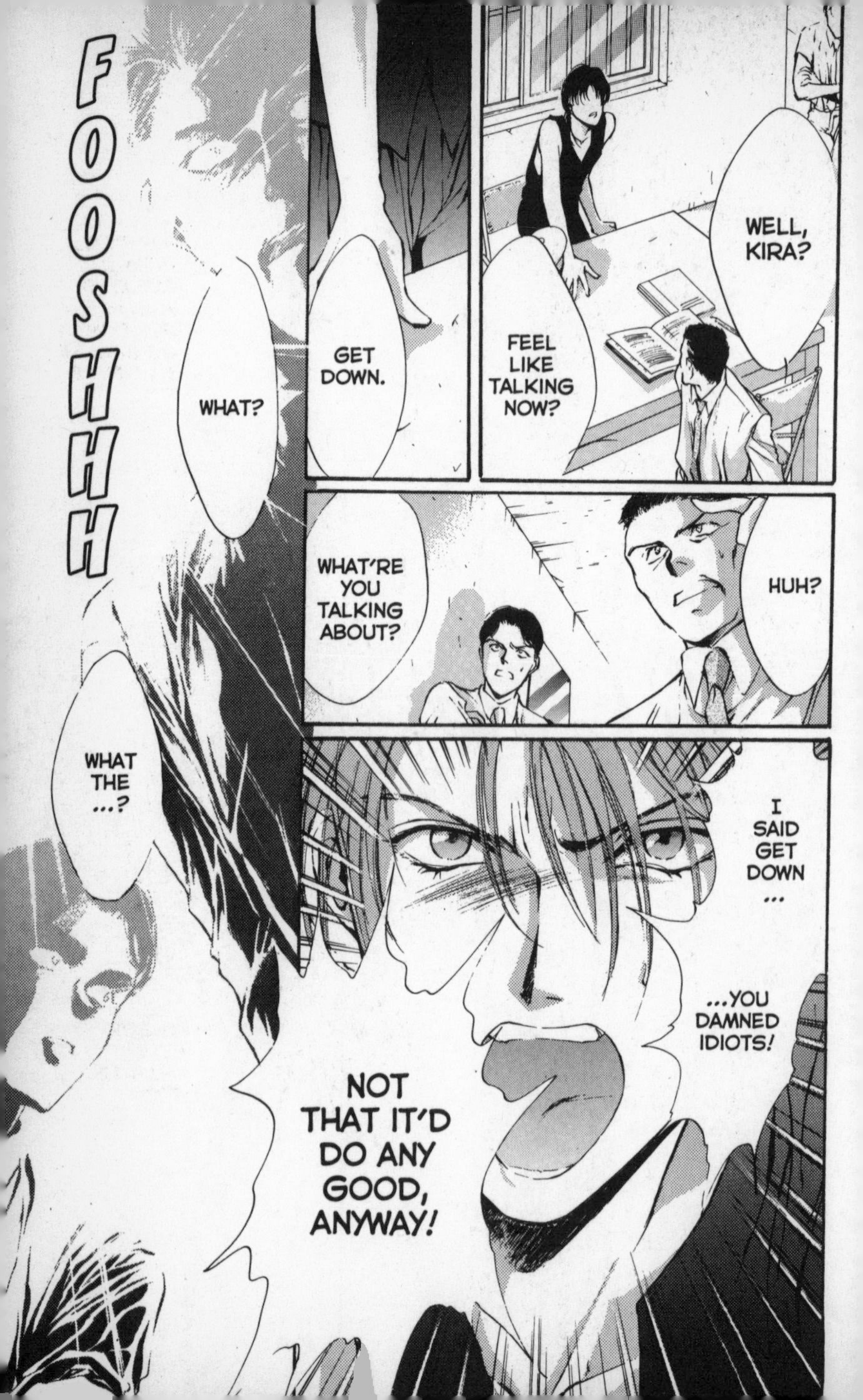
WELL, KIRA?
FEEL LIKE TALKING NOW?
GET DOWN.
HUH?
WHAT'RE YOU TALKING ABOUT?
I SAID GET DOWN...
...YOU DAMNED IDIOTS!
NOT THAT IT'D DO ANY GOOD, ANYWAY!
FOOSHHH
WHAT?
WHAT THE...?

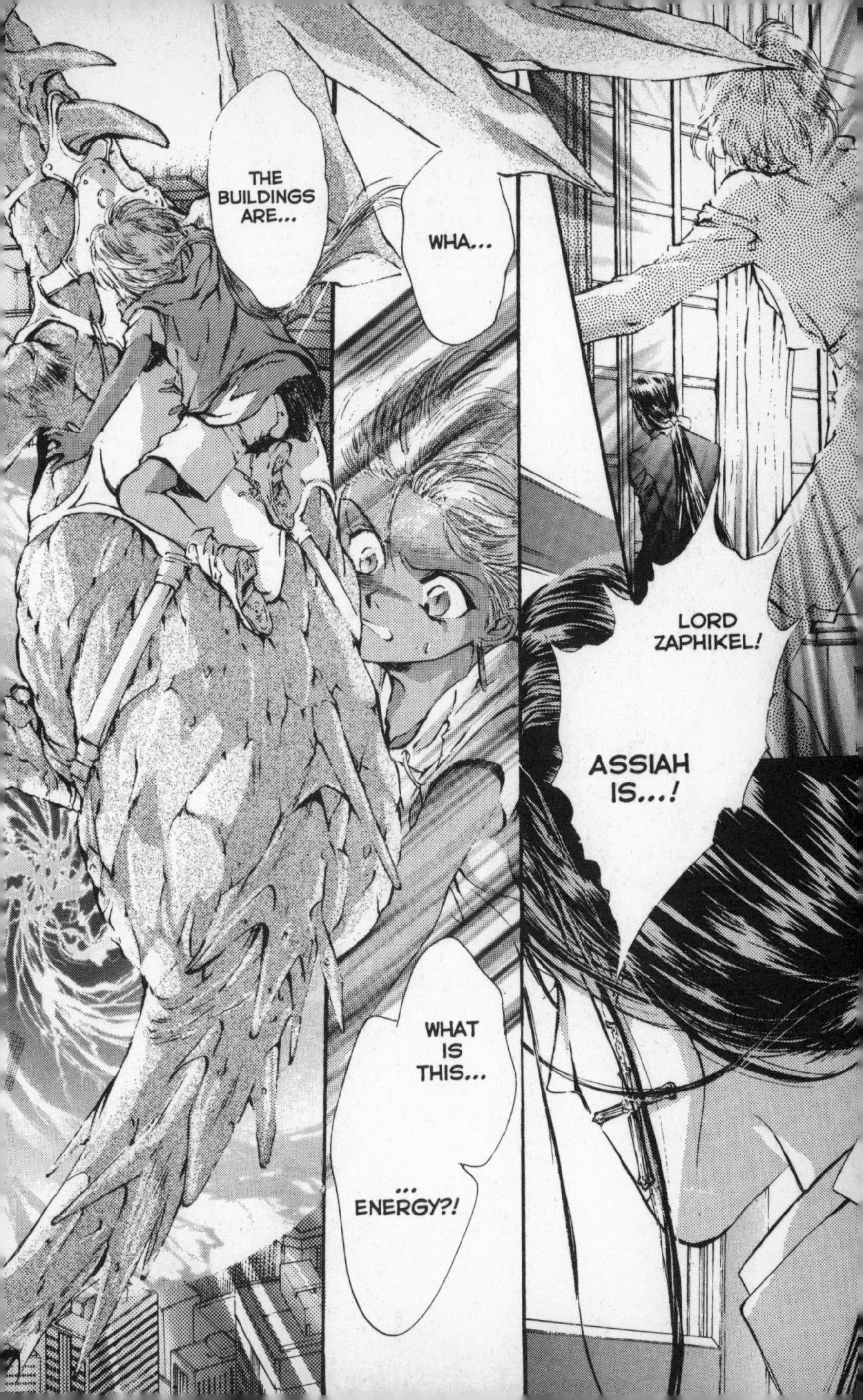
LORD ZAPHIKEL!
ASSIAH IS...!
WHA...
WHAT IS THIS...
...ENERGY?!
THE BUILDINGS ARE...

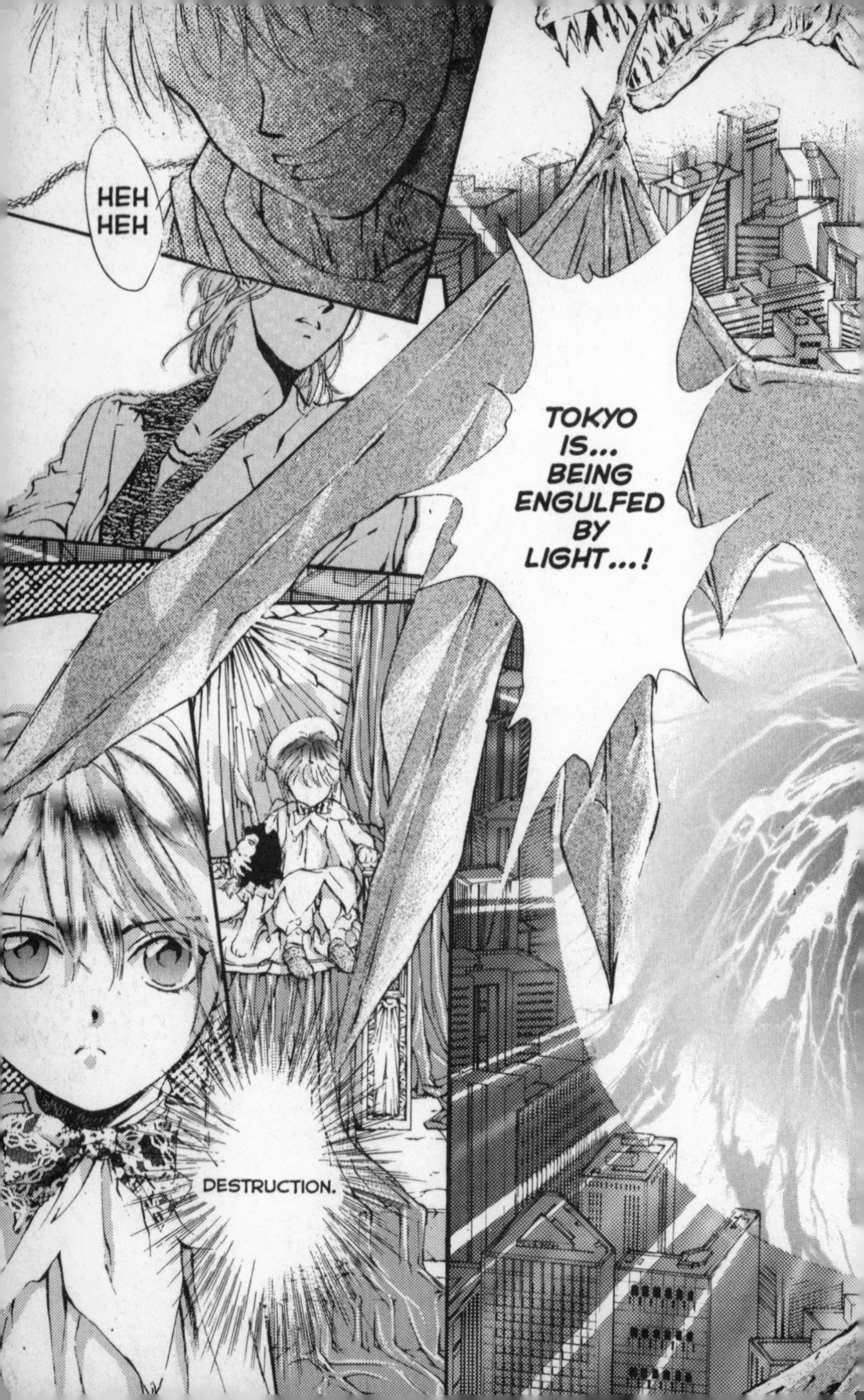
TOKYO IS... BEING ENGULFED BY LIGHT...!
HEH HEH
DESTRUCTION.

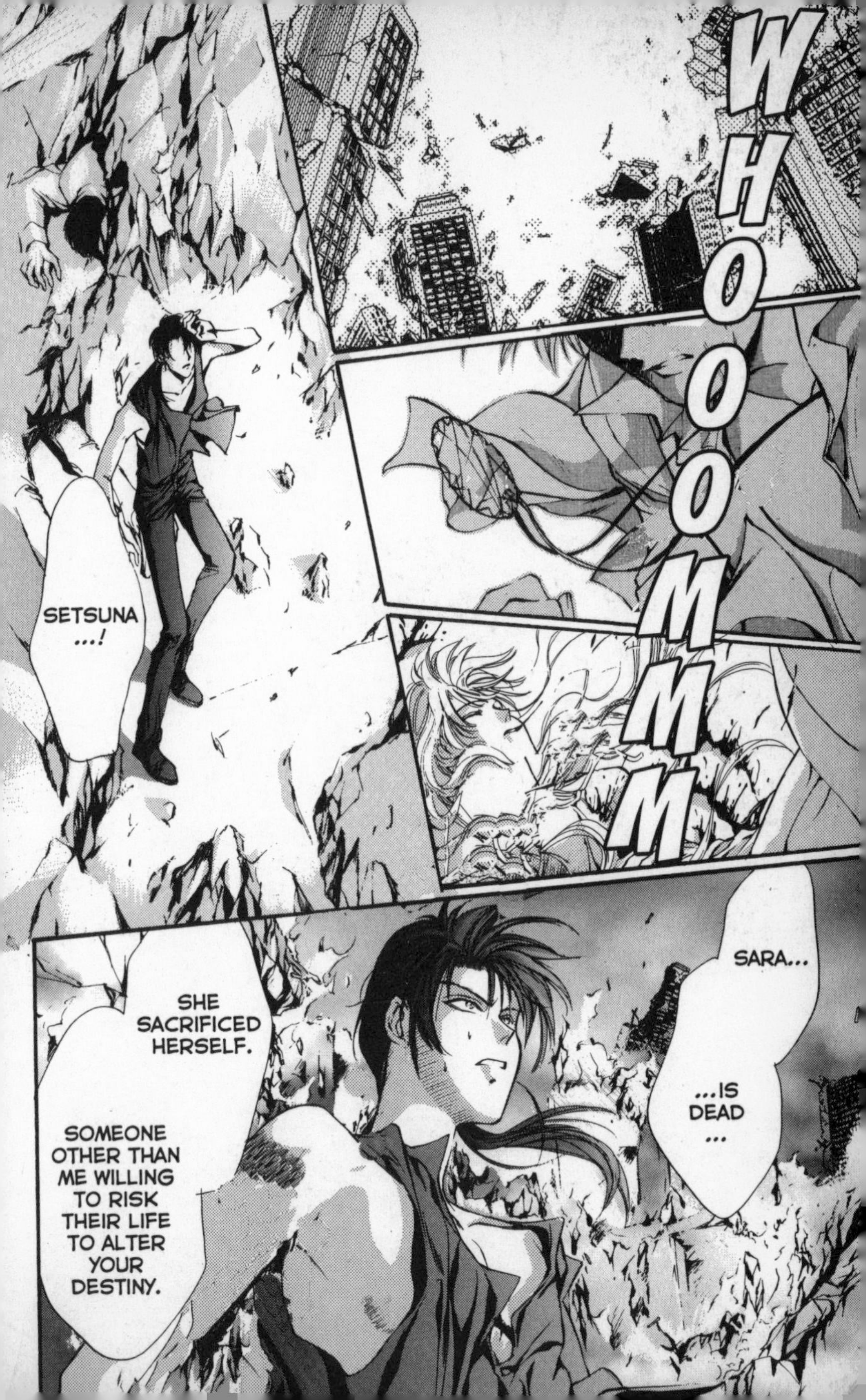
WHOOOMMM
SETSUNA ...!
SARA... ...IS DEAD ...
SHE SACRIFICED HERSELF.
SOMEONE OTHER THAN ME WILLING TO RISK THEIR LIFE TO ALTER YOUR DESTINY.

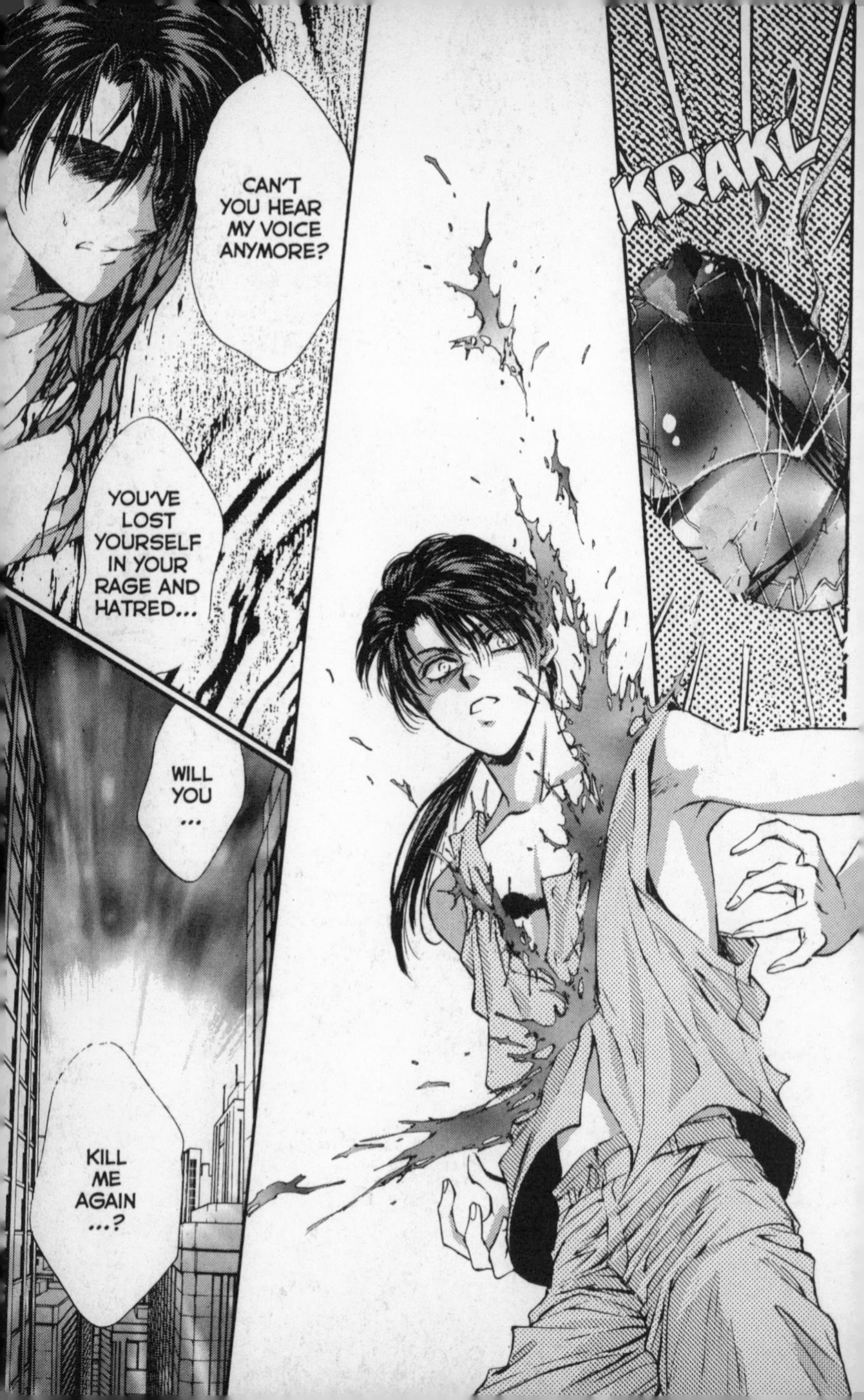
KRAKL
CAN'T YOU HEAR MY VOICE ANYMORE?
YOU'VE LOST YOURSELF IN YOUR RAGE AND HATRED...
WILL YOU ...
KILL ME AGAIN ...?

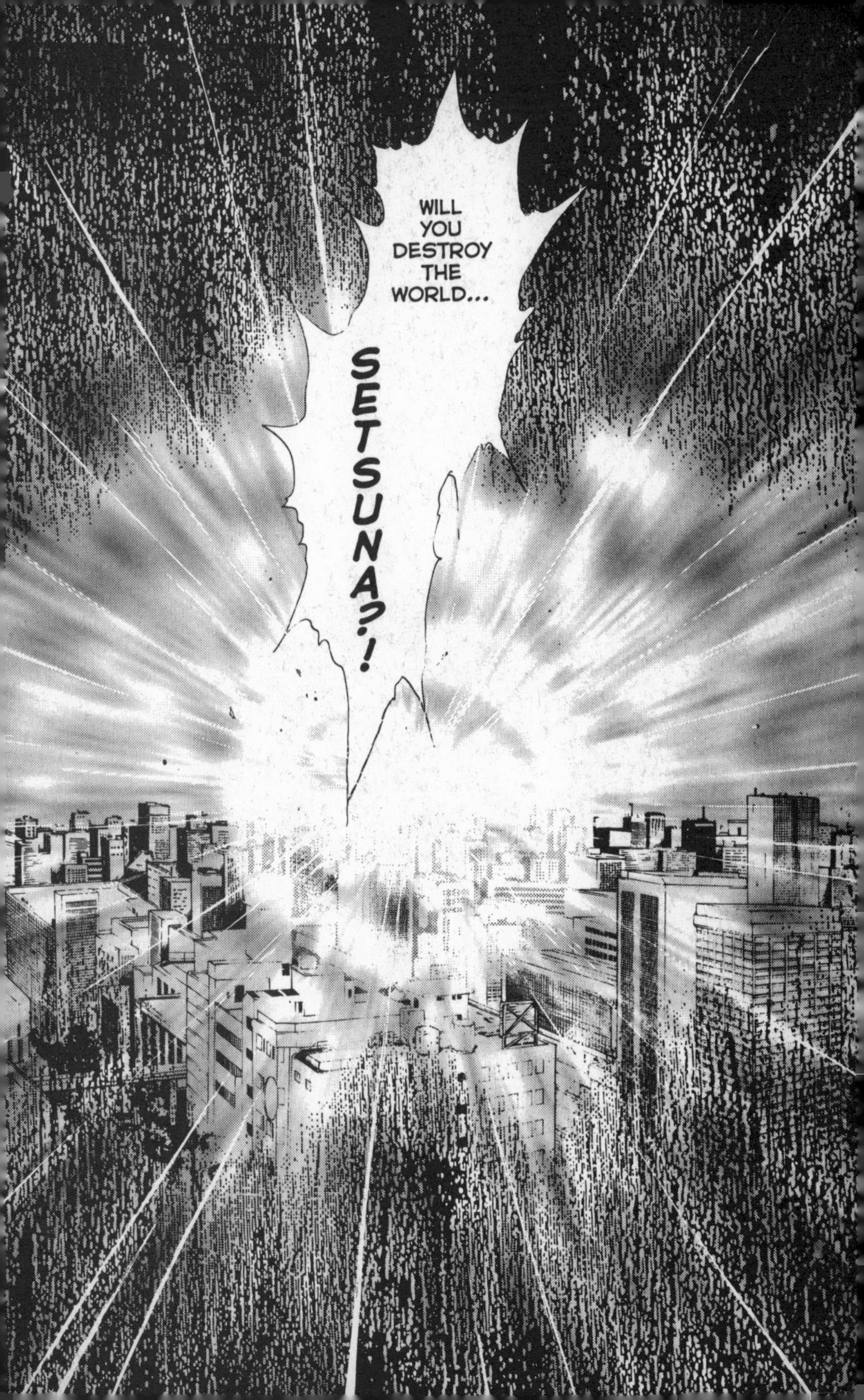
WILL YOU DESTROY THE WORLD...
SETSUNA?!

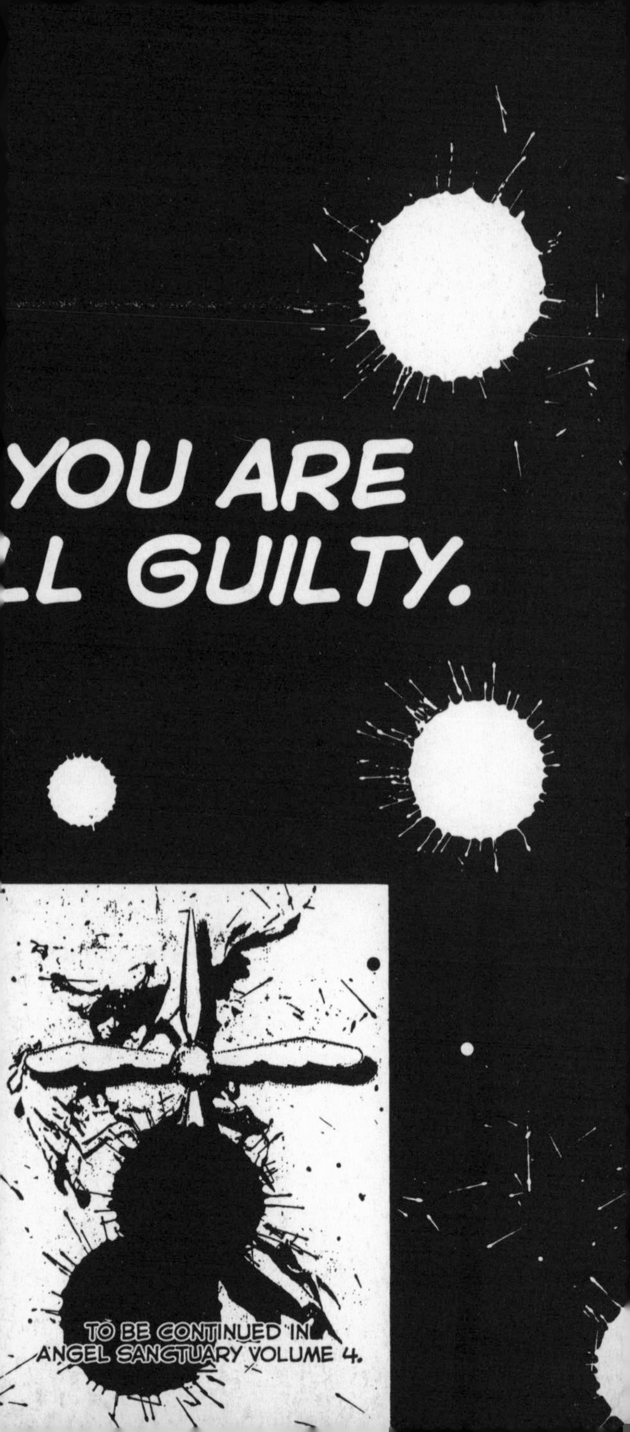
YOU ARE
LL GUILTY.
TO BE CONTINUED IN
ANGEL SANCTUARY VOLUME 4.

Angel ◆ *Sanctuary*

BY
KAORI YUKI

···TO BE CONTINUED

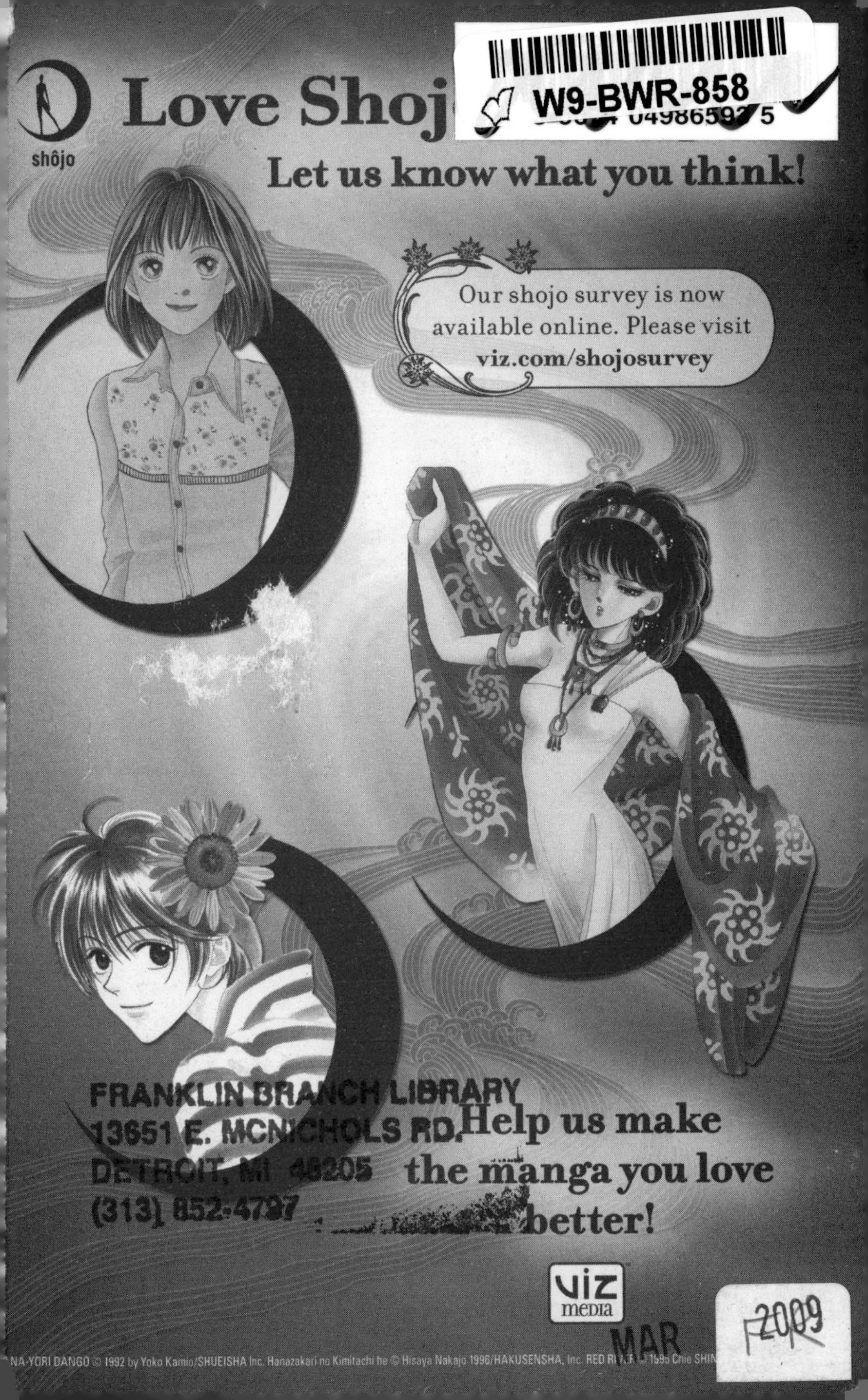
shôjo
Love Shojo
Let us know what you think!
Our shojo survey is now available online. Please visit viz.com/shojosurvey
Help us make the manga you love better!
VIZ media